HTML5

for Masterminds

How to take advantage of HTML5
to create amazing websites
and revolutionary applications

HTML5

for Masterminds

J.D. Gauchat

www.jdgauchat.com

Edited by: **Jessie Colgan**
www.talksciencetome.com

For those who are not here
with me anymore

Table of Contents

Chapter 2—CSS Styling and Box Models

Chapter 3—CSS3 Properties

Chapter 13—Drag and Drop API

Chapter 14—Web Storage API

Chapter 15—IndexedDB API

Chapter 16—File API

Chapter 25—Web Audio API

Chapter 26—Web Workers API

Conclusion

Introduction

HTML5 is not a new version of an old markup language—not even an improvement on this already "ancient" technology—but instead a new concept for the construction of websites and applications in the era of mobile devices, cloud computing and networking.

It all started a long time ago with a simple version of HTML proposed to create the basic structure of web pages, organize their content and share information. The language and the Web itself were born primarily with the intention of communicating information through text.

The narrow scope of HTML motivated companies to develop new languages and software to add characteristics to the Web and improve the user's experience. These initial developments grew into powerful and popular plug-ins. Simple games and animated jokes soon turned into sophisticated applications, providing new possibilities that changed the concept of the Web forever.

Of the options proposed, Java and Flash were the most successful; they were widely adopted and generally considered to be the future of the Internet. However, as soon as the number of users increased and the Internet changed from a way to connect computer lovers to a popular method of business and social interaction, limitations present in both technologies proved to be a death sentence.

The main difficulty with Java and Flash may be described as a lack of integration. Both were conceived as plug-ins, something that is inserted into a structure but basically shares only some space on the screen with that structure. There was no communication and integration between applications and documents.

The lack of integration became critical and paved the way for the evolution of a language that shares space in the document with HTML and that is not affected by plug-in limitations. Javascript, an interpreted language embedded in browsers, clearly was a better way to improve the user's experience and provide functionality for the Web. However, after a few years of failed attempts to promote it and misuses of it, the market never fully adopted the language and its popularity declined. The detractors had good reasons to oppose its adoption. At that time, Javascript couldn't replace the functionality of Java and Flash. And even when it was evident that Java and Flash were limiting the scope of web applications and isolating the Web's content, popular features such as video streaming were becoming a big part of the Web and were only effectively offered through those technologies.

Despite its prevalence, Java was declining. The language's complex nature, slow evolution and lack of integration diminished its importance to the point that today Java is hardly used in mainstream web applications. Without Java, developers turned its attention to Flash. However, the fact that Flash shares the same basic characteristics with its competitor makes it susceptible to the same fate.

While that silent but vigorous competition was taking place, the software to access the Web continued to evolve. Along with new features and faster techniques for Internet access, browsers were also improving their Javascript engines. More power brought more opportunities, and this scripting language was ready to embrace them.

At some point during this process, it became evident to some developers that neither Java nor Flash would be enough to provide the tools they needed to create the applications demanded by an increasing number of users. These developers started to apply Javascript in their applications in a way that had never been seen before. The innovation and the amazing results attracted the attention of more programmers and soon the "Web 2.0" was born. From that point on, the perception of Javascript in the developers' community radically changed.

Javascript was clearly the language that allowed developers to innovate and do things that nobody had done before on the Web. Over the last several years, programmers and web designers all over the world came up with incredible hacks to overcome the limitations of this technology and its initial deficiencies in portability. At some point, it became obvious that Javascript was the third element in a perfect combination of languages, a combination necessary for the evolution of the Web.

HTML5 is the development of that combination, the glue that holds everything together. HTML5 proposes standards for every aspect of the Web as well as a clear purpose for each technology involved. Now, HTML provides the structural elements, CSS manages the structure to make it attractive and useful, and Javascript has the power necessary to provide functionality and build full web applications.

Boundaries between websites and applications have finally disappeared. The required technologies are ready. The future of the Web is promising, and the evolution and combination of these three technologies (HTML, CSS and Javascript) into one powerful specification is turning the Internet into the leading platform for development. HTML5 is clearly leading the way.

> **IMPORTANT:** At the time of writing, not every browser supports HTML5 features, and most of these features are experimental. We recommend you read the chapters and execute the codes with the latest version of Google Chrome and Mozilla Firefox. Google Chrome is a good testing platform. It is based on WebKit, an open source browser engine, and supports almost all the features already implemented in HTML5. On the other hand, Mozilla Firefox is one of the best browsers for developers and provides support for HTML5 as well. The examples in this book were prepared for these two browsers, but for simplification, you will find a few scripts implementing only the experimental methods provided by Google Chrome. For this reason, we recommend you study the codes in **Google Chrome** and then expand your work to other browsers.
>
> Whatever browser you use, always keep in mind that a good developer installs and tests his or her codes in each program available on the market. Test the codes provided in this book with every browser. To download the latest versions, visit the following websites:
>
> - www.google.com/chrome
> - www.apple.com/safari/download
> - www.mozilla.com
> - windows.microsoft.com
> - www.opera.com
> - www.maxthon.com

In the Conclusion, we explore different ways of making your websites and applications accessible from older browsers and those that are not yet HTML5-ready.

Chapter 1
HTML5 Documents

1.1 Basic Components

HTML5 provides three basic features: structure, style and functionality. It was never officially declared but, even when some Javascript APIs and the entire CSS3 specification are not part of it, HTML5 is considered a product of the combination of HTML, CSS and Javascript. These technologies are highly dependable and act as one unit organized under the HTML5 specification. HTML is in charge of the structure, CSS presents that structure and its content on the screen, and Javascript does the rest, which (as we will see later in this book) is quite significant.

Despite the integration of these technologies, the structure is still the fundamental part of a document. It provides the elements necessary to allocate static or dynamic content, and it is also a basic platform for applications. With the variety of devices that access the Internet and the diversity of interfaces used to interact with the Web, the basic aspect of structure becomes a vital part of the document. Now, the structure must provide shape, organization and flexibility, and it must be as solid as the foundations of a house.

To work and create websites and applications with HTML5, we first need to know how that structure is constructed. Creating strong foundations will help us later apply other components to take full advantage of these new possibilities.

So let's start with the basics, step by step. In this first chapter you will learn what HTML is and how to build an essential structure using the new elements of this language.

> **IMPORTANT:** To access additional information and listing examples, visit our website at www.minkbooks.com.

1.2 A Brief Introduction to HTML

The HyperText Markup Language (HTML) is a programming language. Unlike other languages, HTML is not composed of commands or instructions but rather a set of tags that organize and declare a purpose for the content of the document.

In the strict sense, HTML is just text written with a particular syntax that a browser is able to read and implement. The concept behind the creation of this language was the idea of sharing through the Internet not only the text included in documents but also its format. The possibility of differentiating important parts of the content of a document opened the door for the creation of the Web as we know it today, and HTML is the language that made it possible.

IMPORTANT: The concepts explained below are basic but essential for understanding the examples in this book. If you are familiar with this information, please feel free to skip over the parts you already know.

Tags and Elements

An HTML code is not a sequential set of instructions. HTML is a markup language, a set of tags that usually come in pairs and can be nested (fully contained within other elements). These HTML tags are keywords and attributes surrounded by angle brackets (e.g., **<html lang="en">**). Usually, we refer to the individual tags as a "tag" and to the pair of opening-closing tags as an "element". Look at the following example:

```
<!DOCTYPE html>
<html lang="en">
<head>
  <title>My First HTML Document</title>
</head>
<body>
  HELLO WORLD!
</body>
</html>
```

Listing 1-1: Example of a basic HTML document

Some HTML elements are single, composed of only one tag, but most require an opening and a closing tag. In the example in Listing 1-1 we can see several tags, one after another, with text and even other tags in between. Compare every opening and closing tag in this example, and you will see that the closing tag is distinguished by a slash before the keyword. For example, the **<html>** tag indicates the start of the HTML code, while **</html>** declares the end. Everything in between these tags will be treated as HTML code by the browser.

In this example, we have a simple code but already a complex structure. In the first line, there is a single tag with the definition of the document followed by the opening tag **<html lang="en">**. Between the **<html>** tags we insert other tags, like those representing the head and body of the document (**<head>** and **<body>**), that also come in pairs and enclose more content such as text or other elements (**<title>**).

As you can see, to build an HTML document, tags are listed one after another and also in between other tags, resulting in a tree-like structure, with the **<html>** tag as its root.

In general, every element is allowed to be nested, to be a container or to be contained by other elements. Basically, special structural elements like **<html>**, **<head>** or **<body>** have a specific place in an HTML document, but the rest are flexible, as we will see throughout this chapter.

> **Do It Yourself:** An HTML document is a text file. If you don't have any developer software, to create the file you can simply use any text editor such as Windows' Notepad. Create a new file with the code of Listing 1-1, save it with a name and the **.html** extension (e.g., **mycode.html**), and then open the file in your browser (a double click on the file will be enough to execute the file with the browser set to default on your computer). If your editor works with different formats, be sure to save the file as "Plain Text".

IMPORTANT: Don't worry if you don't understand how to create the structure presented in Listing 1-1. We will work on this and the new structural elements introduced in HTML5 in the next part of this chapter.

Attributes

As you probably noticed, the opening `<html>` tag in Listing 1-1 is not only composed of the keyword and angle brackets but also the string `lang="en"`. This is an attribute with a value. The name of the attribute is `lang`, and the value `en` is assigned to the attribute using the symbol =. Attributes provide additional information about an HTML element. In this case, it declares the human language of the HTML code as "English".

Attributes are always declared inside the opening tag and may have a name/value structure, such as the `lang` attribute of our example, or represent a Boolean value, in which case its presence indicates the condition `true` or `false` (e.g., the `disabled` attribute without a specific value will disable a form element).

Since HTML shifted from a general purpose to focus more on the creation of the document's structure, the use of most classic attributes was abandoned and some were even completely replaced by CSS properties, as we will see in following chapters; but a few remain useful, especially four generic attributes that have particular importance in the development of HTML5 websites and web applications:

> **class**—This attribute allows us to work with a group of elements that share some characteristics. For example, using a value for the `class` attribute, we can assign the same font type and styles to text located in different parts of the document.
>
> **id**—This attribute allows us to assign a unique identifier to every element. This is the best way to have access from CSS or Javascript to one specific element.
>
> **style**—This attribute allows us to assign CSS styles to each element individually. As we will see in Chapter 2, it is better practice to avoid the use of this attribute and assign styles to HTML elements by referencing their `class` and `id` attributes.
>
> **name**—This is an old attribute that still has applications when we work with forms. It simply declares a custom name for the element. For more information see Chapter 5.

Besides these, there are more specific attributes, like the `lang` attribute for the `<html>` element introduced before. Two worth mentioning are the `href` attribute for the `<link>` and `<a>` elements and the `src` attribute for media elements such as `<img>` , `<video>`, `<audio>`, etc. Both attributes indicate the path of the file to be loaded or accessed. Try the next example in your browser.

```
<!DOCTYPE html>
<html lang="en">
<head>
  <title>My Second HTML Document</title>
</head>
<body>
  <img src="http://www.minkbooks.com/content/myimage.jpg">
</body>
</html>
```

Listing 1-2: Using the `<img>` *element and the* `src` *attribute to show an image*

Review the Basics: The `<img>` element lets us load and show an image on the screen. It is a single element without a closing tag, and along with the `src` attribute to declare the path of the image, the `width` and `height` attributes may be declared to set its size.

We will study and experiment with these and other attributes in more practical situations throughout the book.

Traditional Elements

In HTML5 some elements were deprecated, some purposes were changed, and some new ones were added. Among those, there are some elements that are no longer considered part of the language, such as `<center>`, `<frame>` or `<font>`. The last one is probably the most significant. The element `<font>`, now usually replaced by the `<span>` element, was used until HTML4 to show text on the screen. Other elements like `<i>` or `<b>`, previously used to emphasize text on the screen, now have a different meaning. While new elements like `<mark>`, `<address>` or `<time>`, for example, were added to provide a better way to describe and represent the document's content.

> **IMPORTANT:** This book focuses on the improvements introduced by HTML5. Concepts already present in the HTML language before HTML5 will be explained only in the **Review the Basics** sections. For a deeper study of the HTML language and to find a complete list of valid HTML elements to use in your projects, please visit our website and follow the links for this chapter.

1.3 Global Structure

HTML documents are strictly organized. Every part of the document is differentiated, declared and enclosed in specific tags. In this part of the chapter, we are going to see how to build the global structure of an HTML document and how this process has been modified in HTML5.

> **Do It Yourself:** Create a new document in a text editor to test in your browser the HTML codes presented later. This will help you remember the new tags and get used to their function.

> **IMPORTANT:** Browsers provide minimum styles to HTML elements. To see the structure created by the HTML code in this chapter on screen, you will have to apply CSS styles. We will study CSS in Chapters 2 and 3.

<!DOCTYPE>

First, we need to indicate the type of document we are creating. Browsers are capable of processing different types of files. To ensure that our document is interpreted correctly as HTML code, we must declare its type at the beginning. In HTML5 this is simple:

```
<!DOCTYPE html>
```

Listing 1-3: Using the `<!DOCTYPE>` *element*

IMPORTANT: This line must be the first line of your file, without any spaces or lines before. This is a way to activate the standard mode and force browsers to interpret HTML5 when it is possible or ignore it otherwise.

Do It Yourself: You can start writing the code in your HTML file now and add each new element studied later.

<html>

After declaring the type of document, we have to build the HTML tree structure. As always, the root element for this tree is the **<html>** element. This element will enclose all our HTML code.

```
<!DOCTYPE html>
<html lang="en">
</html>
```

Listing 1-4: Using the <html> *element*

The attribute **lang** in the opening **<html>** tag is the only attribute we need to specify in HTML5. This attribute defines the human language of the content of the document we are creating—in this case, **en** for English.

IMPORTANT: HTML5 is extremely flexible regarding the structure and the elements used to build it. The **<html>** element may be included without any attributes or may even be ignored. For compatibility, and for a few more reasons not worth mentioning here, we recommend you follow some basic rules. We are going to teach you how to build HTML documents according to what we consider best practices.

To find other languages for the **lang** attribute, you can follow this link: www.w3schools.com/tags/ref_language_codes.asp.

<head>

Let's continue building our document. The HTML code inserted between the **<html>** tags has to be divided into two main sections. Following previous HTML versions, the first section is the head and the second the body. The next step is to create these two sections in the code using the familiar elements **<head>** and **<body>**.

The **<head>** goes first, of course, and like the rest of the structural elements, it has an opening and a closing tag.

```
<!DOCTYPE html>
<html lang="en">
<head>
</head>
</html>
```

Listing 1-5: Using the <head> *element*

The tag itself hasn't changed from previous versions, and its purpose is exactly the same. Within the **<head>** tags we will define the title of our web page, declare the character encoding, provide general information about the document, and incorporate external files with styles, scripts or even images necessary to render the page.

Except for the title and some icons, the rest of the information incorporated in the document between the **<head>** tags is usually not visible to the user.

<body>

The next big section that is part of the main organization of an HTML document is the body. The body is the visible part of the document and is specified with the **<body>** tag. This tag hasn't changed from previous versions of HTML.

```
<!DOCTYPE html>
<html lang="en">
<head>
</head>
<body>

</body>
</html>
```

Listing 1-6: Using the <body> *element*

<meta>

Now it is time to build the document's head. There are a few changes and innovations inside the head, and one of them is the tag that defines the character encoding of the document. This is a **meta** tag, and it specifies how the text has to be presented on the screen.

```
<!DOCTYPE html>
<html lang="en">
<head>
  <meta charset="utf-8">
</head>
<body>
</body>
</html>
```

Listing 1-7: Using the <meta> *element*

The innovation for this element in HTML5, like in most cases, was simplification. The new **meta** tag for the character encoding is shorter and simpler. Of course, you can change **utf-8** for the encoding you prefer to use and other **meta** tags like **description** or **keywords** may be added, as shown in the next example.

```
<!DOCTYPE html>
<html lang="en">
<head>
  <meta charset="utf-8">
  <meta name="description" content="This is an HTML5 example">
  <meta name="keywords" content="HTML5, CSS3, Javascript">
</head>
<body>
</body>
</html>
```

Listing 1-8: Adding more <meta> *elements*

Review the Basics: There are several **<meta>** tags that may be used in a document to declare general information, but this information is not shown in the browser window; it is only important for search engines and devices that need to preview or get a summary of the relevant data of our document. As we mentioned before, aside from the title or some icons, most of the information inserted between the **<head>** tags is not visible to users. In the code in Listing 1-8, the attribute **name** inside the **<meta>** tag specifies its type and the attribute **content** declares its value, but none of these values is shown on the screen. To learn more about **<meta>** tags, go to our website and follow the links for this chapter.

In HTML5, it is not necessary to self-close single tags with a slash at the end, but you can apply self-enclosing for compatibility reasons. You might write the last code this way:

```
<!DOCTYPE html>
<html lang="en">
<head>
  <meta charset="utf-8" />
  <meta name="description" content="This is an example" />
  <meta name="keywords" content="HTML5, CSS3, JavaScript" />
</head>
<body>
</body>
</html>
```

Listing 1-9: Self-closing tags

<title>

The **<title>** tag, as usual, simply specifies the title of the document, and there is nothing new to comment about it.

```
<!DOCTYPE html>
<html lang="en">
<head>
  <meta charset="utf-8">
  <meta name="description" content="This is an HTML5 example">
```

```
  <meta name="keywords" content="HTML5, CSS3, JavaScript">
  <title>This text is the title of the document</title>
</head>
<body>

</body>
</html>
```

Listing 1-10: Using the <title> *element*

> **Review the Basics:** The text between **<title>** tags is the title of the entire document
> we are creating. Usually this text is shown by browsers at the top of the window.

<link>

Another important element that goes in the head of the document is **<link>**. This element is
used to incorporate styles, scripts, images or icons from external files within a document. One of
the most common uses of **<link>** is to incorporate styles by inserting an external CSS file.

```
<!DOCTYPE html>
<html lang="en">
<head>
  <meta charset="utf-8">
  <meta name="description" content="This is an HTML5 example">
  <meta name="keywords" content="HTML5, CSS3, JavaScript">
  <title>This text is the title of the document</title>
  <link rel="stylesheet" href="mystyles.css">
</head>
<body>
</body>
</html>
```

Listing 1-11: Using the <link> *element*

In HTML5, it is no longer necessary to specify what kind of style sheet we are inserting;
consequently, the **type** attribute was eliminated. We only need two attributes to incorporate
our styles' file: **rel** and **href**. The attribute **rel** means relation and specifies the relation
between the document and the file we are incorporating. In this case, the attribute **rel** has the
value **stylesheet** that tells the browser that the file **mystyles.css** is a CSS file with styles
required to render the page.

The **href** attribute, as we explained before, declares the path for the file to be loaded. This
file, of course, must have content according to the value of the **rel** attribute. In this case, the
path points to a CSS file containing styles for the document (the **stylesheet**).

> **Review the Basics:** A style sheet is a group of formatting rules that will help us change
> the appearance of our document—for example, the size and color of the text. Without
> these rules, the text and any other element will be shown on the screen using standard
> styles provided by browsers (default sizes, colors, etc.). Styles are simple rules, usually
> requiring only a few lines of code that may be declared in the same document. As we
> will see later, it is not strictly necessary to get this information from external files, but
> we recommend it as a best practice. Loading the CSS rules from an external document

(another file) will let us organize the main document, increase the load speed of our website and take advantage of the new HTML5 features.

IMPORTANT: In Chapter 2, we will study the CSS language and create the file `mystyles.css` to style our document.

With the last insertion, we can consider the head of our document finished. Now we are able to work on the body, where the magic happens.

1.4 Body Structure

The body structure (the code between `<body>` tags) will generate the visible part of our document. That's the code that will produce our web page.

HTML always offered different ways to build and organize the information in a document's body. One of the first elements provided for this purpose was `<table>`. Tables allowed authors to arrange data, text, images and tools into rows and columns of cells, even when they weren't conceived for that purpose.

In the early days of the Web, tables were a revolution, a big step forward in visualizing the document and improving the users' experience. Gradually later on, other elements replaced the function of tables, providing a different way to do the same thing faster and with less code, thus facilitating creation, portability and maintenance.

The `<div>` element began to dominate the field. With the emergence of more interactive web applications and the integration of HTML, CSS and Javascript, the use of the `<div>` element became common practice. But `<div>`, as well as `<table>`, doesn't provide much information about the parts of the body that the element is representing. Anything from images to menus, text, links, scripts, forms, etc., could go between the opening and closing `<div>` tags. In other words, the keyword `div` only specifies a division in the body, like the cell in a table, but it doesn't give a clue about what kind of division that is, what is the purpose of that division or what is inside.

For users, those clues and indications are not important, but for browsers, the right interpretation of what is inside the document being processed is crucial. After the revolution of portable devices and the emergence of different ways for people to access the Web, the identification of every part of the document is more relevant than ever.

With that in mind, HTML5 incorporates new elements that help identify each part of the document and organize the body. In HTML5, the most important sections of a document are differentiated, and the main structure no longer depends on `<div>` or `<table>` tags.

How we use these new elements is up to us, but the keywords selected for each one will give us a hint about their function. Usually a web page or web application is divided into several visual areas in order to improve the users' experience and interactivity. The keywords representing every new HTML5 element are closely related to those visual areas, as we will see soon.

Organization

Figure 1-1 represents a regular layout currently found in most websites. Despite the fact that every designer creates his or her own designs, in general we will be able to identify every website studied in terms of the following sections:

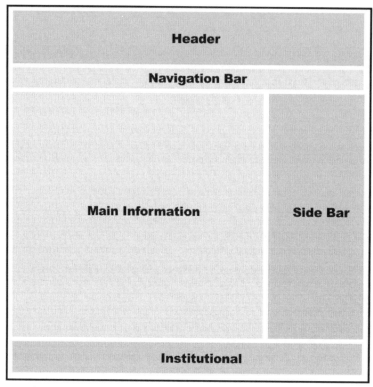

Figure 1-1: Visual representation of a typical web page layout

The top, described as the **Header**, is where you usually have your logo, name, subtitles and short descriptions of your website or web page.

Below, you can see the **Navigation Bar** in which almost every developer offers a menu or list of links for navigation purposes. Users are led from this bar to different pages or documents, usually in the same website.

The most relevant content of the page is usually placed in the middle of the layout. This section presents important information and links. Most of the time, it is divided into several rows and columns. In the example in Figure 1-1, you can see only two columns, **Main Information** and **Side Bar**, but this section is extremely flexible and designers normally adapt it according to their needs by inserting more rows, splitting the columns into smaller blocks or generating different combinations and distributions. The content presented in this part of the layout is usually the top priority. In the example layout, the **Main Information** could have a list of articles, product descriptions, blog entries or any other important information, and the **Side Bar** could show a list of links pointing to each of those items. In a blog, for example, this last column offers a list of links pointing to every blog entry, information about the author, etc.

At the bottom of the typical layout, we have one more bar called the **Institutional** bar. We name it as such because this is the area of the layout where we usually display general information about the website, the author, the company, plus links regarding rules, terms and conditions, maps and all additional data the developer considers worth sharing. The **Institutional** bar is the complement to the **Header**, and it is part of what is now considered the essential structure of a web page.

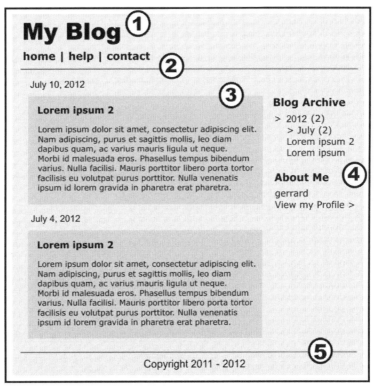

Figure 1-2: *Visual representation of a typical blog layout*

Figure 1-2 is an example of a regular blog. In this example, you can easily identify every part of the design we were considering before.

1. **Header**
2. **Navigation Bar**
3. **Main Information** section
4. **Side Bar**
5. The footer or **Institutional** bar

This simple representation of a blog can help us understand that every section defined in a website has a purpose. Sometimes that purpose isn't clear but the essence is always there, and you will still be able to recognize everywhere any of the sections described above.

HTML5 considers this basic structure and layout, and it provides new elements to differentiate and declare each one of them. Now we can tell browsers what every section is for:

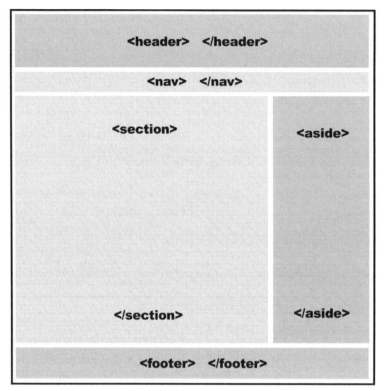

Figure 1-3: *Visual representation of a document's organization using HTML5 tags*

Figure 1-3 shows the typical layout we saw before, but this time with the corresponding HTML5 elements for every section (both opening and closing tags).

\<header>

One of the new elements incorporated in HTML5 is **\<header>**. The **\<header>** must not be confused with the **\<head>** tag, used before to build the head of the document. In the same way that the **\<head>** does, the **\<header>** is intended to provide introductory information (such as titles, subtitles or logos), but the two tags differ in scope. While the **\<head>** tag has the purpose of providing information about the entire document, the **\<header>** is intended only to be used for the body or for sections within the body.

```
<!DOCTYPE html>
<html lang="en">
<head>
  <meta charset="utf-8">
  <meta name="description" content="This is an HTML5 example">
  <meta name="keywords" content="HTML5, CSS3, JavaScript">
  <title>This text is the title of the document</title>
  <link rel="stylesheet" href="mystyles.css">
</head>
```

```
<body>
  <header>
    <h1>This is the main title of the website</h1>
  </header>
</body>
</html>
```

Listing 1-12: *Using the* <header> *element*

In Listing 1-12, we define the title of the web page using the **<header>** tag. Remember that this is not the same as the general title of the document defined previously in the head. The insertion of the **<header>** element represents the beginning of the body and the visible part of the document. From now on we will be able to see the results of the code in the browser window.

> **Do It Yourself:** If you have followed the instructions from the beginning of this chapter, you should already have a text file with the HTML codes studied so far ready to be tested. If not, all you have to do is copy the source code of Listing 1-12 into an empty text file using any text editor (such as Windows' Notepad), save the file with a name and the .**html** extension, and open it in your browser.

> **Review the Basics:** The element **<h1>**, applied in Listing 1-12, is an old HTML element used to define a heading. There is a range of numbers available, from 1 to 6, to indicate the importance of the heading and its content. The element **<h1>** is the highest and **<h6>** is the lowest in importance; therefore **<h1>** will be used to show the main title and the rest for subtitles. Later, we will study how the implementation of these elements was modified in HTML5.

<nav>

The next section of our example is the **Navigation Bar**. This bar is generated in HTML5 with the **<nav>** tag.

```
<!DOCTYPE html>
<html lang="en">
<head>
  <meta charset="utf-8">
  <meta name="description" content="This is an HTML5 example">
  <meta name="keywords" content="HTML5, CSS3, JavaScript">
  <title>This text is the title of the document</title>
  <link rel="stylesheet" href="mystyles.css">
</head>
<body>
  <header>
    <h1>This is the main title of the website</h1>
  </header>
  <nav>
    <ul>
      <li>home</li>
      <li>photos</li>
      <li>videos</li>
      <li>contact</li>
```

```
    </ul>
  </nav>
</body>
</html>
```

Listing 1-13: *Using the* <nav> *element*

As you can see in Listing 1-13, the **<nav>** element is in between the **<body>** tags but falls after the closing tag of the header (**</header>**), not in between **<header>** tags. This is because **<nav>** is not part of the header but instead a new section.

We said before that the structure and the order we choose to use with HTML5 is up to us. That means HTML5 is very versatile and is only giving us the parameters and basic elements to work with, but how to use them is our decision. One example of this versatility is that the **<nav>** tag could be inserted within the **<header>** element or in any other section of the body. However, you must always consider that these new tags were created to provide more information to browsers and to help every new program and device identify the most relevant parts of the document. To keep our HTML code portable and readable, it is best to follow the standards and keep it as clear as possible. The **<nav>** element is intended to contain navigation aids like the main menu or major navigation blocks, and you should use it that way.

> **Review the Basics:** The element **<ul>**, introduced in Listing 1-13, defines a list of items without a specific order. To declare every item of the list we have to use **<li>** elements. These elements are children of **<ul>** (they are introduced in between opening and clossing **<ul>** tags) and are shown on the screen in the order they were declared. To learn more about these traditional HTML elements go to our website and follow the links for this chapter.

<section>

The next parts of our standard design are what we called the **Main Information** bar and the **Side Bar** in Figure 1-1. As we explained before, the **Main Information** bar contains the most relevant information of the document and can be found in different forms—for example, divided into several blocks or more columns. Because the purpose of these columns and blocks is more general, the HTML5 element that specifies these sections was simply called **<section>**.

```
<!DOCTYPE html>
<html lang="en">
<head>
  <meta charset="utf-8">
  <meta name="description" content="This is an HTML5 example">
  <meta name="keywords" content="HTML5, CSS3, JavaScript">
  <title>This text is the title of the document</title>
  <link rel="stylesheet" href="mystyles.css">
</head>
<body>
  <header>
    <h1>This is the main title of the website</h1>
  </header>
  <nav>
    <ul>
      <li>home</li>
```

```
      <li>photos</li>
      <li>videos</li>
      <li>contact</li>
    </ul>
  </nav>
  <section>

  </section>
</body>
</html>
```

Listing 1-14: *Using the* `<section>` *element*

Like the **Navigation Bar**, the **Main Information** bar is a separate section. Therefore, the section for the **Main Information** bar goes below the `</nav>` closing tag.

> **Do It Yourself:** Compare the last HTML code in Listing 1-14 and the layout in Figure 1-3 to understand how the tags are located in the code and what section those tags are generating in the visual representation of the web page.

> **IMPORTANT:** The tags that represent every section of the document are located in the code in a list, one after another, but in the website some of these sections will be side by side (the **Main Information** and **Side Bar** columns, for example). In HTML5, the presentation of these elements on the screen has been delegated to CSS. The design will be achieved by assigning CSS styles to every element. We will study CSS in the next chapter.

<aside>

In the typical website layout (Figure 1-1), the **Side Bar** is beside the **Main Information** bar. This is a column or section that usually contains data related to the main information but is not as relevant nor as important.

In the example of a standard blog layout (Figure 1-2), the **Side Bar** contains a list of links. In that example, the links point to every blog entry and provide additional information about the author of the blog. The information inside this bar is related to the main information but is not relevant by itself. Following the blog example, we can say that the entries of the blog are relevant, but the links and short previews of those entries are only a navigational aid and not what the reader or user will be most interested in.

In HTML5, we are able to differentiate this secondary kind of information with the `<aside>` element.

```
<!DOCTYPE html>
<html lang="en">
<head>
  <meta charset="utf-8">
  <meta name="description" content="This is an HTML5 example">
  <meta name="keywords" content="HTML5, CSS3, JavaScript">
  <title>This text is the title of the document</title>
  <link rel="stylesheet" href="mystyles.css">
</head>
```

```
<body>
  <header>
    <h1>This is the main title of the website</h1>
  </header>
  <nav>
    <ul>
      <li>home</li>
      <li>photos</li>
      <li>videos</li>
      <li>contact</li>
    </ul>
  </nav>
  <section>

  </section>
  <aside>
    <blockquote>Quotation from article number one</blockquote>
    <blockquote>Quotation from article number two</blockquote>
  </aside>
</body>
</html>
```

Listing 1-15: *Using the* <aside> *element*

The **<aside>** element could be located on the right or left side of our sample page; the tag doesn't have a predefined position. The **<aside>** element is only describing the information that is enclosed, not a place in the structure. The **<aside>** element may be located in any part of the layout, and it may be used as long as its content is not considered the main content of the document. For instance, we can use the **<aside>** element inside a **<section>** element, or even within relevant information—for example, for a quotation in a text.

> **Review the Basics:** The **<blockquote>** element used to show information related to each article on the page in Listing 1-15 defines a block of text that is quoted from another part of the document. Browsers style this element by default with margins, providing a specific format for the paragraph they contain.

<footer>

To finish the construction of the elemental structure of our HTML5 document, we only need one more element. We already have the header of the body, sections with navigation aids and important information, and additional information in a side bar. The only thing left is to close the design and give an end to the document's body. HTML5 provides a specific element for this purpose called **<footer>**.

```
<!DOCTYPE html>
<html lang="en">
<head>
  <meta charset="utf-8">
  <meta name="description" content="This is an HTML5 example">
  <meta name="keywords" content="HTML5, CSS3, JavaScript">
  <title>This text is the title of the document</title>
  <link rel="stylesheet" href="mystyles.css">
</head>
```

```
<body>
  <header>
    <h1>This is the main title of the website</h1>
  </header>
  <nav>
    <ul>
      <li>home</li>
      <li>photos</li>
      <li>videos</li>
      <li>contact</li>
    </ul>
  </nav>
  <section>

  </section>
  <aside>
    <blockquote>Quotation from article number one</blockquote>
    <blockquote>Quotation from article number two</blockquote>
  </aside>
  <footer>
    Copyright &copy; 2012-2013
  </footer>
</body>
</html>
```

Listing 1-16: Using the `<footer>` *element*

On the typical web page layout (Figure 1-1), the section named the **Institutional** bar would be defined with **<footer>** tags. This is because the bar represents the end (or foot) of our document, and this part of the web page is commonly used to share general information about the author or the company behind the project, like copyright, terms and conditions, etc.

Usually, the **<footer>** element will represent the end of the body of our document and have the main purpose described above. However, the **<footer>** tag may be used several times within the body to also represent the end of different sections. (The **<header>** tag may be used several times within the body as well.) We will study this use later.

1.5 Deep inside the Body

The body of our document is ready. The basic structure of our website is finished, but we still have to work on the content. The HTML5 elements studied so far help us identify every section of the layout and assign an intrinsic purpose for each one, but what is really important for our website is what is inside those sections.

Most of the elements already examined were created to provide a structure for the HTML document that can be identified and recognized by browsers and new devices. We learned about the **<body>** tags to declare the body or the visible part of the document, the **<header>** tags to enclose important information for the body, the **<nav>** tags to supply navigational aids, the **<section>** tags to contain the most relevant content, and the **<aside>** and **<footer>** tags to provide additional information. But none of these elements declares anything about the content itself. All of them have a very specific structural purpose.

The further inside the document we go, the closer we get to defining the content. This information will be composed of different visual elements such as titles, texts, images, videos and interactive applications, among others. We need to be able to differentiate these elements and establish relationships among them.

<article>

The layout considered before (Figure 1-1) is the most common and basic structure for websites on the Internet today, but it is also representative of how key content is shown on the screen. In the same way that blogs are divided into entries, websites usually present relevant information divided into parts that share similar characteristics. The **<article>** element lets us identify each of these parts.

```html
<!DOCTYPE html>
<html lang="en">
<head>
  <meta charset="utf-8">
  <meta name="description" content="This is an HTML5 example">
  <meta name="keywords" content="HTML5, CSS3, JavaScript">
  <title>This text is the title of the document</title>
  <link rel="stylesheet" href="mystyles.css">
</head>
<body>
  <header>
    <h1>This is the main title of the website</h1>
  </header>
  <nav>
    <ul>
      <li>home</li>
      <li>photos</li>
      <li>videos</li>
      <li>contact</li>
    </ul>
  </nav>
  <section>
    <article>
      This is the text of my first post
    </article>
    <article>
      This is the text of my second post
    </article>
  </section>
  <aside>
    <blockquote>Quotation from article number one</blockquote>
    <blockquote>Quotation from article number two</blockquote>
  </aside>
  <footer>
    Copyright &copy; 2012-2013
  </footer>
</body>
</html>
```

Listing 1-17: Using the <article> *element*

As you can see in the HTML code in Listing 1-17, the **<article>** tags are between the **<section>** tags. The **<article>** tags belong to that section; they are its children, in the same way that every element between the `<body>` tags is a child of the body. But, as with every child of the body, the `<article>` tags are placed one after another. Each one is an independent part of the `<section>`, as shown on Figure 1-4.

> **Review the Basics:** As we explained before, the HTML structure can be described as a tree, with the `<html>` element as its root. Another way to describe the relationships among elements is to name them as parents, children or siblings according to their position in the tree structure. For example, in a typical HTML document the `<body>` element is child of the `<html>` element and sibling of the `<head>` element. Both, `<body>` and `<head>`, has the `<html>` element as their parent.

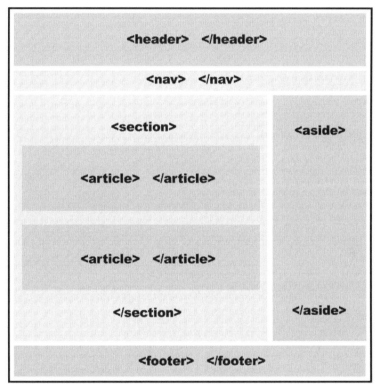

Figure 1-4: *Visual representation of the* `<article>` *tags inside the section created to hold the relevant information of the web page*

The `<article>` element is not limited by its name—so it's not limited to news articles, for example. The `<article>` element is intended to contain an independent item of content; therefore, it may include a forum post, magazine article, blog entry, user's comment, etc. This element will group portions of information that are related to each other regardless of the nature of that information.

As an independent part of the document, the content of every `<article>` element will have its own independent structure. To define this structure, we can take advantage of the versatility of the `<header>` and `<footer>` tags studied before. These tags are portable and can be used not only in the body but also in every section of our document.

```
<!DOCTYPE html>
<html lang="en">
<head>
  <meta charset="utf-8">
  <meta name="description" content="This is an HTML5 example">
  <meta name="keywords" content="HTML5, CSS3, JavaScript">
  <title>This text is the title of the document</title>
  <link rel="stylesheet" href="mystyles.css">
</head>
<body>
  <header>
    <h1>This is the main title of the website</h1>
  </header>
  <nav>
    <ul>
      <li>home</li>
      <li>photos</li>
      <li>videos</li>
      <li>contact</li>
    </ul>
  </nav>
  <section>
    <article>
      <header>
        <h1>Title of post One</h1>
      </header>
      This is the text of my first post
      <footer>
        <p>comments (0)</p>
      </footer>
    </article>
    <article>
      <header>
        <h1>Title of post Two</h1>
      </header>
      This is the text of my second post
      <footer>
        <p>comments (0)</p>
      </footer>
    </article>
  </section>
  <aside>
    <blockquote>Quotation from article number one</blockquote>
    <blockquote>Quotation from article number two</blockquote>
  </aside>
  <footer>
    Copyright &copy; 2012-2013
  </footer>
</body>
</html>
```

Listing 1-18: *Building the structure of the* `<article>`

Both posts inserted in the code in Listing 1-18 were built with the **<article>** element and have a specific structure. First, we have the **<header>** tags containing the title defined with an **<h1>** element. Below it is the content itself, that is the text of the post. And finally, after the text comes the **<footer>** tag specifying the number of comments.

Review the Basics: The `<p>` element declared inside the `<footer>` of every article in Listing 1-18 is used to define a paragraph. Browsers style these tags by default with margins and a line break. Besides the declaration of paragraphs, we can also take advantage of the properties of this element to provide a format to short texts, like in this case.

<hgroup>

Inside each `<header>` element, at the top of the body or at the beginning of every `<article>` of our examples, we incorporated `<h1>` tags to specify a title. Basically, `<h1>` tags are what is needed to create the head line of every part of the document. But sometimes we also need to add subtitles or more information to declare what the web page or the section is about. In fact, the `<header>` element is intended to contain other elements as well—for example, a table of contents, search forms, or short texts and logos.

To build the header, we can take advantage of the rest of the H tags: `<h1>`, `<h2>`, `<h3>`, `<h4>`, `<h5>` and `<h6>`. But for internal processing purposes, and to avoid generating multiple sections or subsections during the interpretation of the document, these tags must be grouped together. To do this, HTML5 provides the `<hgroup>` element.

```
<!DOCTYPE html>
<html lang="en">
<head>
  <meta charset="utf-8">
  <meta name="description" content="This is an HTML5 example">
  <meta name="keywords" content="HTML5, CSS3, JavaScript">
  <title>This text is the title of the document</title>
  <link rel="stylesheet" href="mystyles.css">
</head>
<body>
  <header>
    <h1>This is the main title of the website</h1>
  </header>
  <nav>
    <ul>
      <li>home</li>
      <li>photos</li>
      <li>videos</li>
      <li>contact</li>
    </ul>
  </nav>
  <section>
    <article>
      <header>
        <hgroup>
          <h1>Title of post One</h1>
          <h2>subtitle of the post One</h2>
        </hgroup>
        <p>posted 12-10-2012</p>
      </header>
      This is the text of my first post
      <footer>
        <p>comments (0)</p>
      </footer>
```

```
      </article>
      <article>
        <header>
          <hgroup>
            <h1>Title of post Two</h1>
            <h2>subtitle of the post Two</h2>
          </hgroup>
          <p>posted 12-15-2012</p>
        </header>
        This is the text of my second post
        <footer>
          <p>comments (0)</p>
        </footer>
      </article>
    </section>
    <aside>
      <blockquote>Quotation from article number one</blockquote>
      <blockquote>Quotation from article number two</blockquote>
    </aside>
    <footer>
      Copyright &copy; 2012-2013
    </footer>
  </body>
</html>
```

Listing 1-19: *Using the* <hgroup> *element*

H tags must keep their hierarchy, which means that you must first declare the title with the **<h1>** tag, then use **<h2>** for the subtitle, and so on. However, unlike the older versions of HTML, HTML5 lets you reuse the H tags and build this hierarchy again and again in every section of the document. In the example in Listing 1-19, we add a subtitle and metadata to each post and group the title and subtitle together with **<hgroup>**, reusing the **<h1>** and **<h2>** hierarchy in every **<article>** element.

> **IMPORTANT:** The element **<hgroup>** is necessary when we have a title and subtitle or more H tags together in the same **<header>**. This element can only contain H tags and that's why we kept the metadata outside in the example. If you only have the **<h1>** tag or the **<h1>** tag along with metadata, you don't have to group these elements together. For example, in the **<header>** of the body we didn't use this element because we only have one H element inside. Always remember that **<hgroup>** is only intended to group H tags together just as its name clearly specifies.

Browsers and programs that execute and render websites read the HTML code and create its own internal structure to interpret and process every element. This internal structure is divided into sections that are independent of the divisions in the design or the **<section>** element. These are conceptual sections generated during the interpretation of the code. The **<header>** element doesn't create one of these conceptual sections by itself; this means that the elements inside the **<header>** will represent different levels and could generate internally different sections. The **<hgroup>** element was created with the purpose of grouping H tags together and avoiding misinterpretations by the browser.

> **Review the Basics:** Metadata is a set of data that describes and provides information about another set of data. In the example, the metadata is the date when the articles were inserted.

\<figure\> and \<figcaption\>

The **\<figure\>** tag was created to be more specific in declaring the document's content. Before this element was introduced, we couldn't identify content that was part of the information but self-contained—for example, illustrations, pictures, videos, etc. Usually those elements are part of the relevant content but can be moved away without affecting or interrupting a document's flow. When this type of information is present, **\<figure\>** tags may be used to identify it.

```html
<!DOCTYPE html>
<html lang="en">
<head>
  <meta charset="utf-8">
  <meta name="description" content="This is an HTML5 example">
  <meta name="keywords" content="HTML5, CSS3, JavaScript">
  <title>This text is the title of the document</title>
  <link rel="stylesheet" href="mystyles.css">
</head>
<body>
  <header>
    <h1>This is the main title of the website</h1>
  </header>
  <nav>
    <ul>
      <li>home</li>
      <li>photos</li>
      <li>videos</li>
      <li>contact</li>
    </ul>
  </nav>
  <section>
    <article>
      <header>
        <hgroup>
          <h1>Title of post One</h1>
          <h2>subtitle of the post One</h2>
        </hgroup>
        <p>posted 12-10-2012</p>
      </header>
      This is the text of my first post
      <figure>
        <img src="http://minkbooks.com/content/myimage.jpg">
        <figcaption>
          This is the image of the first post
        </figcaption>
      </figure>
      <footer>
        <p>comments (0)</p>
      </footer>
    </article>
    <article>
      <header>
        <hgroup>
          <h1>Title of post Two</h1>
          <h2>subtitle of the post Two</h2>
        </hgroup>
        <p>posted 12-15-2012</p>
```

```
    </header>
    This is the text of my second post
    <footer>
      <p>comments (0)</p>
    </footer>
  </article>
</section>
<aside>
  <blockquote>Quotation from article number one</blockquote>
  <blockquote>Quotation from article number two</blockquote>
</aside>
<footer>
  Copyright &copy; 2012-2013
</footer>
</body>
</html>
```

Listing 1-20: *Using the* `<figure>` *and* `<figcaption>` *elements*

In the first post in Listing 1-20, we insert an image (`<img src="http://www.minkbooks.com/content/myimage.jpg">`) after the text of the post. This is a common practice; often text is enriched with images or videos. The `<figure>` tags let us enclose these visual complements and differentiate them from the most relevant information.

Also in Listing 1-20, you can see an extra element inside `<figure>`. Usually units of information like images or videos are described with a short text below. HTML5 provides an element to place and identify this descriptive caption. The `<figcaption>` tags enclose the caption related to the `<figure>` and establish a relationship between both elements and their content.

<details> and <summary>

An important feature for websites is the ability to display additional information when it is requested by the user. To avoid the use of Javascript and facilitate the creation of this tool, HTML5 incorporates the elements `<details>` and `<summary>`. The `<details>` element declares the tool. Inside this element we specify the title of the tool with the `<summary>` element and all the information to be disclosed bellow.

```
<details>
  <summary>Click here to expand</summary>
  <p>Hey! I'm visible!</p>
</details>
```

Listing 1-21: *Creating a tool with* `<details>` *and* `<summary>`

▶ Click here to expand   ▼ Click here to expand

                                Hey! I'm visible!

Figure 1-5: *The* `<details>` *element before and after is clicked*

1.6 New and Old Elements

HTML5 was developed in order to simplify, specify and organize the code. To achieve these purposes, elements and attributes were added and HTML was integrated with CSS and Javascript. These incorporations and improvements from previous versions relate not only to new elements but also to the way we use the old ones.

<mark>

The **<mark>** tag was added to highlight part of a text that originally wasn't considered important but is now relevant according to the user's activity. The best example is a search result. The **<mark>** element will highlight the part of the text that matches the search string.

```
<span>My <mark>car</mark> is red</span>
```

Listing 1-22: Using the <mark> *element to highlight the word "car"*

When someone performs a search on a web page for the word "car", the results could be shown with the code in Listing 1-22. The short text represents the results of the search, and the **<mark>** tags in between enclose the text that was searched (the word "car"). In some browsers, this word will be highlighted with a yellow background by default, but you can always overwrite those styles with your own using CSS, as we will see in later chapters.

In the past, we usually achieved the same result using a **<b>** element. However, the addition of **<mark>** helped change the meaning and set up a new purpose for these and other related elements.

- **<em>** is used to indicate emphasis (replacing the **<i>** tag we used before)
- **<strong>** is for importance
- **<mark>** highlights text that is relevant according to the circumstances
- **<b>** should be used only when there is no other element appropriate for the situation
- **<i>** no longer declares italic style for a text, but according to the specification, it represents an alternate voice or mood, such as a thought, a technical term, etc.

<small>

The new specificity of HTML is also evident in elements such as **<small>**. Previously, this element presented any text in small font. The keyword referenced the size of the text, independently of its meaning. In HTML5, the purpose of the **<small>** element is to represent small print, like legal print, disclaimers, etc.

```
<small>Copyright &copy; 2012 MinkBooks</small>
```

Listing 1-23: Legal print with <small>

<cite>

Another element that has become more specific is **<cite>**. Now the **<cite>** tags enclose the title of a work such as a book, movie, song, etc.

```
<span>I love the movie <cite>Temptations</cite></span>
```

Listing 1-24: *Citing a movie with* `<cite>`

<address>

The **<address>** element is an old element that has become a structural element. We didn't have to use it before to build our document, but it can fit perfectly in some situations to represent the contact information for the content of an **<article>** element or the entire **<body>**.

This element should be included inside a **<footer>**, as in the next example:

```
<article>
  <header>
    <h1>Title of post Two</h1>
  </header>
  This is the text of the article
  <footer>
    <address>
      <a href="http://www.jdgauchat.com">J.D. Gauchat</a>
    </address>
  </footer>
</article>
```

Listing 1-25: *Adding contact information to an* `<article>`

> **Review the Basics:** The nature of HTML is hypertext, a text that presents references to other texts and allows readers to move or "navigate" through documents. The **<a>** element, implemented in the example in Listing 1-25, is used to create the hyperlinks necessary to provide this feature. As we already mentioned, this element has an important attribute called **href** to declare the path of the document we are pointing to.

<wbr>

The traditional **
, a single element without a closing tag, was the only element used to insert a line break in a paragraph. Browsers display a line break in the place of this element. But this is only useful when we know exactly where the line break should be generated. HTML5 introduces the new **<wbr> element that suggests the possibility of a line break if it is necessary. This ensures the browser won't break the lines in the wrong places.

In the following example, the browser will generate a line break after displaying the first line of text, and then, according to the space available, will show the second line completely or will generate a second line break after the domain:

```
<article>
  <header>
    <h1>Title of post</h1>
  </header>
  This is the text of the article<br>
  Visit this URL: www.minkbooks.com<wbr>/content/bricks.jpg
</article>
```

Listing 1-26: Implementing the `<br>` *and the* `<wbr>` *elements*

<time>

In every **<article>** in the document of Listing 1-20, we included the date to indicate when the article was posted. We used a simple **<p>** element inside the **<header>** of the articles to show the date, but there is a special element in HTML5 for this specific purpose. The **<time>** element lets you declare a machine-readable timestamp and a human-readable text representing the date and time.

```
<article>
  <header>
    <h1>Title of post Two</h1>
    <time datetime="2012-10-12" pubdate>posted 12-10-2012</time>
  </header>
  This is the text of the article
</article>
```

Listing 1-27: Date and time using the `<time>` *element*

In Listing 1-27, the **<p>** element used in previous examples is replaced by the new **<time>** element to show the date when the article was posted. The attribute **datetime** has a value that represents the machine-readable timestamp. The format of this timestamp usually will follow a pattern as in this example: **2012-10-12T12:10:45**. We also include the attribute **pubdate**, which is added to indicate that the value of the attribute **datetime** represents the publication date.

<data>

For data that are not related to date and time, we can use the **<data>** element. This element uses the **value** attribute to represent the machine-readable value.

```
<data value="32">Thirty Two</data>
```

Listing 1-28: Using the `<data>` *element*

1.7 New and Old Attributes

In the early days of web development, the purpose of attributes was to provide style to the elements they were applied to. With the integration of HTML, CSS and Javascript, that purpose changed. Now attributes are focused on declaring the type of content the element has and the type of functionality it will have. To achieve this, HTML5 altered the characteristics of some old attributes and added new ones.

The Data-* Attribute

If we need to declare additional data not only for the `<data>` and `<time>` elements but for any HTML element, then the `data-*` attribute is our solution. This attribute provides the alternative to assign additional information to an element without exposing it to the user. This information is intended for use by the website and is accessible from Javascript code, as we will study later.

The name of the attribute is composed by the prefix `data-` follow by a custom name.

```
<p data-firstinitial="J" data-last="Gauchat">J.D. Gauchat</p>
```

Listing 1-29: Using the data-* *attribute*

> **IMPORTANT:** We will work with the `data-*` attribute and the `dataset` property in Chapter 4.

Reversed

In the HTML document of Listing 1-20, we took advantage of the traditional `<ul>` and `<li>` elements to generate a list of items. In that case, the order of the items wasn't particularly important so the use of the `<ul>` element was correct, but when the order matters, you should use the `<ol>` element instead. This element generates an ascending list identified with numbers by default. The improvement in HTML5 is the addition of the Boolean attribute `reversed` to create a descending list of items.

```
<ol reversed>
  <li>home</li>
  <li>photos</li>
  <li>videos</li>
  <li>contact</li>
</ol>
```

Listing 1-30: Generating a descending list

The items are always shown in the order they were declared, but the numbers referencing each item will reflect the ascending or descending order.

Ping and Download

The **<a>** element is probably the most important element of HTML. It is the element that defines the most significant characteristic of the language: the hyperlink. It was created to link one document to another, allowing users to "navigate" and easily access the information provided by the website. But now, accessing documents is not the only thing we do. We also need to be able to download those documents and developers need to keep track of our activity. HTML5 incorporates two new attributes that preserve the validity of this element and add the functionality required:

> **ping**—This attribute declares the path for the URLs to be informed when the user clicks on the link. The value could be one or more URLs separated by a space.

> **download**—This is a Boolean attribute which, when present, indicates that instead of reading the file the browser should download it.

```
<a href="http://www.minkbooks.com/content/myfile.pdf"
ping="http://www.jdgauchat.com/control.php" download>Click here to
Download</a>
```

Listing 1-31: Applying the ping *and* download *attributes*

In the example in Listing 1-31, the URL of the hyperlink points to the file **myfile.pdf**. In normal circumstances, a modern browser would show the file's content on the screen, but in this case the **download** attribute forces the browser to download the file. We also include a **ping** attribute pointing to a file called **control.php**. As a result, every time a user clicks on the link, the PDF file is downloaded and the PHP script is executed, allowing the developer to keep track of this activity (we can store user's information in a database, for example).

> **Do It Yourself:** Copy the source code of Listing 1-31 in an empty file, save it with a name and the extension **.html**, and open the file in your browser. When you click on the link, the browser should prompt you to download the file. Try eliminating the **download** attribute to compare the browser's behaviors.

Translate

Most current browsers automatically translate a document when a foreign language is detected, but in some cases there are texts that should remain untouched—such as names, original titles, etc. To control the translation process from HTML, the **translate** attribute was added.

```
<p>Mi película favorita es <span translate="no">Dos Caminos</span></p>
```

Listing 1-32: Using the translate *attribute*

The attribute may have two values: **yes** or **no**. By default the value is **yes**, unless a parent element was changed to **no**. In the example in Listing 1-32, the name of the movie is enclosed by **<span>** tags to specify that this part of the text should be preserved as is.

Review the Basics: The `<span>` element is a generic element used for organization or styling purposes. Due to its characteristics, it is often used to style text, replacing the function of the traditional `<font>` element, currently deprecated. This element shares similar characteristics with the `<div>` element, with the difference that the latter is a block element while `<span>` is an inline element, which makes it suitable for styling and organizing text.

Contenteditable

The ability to edit the content of a webpage has existed for years, but it was never an official feature. Now, with the introduction of the `contenteditable` attribute, we can turn any HTML element into an editable one.

```
<p>My favorite movie is <span contenteditable="true">Casablanca</span>
</p>
```

Listing 1-33: *Using* `contenteditable` *to edit text*

The attribute has two possible values: `true` or `false`. By default none element is editable. Setting the attribute as `true` for an element allows users to edit its content.

Do It Yourself: Copy the source code of Listing 1-33 in an empty file, save it with a name and the extension `.html`, and open the file in your browser. Click on the name of the movie to change it.

Spellcheck

Another feature that is activated automatically by browsers is the spell check. While this is a useful tool and users expect to have it all the time, it can be inappropriate in some circumstances. To activate or deactivate this feature, we can use the `spellcheck` attribute.

```
<p>My favorite movie is <span contenteditable="true"
spellcheck="false">Casablanca</span></p>
```

Listing 1-34: *Deactivating the spell check feature*

This attribute, like those above, has also two possible values: `true` or `false`. The feature is always activated unless we declare the value of this attribute as `false`. In the example in Listing 1-34, the `spellcheck` attribute is applied to the same element we used before. Now, you will be able to change the name of the movie without the browser checking for orthographic or grammatical errors.

Chapter 2
CSS Styling and Box Models

2.1 CSS and HTML

As we previously discussed, the new specification of HTML is not only about tags and HTML itself. The Web demands design and functionality, not just structural organization and section definitions. In this new paradigm, HTML merges with CSS and Javascript as one integrated instrument. So far we have considered the function of every technology and studied the new HTML elements responsible for a document's structure; now, we are going to examine the relevance of CSS in this strategic union and its influence in the presentation of HTML documents.

Officially, CSS has nothing to do with HTML5. CSS is not part of the specification and never was: it was in fact a complement developed to overcome the limitations and reduce the complexity of HTML. Initially, attributes within HTML tags provided some essential styles to every element, but as the language evolved, the code became more complicated to write and maintain and HTML alone no longer could meet the demands of web designers. As a result, CSS was soon adopted as the way to separate structure from presentation. Since then, CSS has thrived but developed in parallel, focused on designers and their needs rather than necessarily being a part of HTML's evolution.

The newest version of CSS, CSS3, follows the same path, but this time with much more compromise. The HTML5 specification was developed implicitly considering CSS in charge of the design. Because of this, the integration between HTML and CSS3 is now vital for web development, and that is why every time we mention HTML5 we also make reference to CSS3, even when officially these are two independent technologies.

Presently, CSS3 features are being implemented and incorporated into HTML5 compatible browsers along with the rest of the specification. In this chapter, we will study the basic concepts of CSS and the new CSS3 techniques available for presentation and structuring. We will also learn about new selectors and pseudo-classes that make the selection and identification of HTML elements easier.

> **IMPORTANT:** The following is a brief introduction to CSS styles. We only mention the techniques and properties necessary to understand the examples in this book. If you don't have any experience with CSS, you can learn from tutorials on the Web. To find this resources, visit our website and follow the links for this chapter.

2.2 A Brief Introduction to CSS

CSS is a language that works with HTML to provide visual styles for the elements of the document, such as size, color, backgrounds, borders, etc. Although each browser grants styles by default to every HTML element, those styles may not match the designer's vision. Usually the styles are far from what we want for our websites. Designers and developers often have to apply their own styles to achieve the look and organization on the screen they desire.

In this part of the chapter, we will review CSS styling and explain basic techniques to define a document's structure.

> **IMPORTANT:** Some of the concepts explained in the following paragraphs are to introduce beginners to CSS and the basics of styling. If you are familiar with this information, please feel free to skip over the parts you already know.

CSS Rules

CSS basically defines how HTML elements are going to be displayed on the screen. To apply the styles, CSS uses properties and values. This construction is called **declaration** and the syntax includes a colon after the name of the property and a semicolon to close the line.

```
color: #FF0000;
```

Listing 2-1: Declaring CSS properties

In the example in Listing 2-1, the property's name is `color` and the value assigned to this property is `#FF0000`. If this property is applied later to an HTML element, that element will be shown on the screen in the color red.

> **Review the Basics:** In CSS, colors are defined by the combination of three basic colors: red, green and blue. To represent those colors we can use hexadecimal numbers (from 00 to FF) or decimal numbers (from 0 to 255). If we decide to use hexadecimal numbers, we have to express the color with a pound sign at the beginning, as in the example in Listing 2-1. For decimal numbers there is a function available called `rgb`, and the colors are declared using the syntax `rgb(255, 0, 0)`. We will study the `rgb()` function and other similar functions later in this book.

Properties can be grouped together using braces (i.e., { }). This group of one or more properties is called **rule** and is identified by a name or *selector*, representing the element or group of elements that will be affected by the rule. We can create as many rules as we want.

```
p {
  color: #FF0000;
  font-size: 24px;
}
```

Listing 2-2: Declaring CSS rules

In Listing 2-2 you can see two properties with their corresponding values surrounded by braces (`color` and `font-size`). This rule is identified with the name `p`. In this case, the name of the rule is a reference to the `<p>` elements. If we apply this rule to our document, the content of every `<p>` element will be red and with a size of 24 pixels.

We can declare as many selectors as we want in a CSS rule, all we have to do is write their names separated by a comma.

```
p, span {
  color: #FF0000;
  font-size: 24px;
}
```

Listing 2-3: Declaring CSS rules

In the example in Listing 2-3, the rule affects all the **<p>** and **<span>** elements found in the document.

We can, as well, reference only elements that are inside a particular element by listing the selectors separated by a space. For example, **<span>** elements that are children of **<p>** elements:

```
p span {
  color: #FF0000;
  font-size: 24px;
}
```

Listing 2-4: Declaring CSS rules

There are different methods to reference HTML elements from CSS. The one we applied in previous examples simply uses the name of the type of elements we want to be affected. This is a general reference, but there are more specific ones that we will study shortly.

Properties

As you can see, properties are the core of CSS. There are dozens of properties and new ones are added for every version of the language. We are going to apply some of those properties in practical situations throughout the book. Meanwhile, here is a list of the most common ones (included since the first version of CSS) that you will find in our examples:

> **font**—This property allows us to declare several styles for a text, such as weight, size, font family, etc. The values must be separated by a space and declared in a specific order (e.g., **font: bold 24px arial,sans-serif**). We can also declare every style independently using the associated properties **font-style, font-variant, font-weight, font-size, line-height** and **font-family** (e.g., **font-size: 24px**).
>
> **color**—This property declares the color of an element. The value may be expressed in hexadecimal (e.g., **color: #FF0000;**) or decimal numbers (e.g., **color: rgb(255, 0, 0);**).
>
> **background**—This property allows us to apply several styles to an element's background, such as color, image, repetition, etc. The values specified must be separated by a space (e.g., **background: #0000FF url('bricks.jpg') no-repeat;**). Every style may be declared independently using individual properties. We will study this and all the associated properties in further detail in Chapter 3.

width—This property declares the width of an element (e.g., `width: 200px`).

height—This property declares the height of an element (e.g., `height: 200px`).

margin—This property declares the external margin for an element. The margin is the space around the element. It may have four values: up, right, bottom and left, in that order and separated by a space (e.g., `margin: 10px 30px 10px 30px;`). However, if only one, two or three parameters are declared, the others will take the same values (e.g., `margin: 10px 30px`). Values can also be declared independently using the associated properties `margin-top`, `margin-right`, `margin-bottom` and `margin-left` (e.g., `margin-left: 10px;`).

padding— This property declares the internal margin of an element. The padding is space around the content of the element and inside its border—for example, the space between the title and the border of the virtual box created by the `<h1>` element that contains that title. The values are declared the same way as for the `margin` property. Values can also be declared independently using the associated properties `padding-top`, `padding-right`, `padding-bottom` and `padding-left` (e.g., `padding-top: 10px;`).

border— This property allows us to declare the width, style and color of an element's border (e.g., `border: 1px solid #990000;`). The possible values for the style are `none`, `hidden`, `dotted`, `dashed`, `solid`, `double`, `groove`, `ridge`, `inset`, `outset` or `inherit`. This property also has associated properties for every side of an element: `border-top`, `border-bottom`, `border-left` and `border-right`. We can also assign values for the width, style and color to each side independently adding the name at the end of the property, but we always have to declare the border before make any change to it (e.g., `border-style: solid; border-top-width: 10px;`).

text-align—This property aligns the element inside its parent. The possible values are `left`, `right`, `center`, `justify` or `inherit`.

IMPORTANT: These are not the only CSS properties available. In this book we will apply only a few of the traditional properties and study the new ones incorporated in CSS3. To learn more about the language, please visit our website and follow the links for this chapter.

Inline Styles

Applying styles to HTML elements changes the way they are presented on the screen. As we said before, by default browsers provide a set of styles that in most cases do not satisfy the needs of designers. To change this, we can overwrite them with our own styles using different techniques. One of those techniques is to assign styles inside the element as an attribute. Listing 2-5, below, provides a simple HTML document showing the `<p>` element modified by the attribute `style` with the value `font-size: 20px`. This property changes the default size of the text inside the `<p>` element to the new size of 20 pixels.

```
<!DOCTYPE html>
<html lang="en">
<head>
  <title>This text is the title of the document</title>
</head>
```

```
<body>
  <p style="font-size: 20px">My text</p>
</body>
</html>
```

Listing 2-5: CSS *styles within HTML tags*

Do It Yourself: In an empty text file, copy the HTML code and open the file in your browser to see how it works. Note that the file must have the `.html` extension to open properly (e.g., `myfile.html`).

Using the technique outlined above is a good way to test styles and see their effects, but it is not recommended for a larger project. The reason is simple: for this technique, we have to write and repeat every style for every element, greatly increasing the document's size, making it impossible to update and maintain. Imagine if you decide that instead of 20 pixels the size of the text in every **<p>** element should be 24 pixels. You would have to change every style in every **<p>** tag in the whole document and in every document of your website.

Embedded Styles

A better alternative to the previous technique is to insert styles in the head of the document and then use references to affect the proper HTML elements.

```
<!DOCTYPE html>
<html lang="en">
<head>
  <title>This text is the title of the document</title>
  <style>
    p { font-size: 20px }
  </style>
</head>
<body>
  <p>My text</p>
</body>
</html>
```

Listing 2-6: Listing s*tyles in the head of the document*

The **<style>** element allows developers to insert CSS styles within documents. In previous HTML versions, it was necessary to specify what kind of styles would be inserted; but in HTML5, the default style is CSS, so we don't need to add any attributes to the opening **<style>** tag.

The highlighted code in Listing 2-6 has the same function as the line of code in Listing 2-5, but in this example, we don't have to write the style inside every **<p>** tag in the document because all **<p>** elements are already affected. With this method we are reducing our code and assigning the style we want to the right elements using references.

External Files

Declaring the styles in the head of the document saves space and makes the code more consistent and maintainable, but it requires a copy of the styles in every document of our website. The solution to this replication is to move all the styles to an external file and then use the **\<link>** element to insert this file to any document that requires styling. This method also allows us to change a whole set of styles simply by including a different file. It also allows us to modify or adapt our documents to every circumstance or device, as we will see at the end of the book.

In Chapter 1, we studied the **\<link>** tag and saw how to insert CSS files in our documents. Using the line **\<link rel="stylesheet" href="mystyles.css">**, we told the browser to load the file **mystyles.css** that contains all the styles needed to render the page. This practice is widely used among designers that already work with HTML5. The **\<link>** tag referencing the CSS file will be inserted in any document where the styles are required.

```
<!DOCTYPE html>
<html lang="en">
<head>
  <title>This text is the title of the document</title>
  <link rel="stylesheet" href="mystyles.css">
</head>
<body>
  <p>My text</p>
</body>
</html>
```

Listing 2-7: Applying CSS styles from an external file

Do It Yourself: From this point on, we will be adding the CSS styles to a file called **mystyles.css**. You have to create that file in the same folder as the HTML file and copy the CSS styles inside this file to see them working.

Review the Basics: CSS files are also regular text files. As well as the HTML files, you can create them using any text editor, such as Windows' Notepad.

References

Putting all our styles together in one external file and linking that file from every document is very convenient. However, we need mechanisms to establish a specific relationship between these styles and the elements inside the document that will be affected by them.

In previous examples, we applied one of the techniques used to assign styles to an element. For example, in Listing 2-6, the style to change the font size referenced every **\<p>** element using the **p** keyword. As a result, the style inserted between the **\<style>** tags assigned that particular CSS style to each **\<p>** element of the document.

There are three basic methods to select which HTML element will be affected by a CSS rule:

- by the keyword of the element
- by the **id** attribute
- by the **class** attribute

However, we will later see that CSS3 is flexible in this regard and incorporates new and more specific ways of doing this.

Referencing by Keyword

Declaring the CSS rule with the keyword of the element will affect every element of that type in the document. For example, the following rule will change the styles of the **<p>** elements:

```
p { font-size: 20px }
```

Listing 2-8: Referencing by keyword

With the keyword **p** in front of the rule, we are telling the browser that this rule must be applied to every **<p>** element found in the HTML document. Conequently, all the texts surrounded by **<p>** tags will have the size of 20 pixels.

Of course, the same will work for any other HTML element in the document. If we specified the keyword **span** instead of **p**, for instance, every text between **<span>** tags would have the size of 20 pixels.

```
span { font-size: 20px }
```

Listing 2-9: Referencing by another keyword

But what happens if we only need to reference one specific tag? Do we need to use the **style** attribute inside that tag? The answer is no. As we discussed before, the **Inline Styles** method (using the attribute **style** within HTML tags) is a deprecated technique, and its use should be reserved only for testing purposes. To select a specific HTML element from the rules in our CSS file, we can use two different attributes: **id** and **class**.

Referencing by the Id Attribute

The **id** attribute is more like a name, an identification of the element. This means that the value of this attribute can't be duplicated. This name must be unique in the entire document.

To reference a particular element using the **id** attribute from our CSS file, the rule has to be declared with the pound sign (**#**) in front of the identification value.

```
#text1 { font-size: 20px }
```

Listing 2-10: Referencing by the value of the id *attribute*

The rule in Listing 2-10 will be applied to the HTML element identified by the attribute **id="text1"**. Now our HTML code should look like this:

```
<!DOCTYPE html>
<html lang="en">
<head>
  <title>This text is the title of the document</title>
```

```
  <link rel="stylesheet" href="mystyles.css">
</head>
<body>
  <p id="text1">My text</p>
</body>
</html>
```

Listing 2-11: Identifying the element <p> *by its* id *attribute*

The impact of this procedure is that every time we make a reference using the identification **text1** in our CSS file, the element with that id value is modified, but the rest of the **<p>** elements, or any other element in the document, won't be affected.

This is an extremely specific way to reference an element and is commonly used for more general elements, such as structural tags. The **id** attribute and its specificity are in fact more appropriate to reference elements from Javascript, as we will see in further chapters.

Referencing by the Class Attribute

Rather than using the **id** attribute, most of the time it is better to use the **class** attribute for styling purposes. This attribute is more flexible and can be assigned to every HTML element in the document that has styles in common.

```
.text1 { font-size: 20px }
```

Listing 2-12: Referencing by the value of the class *attribute*

To work with the attribute **class,** we have to declare the rule with a period before its name. The advantage of this method is that inserting the **class** attribute with the value **text1** will be enough to assign this same rule to any element we choose.

```
<!DOCTYPE html>
<html lang="en">
<head>
  <title>This text is the title of the document</title>
  <link rel="stylesheet" href="mystyles.css">
</head>
<body>
  <p class="text1">My text</p>
  <p class="text1">My text</p>
  <p>My text</p>
</body>
</html>
```

Listing 2-13: Assigning styles through the class *attribute*

The **<p>** elements in the first two lines inside the body in Listing 2-13 have the attribute **class** with the value **text1**. As we said before, the same rule can be applied to different elements in the same document. Therefore, these first two elements share the same styles and are both affected by the rule in Listing 2-12. The last **<p>** element is not affected and will be shown with the styles by default.

CSS Styling and Box Models

Rules assigned by the class attribute are called **classes**. Several classes may be assigned to the same element. All we have to do is declare the names for the classes separated by a space (e.g., `class="text1 text2"`). The class may be declared exclusive for certain types of elements adding a selector before the period.

```
p.text1 { font-size: 20px }
```

Listing 2-14: Declaring a class only for <p> elements

In Listing 2-14, we create a rule that references the class named `text1` but only for the **<p>** elements. If any other element has the same name for its `class` attribute, it won't be modified by this particular rule.

Referencing by Any Attribute

Although these reference methods cover a variety of situations, sometimes they are insufficient for finding the exact element we want to style. The latest versions of CSS have incorporated new ways to reference HTML elements. One of them is the Attribute Selector. Now, we can reference an element not only by `id` and `class`, but also any other attribute.

```
p[name] { font-size: 20px }
```

Listing 2-15: Referencing only <p> elements that has a name attribute

The rule in Listing 2-15 changes only **<p>** elements that have an attribute called **name**. To mirror what we were doing with the attributes `id` and `class`, we can also provide the value of the attribute.

```
p[name="mytext"] { font-size: 20px }
```

Listing 2-16: Referencing <p> elements that has a name attribute with the value mytext

CSS3 lets us combine the symbol "=" with others to make a more detailed selection:

```
p[name^="my"] { font-size: 20px }
p[name$="my"] { font-size: 20px }
p[name*="my"] { font-size: 20px }
```

Listing 2-17: New selectors in CSS3

If you already know Regular Expressions from other languages such as Javascript or PHP, you will recognize the selectors used in Listing 2-17. In CSS3, these selectors produce similar results:

- The rule with the selector ^= will be assigned to any <p> element with a **name** attribute value beginning with "**my**" (e.g., **mytext**, **mycar**).
- The rule with the selector $= will be assigned to any <p> element with a **name** attribute value ending with "**my**" (e.g., **textmy**, **carmy**).
- The rule with the selector *= will match any <p> element with a **name** attribute value containing the substring "**my**" (in this case, the substring could also be in the middle—for example, in **textmycar**).

In these examples, we use the <p> element, the **name** attribute and some random text such as "**my**", but the same technique may be used with any attribute and value you need. To reference any HTML element, you simply write the name of the attribute and the value you are looking for inside square brackets.

Referencing by Pseudo-Classes

Pseudo-classes allow us to reference HTML elements by their characteristics, such as the position in the code or current conditions. CSS3 incorporates new pseudo-classes that make things even more specific. We are going to apply a few here using a simple document and study the rest later in more practical situations.

```
<!DOCTYPE html>
<html lang="en">
<head>
  <title>This text is the title of the document</title>
  <link rel="stylesheet" href="mystyles.css">
</head>
<body>
  <div id="wrapper">
    <p class="mytext1">My text1</p>
    <p class="mytext2">My text2</p>
    <p class="mytext3">My text3</p>
    <p class="mytext4">My text4</p>
  </div>
</body>
</html>
```

Listing 2-18: HTML document to test pseudo-classes

Let's take a look at the new HTML code in Listing 2-18. It has four <p> elements that, considering the HTML structure, are siblings, and all of them are children of the same element <div>.

Using pseudo-classes we can take advantage of this organization and reference a specific element no matter how much we know about its attributes or their values:

```
p:nth-child(2){
  background: #999999;
}
```

Listing 2-19: Pseudo-class :nth-child()

The pseudo-class is added using a colon after the reference and before its name. In the rule in Listing 2-19, we reference `<p>` elements. This rule could also be written as `.myclass:nth-child(2)` to reference every element that is a child of another element and has the value of the `class` attribute equal to `myclass`. The pseudo-classes can be appended to any kind of reference that has been mentioned so far.

The `nth-child()` pseudo-class let us find a specific child. As we already explained, the HTML document of Listing 2-18 has four `<p>` elements that are siblings. This means that all of them have the same parent that is the element `<div>`. What this pseudo-class is really indicating is something like "the child in the position...," so the number between the parentheses will be the number of the position of the child, or index. The rule in Listing 2-19 is referencing every second `<p>` element found in the document.

> **Do It Yourself:** Replace the previous code in your HTML file with the one in Listing 2-18, incorporate the rules presented in Listing 2-19 into the file `mystyles.css`, and open the document in your browser to test this example.

Using this reference method, we can, of course, select any child we want by changing the index number. For example, the following rule will have an impact only on the last `<p>` element of our document:

```
p:nth-child(4){
   background: #999999;
}
```

Listing 2-20: *Pseudo-class* `:nth-child()`

As you probably realized, it is possible to assign styles to every element by creating a rule for every one of them.

```
p:nth-child(1){
   background: #999999;
}
p:nth-child(2){
   background: #CCCCCC;
}
p:nth-child(3){
   background: #999999;
}
p:nth-child(4){
   background: #CCCCCC;
}
```

Listing 2-21: *Creating a list with the pseudo-class* `:nth-child()`

In Listing 2-21, we use the `nth-child()` pseudo-class to generate a list of options that are clearly differentiated by the color of their background.

> **Do It Yourself:** Copy the last code into the CSS file and open the HTML document to check the effect in your browser.

Adding more options to the list could be done by incorporating new **<p>** elements in the HTML code and new rules with the `nth-child()` pseudo-class and the proper index number. However, using this approach would generate lots of code and would be impossible to apply to websites with dynamic content generation. An alternative, to get the same result more effectively, is to take advantage of the keywords **odd** and **even** available for this pseudo-class.

```
p:nth-child(odd){
  background: #999999;
}
p:nth-child(even){
  background: #CCCCCC;
}
```

Listing 2-22: Taking advantage of the keywords odd *and* even

Now there are only two rules for the entire list (no matter how long it is). Even if more options or rows are incorporated to the list, there is no need to add additional rules to the file. The styles will be assigned automatically to every element according to its position. The **odd** keyword for the `nth-child()` pseudo-class affects the elements **<p>** that are children of another element and have an odd index, and the **even** keyword affects those that have an even index.

There are other important pseudo-classes related to this one, some of them recently incorporated, such as `first-child`, `last-child` and `only-child`. The `first-child` pseudo-class references only the first child, the `last-child` references only the last child, and the `only-child` affects an element if it is the only child of its parent. These pseudo-classes in particular don't require keywords or extra parameters and are implemented as in the following example:

```
p:last-child{
  background: #999999;
}
```

Listing 2-23: Using :last-child *to modify only the last* <p> *element of the list*

Another important pseudo-class is the negation pseudo-class, called **not()**.

```
:not(p){
  margin: 0px;
}
```

Listing 2-24: Applying styles to every element except <p>

The rule in Listing 2-24 assigns a margin of 0 pixels to every element in the document except the **<p>** elements. The styles in the rules created with this pseudo-class are assigned to every element but not the ones included between parentheses.

CSS Styling and Box Models

Instead of the keyword of the element, you may use any reference you want. In Listing 2-25, below, every element will be affected except those with the value **mytext2** in their **class** attribute.

```
:not(.mytext2){
  margin: 0px;
}
```

Listing 2-25: Exception using the `class` *attribute*

When you apply this last rule to the HTML code of Listing 2-18, the browser assigns the styles by default to the **<p>** element identified by the class value **mytext2** and provides a margin of 0 pixels to the rest (because the **<p>** element **mytext2** is the one that is NOT going to be affected by the property).

New Selectors

There are a few more selectors that were added or considered part of CSS3 and could be useful for your designs. These selectors use the symbols >, + and ~ to specify a relationship between elements.

```
div > p.mytext2{
  color: #990000;
}
```

Listing 2-26: Applying the > selector

The selector **>** indicates that the element affected is the second element when it has the first element as its parent. The rule in Listing 2-26 modifies the **<p>** elements that are children of a **<div>** element. In this case, we were specific and referenced only the **<p>** element with the class **mytext2**.

The next selector is constructed with the symbol **+**. This selector references the second element when it is immediately preceded by the first element. Both elements must share the same parent.

```
p.mytext2 + p{
  color: #990000;
}
```

Listing 2-27: Applying the + selector

The rule in Listing 2-27 affects the **<p>** element that is after another **<p>** element identified with the class **mytext2**. If you open in your browser the HTML file with the code of Listing 2-18, the text in the third **<p>** element will appear on the screen in the color red because this particular **<p>** element is positioned immediately after the **<p>** element identified with the class **mytext2**.

The last selector is constructed with the symbol ~. This selector is similar to the previous one, but the element affected is not necessarily immediately preceding the first element. Also, there may be more than one element.

```
p.mytext2 ~ p{
  color: #990000;
}
```

Listing 2-28: *Applying the ~ selector*

The rule in Listing 2-28 affects the third and fourth **<p>** elements in our example. The style will be applied to all the **<p>** elements that are siblings and are after the **<p>** element identified with the class **mytext2**. It doesn't matter if other elements are in between; the third and fourth **<p>** element will still be affected. You can experiment with the HTML code in Listing 2-18 by inserting a **<span></span>** element after the **<p>** element with the class **mytext2** to verify that only **<p>** elements are modified by this rule.

2.3 Applying CSS to Our Document

In organizing the structure of a website, every browser basically orders the elements by default according to their type: block or inline. This classification is based on the way the elements are displayed on the screen.

- **Block elements** are positioned one under another down the page.
- **Inline elements** are positioned side-by-side one after another in the same line, without any line break unless there is not enough horizontal space.

Almost every structural element in our document will be treated like a block element by default. That means that every HTML tag that represents a part of the visual organization (for example, **<section>**, **<nav>**, **<header>**, **<footer>**, **<div>**) will be positioned one under another.

In Chapter 1, we created an HTML document to replicate the layout of a typical website. The design included horizontal bars and two columns in the middle. Because of the way browsers render these elements by default, the result on the screen is far from what we expected. Once you open the HTML file with the code from Listing 1-20 (Chapter 1) in your browser, you can immediately identify the misplaced positions of the columns defined by **<section>** and **<aside>**. One column is under the other instead of side by side. This is because every block is rendered by default as wide as possible, as tall as the information it contains and one under another, as shown in Figure 2-1.

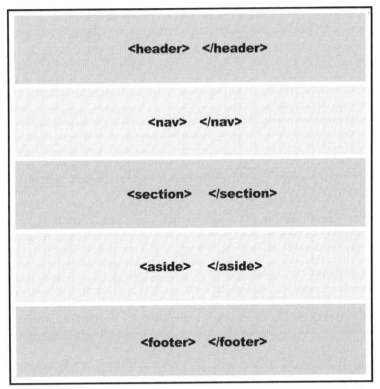

Figure 2-1: *Visual representation of the page layout rendered with default styles*

Box Models

To learn how we can create our own layout, we need to first understand how browsers process HTML code. Browsers consider every HTML element as a box. A webpage is actually a group of boxes put together following certain rules. These rules are made by styles provided by browsers or by designers using CSS.

CSS has a predetermined set of properties to overwrite browsers' styles and achieve the desired design. These properties are not specific; they have to be combined to form rules that later are used to group boxes together and get the right layout. The combination of those rules is usually called a model or layout system. All the rules combined constitute a box model.

There is one standard box model in use today, and several others are experimental. This valid and widely adopted model is called the Traditional Box Model, used since the first version of CSS. Although this model has proven to be effective, some experimental models are trying to address its shortcomings. The most important of these, and the one that is considered part of HTML5, is the new Flexible Box Model, introduced with CSS3.

The Traditional Box Model is currently supported by every browser on the market and is actually a standard for web design. In contrast, the Flexible Box Model, incorporated in CSS3, is still under development, but its advantages over the Traditional Box Model could turn it into the new standard, hence its importance as a subject of study.

Every model can be applied to the same HTML structure, but the structure has to be prepared to be affected by these styles in the right way. Because of the nature of these models, our HTML documents have to be adapted to the box model selected.

IMPORTANT: The Traditional Box Model presented next is not an HTML5 introduction. This model has been available since the first version of CSS and you may already know how to implement it. If this is the case, feel free to jump to the next section of the chapter.

2.4 Traditional Box Model

Web design began with tables. Tables were the elements that unintentionally became the tools for developers to create and organize boxes of content on the screen. This can be considered the first box model for the Web. The boxes were created by expanding cells and combining rows of cells, columns of cells and entire tables, beside one another or even nested. When websites got larger and more complex, this practice presented serious problems related to the size of the files and maintenance of the code necessary to create them.

These initial problems started what now seems natural: the division between structure and presentation. The use of **<div>** tags and CSS styles made possible to replace the function of tables and effectively separate the HTML structure from the presentation. With **<div>** elements and CSS we could create boxes on the screen, position those boxes at one side or another and give a specific size, border, color, etc. CSS provided specific properties to let us organize the boxes as we wished. These properties were powerful enough to create a model of boxes that evolved to what today is known as the Traditional Box Model.

Because of some deficiencies in this model, tables remained in use, but influenced by Ajax's success and a lot of new interactive applications, **<div>** elements and CSS styling gradually turned into the standard. At the end, the Traditional Box Model was adopted on a large scale.

HTML Document

In Chapter 1, we built our HTML5 document. This document has the necessary elements to provide structure and organization for its content, but some additions have to be made to prepare it for CSS styling and the Traditional Box Model.

The Traditional Box Model needs the boxes to be wraped together to provide horizontal order. Because the entire content of the body is created from a group of boxes that have to be centered and sized to a specific value, a **<div>** element has to be added as a wrapper.

The new HTML document will look like this:

```
<!DOCTYPE html>
<html lang="en">
<head>
  <meta charset="utf-8">
  <meta name="description" content="This is an HTML5 example">
  <meta name="keywords" content="HTML5, CSS3, JavaScript">
  <title>This text is the title of the document</title>
  <link rel="stylesheet" href="mystyles.css">
</head>
<body>
<div id="wrapper">
  <header id="main_header">
    <h1>This is the main title of the website</h1>
  </header>
```

```
<nav id="main_menu">
  <ul>
    <li>home</li>
    <li>photos</li>
    <li>videos</li>
    <li>contact</li>
  </ul>
</nav>
<section id="main_section">
  <article>
    <header>
      <hgroup>
        <h1>Title of post One</h1>
        <h2>subtitle of the post One</h2>
      </hgroup>
      <time datetime="2012-12-10" pubdate>posted 12-10-2012</time>
    </header>
    This is the text of my first post
    <figure>
      <img src="http://minkbooks.com/content/myimage.jpg">
      <figcaption>
        this is the image of the first post
      </figcaption>
    </figure>
    <footer>
      <p>comments (0)</p>
    </footer>
  </article>
  <article>
    <header>
      <hgroup>
        <h1>Title of post Two</h1>
        <h2>subtitle of the post Two</h2>
      </hgroup>
      <time datetime="2012-12-15" pubdate>posted 12-15-2012</time>
    </header>
    This is the text of my second post
    <footer>
      <p>comments (0)</p>
    </footer>
  </article>
</section>
<aside id="main_aside">
  <blockquote>Quotation from article number one</blockquote>
  <blockquote>Quotation from article number two</blockquote>
</aside>
<footer id="main_footer">
  Copyright &copy 2012-2013
</footer>
</div>
</body>
</html>
```

Listing 2-29: Preparing the HTML5 document for CSS styling

Listing 2-29 provides a new document ready to be styled. There are two important changes in this code from that in Listing 1-20 (Chapter 1). There are several tags identified with the attributes **id** and **class**. This means that now we can reference a very specific element with the value of its `id` attribute, or we can modify several elements at the same time using the value of their `class` attribute from the CSS rules.

The second important modification from the previous document is the addition of the `<div>` element mentioned before. This `<div>` was identified with the attribute `id="wrapper"`, and it is closed at the end of the body with the closing tag `</div>`. This wrapper will let us apply the box model to the content of the body and designate its horizontal position.

> **Do It Yourself:** Compare the HTML code in Listing 1-20 (Chapter 1) with the code in Listing 2-29 to check the locations of the opening and closing tags of the `<div>` element added as wrapper. Also check which elements are now identified with the `id` attribute and which with the `class` attribute. Confirm that the values of the `id` attributes are unique for every tag. You will also need to replace the code in the HTML file created before by the one in Listing 2-29 to apply the following CSS rules.

With the HTML document ready, it is time to create our style sheet.

Universal Selector *

The universal selector * assigns the same rule to every element in the document. This new selector represents every single element in the document's body and is useful for establishing some basic rules.

Usually, for most elements, we need to customize margins, or simply keep the margins to a minimum. Some elements by default have margins that are different from zero and are sometimes too big. As we progress in the creation of our design, we will find that most of the elements' margins have to be set to zero. To avoid repetitive rules, we can use this selector.

```
* {
  margin: 0px;
  padding: 0px;
}
```

Listing 2-30: Introducing a general CSS rule

The first rule in our CSS file listed in Listing 2-30 ensures that every element will have a margin of 0 pixels. From this point on, we will only need to modify the margins of the elements that we want to be greater than zero.

> **Do It Yourself:** We have to write all the necessary CSS rules in the style sheet file. The file was included in the head of the HTML code with the `<link>` tag, so all you have to do is create a new file with your text editor called `mystyles.css` and insert all the rules presented from Listing 2-30.

Headings

We used the elements `<h1>` and `<h2>` throughout our document to declare the titles and subtitles of different sections. The `<h1>` element, for example, was applied several times, not only for the main title of the entire document, as before, but also for some internal sections, so we have to style them properly:

```
h1 {
  font: bold 20px verdana, sans-serif;
}
h2 {
  font: bold 14px verdana, sans-serif;
}
```

Listing 2-31: Adding styles for <h1> *and* <h2> *elements*

The property **font**, discussed earlier, changes the type, size and font family of every text inside **<h1>** and **<h2>** elements to the values we want.

Declaring New HTML5 Elements

Another basic rule that has to be declared at the beginning of a document is the default definition of the HTML5 structural elements. Some browsers do not recognize these elements or treat them as inline elements. We need to declare these elements as block elements to ensure that they will be treated like **<div>** elements and that we are able to build our box model.

```
header, section, footer, aside, nav, article, figure, figcaption, hgroup{
  display: block;
}
```

Listing 2-32: Defining HTML5 elements as block elements

Now the elements affected by the rule in Listing 2-32 will be positioned on top of one another unless we later specify otherwise.

> **Review the Basics:** The property **display** assigns a different type to the element affected. If we want to turn an inline element into a block element, all we have to do is use the declaration **display: block**. There are several possible values for this property, such as **block**, **inline**, **inline-block**, etc. For a complete list, please visit our website and follow the links for this chapter.

Centering the Body

The first element of the box model is always **<body>**. Usually the content of this element has to be positioned horizontally for one reason or another. We have to specify its size or a maximum size to have a consistent design through different configurations.

```
body {
  text-align: center;
}
```

Listing 2-33: Centering the body

By default, the **<body>** tag has a width value of 100%. This means that the body will occupy the complete width of the browser window. To center the page in the window, we need to center the content inside the body. With the rule added in Listing 2-33, everything inside the **<body>** is centered, thus centering the entire web page.

Creating the Main Box

Next, we have to specify the maximum size or a fixed size for the content of the body. If you remember, in Listing 2-29 of this chapter, a **<div>** element was added to our document to wrap the whole body's content. This **<div>** will be considered the main box that contains everything else inside. Therefore, the size of this box will be the maximum size of the rest of the elements.

```
#wrapper {
  width: 960px;
  margin: 15px auto;
  text-align: left;
}
```

Listing 2-34: *Defining the properties of the main box*

The rule in Listing 2-34 for the first time references an element by the value of its **id**. The character **#** is telling the browser that the element affected by these styles has the attribute **id** with the value **wrapper**.

This rule provides three styles for the main box. The first is setting its fixed width to 960 pixels; therefore, this box will always be 960 pixels wide. (The common values for a website presently are between 960 and 980 pixels wide.

The second style is part of the Traditional Box Model. In the previous rule (Listing 2-33), we specified that the content of the body will be horizontally centered with the style **text-align: center**, but that only affected inline content such as text or images. For block elements such as **<div>**, we need to set a specific value for its margin that automatically adjusts them to the size of the parent. In Listing 2-34, the style **margin: 15px auto** assigns 15 pixels to the margin at the top and the bottom of the **<div>** element that it is referencing and sets the size for the left and right margins as automatic. As a result, we will have a space of 15 pixels at the top and bottom of the body and the space at the left and right is automatically calculated according to the size of the body and the size of the **<div>**, effectively centering the content on the screen.

The web page is now centered and has a fixed size of 960 pixels. The next step is to prevent a problem that occurs in some browsers. The property **text-align** is hereditary. That means that all the elements inside the body will be centered, not only the main box, and the style will be transferred to every child of the **<body>**. We have to change this style for the rest of the document back to its default value. The third and last style in the rule of Listing 2-34 accomplishes this. The result is that the content of the body is centered, but the content of the main box (the **<div>** wrapper) is again aligned to the left, and therefore, the rest of the code will inherit this style and use it by default.

> **Do It Yourself:** If you haven't already done so, copy every rule we listed up to this point into an empty file named **mystyles.css**. This file must be placed in the same folder or directory as the HTML file with the code of Listing 2-29. After this is complete, you should have two files, one with the HTML code and **mystyles.css** with all the CSS

CSS Styling and Box Models

styles we studied since Listing 2-30. Open the HTML file in your browser, and on the screen you will be able to see the box created.

The Header

Let's continue with the rest of the structural elements. Following the opening tag of the **<div>** wrapper is the first HTML5 structural element: **<header>**. This element contains the main title of our web page and will be located at the top of the screen. The **<header>** was identified in the code with the attribute **id="main_header"**.

By default, every block element, as well as the body, has a width of 100%. That means that the element will occupy all the horizontal space available. In the case of the body, as we already discussed, that space is the width of the browser window, but for the rest of the elements, the maximum space will be determined by the size of their parent. In our example, the maximum space of the elements inside the main box will be 960 pixels, because their parent is the main box, which has a width previously set as 960 pixels.

```
#main_header {
  background: #FFFBB9;
  border: 1px solid #999999;
  padding: 20px;
}
```

Listing 2-35: *Adding styles for* <header>

Because the **<header>** will occupy all the horizontal space available in the main box, and will already be treated like a block element and positioned at the top of the page, the next step is to assign styles that will let us recognize it when it is presented on the screen. In the rule shown in Listing 2-35, we give the **<header>** a yellow background, a solid border of 1 pixel and an inside margin of 20 pixels using the property **padding**.

Navigation Bar

Following the **<header>**, the next structural element is **<nav>**, which has the purpose of facilitating navigation. The links grouped inside this element will represent the menu of our website. This menu will just be a single bar below the header. Because of this, as in the **<header>** element, most of the styles we need to position the **<nav>** element are already assigned: **<nav>** is a block element, therefore will be located below the previous element; the default width is 100%, so it will be as wide as its parent (the wrapper **<div>**); and (also by default) it will be as tall as its content and specified margins. Therefore, we only need to make it more aesthetically pleasing. We do this by adding a gray background and a small internal margin to separate the menu options from the border.

```
#main_menu {
  background: #CCCCCC;
  padding: 5px 15px;
}
```

```
#main_menu li {
  display: inline-block;
  list-style: none;
  padding: 5px;
  font: bold 14px verdana, sans-serif;
}
```

Listing 2-36: Adding styles for <nav>

In Listing 2-36, the first rule is referencing the **<nav>** element by its **id**, changing its background and adding internal margins of **5px** and **15px** with the property **padding**.

Inside the navigation bar, a list is created with the **<ul>** and **<li>** elements. By default, the items of a list are positioned below one another. To change this and put every option of the menu side by side on the same line, we reference the **<li>** elements inside this particular **<nav>** element with the selector **#main_menu li** and then assign the style **display: inline-block** to turn them into inline boxes. Unlike the block elements, the elements affected by **inline-block**, standardized in CSS3, don't generate line breaks, but let us treat the elements as blocks and declare a width value for them. This parameter also sets the size of the element according to the size of its content when no width is specified.

> **Review the Basics:** The property **list-style** affects the small graphics generated in front of every item of the list (usually called **bullets**). In our example, we assigned the value **none** to this property to remove those graphics. However, there are many graphics available, such as **square**, **circle**, **decimal**, etc. The property lets us declare not only the type of graphic but also the position (**inside** or **outside**) and a custom image (e.g., **list-style: url('mybullet.jpg');**).

Section and Aside

The next structural elements in our code are two boxes placed horizontally. The Traditional Box Model is built over CSS styles that let us specify the position of every box. Using the property **float**, we can position these boxes on the right or left side of the screen according to our needs. The elements we use in our HTML document to create them are **<section>** and **<aside>**, each one identified with the attribute **id** and the values **main_section** and **main_aside** respectively.

```
#main_section {
  float: left;
  width: 660px;
  margin: 20px;
}
#main_aside {
  float: left;
  width: 220px;
  margin: 20px 0px;
  padding: 20px;
  background: #CCCCCC;
}
```

Listing 2-37: Creating two columns with the property float

CSS Styling and Box Models

The CSS property `float` is one of the properties widely used to apply the Traditional Box Model. It makes the element float to one side or the other in the available space. The elements affected by `float` act as block elements—with the difference that they are laid out according to the value of this property and not the normal flow of the document. The elements are moved to the left or to the right of the available area, as far as possible, responding to the value of `float`.

With the rules in Listing 2-37, we declare the position of both boxes and their sizes and thus generate the visible columns on the screen. The property `float` moves the box to the available space at the side specified by its value, `width` assigns a horizontal size, and `margin`, of course, assigns the margin of the element.

Once affected by these styles, the content of the `<section>` element will be aligned on the left of the screen, with a size of 660 pixels, plus 40 pixels of margins, occupying a total space of 700 pixels wide.

The `float` property of the `<aside>` element also has the value `left`. This means that the box generated will move to the space available at its left. Because the previous box created by the element `<section>` was also moved to the left of the screen, now, the space available will be the space remaining. The new box will be in the same line as the first box but to its right, occupying the rest of the space in the line, creating a second column for the design. We could have used the value `right` for the `float` property of `<aside>`, because we only have two columns, one on the left and one on the right side of the screen, but using `left` leaves our options open in case we want to add new columns to the design later.

We also declare a size of 220 pixels for this second box, add a gray background and set an internal margin of 20 pixels. As a result, this box's horizontal size will be 220 pixels, plus 40 pixels added by the `padding` property. (The side margins are set as `0px`.)

> **Review the Basics:** The size of an element and its margins are added to get the real value. If we have an element 200 pixels wide and a margin of 10 pixels at each side, the real width of the element will be 220 pixels. The total 20 pixels of the margins are added to the 200 pixels of the element, and the final value is represented on the screen. The same happens for the properties `padding` and `border`. Every time we add a border to an element, or create a space between the content and the border with the property `padding`, those values will be added to the total width of the element to get the real value when it is shown on the screen. The real value is calculated by the formula: `size + margin + padding + borders`.

> **Do It Yourself:** Review Listing 2-29. Check every CSS rule we have created so far and find the HTML element in the document corresponding to each of those rules. Follow the references, elements' keywords (like `h1`) and `id` attributes (like `main_header`), to understand how the references work and how styles are assigned to every element.

Footer

To finish the application of the Traditional Box Model, another CSS property has to be applied to the `<footer>` element. This property recovers the normal flow of the document and lets us position the `<footer>` under the last element rather than at the side.

```
#main_footer {
  clear: both;
  text-align: center;
```

```
  padding: 20px;
  border-top: 2px solid #999999;
}
```

Listing 2-38: Styling the `<footer>` *and recovering the normal flow*

Listing 2-38 declares a border of 2 pixels at the top of the `<footer>`, an internal margin (or padding) of 20 pixels and centers the text inside the element. As well, it restores the normal flow of the document with the property `clear`. This property simply clears the area occupied by the element, not allowing it to position adjacent to a float box. The usual value is `both`, which means that both sides will be cleared, and the element will follow the regular flow (the element no longer floats). For a block element, this means that it will be positioned below the last element, in a new line.

The property `clear` also pushes the elements vertically, making the float boxes occupy a real area on the screen. Without this property, the browser renders the document as if the float elements don't exist, and the boxes would overlap.

When we have boxes positioned side by side in the Traditional Box Model, we always need to create an element with the style `clear: both` to be able to continue placing other boxes below. Figure 2-2 shows a visual representation of this model with basic CSS styles necessary to create the layout.

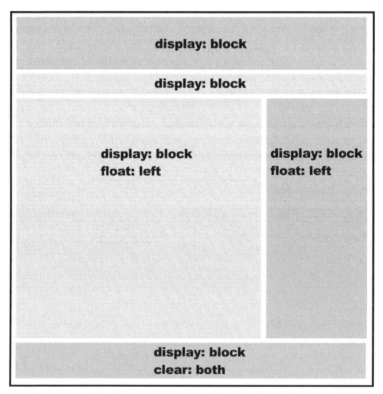

Figure 2-2: Visual representation of the Traditional Box Model

The values `left` and `right` in the property `float` do not necessarily mean that the box must be positioned to the left or the right side of the window. What the values do is turn float that specific side of the element, breaking the normal flow of the document. If the value is `left`, for example, the browser will try to position the element at the left side of the available space. If there is space available next to a previous element, this new element will be situated at its right, because the left side of the element has been set to `float`. The value will make it float to the left until it finds something that blocks it, such as another element or the edge of its parent. This is important when we want to create a layout with several columns. In that case, every column will have the value `left` in the property `float` to ensure that one column will be positioned next to the other in the correct order. Every column will be floating to the left until is blocked by another column or the edge of the parent. This practice will position the boxes side by side in the same line, creating a set of columns in the visual representation on the screen.

Finishing Touches

The last step is to work on the content's design. There are a few more HTML5 elements that can be styled for this purpose:

```
article {
  background: #FFFBCC;
  border: 1px solid #999999;
  padding: 20px;
  margin-bottom: 15px;
}
article footer {
  text-align: right;
}
time {
  color: #999999;
}
figcaption {
  font: italic 14px verdana, sans-serif;
}
```

Listing 2-39: Adding the finishing touches for the basic design

The first rule in Listing 2-39 references all the **<article>** elements and provides them with some styles (background color, a solid 1 pixel border, padding and a bottom margin). The bottom margin of 15 pixels vertically separates one article from the next.

Every article also has a **<footer>** element that shows the number of comments received. To reference a **<footer>** inside an **<article>** element, we use the selector **article footer** that means "every **<footer>** inside an **<article>** will be affected by the following styles." This reference technique is applied here to align the text inside the **<footer>** of every article to the right.

At the end of the code in Listing 2-39, we change the color inside every **<time>** element and differentiate the caption of the image from the rest of the text in the article using a different font.

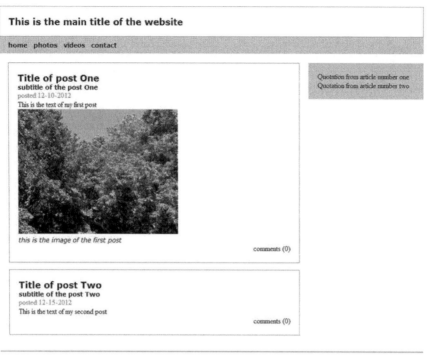

Figure 2-3: The Traditional Box Model applied to our document

Do It Yourself: If you haven't done it yet, copy every CSS rule listed in this chapter since Listing 2-30, one after another, inside the file `mystyles.css`, and then open the HTML file with the document created in Listing 2-29 in your browser. The result should be similar to Figure 2-3.

Box-Sizing

There is an additional property incorporated to CSS3 regarding structure and the Traditional Box Model. The `box-sizing` property allows us to change how the size of an element is calculated and force browsers to include the padding and border in the original value.

As we explained before, every time the total area occupied by an element is calculated, the browser gets the final number through the following formula: `size + margin + padding + borders`. Therefore, if we set the `width` property to 100 pixels, `margin` to 20 pixels, `padding` to 10 pixels and `border` to 1 pixel, the total horizontal area occupied by the element will then be `100 + 40 + 20 + 2 = 162` pixels. (Notice that we had to double the values of the `margin`, `padding` and `border` in the formula because we assumed the same values were assigned to the left and right side of the box.) This means that every time you declare the size of an element with the property `width`, you have to remember the real area necessary to place the element will usually be larger.

Depending on your preferences, it might be good to force the browser to include the `padding` and `border` in the value of `width`, so the new formula will be just `size + margin`.

```
div {
  width: 100px;
  margin: 20px;
  padding: 10px;
  border: 1px solid #000000;

  -moz-box-sizing: border-box;
  -webkit-box-sizing: border-box;
  box-sizing: border-box;
}
```

Listing 2-40: Including padding and border in the size of the element

The **box-sizing** property may take one of three values. By default, it is set to **content-box**, which means the browser will add the **padding** and **border** to the size specified by **width**. In contrast, the value **padding-box** will draw the padding inside the element, and **border-box** will also include the border.

Listing 2-40 shows the application of this property on a **<div>** element. This is just an example and we are not going to use it in our document, but it could be useful for some designers depending on how familiar they are with the traditional methods of calculation used in previous versions of CSS.

> **IMPORTANT:** Because the CSS properties we are studying are experimental at the moment, most of them have to be declared with a specific prefix according to the rendering engine. In the future, we will be able to declare only **box-sizing: border-box**, but until the experimental phase is over, we have to code as shown in Listing 2-40. The prefixes for the most common browsers are:
>
> - **-moz-** for Mozilla Firefox
> - **-webkit-** for Safari and Google Chrome
> - **-o-** for Opera
> - **-khtml-** for Konqueror
> - **-ms-** for Internet Explorer

2.5 Flexible Box Model

The main purpose of a box model is to provide a mechanism for dividing the window's space into several boxes and creating the rows and columns that are part of a regular web design. However, the Traditional Box Model, implemented since the first version of CSS and widely used these days, fails in this regard. Defining how boxes are distributed and specifying their horizontal and vertical sizes, for example, can't be done efficiently with this model without using tricks or a set of intricate rules programmed by a clever guy somewhere.

The difficulty of creating common design effects (for example, expanding several columns according to the space available, vertically centering the content or extending a column from top to bottom independently of its content) made developers think about new possible models to apply to their documents. Several models were developed, but none received more attention than the Flexible Box Model.

The Flexible Box Model solves the Traditional Box Model's problems in an elegant manner. In this new model, the boxes finally represent those virtual rows and columns that are, in fact, what designers and users really see and care about. Now we have total control over the layout, the position and size of the boxes, the distribution of the boxes inside other boxes, and how they share and use the available space. The code satisfies the designers' needs once and for all.

In this section of the chapter, we will see how the Flexible Box Model works, its advantages, and how we can apply it to our document.

> **IMPORTANT:** Although the Flexible Box Model has advantages over the previous model, it is still experimental and cannot be adopted by browsers and developers for at least a few more years. Presently, there are two specifications available, and the new one is so far only supported by Google Chrome. This is why we discussed the use of the Traditional Box Model in depth. You should consider these issues before choosing to apply one model or another. At the end of the book we will explain how to develop different versions of a website to support both, HTML5 compatible and non-compatible browsers.

Flex Container

The main reason for the creation of the Flexible Box Model was the need to distribute the space in the window among the elements of the document. The elements had to be reduced or increased in size according to the space available. In order to know the amount of space to be distributed, we had to know the exact size of the container, which led to the definition of **flex containers**.

A flex container is an element that allows its content to be flexible. Some important features of this model, such as vertical and horizontal orientation, are declared in these containers. Flexible elements must have a common parent to be able to organize them. In this new model, every set of boxes on the screen has to have a parent box.

HTML Document

The following is the HTML code we are going to use from now on to test the examples:

```
<!DOCTYPE html>
<html lang="en">
<head>
  <title>Flexible Box Model</title>
  <link rel="stylesheet" href="test.css">
</head>
<body>
<section id="parentbox">
  <div id="box-1">Box 1</div>
  <div id="box-2">Box 2</div>
  <div id="box-3">Box 3</div>
  <div id="box-4">Box 4</div>
</section>
</body>
</html>
```

Listing 2-41: Basic HTML document for testing the Flexible Box Model

CSS Styling and Box Models

Do It Yourself: Create another empty text file with a name and the `.html` extension. Copy the HTML code in Listing 2-41 into the file. This is the document we will use to experiment with the properties of the Flexible Box Model. The CSS rules will be included from an external file called `test.css`. Create this file and add the rules provided later. Check the results of applying every rule by opening the HTML file in your browser.

Display

A flex container is defined by the property `display`, and it may be determined as a block element with the value `flex` or inline element with the value `inline-flex`. We will define our container as `flex`:

```
#parentbox {
  display: flex;
}
```

Listing 2-42: Declaring the element `parentbox` *as a flex container*

IMPORTANT: Always keep in mind that, at the moment, these properties are experimental. To use them, you have to declare every one by adding the prefixes `-moz-` or `-webkit-` according to the browser you are using. For example, `display: flex` must be written as `display: -webkit-flex` for the WebKit engine. We don't include the prefixes in this part of the chapter to make the source code easy to understand.

Axes

A flex container uses axes to describe the orientation of its content. The specification declares two axes that are independent of the orientation: the main axis and the cross axis. The main axis is the one on which the content is laid out (usually equivalent to horizontal orientation), and the cross axis is the one perpendicular to the main axis (usually equivalent to vertical orientation). If the orientation changes, the axes are displaced along with the content:

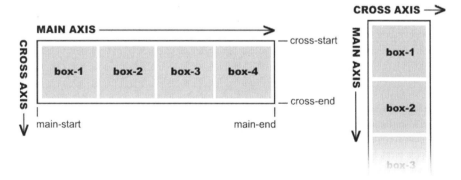

Figure 2-4: Axes of flex containers

The properties for this model work with axes, organizing elements from the extremes of every axis: main-start, main-end, cross-start and cross-end. This is similar to left to right and top to bottom used to describe horizontal and vertical directions, but in this model that relationship is inverted when the orientation changes. When one of the extremes, such as main-start, is mentioned in the description of a property, you have to remember that its meaning could be *left* or *top*, according to the current orientation of the container (in the left diagram in Figure 2-4, for example, main-start is referencing the left side of the container).

Flex Property

For an element inside a flex container to become flexible it has to be declared as such using the `flex` property. The `flex` property declares a box as flexible or inflexible, and it helps to distribute space among the boxes. It can take three possible parameters, separated by a space: `flex-grow`, `flex-shrink` and `flex-basis`. By giving a value of at least 1 to the first parameter, `flex-grow`, we declare the box as flexible. This first parameter declares the ratio for the expansion of the element, in other words how much the element will grow considering its siblings. The second parameter, `flex-shrink`, declares the ratio for reduction, or how much the element will shrink according to the configuration of its siblings. Finally, the third parameter, `flex-basis`, indicates an initial size for the element that is considered when the free space is distributed among all the children.

Flexible boxes will be expanded or reduced to fill the extra space inside their parent. The distribution of the space depends on the properties of the rest of the boxes. If all of the children are set as flexible, the size of each one will depend on the size of their parent and the value of the `flex` property. Let's see an example:

```
#parentbox {
  display: flex;
  width: 600px;
}
#box-1{
  flex: 1;
}
#box-2{
  flex: 1;
}
#box-3{
  flex: 1;
}
#box-4{
  flex: 1;
}
```

Listing 2-43: *Making the boxes flexible with* `flex`

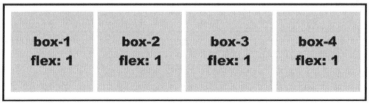

parentbox 600px

Figure 2-5: *The space is distributed equally*

CSS Styling and Box Models

In the example in Listing 2-43, we declare only the `flex-grow` value for the `flex` property to determine how the boxes will expand. The size of each box is calculated by multiplying the value of the size of the parent by the value of its `flex` property and then dividing by the sum of the `flex-grow` values of all the children. For example, the formula for the element **box-1** is **600 × 1 / 4 = 150**. The value **600** is the size of the parent, **1** is the value of the property `flex` for **box-1** and **4** is the sum of the values of the property `flex` of every child. Because each box in our example has the same value of **1** for the `flex` property, the size of every child is 150 pixels.

> **Do It Yourself:** Copy the CSS code in Listing 2-43 into the `test.css` file and open the HTML document of Listing 2-41 in your browser. Remember to add the corresponding prefixes to these new properties before testing (e.g., `-webkit-flex`).

The potential of this property is evident when we start providing different values and combinations:

```css
#parentbox {
  display: flex;
  width: 600px;
}
#box-1{
  flex: 2;
}
#box-2{
  flex: 1;
}
#box-3{
  flex: 1;
}
#box-4{
  flex: 1;
}
```

Listing 2-44: Creating an uneven distribution

In Listing 2-44, we change the value of the `flex` property for **box-1** to **2**. Now the formula to calculate the size of this box is **600 × 2 / 5 = 240**. Because we didn't change the size of the parent box, the first value of the formula is the same, but the second value is now **2** (the new value of the `flex` property for **box-1**). And now, of course, the sum of the values of all the children's properties is **5** (**2** for **box-1** and **1** for each of the other three boxes). Applying the same formula for the rest of the children we get their sizes: **600 × 1 / 5 = 120**.

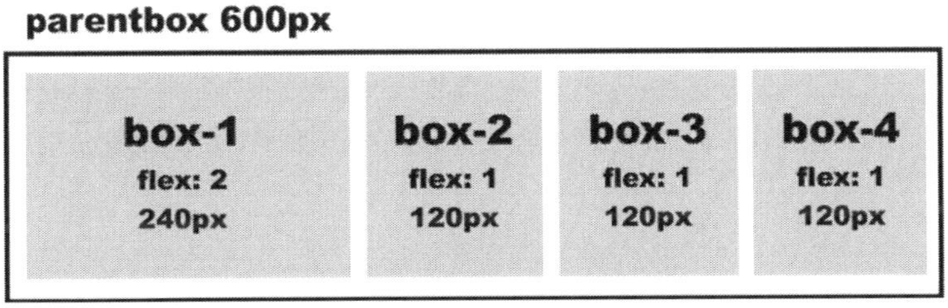

Figure 2-6: The space is distributed according to the value of `flex`

Comparing the results we can see how the space is distributed. The available space is divided into portions according to the sum of the values of the `flex` property of each child (a total of **5** in our example). Then, the portions are distributed among the boxes. The element `box-1` gets two portions and the rest of the children get just one portion each because the value of their `flex` property is just **1**.

The effect of this property is represented in Figure 2-6. The advantage is that when you add a new child you don't have to calculate the size; it is recalculated automatically.

This is interesting, but there are more scenarios. For example, when one of the children is inflexible and has an explicit size, the other children will share the rest of the space available.

```
#parentbox {
  display: flex;
  width: 600px;
}
#box-1{
  width: 300px;
}
#box-2{
  flex: 1;
}
#box-3{
  flex: 1;
}
#box-4{
  flex: 1;
}
```

Listing 2-45: Combining inflexible and flexible children

The first box of the example in Listing 2-45 has a size of 300 pixels, so the available space to distribute between the rest of the children is 300 pixels (**600 − 300 = 300**). The browser will calculate the size of every flexible box with the same formula we used before: **300 × 1 / 3 = 100**.

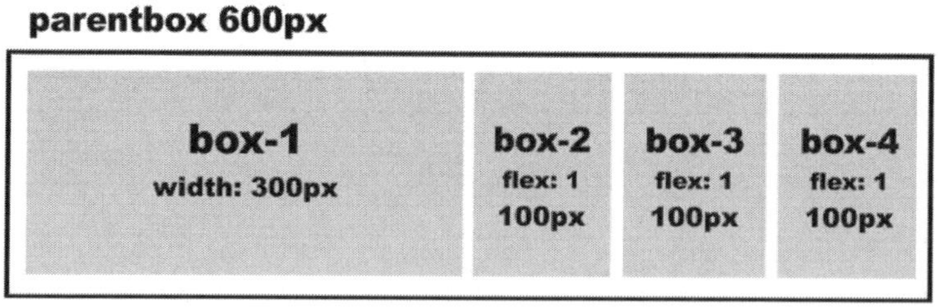

parentbox 600px

Figure 2-7: Only the free space is distributed

Just as you might have one box of an explicit size, you may have several. The principle is the same: only the free space is distributed among the flexible boxes.

There is a possible scenario in which we could have to declare a size for the element but keep it flexible. To do this we can take advantage of the rest of the parameters available for the `flex` property (`flex-shrink` and `flex-basis`). Let's see an example:

```
#parentbox {
  display: flex;
}
#box-1{
  flex: 1 1 200px;
}
#box-2{
  flex: 1 5 100px;
}
#box-3{
  flex: 1 5 100px;
}
#box-4{
  flex: 1 5 100px;
}
```

Listing 2-46: *Controlling how the elements shrink*

This time three parameters were provided for the `flex` property of each box. All the boxes have the value 1 for the first parameter (`flex-grow`), declaring the same expansion ratio. The difference is determined by the addition of the values for the `flex-shrink` and `flex-basis` parameters.

The `flex-shrink` parameter works similar to `flex-grow` but determines the ratio in which the boxes will be reduced to fit into the space available. In our example, the value of this parameter is 1 for **box-1** and 5 for the rest of the boxes, which will assign more space to **box-1**.

The `flex-basis` parameter, as we mentioned before, establishes an initial value for the element. To calculate the reduction or expansion values of flexible elements, the value of the `flex-basis` parameter is considered. When this value is 0 or isn't declared, the value taken into account is the size of the elements' content. We can also use the keyword `auto` to let the browser use the value of the `width` property as a reference, as we will see in the next example.

> **IMPORTANT:** A value 0 for `flex-grow` or `flex-shrink` will not allow the element to be expanded or reduced, respectively. To declare flexibility, the values for these parameters must be 1 or higher.

> **Do It Yourself:** Copy the CSS code in Listing 2-46 into the `test.css` file to check the effects of the different combinations of the three parameters of the `flex` property. We didn't declared the size for the `parentbox` element, so when the browser window is expanded, the parent element will expand as well and all the elements will grow at the same ratio. On the contrary, when the window's size is reduced, the element **box-1** will be reduced at different ratio due to the value specified for `flex-shrink` (1 instead of 5). As we recommended before, add other properties to the elements, such as a color background, height or a border, to get a better look and be able to identify each one on the screen.

Let's see an example using the `width` property. In this case, the `flex-basis` parameter has to be declared as `auto` for the value of `width` to be set as the initial size.

```
#parentbox {
  display: flex;
  width: 600px;
}
#box-1{
  width: 200px;
  flex: 1 1 auto;
}
#box-2{
  width: 100px;
  flex: 1 1 auto;
}
#box-3{
  width: 100px;
  flex: 1 1 auto;
}
#box-4{
  width: 100px;
  flex: 1 1 auto;
}
```

Listing 2-47: Defining flexible boxes with a preferred size

In Listing 2-47, every box has a preferred `width` value, but after all the boxes are positioned there is a space of 100 pixels remaining. This extra space will be divided among the flexible boxes. To calculate the portion of space assigned to every box, we use the same formula: **100 × 1 / 4 = 25**. This means that 25 pixels of extra width is added to the preferred size of each box.

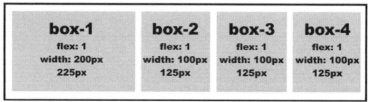

Figure 2-8: Adding free space to every box's width

Flex-Direction

If we want to customize the order and orientation of a flex container's content, we have to use the `flex-direction` property. This property has four possible values: `row`, `row-reverse`, `column` and `column-reverse`, with `row` as the default value.

row—This value sets the orientation according to the orientation of the text (usually horizontal) and orders the children from main-start to main-end (usually left to right).

row-reverse—This value sets the same orientation as `row` but inverts the order of the elements from main-end to main-start (usually right to left).

column—This value sets the orientation according to the orientation in which blocks of texts are laid out (usually vertical) and orders the children from main-start to main-end (usually top to bottom).

column-reverse—This value sets the same orientation as `column` but inverts the order of the elements from main-end to main-start (usually bottom to top).

```
#parentbox {
  display: flex;
  flex-direction: row;
}
#box-1{
  flex: 1;
}
#box-2{
  flex: 1;
}
#box-3{
  flex: 1;
}
#box-4{
  flex: 1;
}
```

Listing 2-48: Changing children's orientation

Review the Basics: There is a property called `writing-mode` that sets the orientation of the lines of text (horizontal or vertical), and this is the reason why the result of the Flexible Box Model's properties always depends on the orientation previously set for the text. To learn more about this property, please visit our website and follow the links for this chapter.

Order

The order of the children may also be customized. The `order` property lets us declare a specific place for each box:

```
#parentbox {
  display: flex;
}
#box-1{
  flex: 1;
  order: 2;
}
#box-2{
  flex: 1;
  order: 4;
}
#box-3{
  flex: 1;
  order: 3;
}
```

```
#box-4{
  flex: 1;
  order: 1;
}
```

Listing 2-49: *Defining the position of each box*

As you can see in Listing 2-49, the property must be assigned to the children. If the value is duplicated, those boxes will follow their order in the source code.

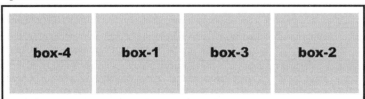

Figure 2-9: *Specific positions for every box according to Listing 2-49*

Justify-Content

One of the most important features of the Flexible Box Model is also the capacity to lay out free space. When the size of the children does not fill the entire container, there will be free space that has to be placed somewhere in the design. Let's see an example:

```
#parentbox {
  display: flex;
  width: 600px;
}
#box-1{
  width: 100px;
}
#box-2{
  width: 100px;
}
#box-3{
  width: 100px;
}
#box-4{
  width: 100px;
}
```

Listing 2-50: *Distributing free space in the flex container*

Do It Yourself: Add other properties to the elements, such as a color background, height or a border, to see and be able to identify each one on the screen.

In Listing 2-50, the size of our flex container is set as 600 pixels and each child is 100 pixels wide. Therefore, there are 200 pixels of free space.

         CSS Styling and Box Models

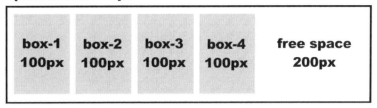

parentbox 600px

box-1 100px | box-2 100px | box-3 100px | box-4 100px | free space 200px

Figure 2-10: Boxes and free space inside a flex container

We can choose different ways to distribute the free space. By default, the children are ordered according to Figure 2-10, from the main-start to main-end (usually left to right), leaving the free space at the end. However, the `justify-content` property will give us alternatives.

The `justify-content` property specifies how the children and the additional space are distributed on the main axis of a flex container. This property can take five values: `flex-start`, `flex-end`, `center`, `space-between` and `space-around`. If the property is not present, `flex-start` is the value by default, which aligns the elements to the main-start and the free space to the main-end (left and right or top and bottom).

```
#parentbox {
  display: flex;
  width: 600px;
  justify-content: flex-end;
}
#box-1{
  width: 100px;
}
#box-2{
  width: 100px;
}
#box-3{
  width: 100px;
}
#box-4{
  width: 100px;
}
```

Listing 2-51: Distributing free space with justify-content

The following figures show the potential of this property and the competence of the Flexible Box Model.

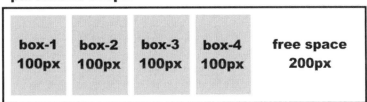

parentbox 600px

box-1 100px | box-2 100px | box-3 100px | box-4 100px | free space 200px

Figure 2-11: Free space distributed with justify-content: flex-start

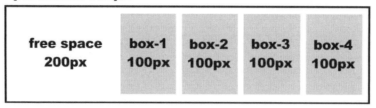

Figure 2-12: Free space distributed with `justify-content: flex-end`

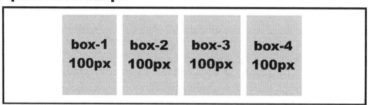

Figure 2-13: Free space distributed with `justify-content: center`

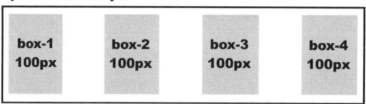

Figure 2-14: Free space distributed with `justify-content: space-between`

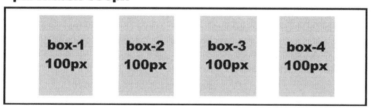

Figure 2-15: Free space distributed with `justify-content: space-around`

Align-Items

Another property that will help us distribute space is **align-items**. This property works like **justify-content** but aligns the boxes in the cross-axis. This quality makes the property appropriate for vertical alignment—something that has been missing since the use of tables was deprecated.

```
#parentbox {
  display: flex;
  align-items: center;
  width: 600px;
  height: 200px;
}
#box-1{
  flex: 1;
  height: 100px;
}
#box-2{
  flex: 1;
  height: 100px;
}
#box-3{
  flex: 1;
  height: 100px;
}
#box-4{
  flex: 1;
  height: 100px;
}
```

Listing 2-52: *Distributing vertical space*

In Listing 2-52, we provide a specific height for every box, including the parent. There is a free space of 100 pixels that will be laid out according to the value of the `align-items` property.

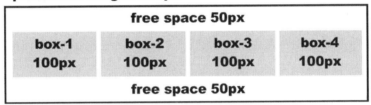

Figure 2-16: *Vertical alignment with* `align-items: center`

The possible values for the `align-items` property are `flex-start`, `flex-end`, `center`, `baseline` and `stretch`. The last value will stretch the boxes from top to bottom to adjust the children to the available space. This characteristic is so important that the value `stretch` is set by default when a flex container is created. The effect of the value `stretch` is that when the height for the children is not declared they automatically adopt the height of their parent.

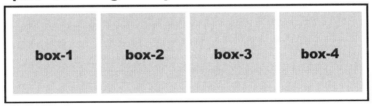

Figure 2-17: *Stretching the children with* `align-items: stretch`

This is extremely useful when we have columns in our design that are stretched vertically by their content but the different amounts of content leave one shorter than the other. Using the `stretch` value for the `align-items` property, the shorter columns will match the size of the longest one.

We also count on the `flex-start` value to align the boxes at the start of the line, which is determined by the orientation of the container (usually left or top):

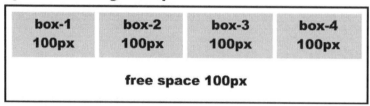

Figure 2-18: Aligning the children with `align-items: flex-start`

The `flex-end` value aligns the boxes to the end of the container (usually right or bottom):

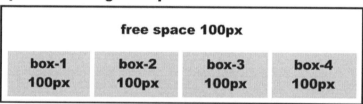

Figure 2-19: Aligning the children with `align-items: flex-end`

Finally, the `baseline` value aligns the boxes by the base line of the first line of content:

Figure 2-20: Aligning the children with `align-items: baseline`

Do It Yourself: Use the CSS code in Listing 2-56 to test different values for the `align-items` property. Erase the `height` property for every element and write some content for `box-1`. Using the `stretch` value for the `align-items` property (or not declaring this property at all) will let you see how the rest of the boxes expand to match the height of `box-1`. You can also declare the property `font-size: 50px` for the element `box-2`, as shown in Figure 2-20, to test how the `baseline` value aligns the boxes by the base line of the first line of content.

CSS Styling and Box Models

Align-Self

Sometimes it may be useful to align boxes independently of the alignment set by their parent. The property `align-self` works exactly like `align-items` but for the children.

```
#parentbox {
  display: flex;
  align-items: flex-end;
  width: 600px;
  height: 200px;
}
#box-1{
  flex: 1;
  height: 100px;
}
#box-2{
  flex: 1;
  height: 100px;
  align-self: center;
}
#box-3{
  flex: 1;
  height: 100px;
}
#box-4{
  flex: 1;
  height: 100px;
}
```

Listing 2-53: *Changing the alignment for* box-2

The CSS code in Listing 2-53 aligns the elements to the bottom of the flex container, but the `align-self` property displace the element **box-2** to the center, as shown in Figure 2-21.

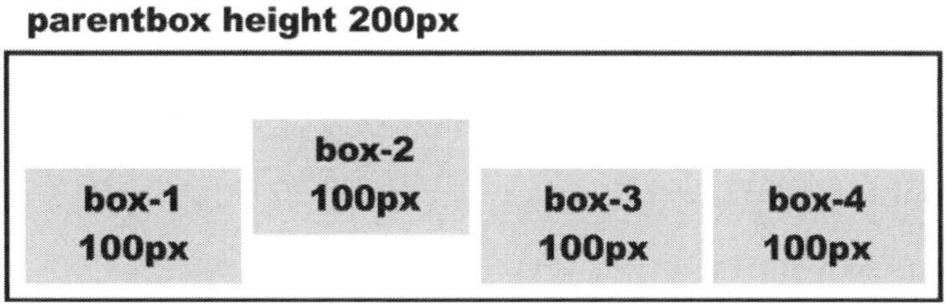

parentbox height 200px

Figure 2-21: *Using* align-self *to align a specific box*

Flex-Wrap

A flex container can be single-line or multi-line; we can have only one line of boxes in the container or several. The **flex-wrap** property declares this condition using three possible values: **nowrap**, **wrap** and **wrap-reverse**. The value **nowrap** will set the flex container as a single-line container (no lines will be wrapped). On the other hand, the value **wrap** will declare the container as multi-line, and it will order the lines from cross-start to cross-end (usually left to right or top to bottom). To reverse this order we can use the last value available called **wrap-reverse**.

```
#parentbox {
   display: flex;
   justify-content: center;
   flex-wrap: wrap;
   width: 600px;
}
#box-1{
   width: 100px;
}
#box-2{
   width: 100px;
}
#box-3{
   width: 100px;
}
#box-4{
   flex: 1 1 400px;
}
```

Listing 2-54: Creating two lines of boxes with the flex-wrap *property*

In Listing 2-54, the first three boxes have a size of 100 pixels, enough to fit in one single line of a 600 pixel-wide container, but the last box is declared as flexible with an initial size of 400 pixels (**flex-basis**). There is not enough space in the container to lay out all the boxes. The browser has two options: reduce the size of the flexible box to make it fit into the available space or generate a new line. Since the **flex-wrap** property was declared with the value **wrap**, a new line is created, as shown in the next figure.

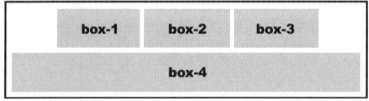

Figure 2-22: A multi-line flex container

The element **box-4** was declared as flexible by its **flex** property, so it is not only placed in a second line but also expanded to occupy the total space available in the line (remember that the 400 pixels declared by the **flex-basis** parameter is just the initial value, not a declaration of size). Also, the boxes in the first line are aligned to the center due to the new available space in the first line and the value of the **justify-content** property.

The order of the lines can be inverted with the value **wrap-reverse**, as shown in the next figure.

CSS Styling and Box Models

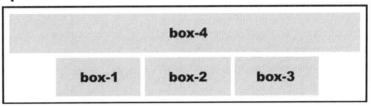

Figure 2-23: *New line order using* `flex-wrap: wrap-reverse`

Align-Content

When we have multi-line flex containers, there is a chance we will need to align them. There is a special property called **align-content** that will align the lines inside a flex container. It works like **align-items** but for multi-line containers.

```
#parentbox {
  display: flex;
  flex-wrap: wrap;
  align-content: flex-start;
  width: 600px;
  height: 200px;
}
#box-1{
  flex: 1 1 100px;
}
#box-2{
  flex: 1 1 100px;
}
#box-3{
  flex: 1 1 100px;
}
#box-4{
  flex: 1 1 400px;
}
```

Listing 2-55: *Aligning multiple lines with the* align-content *property*

For the lines to align, there has to be free space available, that's why in Listing 2-55 we add the **height** property for the container. Each box is declared as flexible with an initial size, and the element **parentbox** is defined as a multi-line container with the **flex-wrap** property. This creates a flex container with two lines similar to the example in Listing 2-54, but now we have a vertical free space to play around.

The **align-content** property can take six values: **flex-start**, **flex-end**, **center**, **space-between**, **space-around** and **stretch**. The value **stretch** is set by default and will expand the lines to fill the space available, unless a fix size was declared for the elements.

Let's see how different values work:

parentbox

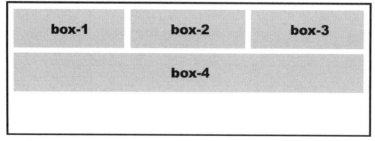

Figure 2-24: Lines aligned with `align-content: flex-start`

parentbox

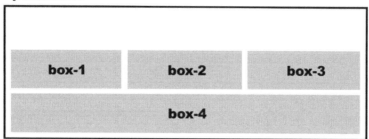

Figure 2-25: Lines aligned with `align-content: flex-end`

parentbox

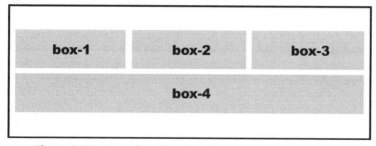

Figure 2-26: Lines aligned with `align-content: center`

parentbox

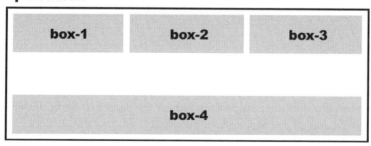

Figure 2-27: Lines aligned with `align-content: space-between`

CSS Styling and Box Models

parentbox

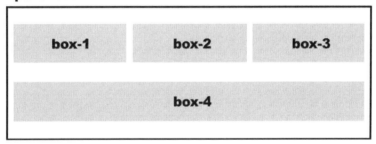

Figure 2-28: Lines aligned with `align-content: space-around`

parentbox

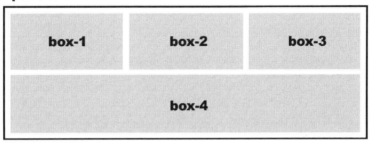

Figure 2-29: Lines aligned with `align-content: stretch`

Do It Yourself: Try the different values available for the **align-content** property using the CSS code in Listing 2-55. Remember again to add other properties to the elements, such as a color background, height, or a border, to see and identify each one of them on the screen.

IMPORTANT: Remember that for every new property to work we have to specify the corresponding prefix. As mentioned, at the moment, Google Chrome is the only browser with a working implementation of the Flexible Box Model. Therefore, you will be only able to test the examples using that browser and the **-webkit-** prefix (e.g., **-webkit-align-content: center;**).

CSS Styling and Box Models

Chapter 3
CSS3 Properties

3.1 The New Rules

The Web changed forever when in the early 2000s new applications that were developed over Ajax implementations improved designs and users' experience. Web 2.0, a name assigned to describe a new level of development, represented a change not only in the way the information was transmitted but also in how websites and applications were designed.

The codes implemented in this new generation of websites soon became the standard. The innovations were so important in the success of everything on the Internet that programmers developed entire Javascript libraries to overcome limitations and satisfy designers' requirements.

The lack of browser support was evident, but the W3C, the organization responsible for Web standards, didn't seriously consider the market and tried to continue on its own path. Fortunately, some bright programmers continued to develop new standards and soon HTML5 was born. After the dust settled, the integration of HTML, CSS and Javascript under the HTML5 umbrella was like a victorious, brave knight who had led the troops towards the enemy's palace.

Despite the recent turmoil, the battle began a long time ago, with the first specification of the third version of CSS. When finally, in 2005, this technology was officially considered a standard, CSS was ready to provide the features required by developers that programmers had been creating for years using complicated and not always compatible Javascript codes.

In this chapter, we will study the contributions of CSS3 to HTML5 and all the new properties that simplify the lives of designers and programmers.

CSS3 Goes Crazy

CSS was always about appearance and formatting, but not anymore. In an attempt to reduce the use of Javascript code and in order to standardize popular features, CSS3 addresses not only design and web styles but also form and movement. The CSS3 specification is presented in modules that provide a standard specification for every aspect involved in the visual presentation of the document. From round corners and shadows to transformations and rearrangement of the elements already rendered on the screen, every possible effect previously applied using Javascript was included. With this level of change, CSS3 was turn into almost an entirely new technology compared with previous versions.

HTML Document

The new CSS3 properties are extremely powerful and must be studied individually, but to make things easier, we are going to apply all of them to the same HTML document. So let's start with the HTML code and some basic styles:

```
<!DOCTYPE html>
<html lang="en">
<head>
  <title>New CSS3 styles</title>
  <link rel="stylesheet" href="newcss3.css">
</head>
<body>
  <header id="mainbox">
    <span id="title">CSS Styles Web 2.0</span>
  </header>
</body>
</html>
```

Listing 3-1: A simple document to test new properties

Our document has only one box with a short text inside. The **<header>** element used for this box could be replaced by **<div>**, **<nav>**, **<section>** or any other structural element according to the location in the design and its function. After the styling, the box in Listing 3-1 will look like a header, hence the **<header>** element.

Because the **<font>** element was deprecated in HTML5, as we explained before, the elements used to display texts are usually **<span>** for short lines and **<p>** for paragraphs, among others. For this reason, the text in our document is inserted between **<span>** tags.

> **Do It Yourself:** Use the code provided in Listing 3-1 as the document for this chapter. You will also need to create a new CSS file called **newcss3.css** to store the CSS styles.

The following are the basic styles for our document:

```
body {
  text-align: center;
}
#mainbox {
  display: block;
  width: 500px;
  margin: 50px auto;
  padding: 15px;
  border: 1px solid #999999;
  background: #FFFFFF;
}
#title {
  font: bold 36px verdana, sans-serif;
}
```

Listing 3-2: Basic CSS rules for this chapter

There is nothing new in the rules in Listing 3-2—just the styles necessary to shape our header and create a long box, positioned at the center of the window, with a gray background, a border of 1 pixel and large text inside that reads "CSS Styles Web 2.0".

Figure 3-1: Header with traditional styles

Border-Radius

For so many years developers suffered trying to get beautiful round corners for the boxes on their web pages, usually an exhausting and painful process. If you watch any early video presentation about the features incorporated in HTML5, every time someone talked about the CSS property that makes round corners easy to generate, the audience went wild. Round corners were the kind of thing that made you think: "It should be easy to do". However, for many years, they weren't an easy task. That's why, among all the new possibilities and amazing properties incorporated in CSS3, the first one we will explore is **border-radius**.

```
body {
  text-align: center;
}
#mainbox {
  display: block;
  width: 500px;
  margin: 50px auto;
  padding: 15px;
  border: 1px solid #999999;
  background: #FFFFFF;

  border-radius: 20px;
}
#title {
  font: bold 36px verdana, sans-serif;
}
```

Listing 3-3: Generating round corners

Figure 3-2: Round corners

Do It Yourself: In some browsers these new properties are still experimental. If you can't see the effect they are supposed to produce on the screen, try to add the corresponding prefixes for the browser you are using (e.g., **-moz-**, **-webkit-**, etc.), just as we did before with the properties studied in Chapter 2.

If every corner takes the same value, we can declare just one value for this property. However, as with the **margin** and **padding** properties, we can select a different value for each corner.

```
body {
   text-align: center;
}
#mainbox {
   display: block;
   width: 500px;
   margin: 50px auto;
   padding: 15px;
   border: 1px solid #999999;
   background: #FFFFFF;

   border-radius: 20px 10px 30px 50px;
}
#title {
   font: bold 36px verdana, sans-serif;
}
```

Listing 3-4: *Declaring different values for every corner*

As you can see in Listing 3-4, the four values assigned to the **border-radius** property represent four different locations. Going clockwise, the order of these values is top-left corner, top-right corner, bottom-right corner and bottom-left corner. The values are always given clockwise starting from the top-left corner.

CSS Styles Web 2.0

Figure 3-3: *Different values for every corner*

As with **margin** or **padding**, **border-radius** can also work with just two values. The first value is assigned to the first and third corners (top-left, bottom-right) and the second to the second and forth corners (top-right, bottom-left)—again, with the corners always ordered clockwise, starting from the top-left corner.

We can also shape the corners by providing new values separated by a slash. The values to the left of the slash represent the horizontal radius and the values at the right the vertical radius; the combination of these values generates an ellipse.

```
body {
   text-align: center;
}
#mainbox {
   display: block;
   width: 500px;
   margin: 50px auto;
   padding: 15px;
   border: 1px solid #999999;
```

```
  background: #FFFFFF;

  border-radius: 20px / 10px;
}
#title {
  font: bold 36px verdana, sans-serif;
}
```

Listing 3-5: Generating elliptic corners

CSS Styles Web 2.0

Figure 3-4: Elliptic corners

Do It Yourself: Copy the styles you want to test into the CSS file called `newcss3.css` and open the HTML file in Listing 3-1 in your browser. Change every value to learn how the property works.

Box-Shadow

Now that we finally have nice corners, we can go further. Another great effect, which had also been extremely complicated to get before, is shadows. For years designers have combined images, elements and some CSS properties to generate shadows. Thanks to CSS3 and the new property `box-shadow`, we are able to do that for our box with just one single line of code:

```
body {
  text-align: center;
}
#mainbox {
  display: block;
  width: 500px;
  margin: 50px auto;
  padding: 15px;
  border: 1px solid #999999;
  background: #FFFFFF;

  box-shadow: rgb(150,150,150) 5px 5px;
}
#title {
  font: bold 36px verdana, sans-serif;
}
```

Listing 3-6: Adding a shadow to our box

The `box-shadow` property needs at least three values. The first one, which you can see in the rule in Listing 3-6, is the color. This value is built here using `rgb()` and decimal numbers, but you can write it in hexadecimal (as we did before for other properties in this book).

The next two values, expressed in pixels, set the offset of the shadow. The offset may be positive or negative. The values indicate the horizontal and the vertical distance, respectively, from the shadow to the element. Negative values position the shadow at the left and above the element; whereas, positive values create a shadow at the right and below the element. Values of 0 place the shadow behind the element, providing the possibility of generating a blur effect all around it, as we will see next.

Figure 3-5: Basic shadow

Do It Yourself: To test the different parameters and possibilities to create a shadow for a box, copy the code in Listing 3-6 into the CSS file and open the HTML file of the document of Listing 3-1 in your browser. Now you can experiment with the values of the property `box-shadow` and use the same code for the new parameters that we study next.

The shadow we get, so far, is solid, with no gradient and transparency—not how a shadow really appears. There are a few more parameters and changes we can make to improve the shadow's appearance.

A fourth possible value to add to the **box-shadow** property is the blur distance. With this effect, the shadow will now look like a real shadow. You can try this parameter by declaring a value of 10 pixels in the rule in Listing 3-6, as in the following example:

```
box-shadow: rgb(150,150,150) 5px 5px 10px;
```

Listing 3-7: Adding the blur value to box-shadow

Figure 3-6: Real shadow

Adding another value in pixels at the end of the property will spread the shadow. This effect slightly changes the appearance of the shadow by expanding the area that it covers.

Do It Yourself: Try to add a value of 20 pixels at the end of the style in Listing 3-7. Combine that code with the code in Listing 3-6 and test it.

IMPORTANT: Always keep in mind that, presently, these properties are experimental in some browsers. To use them, you have to declare every one by adding the prefixes – **moz-** or **-webkit-** according to the browser (e.g., Mozilla Firefox, Google Chrome, etc.).

The last possible value for **box-shadow** is not a number but rather the keyword **inset**. This keyword turns the external shadow into an inner shadow that provides a depth effect to the box.

```
box-shadow: rgb(150,150,150) 5px 5px 10px inset;
```

Listing 3-8: Inner shadow

The style in Listing 3-8 generates an internal shadow of 5 pixels from the border of the box and a blur effect of 10 pixels, as shown in the next figure.

Figure 3-7: Inner shadow

Do It Yourself: The styles in Listing 3-7 and 3-8 are just examples. To check the effect in your browser, you must apply those changes to the complete set of rules in Listing 3-6.

IMPORTANT: Shadows don't expand the element nor increase its size, so you have to check carefully that the available space will allow the shadow to be seen.

Text-Shadow

Now that we know everything about shadows, you probably want to generate one for every element in your document. The **box-shadow** property was designed specifically for boxes. If you try to apply this effect to a **<span>** element, for example, the invisible box occupied by this element on the screen will have a shadow, not the content of the element. So, to create shadows for the irregular shapes present in texts, there is a special property called **text-shadow**.

```
body {
  text-align: center;
}
#mainbox {
  display: block;
  width: 500px;
  margin: 50px auto;
  padding: 15px;
  border: 1px solid #999999;
  background: #FFFFFF;
}
#title {
  font: bold 36px verdana, sans-serif;
  text-shadow: rgb(150, 150, 150) 3px 3px 5px;
}
```

Listing 3-9: Adding a shadow to the title

The values for **text-shadow** are similar to those for **box-shadow**. We can set the color of the shadow, the horizontal distance from the shadow to the object, the vertical distance and the blur radius. In Listing 3-9, a shadow is applied to the title of our header with a distance of only 3 pixels and a blur radius of 5, as shown in the next figure.

Figure 3-8: Text shadow

@font-face

A text shadow is a pretty good trick—hard to get with previous methods—but it just provides a three-dimensional effect rather than changing the text itself. A shadow is like painting an old car; at the end it will be the same car. In this case, it will be the same font.

The problem with fonts is as old as the Web. Regular web users often have a limited number of fonts installed, they don't always have the same families of fonts, and some users will likely have a font that others don't. For years, websites could only use a minimum set of reliable fonts—a basic group that most users have—to render and show the information on the screen.

The function @font-face allows designers to provide a specific font file to display text on a web page. Now we can include any font we want in a website by providing the file for it.

```css
body {
  text-align: center;
}
#mainbox {
  display: block;
  width: 500px;
  margin: 50px auto;
  padding: 15px;
  border: 1px solid #999999;
  background: #FFFFFF;
}
#title {
  font: bold 36px MyNewFont, verdana, sans-serif;
}
@font-face {
  font-family: 'MyNewFont';
  src: url('font.ttf');
}
```

Listing 3-10: New font for the title

Do It Yourself: Download the file `font.ttf` from our website or use one of your own, and copy it to the same folder or directory of your CSS file (to download the file, go to www.minkbooks.com/content/). You can get more free fonts like this one at: www.moorstation.org/typoasis/designers/steffmann/

IMPORTANT: The font's file must be on the same domain as the web page (or in the same computer, in this case). This is a restriction of some browsers, such as Mozilla Firefox.

The @font-face function needs at least two properties to declare the font and load the file. The **font-family** property specifies the name we want to use to reference that particular font, and the `src` property indicates the URL of the file with the specifications for the font. In Listing 3-10, the name `MyNewFont` is assigned to our font and the `font.ttf` file is indicated as the source.

Once the font is loaded, we are able to use it in any element of the document just by writing its name (`MyNewFont`). In the style `font` of the rule in Listing 3-10, we specify that the title will be rendered with the new font or with the alternatives `verdana` and `sans-serif` if the font is not loaded properly.

Figure 3-9: *Custom font for the title*

Linear Gradient

Gradients are one of the most attractive features among those incorporated to CSS3. They were almost impossible to implement using previous techniques but are now really easy to do in CSS. A **background** property with a few parameters is sufficient to turn your document into a web page that looks professional.

```
body {
  text-align: center;
}
#mainbox {
  display: block;
  width: 500px;
  margin: 50px auto;
  padding: 15px;
  border: 1px solid #999999;

  background: -webkit-linear-gradient(top, #FFFFFF, #666666);
  background: -moz-linear-gradient(top, #FFFFFF, #666666);
}
#title {
  font: bold 36px verdana, sans-serif;
}
```

Listing 3-11: *Adding a beautiful gradient background to our box*

Gradients are set as backgrounds, so we can apply them using the properties `background` or the more specific `background-image`. The syntax to create linear gradients with these properties is `linear-gradient(starting position, from color, to color)`. The attributes for the `linear-gradient()` function indicate the starting point and the colors used to create the gradient. The first value is declared using the keywords `top`, `bottom`, `left` and `right` (as we did in the example in Listing 3-11).

CSS Styles Web 2.0

Figure 3-10: Linear gradient

The keywords may also be combined to point to a corner of the element, as in the following example:

```
background: -webkit-linear-gradient(top right, #FFFFFF, #666666);
background: -moz-linear-gradient(top right, #FFFFFF, #666666);
```

Listing 3-12: Combining keywords

CSS Styles Web 2.0

Figure 3-11: Different starting position for a linear gradient

IMPORTANT: The new specification declares the keywords with the prefix **to**, which inverts the direction of the gradient (e.g., **to top**), but not every browser currently understands this new syntax, and it is not clear whether the syntax presented in this chapter will be preserved or deprecated. To learn more about the history of gradient syntaxes, please visit our website and follow the links for this chapter.

The starting position may be also expressed by an angle.

```
background: -webkit-linear-gradient(30deg, #FFFFFF, #666666);
background: -moz-linear-gradient(30deg, #FFFFFF, #666666);
```

Listing 3-13: Creating a gradient with a direction of 30 degrees

CSS Styles Web 2.0

Figure 3-12: Starting position in degrees for a linear gradient

We may add more values to generate a multicolor gradient:

```
background: -webkit-linear-gradient(top, #000000, #FFFFFF, #999999);
background: -moz-linear-gradient(top, #000000, #FFFFFF, #999999);
```

Listing 3-14: Creating a multicolor gradient

CSS Styles Web 2.0

Figure 3-13: Multicolor linear gradient

Using the keyword `transparent`, we are able to merge the gradient with the background (this effect can also be achieved with the `rgba()` function studied later).

```
body {
  text-align: center;
  background: url(http://www.minkbooks.com/content/bricks2.jpg);
}
#mainbox {
  display: block;
  width: 500px;
  margin: 50px auto;
  padding: 15px;
  border: 1px solid #999999;

  background: -webkit-linear-gradient(top, transparent, #666666);
  background: -moz-linear-gradient(top, transparent, #666666);
}
#title {
  font: bold 36px verdana, sans-serif;
}
```

Listing 3-15: Creating a transparent gradient

In the example in Listing 3-15, we add a background image to the **<body>** element to be able to see the effect of the **transparent** keyword on the screen. The result is shown in Figure 3-14 below.

Figure 3-14: Transparent gradient

The parameters for the colors are described in the specification with the name *color-stop*. This is because by including an additional value we can determine the starting and ending point of each color and customize the gradient.

```
background: -webkit-linear-gradient(top, #FFFFFF 50%, #666666 90%);
background: -moz-linear-gradient(top, #FFFFFF 50%, #666666 90%);
```

Listing 3-16: Setting color-stops

CSS Styles Web 2.0

Figure 3-15: Adding color-stop values

Radial Gradient

The current standard syntax for radial gradients is not that different from the syntax for linear gradients we just studied. We use the `radial-gradient()` function and include a parameter for the shape, which can be either `circle` or `ellipse`.

```
background: -webkit-radial-gradient(center, ellipse, #FFFFFF, #000000);
background: -moz-radial-gradient(center, ellipse, #FFFFFF, #000000);
```

Listing 3-17: Creating a radial gradient

The first value in the `radial-gradient()` function in Listing 3-17 determines the starting position. This position is the origin of the gradient and can be declared either as pixels, as percentage or a combination of the keywords `center`, `top`, `bottom`, `left` and `right`.

CSS Styles Web 2.0

Figure 3-16: Radial gradient

Except for the shape (circle or ellipse), the rest of the function works exactly like `linear-gradient()`. The position may be customized, and we can use several colors with the second value for color-stops to determine the limit of each of them.

```
background: -webkit-radial-gradient(30px 50px, ellipse, #FFFFFF 50%,
#666666 70%, #999999 90%);
background: -moz-radial-gradient(30px 50px, ellipse, #FFFFFF 50%, #666666
70%, #999999 90%);
```

Listing 3-18: Creating a multicolor radial gradient

CSS Styles Web 2.0

Figure 3-17: Adding color-stops to a radial gradient

IMPORTANT: Mozilla proposed a new syntax for both types of gradients that has not yet been adopted by other browsers' vendors. The new specification includes the word `at` to describe the position of radial gradients. Please check our website for updates.

RGBA

Up to this point, colors have been declared as solid, with hexadecimal numbers or the function `rgb()` for decimals. CSS3 has added a new function called `rgba()` that simplifies the declaration of colors and transparencies and solves a previous problem cause by the `opacity` property.

The `rgba()` function has four attributes. The first three values are similar to `rgb()` and simply declare the combination of colors. The last one is for the opacity; its value ranges from 0 to 1, with 0 as fully transparent and 1 as fully opaque.

```
#title {
  font: bold 36px verdana, sans-serif;
  text-shadow: rgba(0,0,0,0.5) 3px 3px 5px;
}
```

Listing 3-19: *Improving the shadow with transparency*

Listing 3-19 shows a simple example to demonstrate how shadow effects are improved by the use of transparency. We replaced the function `rgb()` by `rgba()` in the shadow of the title of our example in Listing 3-9 to add an opacity value of 0.5. Now the shadow of our title is merged with the background of the box, creating a more natural effect.

In previous versions of CSS, we had to use different techniques for different browsers to make an element transparent. All of them presented the same problem: the opacity value for an element was inherited by all its children. That problem was solved by `rgba()` and now you can assign an opacity value to the background of a box and its content won't be affected.

> **Do It Yourself:** Replace the corresponding code in Listing 3-9 with the code in Listing 3-19 to test the effect in your browser.

HSLA

Just as the `rgba()` function adds the opacity value for `rgb()`, the function `hsla()` does the same for the previous `hsl()` function.

The function `hsla()` is simply another function to generate the color for an element, but it is more intuitive than `rgba()`. Some designers will find it easier to create a personal set of colors using `hsla()`. The syntax is `hsla(hue, saturation, lightness, opacity)`.

```
#title {
  font: bold 36px verdana, sans-serif;
  text-shadow: rgba(0,0,0,0.5) 3px 3px 5px;
  color: hsla(120, 100%, 50%, 0.5);
}
```

Listing 3-20: *Generating a color for the title with* `hsla()`

According to the syntax, hue represents the color extracted from an imaginary wheel, and it is expressed in degrees from 0 to 360. Around 0 and 360 are reds, close to 120 are greens and close to 240 are blues. Saturation is represented as a percentage, from 0% (gray scale) to 100% (full color or fully saturated). Lightness is also a percentage value, from 0% (completely black) to 100% (completely white); the value of 50% is average lighting. And the last value, as in `rgba()`, represents the opacity.

> **Do It Yourself:** Replace the corresponding code in Listing 3-2 with the code in Listing 3-20 to test the effect in your browser.

Outline

The property `outline` is an old CSS property that has been expanded in CSS3 to include an offset. This property is used to create a second border, and now that border can be rendered away from the edge of the element.

```
#mainbox {
  display: block;
  width: 500px;
  margin: 50px auto;
  padding: 15px;
  border: 1px solid #999999;
  background: #FFFFFF;

  outline: 2px dashed #000000;
  outline-offset: 15px;
}
```

Listing 3-21: Adding an outline for the header box

In Listing 3-21, we add an outline of 2 pixels with an offset of 15 pixels to the styles originally assigned to the box of our document. The `outline` property has similar characteristics, and it uses the same parameters as `border`. The `outline-offset` property only needs one value in pixel units.

Figure 3-18: Adding a second border

> **Do It Yourself:** Replace the corresponding code in Listing 3-2 with the code in Listing 3-21 to test the effect in your browser.

Border-Image

The effects achieved by the properties `border` and `outline` are limited to single lines and a few configuration options. The new `border-image` property is intended to overcome these limitations and allow designers to determine the quality and variety of borders, providing the alternative to use custom images.

> **Do It Yourself:** We will use a PNG image of diamonds to test this property. Follow the link to download the file `diamond.png` from our website (www.minkbooks.com/content/) and then copy the file in the same folder or directory as your CSS file.

The `border-image` property takes an image as a pattern. According to the values provided, the image is sliced like a cake to get the pieces and then these pieces are placed around the object to build the border.

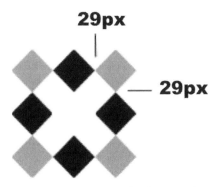

Figure 3-19: The pattern we will build our border from, with each piece 29 pixels wide

To accomplish this, we need to declare three attributes: the name of the image file and its location, the size of the pieces we want to get from the pattern and a few keywords to specify how those pieces will be distributed around the object.

```
#mainbox {
  display: block;
  width: 500px;
  margin: 50px auto;
  padding: 15px;

  border: 29px solid;
  border-image: url("diamonds.png") 29 stretch;
}
```

Listing 3-22: Creating a custom border for the header box

With the modifications in Listing 3-22, we set a border of 29 pixels for the header box and then load the image `diamonds.png` to build the border. The value 29 in the `border-image` property declares the size of the pieces, and `stretch` is one of the methods available to distribute these pieces around the box.

There are three possible values for the last attribute. The keyword **repeat** will repeat the pieces taken from the image as many times as needed to cover the side of the element. In this case, the size of the pieces is preserved and the image will be cut if there is not enough space to place it. The keyword **round** will calculate how long the side is and then strech the pieces to make sure that none of the pieces is cut. Finally, the keyword **stretch** (used in Listing 3-22) stretches one piece to cover the whole side.

We used the **border** property to set the size of the border, but you can also use **border-with** to specify a different size for each side of the element. (The **border-with** property uses four parameters, similar to the syntax of **margin** and **padding.**) The same happens with the size of every piece; up to four values can be declared to get different images of different sizes from the pattern.

Figure 3-20: *Border image for our header*

Do It Yourself: Replace the corresponding code in Listing 3-2 with the code in Listing 3-22 to test the effect in your browser. Test each keyword for the **border-image** property (**repeat**, **round** and **stretch**).

Background

The **background** property has incorporated new parameters and features such as size, positioning or painting area, and it can include several images. The new syntax is **background: color image position size repeat origin clip attachment**, which is shorthand for the following properties:

> **background-color**—This property assigns a background color to an element. The value can be expressed in hexadecimal (e.g., **#FF0000**), in decimal numbers using the **rgb()** function (e.g., **rgb(255,0,0)**), or with a keyword such as **yellow, white, black**, etc.
>
> **background-image**—This property assigns one or more images for the background of an element. The URL to the file is declared by the **url()** function (e.g., **url('bricks.jpg')**). If more than one image is provided, the values must be separated by a comma.
>
> **background-position**—This property declares the starting position of a background image. The values must be specified in percentage, pixels or using a combination of the following keywords: **center, left, right, top, bottom.**
>
> **background-size**—This property declares the size of the background image. The values can be specified as percentage, as pixels or by the keywords **cover** and **contain**. The keyword **cover** will scale the image until at least its width or its height fits into the element, while **contain** will scale the entire image to fit into the element.
>
> **background-repeat**—This property determines how a background image will be distributed using four keywords: **repeat, repeat-x, repeat-y** and **no-repeat**. The keyword **repeat** will repeat the image horizontally and vertically, while **repeat-x** and

repeat-y will do so only for the horizontal axis or the vertical axis, respectively. Finally, no-repeat will show the background image only once.

background-origin—This property uses the same keywords as background-clip to set the image relative to the border, the padding or the content of the box.

background-clip—This property declares the area to be painted using three keywords: border-box, padding-box and content-box. The first clips the image to the border of the box, the second clips the image to the padding of the box and the third clips the image to the content of the box.

background-attachment—This property determines whether the image is fixed or scrolls with the rest of the elements using two keywords: scroll and fixed. The first keyword is the value by default and makes the image scroll with the page. The second keyword, fixed, fixes the background image in the place where it was declared.

```
#mainbox {
  display: block;
  width: 500px;
  margin: 50px auto;
  padding: 15px;
  border: 1px solid #999999;

  background: #CCCCCC url("bricks2.jpg") 10px 10px / 510px 55px no-repeat
scroll border-box;
}
```

Listing 3-23: Generating a custom background for the header box

In Listing 3-23, the background is created using the shorthand property background and the values are separated by a space. Notice that when both position and size are declared they must be separated by a slash. We declare the color, image, position and size of the background image in that order. The values no-repeat, scroll and border-box at the end correspond to the values for background-repeat, background-attachment and background-origin.

Figure 3-21: Testing the background *property*

Some values can be interchanged and in some cases you will be able to use the background property to declare just a few of them, such as in background: #CCCC99.

Do It Yourself: Replace the corresponding code in Listing 3-2 with the code in Listing 3-23 to test the effect in your browser. Some of the new parameters for the background property are currently only implemented by Google Chrome. To download the image used as background in this example, go to www.minkbooks.com/content/.

Columns

CSS3 incorporates a group of properties to facilitate the creation of columns inside a box. We can have a multi-column content by adding a simple rule.

```
#mainbox {
  display: block;
  width: 500px;
  margin: 50px auto;
  padding: 15px;
  border: 1px solid #999999;
  background: #FFFFFF;

  column-count: 2;
  column-gap: 10px;
  column-rule: 1px solid #000000;
}
```

Listing 3-24: Generating columns for text

The property `column-count`, applied in Listing 3-24, declares the number of columns to be created. With `column-gap` we declare the gap between columns, and finally `column-rule` specifies a rule, a visible division for the columns on the screen. In this case, the division is a black solid line 1 pixel wide. The syntax for this last property is the same as for the `border` property: `width style color` (separated by a space).

Figure 3-22: Two columns for our header

There are other properties available to customize the columns. Some of the most interesting are `column-width` and `column-span`:

> **column-width**—This property declares a specific width for the columns. The values can be `auto` (by default) or a length in any valid CSS unit, such as pixels.

> **column-span**—This property is applied to elements inside the box and determines if the element will be placed inside one column or spanned across multiple columns. The possible values are `all`, meaning "all the columns", and `none` (by default).

> **Do It Yourself:** If you test this example using the CSS code in Listing 3-2, you will see the title of the header divided into two columns, as shown in Figure 3-22. Remember to add the corresponding prefixes to the `colum-` properties (e.g., `-webkit-`, `-moz-`, etc.).

Filters

Filters allow us to add effects to an image. They have been well used by graphic designers for a long time, and we can find them in photo editing programs or video editors, for example. But programmers never expected they would be available on the Web, unless we spent hours coding the filters ourselves. CSS3 changed this with the introduction of several new functions of the old `filter` property to affect not only images but any element in the document.

> **IMPORTANT:** At the moment, filters are only available on Google Chrome. The implementation is still in the experimental stage, so we must use the **-webkit-** prefix to apply the `filter` property.

```
#mainbox {
  display: block;
  width: 500px;
  margin: 50px auto;
  padding: 15px;
  border: 1px solid #999999;

  background: #CCCC99 url("bricks2.jpg");
  -webkit-filter: blur(5px);
}
```

Listing 3-25: Applying a filter to the header

Figure 3-23: A blurry header

The `filter` property in Listing 3-25 applies the `blur()` function to provide a blur effect to the header of the document (and all its content). Here are all the functions now available for this property:

blur(value)—This function produces a blur effect. It takes a value in pixels from **1px** to **10px**.

grayscale(value)—This function gradually turns the element's colors into a gray scale. It takes a decimal number from **0.1** to **1**.

drop-shadow(x, y, size, color)—This function produces a simple shadow for the element. The **x** and **y** attributes determine the distance the shadow will be from the element, the **size** attribute specifies the size of the shadow and the **color** attribute declares its color.

sepia(value)—This function gives the element's colors a sepia tone. It takes a decimal number from **0.1** to **1**.

brightness(value)—This function changes the element's brightness. It takes a decimal number from **0.1** to **10**.

contrast(value)—This function changes the element's contrast. It takes a decimal number from 0.1 to 10.

hue-rotate(value)—This function applyies a rotation to the element's hue. It takes a value in degrees from 1deg to 360deg.

invert(value)—This function inverts the element's colors, producing a negative. It takes a decimal number from 0.1 to 1.

saturate(value)—This function saturates the element's colors. It takes a decimal number from 0.1 to 10.

opacity(value)—This function produce an opacity effect. It takes a decimal number from 0 to 1 (with 0 defining full transparency and 1 full opacity).

Do It Yourself: Replace the corresponding code in Listing 3-2 with the code in Listing 3-25 to test the effect in your browser. Replace the `blur()` function with the one you want to apply.

3.2 Transform

Once created, HTML elements are like solid immovable blocks. They may be moved using customized Javascript code or by taking advantage of some popular libraries, such as jQuery (www.jquery.com), but there was no standard procedure until CSS3 arrived with the `transform` and `transition` properties. Now, we don't have to think about how to do this. Instead, we have to know a few parameters and our website can be as dynamic as we imagined it.

The `transform` property can perform four basic transformations of an object: `scale`, `rotate`, `skew` and move or `translate`. Let's see how they work.

Transform: Scale

The `scale()` function receives two parameters, the `X` value for horizontal scaling and the `Y` value for vertical scaling. If only one value is given, the same value is applied to both parameters.

```
#mainbox {
  display: block;
  width: 500px;
  margin: 50px auto;
  padding: 15px;
  border: 1px solid #999999;
  background: #FFFFFF;

  -webkit-transform: scale(2);
  -moz-transform: scale(2);
}
```

Listing 3-26: Scaling the header box

In the example in Listing 3-26, we take the basic styles used in Listing 3-2 for the header box and transform it by scaling the element to double its size. Integer and decimal values can be provided for the scaling, and it is calculated using a matrix. Values between 0 and 1 will reduce the element, a value of 1 will keep the original proportions, and values greater than 1 will increase the dimensions of the object linearly.

An interesting effect possible with this function can be achieved by using negative values.

```
#mainbox {
  display: block;
  width: 500px;
  margin: 50px auto;
  padding: 15px;
  border: 1px solid #999999;
  background: #FFFFFF;

  -webkit-transform: scale(1,-1);
  -moz-transform: scale(1,-1);
}
```

Listing 3-27: Creating a mirror image with scale

In Listing 3-27, two parameters are declared to scale the **mainbox**. The first value, 1, keeps the original proportion for the horizontal dimension. The second value also keeps the original proportion but inverts the element vertically to produce a mirror effect.

CSS Styles Web 2.0

Figure 3-24: Mirror image with scale()

There are two more functions similar to **scale** but restricted to horizontal and vertical dimensions: **scaleX()** and **scaleY()**. These functions, of course, have only one parameter.

> **Do It Yourself:** Replace the corresponding code in Listing 3-2 with the code in Listing 3-26 or 3-27 to test the effect in your browser.

Transform: Rotate

The **rotate()** function rotates the element and its content clockwise. The value must be specified in degrees using the "**deg**" unit.

```
#mainbox {
  display: block;
  width: 500px;
  margin: 50px auto;
  padding: 15px;
  border: 1px solid #999999;
  background: #FFFFFF;
```

```
    -webkit-transform: rotate(30deg);
    -moz-transform: rotate(30deg);
}
```

Listing 3-28: Rotating the box

If a negative value is specified, it will change the direction in which the element is rotated.

Do It Yourself: Replace the corresponding code in Listing 3-2 with the code in Listing 3-28 to test the effect in your browser.

Transform: Skew

The `skew()` function changes the symmetry of the element by degrees in both dimensions.

```
#mainbox {
    display: block;
    width: 500px;
    margin: 50px auto;
    padding: 15px;
    border: 1px solid #999999;
    background: #FFFFFF;

    -webkit-transform: skew(20deg);
    -moz-transform: skew(20deg);
}
```

Listing 3-29: Skew horizontally

This function has two parameters, but unlike other functions, each parameter for `skew()` only affects one dimension, thus the parameters are independent of one another. In Listing 3-29, we perform a `transform` operation to the header box in order to skew it. Only the first parameter is declared, so only the horizontal dimension is modified. If we use both parameters, we can alter both dimensions of the object. Alternatively, we could use independent functions for this purpose: `skewX()` and `skewY()`.

Figure 3-25: Effect using skew()

Do It Yourself: Replace the corresponding code in Listing 3-2 with the code in Listing 3-29 to test the effect in your browser.

Transform: Translate

Similar to the old `top` and `left` CSS properties, the `translate()` function moves the element on the screen to a new position.

```
#mainbox {
  display: block;
  width: 500px;
  margin: 50px auto;
  padding: 15px;
  border: 1px solid #999999;
  background: #FFFFFF;

  -webkit-transform: translate(100px);
  -moz-transform: translate(100px);
}
```

Listing 3-30: Moving the header box to the right

The `translate()` function considers the screen as a grid of pixels, with the original position of the element used as the reference point. The top-left corner of the element is the `0,0` position, so negative values will move the object to the left or above the original position, and positive values will move it to the right or below.

In Listing 3-30, we move the header box to the right by 100 pixels from the original position. Two values may be declared for this function to move the element both horizontally and vertically, or the `translateX()` and `translateY()` functions can be used to do this independently.

> **Do It Yourself:** Replace the corresponding code in Listing 3-2 with the code in Listing 3-30 to test the effect in your browser.

Transforming All at Once

Sometimes it may be useful to apply several transformations to one single element. To get a compound **transform** property, we just have to separate the functions with a space.

```
#mainbox {
  display: block;
  width: 500px;
  margin: 50px auto;
  padding: 15px;
  border: 1px solid #999999;
  background: #FFFFFF;

  -webkit-transform: translateY(100px) rotate(45deg) scaleX(0.3);
  -moz-transform: translateY(100px) rotate(45deg) scaleX(0.3);
}
```

Listing 3-31: Moving, scaling and rotating the element in just one line

One of the things you must remember here is that the order of transformations is important. Because some functions modify the origin point and the center of the object, they change the parameters the rest of the functions will operate from.

Do It Yourself: Replace the corresponding code in Listing 3-2 with the code in Listing 3-31 to test the effect in your browser.

Dynamic Transformations

What we have learned so far changes our web, page but the elements remain static. However, we can take advantage of the combination of transformations and pseudo-classes to turn our document into a dynamic application.

```
#mainbox {
  display: block;
  width: 500px;
  margin: 50px auto;
  padding: 15px;
  border: 1px solid #999999;
  background: #FFFFFF;
}
#mainbox:hover{
  -webkit-transform: rotate(5deg);
  -moz-transform: rotate(5deg);
}
```

Listing 3-32: Responding to user's activity

The original rule for the header box introduced in Listing 3-2 remains the same, but a new rule is added in Listing 3-32 to apply the transformation effect using the :hover pseudo-class. The result is that every time the mouse pointer is over the header box, the **transform** property rotates it 5 degrees, and when the mouse pointer is outside the box, the header is rotated back to its previous position. This achieves a basic but useful animation, using no more than CSS properties.

> **Review the Basics:** The :hover pseudo-class, as well as the rest of the pseudo-classes studied in Chapter 2, add a special effect to a rule. In this case, the styles are applied only when the mouse pointer is over the element referenced by the rule. To get a complete list of pseudo-classes, visit our website and follow the links for this chapter.

> **Do It Yourself:** Replace the corresponding code in Listing 3-2 with the code in Listing 3-32 to test the effect in your browser.

3D Transformations

In the same way we can make two-dimensional transformations, we can also perform three-dimensional operations on HTML elements. CSS3 provides functions and properties to produce amazing 3D effects for our webpages with just a few lines of code.

```
#mainbox {
  display: block;
  width: 500px;
```

```
    margin: 50px auto;
    padding: 15px;
    border: 1px solid #999999;
    background: #FFFFFF;

    -webkit-transform: perspective(500px) rotate3d(0, 1, 0, 45deg);
    -moz-transform: perspective(500px) rotate3d(0, 1, 0, 45deg);
}
```

Listing 3-33: *Adding a three-dimensional effect to the header*

As you can see in Listing 3-33, there are new functions available for the **transform** property to produce 3D transformations. In this first example, we assign perspective to the header of our document of Listing 3-1 and perform a 3D rotation.

Figure 3-26: *3D effect*

Except **perspective()**, the rest of the 3D functions available for the **transform** property are similar to those for 2D effects.

> **perspective()**—This function adds depth to the scene, making the elements bigger when they are closer to the viewer. It is necessary to apply this function first to be able to see the 3D effects on the screen.
>
> **translate3d(x, y, z)**—This function moves the element to a new position in 3D space. It takes three values in pixels for the **x**, **y** and **z** axis.
>
> **scale3d(x, y, z)**—This function provides a new scale for the element in 3D space. It takes three values in decimal numbers to set the scale for the **x**, **y** and **z** axis. As in 2D transformations, a value of 1 will preserve the original scale.
>
> **rotate3d(x, y, z, angle)**—This function rotates the element according to the values provided for every axis and the angle. The axis values must be specified in decimal numbers and the angle expressed as **angle deg** (e.g., **30deg**). The values for the axes determine a vector for the rotation, which is why the relation between the values is important, not the values themselves. For example, **rotate3d(5, 2, 6, 30deg)** will produce the same effect as **rotate3d(50, 20, 60, 30deg)**, because the resulting vector is the same.

As before, we can apply all the transformations we want at once.

```
#mainbox {
    display: block;
    width: 500px;
    margin: 50px auto;
    padding: 15px;
    border: 1px solid #999999;
    background: #FFFFFF;
```

```
    -webkit-transform: perspective(500px) translate3d(0, 0, -300px)
rotate3d(0, 1, 0, 50deg);
    -moz-transform: perspective(500px) translate3d(0, 0, -300px)
rotate3d(0, 1, 0, 50deg);
}
```

Listing 3-34: Translating and rotating in 3D

There are a few properties also available to get a more realistic effect:

> **perspective**—This is the same as the `perspective()` function but works in a parent box. It creates a containing box to provide the perspective effect for its children.

> **perspective-origin**—This property changes the `X` and `Y` coordinates of the viewer. It takes two values in percentage, pixels or by the keywords `center`, `left`, `right`, `top` and `bottom`. The values by default are `50% 50%`.

> **backface-visibility**—This property determines whether the back of an element will be visible or not. It has two values: `visible` or `hidden`, with `visible` set by default.

```
body {
  text-align: center;

  -webkit-perspective: 500px;
  -moz-perspective: 500px;

  -webkit-perspective-origin: 50% 90%;
  -moz-perspective-origin: 50% 90%;
}
#mainbox {
  display: block;
  width: 500px;
  margin: 50px auto;
  padding: 15px;
  border: 1px solid #999999;
  background: #FFFFFF;

  -webkit-transform: rotate3d(0, 1, 0, 135deg);
  -moz-transform: rotate3d(0, 1, 0, 135deg);
}
#title {
  font: bold 36px verdana, sans-serif;
}
```

Listing 3-35: Declaring a different origin for the viewer

The `perspective` property has to be assigned to the parent box of the element we want to affect. In the document of Listing 3-1, the parent box of the header is the body of the document. The result is the same as using the `perspective()` function for the child, but by declaring the perspective in this way, we were able to use the `perspective-origin` property and change the coordinates for the viewer as well.

CSS3 Properties

Figure 3-27: *3D effect using the* `perspective` *property*

Do It Yourself: Replace the corresponding code in Listing 3-2 with the code in Listing 3-35 to test the effect in your browser. Try adding the **backface-visibility** property with the value **hidden** to the **mainbox** to make the header invisible when it's backwards.

3.3 Transitions

Beautiful effects with dynamic transformations are accessible and easy to implement in our designs using CSS3. However, a real animation requires a transition between the two steps of the process.

The **transition** property was created to smooth the shift out, to magically create the rest of the steps implicit in the movement. By adding this property, we force the browser to handle the situation, create all those invisible steps and generate a smooth transition from one status to another.

```
#mainbox {
  display: block;
  width: 500px;
  margin: 50px auto;
  padding: 15px;
  border: 1px solid #999999;
  background: #FFFFFF;

  -webkit-transition: -webkit-transform 1s ease-in-out 0.5s;
  -moz-transition: -moz-transform 1s ease-in-out 0.5s;
}
#mainbox:hover{
  -webkit-transform: perspective(500px) rotate3d(0, 1, 0, 360deg);
  -moz-transform: perspective(500px) rotate3d(0, 1, 0, 360deg);
}
```

Listing 3-36: *Creating a beautiful 3D rotation using* `transition`

As we can see in Listing 3-36, the **transition** property can take up to four parameters separated by space. The first value is the property that will be considered to create the transition (in our example is **transform**). This is necessary because several properties can change at the same time and we likely will only need to create steps for one of them. The second parameter sets the time the transition will take from the initial position to the end (1 second in our example). The third parameter can be one of five keywords: **ease**, **linear**, **ease-in**, **ease-out** or **ease-in-out**. These keywords determine how the transition will take place based on a Bézier curve. Each keyword represents a different Bézier curve, and the only way to know which one is best for a transition is by testing them on the screen. The last parameter for the `transition` property is the delay. It indicates how long it will take for the transition to start.

To produce a transition for all the properties that are changing in an element, the `all` keyword may be specified. We can also declare every property to be affected by listing them separated by commas.

> **Do It Yourself:** Replace the corresponding code in Listing 3-2 with the code in Listing 3-36 to test the effect in your browser.

> **IMPORTANT:** In Listing 3-36, we perform a transition with the `transform` property. Not every CSS property is supported by the `transition` property and by every browser at present, but this will change over time. You will have to test them by yourself or visit the website of every browser to find more information.

3.4 Animations

The most complex effect we can probably achieve with CSS is animations. In the previous section, we saw how to create a basic animation using the `transition` property, but the process involved only two steps: the initial state and the final state. For a real animation we need to declare several frames, as in a movie. CSS3 will let us do that with the `@keyframes` function and the `animation` property. The function defines the animation and the property provides all the configuration parameters, as shown in Listing 3-37 below.

> **IMPORTANT:** Currently, browser vendors are eliminating the prefixes for the `transform`, `transition` and `animation` properties, but it is still likely that you will need to add the prefixes for these examples to work. The `@keyframes` function uses the prefix in between the @ symbol and the name (e.g., `@-webkit-keyframes`).

```
body {
  text-align: center;
}
#mainbox {
  display: block;
  width: 500px;
  margin: 50px auto;
  padding: 15px;
  border: 1px solid #999999;
  animation: myanimation 1s ease-in-out 0s infinite normal none;
}
@keyframes myanimation {
  0% {
    background: #FFFFFF;
  }
  50% {
    background: #FF0000;
  }
  100% {
    background: #FFFFFF;
  }
}
```

```
#title {
  font: bold 36px verdana, sans-serif;
}
```

Listing 3-37: A first approach to CSS animations

The frames are set by the @**keyframes** function using values in percentage and grouping the styles for every frame with braces. The value 0% is the first frame or the start of our movie and 100% is the final frame or the end. These values can be ignored or even replaced by the keywords **from** (0%) and **to** (100%). We can start the movie whenever we want and declare all the frames we need.

```
body {
  text-align: center;
}
#mainbox {
  display: block;
  width: 500px;
  margin: 50px auto;
  padding: 15px;
  border: 1px solid #999999;

  animation: myanimation 1s ease-in-out 0s infinite normal none;
}
@keyframes myanimation {
  20% {
    background: #FFFFFF;
  }
  35% {
    transform: scale(0.5);
    background: #FFFF00;
  }
  50% {
    transform: scale(1.5);
    background: #FF0000;
  }
  65% {
    transform: scale(0.5);
    background: #FFFF00;
  }
  80% {
    background: #FFFFFF;
  }
}
#title {
  font: bold 36px verdana, sans-serif;
}
```

Listing 3-38: Declaring more frames for our animation

In Listing 3-38, the animation starts at 20% and ends at 80%, with a total of 5 frames involved. The properties in each frame indicate how the element will be styled in that step of the animation process but not how the animation will occur. To configure that, we have the **animation** property. This property is shorthand for several properties available to control the whole animation process:

animation-name—This property provides the name used to create the frames in the `@keyframe` function for an effective way to connect the frame to the configuration of the animation. It can be used to configure several animations at once declaring the names separated by a comma.

animation-duration—This property is used to declare how much time the animation will take per cycle. The value must be specified in seconds (e.g., `1s` for 1 second).

animation-timing-function—This property works exactly as in the `transition` property we studied before. It determines how the animation process will take place based on a Bézier curve declared by the keywords `ease`, `linear`, `ease-in`, `ease-out` and `ease-in-out`.

animation-delay—This property delays the start of the animation. It must be declared in seconds (e.g., `1s` for 1 second), with a value by default of `0s`.

animation-iteration-count—This property declares the number of times the animation will be executed. It takes an integer number for a value or the keyword `infinite`, which will run the animation indefinitely. The value by default is `1`.

animation-direction—This property sets the direction of the animation. It can take four values: `normal`, `reverse`, `alternate` and `alternate-reverse`. The value `normal` is the one set by default, and it won't produce any changes. The second value, `reverse`, inverts the direction of the animation, showing the frames in the opposite direction they were declared. The value `alternate` mixes the cycles of the animation, playing the ones that have an odd index in normal direction and the rest in reverse direction. Finally, the value `alternate-reverse` simply does the same as `alternate`, but in reverse.

animation-fill-mode—This property can take four values to define how the animation will interact with the styles of the element: `none`, `forwards`, `backwards` and `both`. The value `none` is set by default and doesn't affect the styles of the element. The value `forwards` will keep the element styled with the properties applied in the last frame of the animation (defined by `100%` or the keyword `to`), whereas `backwards` will apply the styles of the first frame (defined by `0%` or the keyword `from`) to the element as soon as the animation is defined (before it is executed). Finally, the value `both` will, of course, produce both effects.

As we saw in our examples, we can declare all these properties at once using the `animation` property and the following syntax (the order is important): `animation: name duration timing-function delay iteration-count direction fill-mode`.

> **IMPORTANT:** Remember to add the corresponding prefixes to the `animation` property and the `@keyframes` function to test these examples (e.g., `-webkit-animation`, `@-webkit-keyframes`).

Chapter 4
Javascript

4.1 A Brief Introduction to Javascript

HTML5 may be thought of as a building supported by three columns: HTML, CSS and Javascript. We have already examined the elements incorporated in HTML and the new properties that make CSS the ideal tool for designers. Now it is time to unveil what may be considered one of the strongest aspects of this specification: Javascript.

Javascript is an interpreted language used for multiple purposes but was so far considered just as a complement of HTML and CSS. One of the innovations that helped change how we see Javascript was browsers' new engines, developed to accelerate script processing. What these innovative engines did was to turn scripts into machine code in order to reach execution speeds similar to those in desktop applications. This improved capacity overcame previous Javascript performance limitations and confirmed this language as the best coding option for the Web.

Javascript needs a hosting environment to run, but thanks to new interpreters and compilers like V8 from Google, it has become a more independent and powerful language. Now, it runs almost everywhere and is responsible for the Internet revolution as well as the rise of the mobile market.

To take advantage of this promising architecture, Javascript has been enhanced for portability and integration. Additionally, full application programming interfaces (APIs) have been incorporated by default in every browser to assist the language with elemental features. These new APIs (such as Web Storage, Canvas and others) are the interfaces for libraries embedded in browsers. The idea is to make powerful features available everywhere through simple and standard programming techniques, expanding the language's scope and facilitating the creation of compelling and useful software for the Web.

Javascript is the most popular and promising language in the world at present, and HTML5 is turning it into an essential tool for web and mobile developers. In this chapter, we will study basic concepts of Javascript, how to incorporate the scripts into our HTML documents and introduce recent additions to the language to prepare you for the rest of the book.

> **IMPORTANT:** Our approach to Javascript in this book is introductory. We work with basic and complex features but only apply elemental concepts necessary to take advantage of the innovations introduced in HTML5. To expand your knowledge about the language, visit our website and follow the links for this chapter. If you are familiar with this information, please feel free to skip over the parts you already know.

The Language

Javascript is a programming language, something completely different from HTML and CSS. HTML is a markup language, like a cryptic code that browsers interpret to organize information, and CSS can be considered as a sheet of styles (although the new specification has turned it into a more dynamic tool). Javascript, on the other hand, is a scripting language but is comparable to any full programming language such as C++ or Java. The only significant difference between most programming languages and Javascript is its nature. While other modern languages are object-oriented, Javascript is a prototype-based scripting language, which, paradoxically, makes it more focused on objects than any other, as we will see soon.

Javascript can perform numerous tasks, from providing instructions to calculating complex algorithms, but the most important characteristic, as in every programming language, is the capacity to store and process information, which is done through variables.

Variables

The memory of a computer or mobile device is like a huge honeycomb with millions and millions of cells available to store information. Those cells have an address, a consecutive number that identifies each one. Cells have limited space, and usually the combination of several cells is necessary to store large amounts of data. Because of the complexity of the manipulation of this storage space, programming languages incorporated the concept of *variables* to facilitate the identification of each value stored in memory.

Variables are just names assigned to a "cell" or a group of "cells" where the data are going to be stored. For example, if we want to store the value 5 in memory, we need to know where that number was stored to be able to retrieve it later. Creating a variable allows us to identify that space by a name and retrieve the content of that "cell" using the corresponding name.

To declare a variable, Javascript uses the keyword **var**.

```
<script>
  var mynumber = 2;
</script>
```

Listing 4-1: Declaring a variable in Javascript

Review the Basics: The `<script>` tag is used to inform the browser that the source code in between was written in Javascript. This is one of the possible ways to incorporate Javascript code in an HTML document. We will look at other alternatives soon.

In listing 4-1, we create the variable **mynumber** and store in that variable the value 2. This process is usually called **assign**. In those terms, what we do is "assign the value 2 to the variable **mynumber**".

Javascript reserves a space in memory, stores the number 2, creates a reference to that space and assigns that reference to the name **mynumber**. So every time we use that reference (the name **mynumber**), we get the number 2 .

```
<script>
  var mynumber = 2;
  alert(mynumber);
</script>
```

Listing 4-2: Using the content of a variable

In Listing 4-2, we create the variable and then assign the value 2 to it. Now the content of the variable **mynumber** is 2. Using the **alert()** method, the content of this variable is shown on the screen.

> **Review the Basics:** The **alert()** method is a predefined Javascript method used to generate a pop-up window to show some information on the screen. The method will show any value declared between parentheses (e.g., **alert("Hello World");**) in the window. We will study this and other similar methods later.

> **Do It Yourself:** For testing purposes, we don't need to create the entire HTML structure. The source code in Listing 4-2 is more than enough for browsers to interpret Javascript. Copy this source code in an empty text file, save it with a name and the **.html** extension (e.g., **jscode.html**), and open the file in your browser. You will see a pop-up window with the value 2.

Variables are called variables because they are not constant. We can change the value assigned to them any time we want, and that is, in fact, their most important characteristic.

```
<script>
  var mynumber = 2;
  mynumber = 3;
  alert(mynumber);
</script>
```

Listing 4-3: Assigning a new value for the variable

In Listing 4-3, after the creation of the variable, we assign a new value to **mynumber**. Now the **alert()** method will show the number 3. There is no need for the use of the **var** keyword, just the name of the variable and the = sign is now enough to assign the new value.

In a more practical situation, we would probably use the value of the variable to perform an operation and assign the result to that same variable:

```
<script>
  var mynumber = 2;
  mynumber = mynumber + 1;
  alert(mynumber);
</script>
```

Listing 4-4: Using the value stored in the variable

In this example, a value of 1 is added to the current value of **mynumber** and the result is assigned to the same variable. This is the same as performing 2 + 1, with the difference that when using a variable instead of a number its value can change all the time. This is because during the execution of the code, the value of variables can be modified. We could have had the number 5 instead of 2 stored in the variable by a previous process, and the result of the addition would have been 6, not 3.

This gives us a glance at the power of variables. We can perform any mathematical operation or concatenate text, and variables will always keep the last value assigned to them.

> **Review the Basics:** Besides the + operator, there are numerous operators available in Javascript. The most common are + (addition), – (substraction), * (multiplication) and / (division), but the language also provides logical operators, such as && (and) or || (or), comparison operators, such as == (equal), != (not equal), < (less than), > (greater than), and more. We will use and study several of them throughout the book. For a complete list, please visit our website and follow the links for this chapter.

Variables can store numbers, text, and predefined values, such as Boolean values (**true** or **false**), or elemental values such as **null** or **undefined**. Numbers are expressed as in previous examples, but text has to be enclosed by single or double quotes.

```
<script>
  var mytext = "Hello World!";
  alert(mytext);
</script>
```

Listing 4-5: Assigning a string to a variable

Variables can also store several values at once in a structure called **arrays**. These are multidimensional variables. Arrays may be created using a simple notation of square brackets with commas to separate each value. The values are later identified by an index, starting from 0.

```
<script>
  var myarray = ["red", "green", "blue"];
  alert(myarray[0]);
</script>
```

Listing 4-6: Creating multidimensional variables

In Listing 4-6, we create an array called **myarray** with three values: *red, green* and *blue*. Javascript automatically assigns the index 0 for the first value, 1 for the second value and 2 for the third value. To retrieve this information, we have to mention the index every time we want to use the array. This is done enclosing the index number in square brackets after the name of the variable. For example, to get the first value of **myarray** we have to write **myarray[0]**, as we did in our example.

Arrays, like variables, can take any type of value. We can create an array like the one in Listing 4-6 using numbers, strings, Boolean values or even declare the value as **null** or **undefined**.

```
<script>
  var myarray = ["red", , 32, null, "HTML5 is awesome!"];
  alert(myarray[1]);
</script>
```

Listing 4-7: Using different type of values

Review the Basics: The values `null` and `undefined` are native Javascript values. Basically, both represent the absence of a value, but `undefined` is also returned when an object's property or an array element was not defined. In the example in Listing 4-7, the second element of the array was not defined. If we try to retrieve this element, the value `undefined` is returned.

Do It Yourself: Copy the code in Listing 4-7 in an empty text file, save it with a name and the `.html` extension (e.g., `jscode.html`), and open the file in your browser. Change the index to see every value of the array.

Of course, we can also perform operations over the values of an array and store the result, as we did before for single variables.

```
<script>
  var myarray = ["red", 32];
  alert(myarray[0]);
  myarray[0] = myarray[0] + " color";
  myarray[1] = myarray[1] + 10;
  alert(myarray[0] + " " + myarray[1]);
</script>
```

Listing 4-8: Working with arrays

With the script in Listing 4-8 we learn not only how to modify the value of an array but also how to concatenate text. Arrays operate exactly like single variables, with the exception that we have to mention the index every time we want to use them. Using the line `myarray[1] = myarray[1] + 10` we tell the Javascript interpreter to take the current value of `myarray` at index 1 (32), add 10 to that value and store the result (42) in the same array at the same index; so now the value of `myarray[1]` will be 42.

The + operator works for numbers and strings, but in the case of strings, it will concatenate the text and generate a new string that includes both values. In our example, the value of `myarray[0]` was "red," but later the string " color" was added and now the value of `myarray` at index 0 is "red color".

Review the Basics: At the end of the last script, the `alert()` method shows both values of the array separated by a space. The values and the space are linked by the + operator. This operator can be used not only to perform operations but also to concatenate values and strings for styling purposes (numbers are converted to strings automatically).

Javascript provides a simple way to work with arrays. We can extract or add values using the following methods:

push(value)—This method adds a new value to the end of the array. The **value** attribute is the value to be added.

shift()—This method removes and returns the first value of the array.

pop()—This method removes and returns the last value of the array.

```
<script>
  var myarray = ["red", 32];
  myarray.push('car');
  alert(myarray[2]);
  alert(myarray.shift());
</script>
```

Listing 4-9: Adding and extracting values from the array

The value added by the **push()** method is assigned to the next index available in the array. In Listing 4-9, the value inserted by **push()** gets the index 2. Then, using this index, the same value is shown on the screen.

At the end of the script, we extract and show the first value of the array on the screen. Values extracted with the **shift()** and the **pop()** methods are no longer part of the array. After running the script of this example, the array will only have two values left: 32 and **car**.

Conditionals and Loops

A computer program is not a program if we can't establish conditions and set complex processing cycles. Javascript provides a total of four statements to process code according to conditions determined by the programmer: **if, switch, for** and **while**.

```
<script>
  var myvariable = 9;
  if(myvariable < 10) {
    alert("the number is smaller than 10");
  }
</script>
```

Listing 4-10: Checking a condition with if

> **Review the Basics:** It is recommended to close every line in Javascript using a semicolon, but this is not necessary after a block statement (a block of code enclosed in braces).

The **if** statement simply checks the expression in parentheses and processes the instructions between braces if the condition is true. In the script in Listing 4-10, the value 9 is assigned to **myvariable,** and then using **if** we compare the variable with the number 10. If the value of the variable is smaller than 10, then the **alert()** method shows a message on the screen.

There is an important addition we can make to this statement that lets us perform an action whether the condition is true or not. The construction `if else` will check the condition in parentheses and perform a different action in each case.

```
<script>
  var myvariable = 9;
  if(myvariable < 10) {
    alert("the number is smaller than 10");
  }else{
    alert("the number is 10 or bigger");
  }
</script>
```

Listing 4-11: *Checking two conditions with* `if else`

In this example, the script checks for two conditions: when the number is smaller than 10 and when the number is equal to or larger than 10.

To check for multiple conditions, Javascript provides the `switch` statement.

```
<script>
  var myvariable = 9;
  switch(myvariable) {
    case 5:
      alert("the number is five");
      break;
    case 8:
      alert("the number is eight");
      break;
    case 10:
      alert("the number is ten");
      break;
    default:
      alert("the number is " + myvariable);
  }
</script>
```

Listing 4-12: *Using the* `switch` *statement*

The `switch` statement evaluates an expression (usually just a variable), matches the result with the `case` statements in between braces and, in case of success, executes the instructions declared for that case. In the example in Listing 4-12, `switch` evaluates the variable `myvariable` and gets its value. Then, it compares that value with every case. In case the value is 5, for example, the control will be transferred to the first `case` and the `alert()` method will show the text "the number is five" on the screen. If this first `case` doesn't match the value of the variable, then the next case will be evaluated, and so on. If no case matches the value, the instructions in the case labeled `default` will be executed.

The code in every `case` must end with `break`. This instruction informs the Javascript interpreter that there is no need to continue evaluating the rest of the statements.

The `switch` and `if` statements are useful but perform a simple task: they evaluate an expression, execute a group of instructions according to the result and return the control to the script afterwards. There are certain situations in which this won't be sufficient. We could have to execute the instructions several times for the same condition or evaluate the condition again after a possible change during the process. There are two statements we can use for those situations: `for` and `while`.

```
<script>
  var myvariable = 9;
  for(var f = 0; f < myvariable; f++) {
    alert("The current number is " + f);
  }
</script>
```

Listing 4-13: Using the `for` *statement*

The `for` statement will execute the code between braces while the condition declared as the second parameter is true. It uses the syntax `for(initialization; condition; increment)`. The first parameter establishes the initial values for the loop; the second parameter is the condition to be checked; and the last parameter is an instruction that will determine how the initial values will evolve in every cycle.

In the script in Listing 4-13, we declare a single variable called `f` and assign the value 0 as the initialization value. The condition in this example determines if the value of the variable `f` is smaller than the value of the variable `myvariable`. In case this is true, the code between braces is executed. After that, the Javascript interpreter executes the last parameter of `for` and checks the condition again. If the condition is true, the instructions are executed one more time. The loop continues until the condition is false.

The variable `f` is initialized with the value 0. After the first cycle is over, the instruction `f++` increases the value of `f` by 1, and the condition is checked again. In every cycle the value of `f` is increased by 1. This process continues until `f` reaches a value of 9, which makes the condition false (9 is not smaller than 9), and the loop is interrupted.

> **Review the Basics:** The ++ operator is another Javascript operator for addition. It adds a value of 1 to the value of the variable and stores the result back in the variable. It is a shortcut for the construction `variable = variable + 1`.

The `for` statement is useful when we are able to predetermine certain conditions, such as the initial value for the loop or how those values will evolve. When conditions are unclear, we can take advantage of the `while` statement.

```
<script>
  var myvariable = 9;
  while(myvariable < 100) {
    myvariable++;
  }
  alert("The final value of myvariable is " + myvariable);
</script>
```

Listing 4-14: Using the `while` *statement*

The `while` statement only requires the declaration of the condition in parentheses and the code to be executed between braces. The loop will run until the condition is false. If the first evaluation of the condition returns **false**, the code is never executed. If you want the instructions to be executed at least once, no matter what the result of the condition is, then you use the **do while** construction.

```
<script>
  var myvariable = 9;
  do{
    myvariable++;
  }while(myvariable > 100);
  alert("The final value of myvariable is " + myvariable);
</script>
```

Listing 4-15: *Using the* do while *statement*

In the example in Listing 4-15, we change the condition to "**myvariable** greater than 100". Since the initial value assigned to the variable was 9, this condition is false, but because we are using the **do while** construction, the code inside the loop is executed once before the condition is evaluated. At the end, the window pop-up shows the value **10** (9 + 1 = 10).

Functions and Anonymous Functions

Thus far, we have being working in the global space. This is a main space in which the code is processed at the time it is read by the interpreter. Instructions are executed sequentially in the order they were listed in the code, but we can change that using functions.

Basically, a function is a block of code identified by a name. There are several advantages of declaring the code inside a function instead of doing it in the global space. The most important is that functions are declared but not executed until we called them by their name.

```
<script>
  function myfunction(){
    alert("I'am a function");
  }
  myfunction();
</script>
```

Listing 4-16: *Declaring functions*

> **Review the Basics:** Quotes in Javascript are interchangeable. A string can be declared using double or single quotes (e.g., **"Hello"** or **'Hello'**). If a string includes the same type of quote we used to declare it, then we have to escape the character using a backslash (e.g., **'I\'m Tom'**).

Functions are declared using the keyword **function**, the name, and the code between braces. To call the function (execute it), we just use its name with a pair of parentheses at the end, as shown in Listing 4-16.

As with variables, the Javascript interpreter reads the function, stores its content in memory and assigns a reference to the name of the function. When we call the function, the interpreter checks the reference and reads the function from memory. This allows us to call the function again and again, every time we need it, turning functions into powerful processing units.

```
<script>
  var myvariable = 5;
  function myfunction(){
    myvariable = myvariable * 2;
  }
  for(var f = 0; f < 10; f++){
    myfunction();
  }
  alert("The value of myvariable is now " + myvariable);
</script>
```

Listing 4-17: Processing data with functions

The example in Listing 4-17 combines different statements already studied. First, it declares a variable and assigns it the value **5**. Then, a function called **myfunction()** is declared (but not executed). Next, a **for** statement is used to create a loop, which will run as long as the value of the variable **f** is less than 10. And finally, the last value stored in the variable **myvariable** is shown on the screen.

The code inside the loop simply calls the function, so every cycle of the loop will execute **myfunction()**. This function multiplies the value of **myvariable** by 2 and stores the result in the same variable. Every time the function is executed, the value of **myvariable** is increased. This demonstrates the potential of functions as processing units: we declare them once, give them a name for a reference and then can use them any time we want.

Another way to declare a function is to use an anonymous function and assign it to a variable. The name of the variable will be the name we use later to call the function. This technique is used to define functions inside other functions, turn functions into object constructors and create complex programming patterns, as we will see later.

```
<script>
  var myvariable = 5;
  var myfunction = function(){
    myvariable = myvariable * 2;
  }
  for(var f = 0; f < 10; f++){
    myfunction();
  }
  alert("The value of myvariable is now " + myvariable);
</script>
```

Listing 4-18: Declaring functions with anonymous functions

Anonymous functions are functions without a name or identifier (hence "anonymous"). We can assign these functions to variables, create methods for objects, pass them as arguments to (or return them from) another functions, etc. These functions are extremely useful in Javascript. Complex programming patterns wouldn't be possible without these kinds of constructions.

IMPORTANT: The study of anonymous functions and complex Javascript patterns is not the intended purpose of this book, but we will see more examples of Javascript patterns and anonymous functions in this and following chapters.

In past examples, we used a variable defined in the global space. Variables can have different scopes. The ones defined in the global space have global scope; they can be used anywhere in the code. But variables declared inside functions have local scope, which means they can only be used inside the function in which they were declared. This is another advantage of functions they are special places in the code where we can store private information that won't be accessible from other parts of the code. This segregation helps us avoid duplicates that may lead to mistakes or accidental overwrites of variables and values. Two variables with the same name one in the global space and another inside a function will be considered two different variables.

```
<script>
  var myvariable = 5;
  function myfunction(){
    var myvariable = "this is a function variable";
    alert(myvariable);
  }
  myfunction();
  alert(myvariable);
</script>
```

Listing 4-19: Declaring global and local variables

In the script above, we declare two variables called **myvariable**, one in the global space and the other inside the function **myfunction()**. There are also two **alert()** methods in the code, one inside the function and the other in the global space at the end of the script. Both methods show the content of **myvariable**; but, as you will see if you run the script on your browser, they are different variables. The variable inside the function is referencing a space in memory that contains the string "this is a function variable," while the variable in the global space (declared first) is referencing a space in memory containing the value 5.

Global variables are useful when functions have to share common values. They are accessible from every function in the script. But as a result, there is always the possibility of accidentally overwriting their values or erasing them from somewhere in the script, or even from other scripts (every script in the document shares the same global space). Therefore, we recommend you avoid using them whenever possible.

IMPORTANT: Global variables can also be created from functions. Omitting the **var** keyword when we are declaring a variable inside a function will be enough to set that variable as global.

Review the Basics: A common practice to avoid the use of global variables is to declare a global object and then create our application within this object. We will study objects next.

We can read global variables from inside a function but not the other way around. That is why Javascript provides different alternatives to communicate between a function and the global space. We can send data to the function through the function's arguments or we can send back data from the function through the **return** statement.

```
<script>
  var myvariable = 5;
  var myresult;
  function myfunction(count){
    count = count + 12;
    return count;
  }
  myresult = myfunction(myvariable);
  alert(myresult);
</script>
```

Listing 4-20: Communicating with functions

Arguments are variables that are defined between the parentheses of the function and can be used inside the function as regular variables. They take the values sent by the script when the function is called. In Listing 4-20, the function **myfunction()** is declared with one argument called **count**. Later, we call the function with the variable **myvariable** between parentheses. This is the value the function will receive and assign to **count**. When the function is called, the initial value of **count** is **5** (because that is the initial value declared for **myvariable**). Inside **myfunction()**, the value **12** is added to **count** and the result is returned by the **return** statement. Back to the global space, the value returned by the function (**17**) is assigned to the variable **myresult**, and the content of that variable is shown on the screen.

Notice that at the beginning we declare the variable **myresult** but don't assign a value to it. This is perfectly acceptable and is recommended. It is good to declare all the variables we are going to work with at the beginning, to avoid confusion and be able to identify each one later from other parts of the code.

> **IMPORTANT:** We will study more aspects of functions and practice all these techniques later in the book.

Objects

Objects are like large variables, capable of containing other variables (called **properties**) as well as functions (called **methods**). There are different ways to declare objects; the most simple is to use a literal notation.

```
<script>
  var myobject = {
    name: "John",
    age: 30
  }
</script>
```

Listing 4-21: Creating objects

The object is declared using the **var** keyword and braces. Properties and methods require a name and a value. They are declared between the braces using a colon after the name and a comma to separate each declaration (the last declaration doesn't require a comma).

In the example in Listing 4-21, we declare the object **myobject** with two properties: **name** and **age**. The value of the property name is **John** and the value of the property age is **30**. In contrast to variables, we can't access the properties values using simply their name. First we must specify the object they belong to, and we have two ways to do this: using dot notation or using square brackets.

```
<script>
  var myobject = {
    name: "John",
    age: 30
  }
  alert("My name is " + myobject.name);
  alert("I'm " + myobject['age'] + " years old");
</script>
```

Listing 4-22: Accessing properties

In Listing 4-22, we use both notations to access the object's properties. On the screen, we get two alert messages: "My name is John" and "I'm 30 years old". The use of any notation is irrelevant, except in some circumstances. For example, when we need to access the property through the value of a variable we have to use square brackets.

```
<script>
  var myvariable = "name";
  var myobject = {
    name: "John",
    age: 30
  }
  alert(myobject[myvariable]);
</script>
```

Listing 4-23: Accessing properties using variables

In Listing 4-23, we couldn't have accessed the property with dot notation (**myobject.myvariable**) because the interpreter would have try to find a property called **myvariable** that doesn't exist. Using square brackets, first the variable is resolved and then the object is accessed with the value of the variable (**name**) instead of its name. The result on the screen will be "John".

It is also necessary to access the property using square brackets when its name is considered invalid for a variable (it includes invalid characters, a space, or starting with a number). In the following example, the object includes a property declared with a string as a name. We are allowed to declare names of properties as quoted strings, but because this particular string has a space, the code **myobject.my age** would return an error, so we have to use square brackets to access the property.

```
<script>
  var myvariable = "name";
  var myobject = {
    name: "John",
    'my age': 30
  }
  alert(myobject['my age']);
</script>
```

Listing 4-24: Properties with invalid names

Besides reading the value of properties, we can also set or modify them using both notations. In the next example, we are going to modify the value of the **name** property and add a new property called **job**. So the object will have three properties: **name**, **age** and **job**. At the end of the script, we will show all the values on the screen.

```
<script>
  var myobject = {
    name: "John",
    age: 30
  }
  myobject.name = "Martin";
  myobject.job = "Programmer";
  alert(myobject.name + " " + myobject.age + " " + myobject.job);
</script>
```

Listing 4-25: Updating values and adding new properties to the object

As we mentioned before, objects can also include functions. Functions inside an object are called **methods**. They turn an object into a unit capable of containing and processing information independently.

```
<script>
  var myobject = {
    name: "John",
    age: 30,
    showname: function(){
        alert(myobject.name);
    },
    changename: function(newname){
      myobject.name = newname;
    }
  }
  myobject.showname();
  myobject.changename('Jonathan');
  myobject.showname();
</script>
```

Listing 4-26: Including functions inside the object

The script in Listing 4-26 shows not only how to include methods in an object but also how to use them. Methods have the same syntax as properties: they require a colon after the name and a comma to separate each declaration. The difference from properties is that methods don't take direct values; they are built using anonymous functions.

In this example, we create two methods, `showname()` and `changename()`. The `showname()` method shows a pop-up window with the value of the **name** property, and the `changename()` method assigns the value received from the **newname** attribute to the **name** property. These are two independent methods that work on the same property. To execute the methods, we use the dot notation and parentheses after the name. As with functions, methods can take attributes and return values using the `return` statement (in this example, `changename()` requires an attribute with the new name).

Objects can also contain other objects. The structure can get more and more complex according to our needs. To access the properties and methods of these internal objects, we have to concatenate their names using the dot notation.

```
<script>
  var myobject = {
    name: "John",
    age: 30,
    bike: {
      model: "Susuki",
      year: 1981
    },
    showcar: function(){
      alert(myobject.name + " owns a " + myobject.bike.model);
    }
  }
  myobject.showcar();
</script>
```

Listing 4-27: Creating objects inside objects

As you can probably see by now, objects are powerful and independent processing units. They are so important in Javascript that the language not only offers different alternatives to create your own objects but also provides its own. In fact, almost everything in Javascript is an object. We can use native objects, create our own from scratch, and modify or expand them. But one of the most important characteristics of objects is the possibility to create new ones that inherit properties and methods from the objects they were created from.

Inheritance in Javascript (how objects get the same properties and methods from other objects) is done through prototypes. Every object has a prototype, and new objects are created from that prototype.

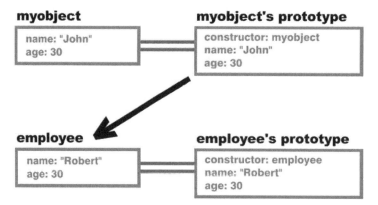

Figure 4-1: *Prototypal inheritance*

The object **myobject** from previous examples automatically got its own prototype when it was created. If we decide to create a new object based on **myobject**, the new one will be created from **myobject**'s prototype, not from the object itself. In Figure 4-1, the object **employee** is created from **myobject**'s prototype. The new object also gets its own prototype. If later on, new objects are created from **employee**, they will be based on **employee**'s prototype. This construction can go forever, creating a chain of objects called **prototype chain**. Modifications introduced in one prototype will affect all the objects down the chain. If we introduce changes to **myobject**'s prototype, for example, **employee** and all the objects based on **employee**'s prototype will inherit those changes.

The techniques available to achieve this type of inheritance were messy and inconsistent with other object-oriented languages, which deterred some programmers from Javascript for a while. The new **create()** method changes this situation. This method is part of a native object called Object. It uses an existing object as a prototype for a new one, so we don't have to worry about how to work with prototypes anymore.

```
<script>
  var myobject = {
    name: "John",
    age: 30,
    showname: function(){
        alert(this.name);
    },
    changename: function(newname){
      this.name = newname;
    }
  }
  var employee = Object.create(myobject);
  employee.changename('Robert');
  employee.showname();
  myobject.showname();
</script>
```

Listing 4-28: *Generating new instances*

An important thing to notice in Listing 4-28 is how we reference the object we are working with. Objects can reference themselves using the keyword **this**. In this example, we use **this** instead of the name of the object (**myobject**) to have access to the **name** property from inside the object. The keyword is declaring "this object" instead of providing the object's name. The reason for the use of **this** is because this object serves as a blueprint for the creation of new ones (instances). These copies will have their own name, which won't be the same as the original object. The use of **this** is necessary in cases like this to represent the name of the object we are working with, regardless of whether it is the original or one of the copies. For example, in the object **employee**, created from **myobject** in the script in Listing 4-28, the keyword **this** represents the **employee** object, so the construction **this.name** in this object will return the same value than **employee.name**.

The object **employee** is created using the **create()** method. This method only requires the name of the object that is going to be a prototype for the new one. It returns a new object that we can assign to a variable. In Listing 4-28, the instance is first created with **Object.create()** and is then assigned to the variable **employee**. Once we have the instance, we can update its values. Using the **changename()** method we change the name for **employee** to "Robert" and then show the value of each **name** property on the screen.

> **IMPORTANT:** The **create()** method is a new method introduced in recent versions of the language. To emulate this method in old browsers, Douglas Crockford, on his website (www.crockford.com) and in his book *Javascript: The Good Parts* (published by O'Reilly Media/Yahoo Press), recommends the use of the following script:
>
> ```
> if(typeof Object.create !== 'function') {
>   Object.create = function(o) {
>     function F() {}
>     F.prototype = o;
>     return new F();
>   };
> }
> ```

Now we have two individual objects, **myobject** and **employee**, with their own properties, methods and values, but linked through the prototype chain. The new **employee** object is not just a copy; it is an instance, an object that keeps a link to its prototype. When the prototype changes the instances inherit those changes.

```
<script>
  var myobject = {
    name: "John",
    age: 30,
    showname: function(){
        alert(this.name);
    },
    changename: function(newname){
      this.name = newname;
    }
  }
  var employee = Object.create(myobject);
  employee.age = 24;
```

```
  myobject.showage = function(){
    alert(this.age);
  };

  employee.showage();
</script>
```

Listing 4-29: Adding a new method to the prototype

In Listing 4-29, the `employee` object is created using `myobject` as a prototype, as we have done before. Then, the `age` property of this new object is updated with the value 24. And finally, a method called `showage()` is added to the prototype object (`myobject`). Because of the prototype chain, this new method is now accessible from the instances as well. When we call the `showage()` method of `employee` at the end of the script, the interpreter looks for the method in `employee` and continues searching up the prototype chain until it finds it in `myobject`. When the method is finally found, it shows the value 24 on the screen. This is because, even when the `showage()` method belongs to `myobject`, the `this` keyword in this method points to the object we are working with (`employee`). Due to the prototype chain, the `showage()` method can be invoked from `employee`, and due to the `this` keyword, the `age` property shown on the screen is the one that belongs to `employee`.

The `create()` method is as simple as it is powerful. It takes an object and turns it into the prototype for a new one. This allows us to build a chain of objects where each one inherits properties and methods from its predecessors. In the next example, we will demonstrate this attribute, creating a total of four objects. The initial object `myobject` is the prototype for `employee1`, but then we use `employee1` as a prototype for `employee2` and `employee2` as a prototype for `employee3`. These are all independent objects but are connected to each other by the prototype chain. When properties or methods are added to one of the objects (a prototype), the rest of the objects down the chain have also access to them.

```
<script>
  var myobject = {
    name: "John",
    age: 30,
    showname: function(){
        alert(this.name);
    },
    changename: function(newname){
      this.name = newname;
    }
  }
  var employee1 = Object.create(myobject);
  var employee2 = Object.create(employee1);
  var employee3 = Object.create(employee2);

  employee2.showage = function(){
    alert(this.age);
  };
  employee3.age = 24;
  employee3.showage();
</script>
```

Listing 4-30: Testing the prototype chain

In Listing 4-30, the prototype chain is demonstrated adding the method `showage()` for `employee2`. Now `employee2` and `employee3` (and also any object created later based on these two objects) have access to this method, but if you try to call the method in `employee1` it won't work. This is because inheritance works down the chain, not up.

Despite the simplicity of `Object.create()`, sometimes it has to be complemented with complex patterns and supporting functions to enable certain characteristics in our code, such as dynamic creation of objects, initialization values, and private properties and methods.

Depending on your needs, it may be better to create your objects with an alternative technique that combines literal notation, anonymous functions and the `return` statement.

```
<script>
  var constructor = function(initialname){
    var obj = {
      name: initialname,
      age: 30,
      showname: function(){
          alert(this.name);
      },
      changename: function(newname){
        this.name = newname;
      }
    };
    return obj;
  };
  employee = constructor("John");
  employee.showname();
</script>
```

Listing 4-31: Using anonymous functions to create objects

In the example in Listing 4-31, we use an anonymous function to create an object. The anonymous function is assigned to the variable `constructor` and through this variable we call the function with an initial value `John`. This value is taken by the function's attribute `initialname` and assigned to the `name` property of the object. Finally, the object called `obj` is returned by the `return` statement and assigned to the variable `employee`.

Using this technique we are able to create new objects dynamically, providing initial values, or even perform some processing at the beginning of the function and then return an object created by that processing.

As you can see, this is more than creating and duplicating an object. The most important advantage of this technique is the possibility to define private properties and methods. All the objects and instances we have created so far have public properties and methods; that means the content of the objects can be accessed and modified from anywhere in the code. To avoid this and make the properties and methods available only for the object that created it, we have to make them private using a technique called **closure**.

As we explained before, variables created in the global space are accessible from everywhere in the code, while variables created inside functions are only accessible from those functions. What we didn't mention is that functions, and therefore methods, always keep a link to the environment they were created in, and they are always bound to its variables. When we return an object from a function, its methods will be able to access the function's variables, even when they are no longer in the same scope. Let's see an example:

```
<script>
  var constructor = function(){
    var name = "John";
    var age = 30;
    var obj = {
      showname: function(){
          alert(name);
      },
      changename: function(newname){
        name = newname;
      }
    };
    return obj;
  };
  employee = constructor();
  employee.showname();
</script>
```

Listing 4-32: Creating private properties for an object

The script in Listing 4-32 is exactly the same from the previous example except instead of declaring **name** and **age** as properties of the object we declare them as variables of the function that is returning the object. The object returned will remember these variables, but the object will be the only one to have access to them. There is no way to modify the value of those variables from other elements in the code other than to use the methods of the object returned (in this case, **showname()** and **changename()**). This is called **closure**. The function is closed and its environment is no longer accessible, but we keep an element bonded to it (an object in our example).

Of course, every new instance created from this function will have the same structure and will have access to its own private properties.

> **Do It Yourself:** Create new objects from the function in Listing 4-32 and use the **changename()** and **showname()** methods to access their properties (e.g., **employee2 = myobject();**).

Constructors

The functions we used to create objects in the previous examples are called **constructors**. Javascript includes a special kind of constructor that works with the **new** operator to get a new object. This method is not part of a prototypal language but was introduced in Javascript to maintain consistency with other object-oriented languages.

These kinds of constructors don't return an object; they are like blueprints from which objects are created. As a result, they require the use of the keyword **this** to declare or access properties and methods.

```
<script>
  function Myobject(){
    this.name = "John";
    this.age = 30;
```

Javascript

```
    this.showname = function(){
        alert(this.name);
    };
    this.changename = function(newname){
      this.name = newname;
    };
  }
  var employee = new Myobject();
  employee.showname();
</script>
```

Listing 4-33: Using constructors

Except for the use of **this**, constructors and functions look almost the same. To signal the presence of these constructors, we recommend starting their name with a capital letter, as in the example in Listing 4-33.

To create an object from a constructor we have to use the **new** operator. This operator takes the name of the constructor and returns an object. The constructor may include attributes to provide initial values for the new object.

```
<script>
  function Myobject(initialname, initialage){
    this.name = initialname;
    this.age = initialage;
    this.showname = function(){
        alert(this.name);
    };
    this.changename = function(newname){
      this.name = newname;
    };
  }
  var employee = new Myobject("Robert", 55);
  employee.showname();
</script>
```

Listing 4-34: Defining initial values for the object

This constructor doesn't turn an object into a prototype of another, as the **create()** method does. Instead, it creates new instances from the prototype of the constructor (**Myobject.prototype**). Because of this, if we want to introduce modifications to affect the instances, we can't work directly with the initial object, as we did before. We have to access the constructor's prototype using the **prototype** property.

```
<script>
  function Myobject(initialname, initialage){
    this.name = initialname;
    this.age = initialage;
    this.showname = function(){
        alert(this.name);
    };
```

```
    this.changename = function(newname){
      this.name = newname;
    };
  }
  Myobject.prototype.showage = function(){
    alert(this.age);
  };
  var employee = new Myobject("Robert", 55);
  employee.showage();
</script>
```

Listing 4-35: Augmenting the prototype

The constructor in Listing 4-35 is the same as the previous example. Here, we add a new method called **showage()** to the prototype of **Myobject**. From now on, every instance will include this new method.

> **IMPORTANT:** Prototypes are the essence of Javascript but are difficult to assimilate. If you get used to working with the **create()** method and the literal notation studied at the beginning of this chapter, in most cases you will not need the use of about prototypes, constructors and the **new** keyword. In fact, the **create()** method should be the way we work with Javascript, creating objects and instances without getting into the complexity of their prototypal nature; however, these techniques are still necessary in some circumstances, and elemental libraries and APIs require their use all the time, as we will see later, so it is good to be familiar with them. The options offered by Javascript in this aspect are almost unlimited. To learn more about Javascript patterns and how to work with objects, please visit our website and follow the links for this chapter.

The Window Object

Every time the browser starts, a global object called Window is created to reference the browser window and provide some essential methods and properties. Everything is included inside this object, from scripts to the entire document.

The Window object is accessible from Javascript through the **window** property. This property should be mentioned every time we want to access Javascript properties and methods, but it is not strictly necessary. Since it is the global object, the interpreter infers that anything that doesn't have a reference belongs to it. For example, we can write the Window method **alert()** as we did in previous examples or as **window.alert()**.

Here is a list of the most common properties and methods offered by this object:

> **alert(text)**—This method shows a pop-up window on the screen with the value between parentheses (see previous examples in this chapter).
>
> **confirm(text)**—This method is similar to **alert()**, but it offers two buttons, "yes" and "no", for the user to choose from. It returns **true** or **false**, according to the user's response (see the example in Chapter 14, Listing 14-6).
>
> **setTimeout(function, milliseconds)**—This method executes the function specified in the first attribute after the time in milliseconds specified by the second attribute. We can assign this method to a variable and then cancel the process using **clearTimeout()** and the name of the variable between parentheses (e.g., **var time**

= setTimeout(function(){ alert("Hello"); }, 5000);). An example of the application of this method is provided in Chapter 11, Listing 11-13.

setInterval(function, milliseconds)—This method is similar to `setTimeout()` but will call the function repeatedly every given time until the process is canceled by `clearInterval()` (e.g., `var time = setInterval(function(){ alert("Hello"); }, 2000);`). Some examples of this method are provided in Chapter 6 and 10.

location—This object has several properties to return information about the URL of the current document. It can be also used as a property to set or return the URL of the document (e.g., `window.location = "http://www.minkbooks.com"`).

history—This object provides methods to navigate through the history of the window. It includes methods like `back()`, to load the previous document, `forward()`, to load a more recent document in the list, and `go()`, to load any document in the window's history. We will study these methods along with the History API in Chapter 18.

The Document Object

As we mentioned before, almost everything in Javascript is an object, from the customized objects we created in the examples in this chapter to functions, arrays, strings or even numbers. So you may not be surprised to learn that the entire HTML document and each of the HTML elements are objects too.

In a browser environment, an internal structure is created to process the HTML document. The structure is called DOM (Document Object Model) and is composed of objects representing each HTML element. The DOM starts with the Document object, accessible from Javascript through the **document** property. Using this property we can access or modify any HTML element in the document.

The Document object is a member of the Window object and provides properties and methods to work with the document. We will study and apply some of these methods later in this chapter.

4.2 An Introduction to Events

In Javascript, a user's actions are called **events**. When the user performs an action, such as clicking the mouse or pressing a key, an event specific for each action is fired. Besides the events produced by a user, there are also events fired by the system—for example, the **load** event that fires when the document is fully loaded. These events are handled by codes or entire functions. The code that responds to the event is called the **event handler**. When we register an event handler, we define how our application will respond to the event. The standardization of the **addEventListener()** method changed how we called this procedure; instead of registering a handler for the event we add an event listener. The handler is now called the listener.

This leaves us with three different ways to register an event handler for an HTML element: add a new event attribute to the element, register an event handler with an event property, or use the new standard method **addEventListener()**.

> **IMPORTANT:** We will present the theory here and see examples of how to apply these techniques in the next part of this chapter.

Event Attributes

HTML provides attributes to insert Javascript code in our documents. These attributes are associated with events that execute code according to the user's response or the current state of the document and the elements. The attributes are called **event attributes**, and their values are Javascript codes that handle the events (e.g., `<p onclick="alert('Hello')">Click Me</p>`).

The names of the event attributes are made by adding the prefix `on` to the name of the event. For example, the name of the event attribute for the `click` event is `onclick`.

The most commonly used event attributes are mouse-related, such as `onclick`, `onMouseOver` or `onMouseOut`. However, there are also event attributes that respond to keyword and window events, performing actions after a key is pressed or after a change in the condition of the document (for example, `onload` or `onfocus`). Here is a list of the most common event attributes:

> **onLoad**—This attribute handles the `load` event. This event is fired when the document has loaded.
>
> **onClick**—This attribute handles the `click` event. This event is fired when the user clicks the mouse.
>
> **onMouseover**—This attribute handles the `mouseover` event. This event is fired when the mouse's pointer moves over the element.
>
> **onMouseout**—This attribute handles the `mouseout` event. This event is fired when the mouse pointer moves off the element.
>
> **onKeypress**—This attribute handles the `keypress` event. This event is fired when a key is pressed and released.
>
> **onKeydown**—This attribute handles the `keydown` event. This event is fired when a key is pressed.
>
> **onKeyup**—This attribute handles the `keyup` event. This event is fired when a key is released.
>
> **onChange**—This attribute handles the `change` event. This event is fired when an element changes (usually an input field in a form).
>
> **IMPORTANT:** HTML5 introduces several new events that we will study in following chapters along with their corresponding APIs. For a complete list of traditional events, please visit our website and follow the links for this chapter.

Event Properties

Event properties are the same as event attributes with the difference that they are applied in the script as properties of the elements. Using Javascript selectors, we can reference an HTML element and assign to that element the right event property (e.g., `element.onclick = myfunction;`).

Prior to HTML5, this was the only cross-browser technique available to register events in Javascript. Some browser vendors were developing their own systems but nothing caught on until the new standard `addEventListener()` was adopted.

We will see examples of event properties in the next part of this chapter.

The AddEventListener() Method

The `addEventListener()` method is the ideal technique for listening to events and is implemented as standard by HTML5. It uses the syntax `addEventListener(event, listener, Capture)`. The first attribute is the event's name (without the prefix **on**); the second attribute is a function that will respond to the event, usually called **listener function** (this could be a function's reference or an entire anonymous function); and the third attribute will set how multiple events will fire in the HTML tree using **true** or **false**. The third attribute can be useful for debugging or in other circumstances where we need to propagate the event fired by an element to all the elements up the tree, but usually the value **false** is enough for most situations (this is the value by default).

Even when the results of applying this technique and the previous one are similar, `addEventListener()` lets us add as many event listeners as we want for the same element. This distinction gives `addEventListener()` an advantage over other methods, making it the ideal technique for HTML5 applications.

> **IMPORTANT:** Javascript also offers the `removeEventListener()` method to remove a listener from an element. This method requires the same attributes as `addEventListener()`. See Chapter 12, Listing 12-3, for an example of how to implement this method.

4.3 Incorporating Javascript

Following the same approach as with CSS, there are three different techniques to incorporate Javascript code within an HTML document: *Inline*, *Embedded* and *External Files*.

Inline

The Inline technique takes advantage of the event attributes studied previously. This is a deprecated technique but is still useful and practical in some circumstances. To make an element respond to an event, all we have to do is add the corresponding attribute with the code to handle it.

```
<!DOCTYPE html>
<html lang="en">
<head>
  <title>Javascript</title>
</head>
<body>
  <section id="main">
    <p onclick="alert('you clicked me!')">Click Me</p>
    <p>You Can't Click Me</p>
  </section>
</body>
</html>
```

Listing 4-36: Inline Javascript

Using the event attribute `onclick` in Listing 4-36, a Javascript code is executed every time the user clicks on the text "Click Me". The `onclick` attribute says something like, "when someone clicks on this element execute this code," and the code is (in this case) the predefined Javascript function `alert()` that shows a small window with the message "you clicked me!".

Try to change the `onclick` attribute to `onMouseOver`, for example, and the code will be executed just by hovering the mouse pointer over the element.

The use of Javascript inside HTML elements is allowed by HTML5, but for the same reasons as CSS, this practice is not recommended. The HTML code is extended unnecessarily and is hard to maintain or update; as well, the code is distributed all over the document complicating the development of useful applications.

> **Do It Yourself:** Copy the code in Listing 4-36 and the following codes in this chapter into a new empty HTML file. Then, open the file in your browser to test them.

Embedded

To work with extensive codes and customized functions we have to group the scripts together between `<script>` tags. The `<script>` element acts exactly like the `<style>` element for CSS, organizing the code in one place and affecting the rest of the elements in the document using references.

Just as with the `<style>` element for HTML5, we no longer have to use the `type` attribute to specify the language in the `<script>` tag. In HTML5, Javascript is assigned by default.

```
<!DOCTYPE html>
<html lang="en">
<head>
  <title>Javascript</title>
  <script>
    function clickme(){
      var elem = document.getElementsByTagName('p')[0];
      elem.addEventListener('click', showalert);
    }
    function showalert(){
      alert('you clicked me!');
    }
    addEventListener('load', clickme);
  </script>
</head>
<body>
  <section id="main">
    <p>Click Me</p>
    <p>You Can't Click Me</p>
  </section>
</body>
</html>
```

Listing 4-37: Embedded Javascript

The `<script>` element and its content can be located anywhere in the document, inside other elements or between them. For clarity, we recommend you always locate scripts inside the head of the document (as in the example in Listing 4-37) and then use references to access the

HTML elements from the Javascript code. The Document object includes three methods for this purpose:

> **getElementsByTagName()**—This method references elements by its keyword.
>
> **getElementById()**—This method references an element by the value of its `id` attribute.
>
> **getElementsByClassName()**—This method is a new incorporation that let us reference elements using the value of the `class` attribute.

Even when following the recommended practice (positioning the scripts inside the head of the document), you must consider a situation: the code is read sequentially by the browser and we can't reference an element that hasn't been created yet.

In Listing 4-37, the script is positioned in the head of the document and is read prior to the creation of the `<p>` elements. If we had tried to affect the `<p>` element from this code with a reference, we would have received an error message explaining that the element doesn't exist. To avoid this problem, the reference to the `<p>` element and the registration of the event are listed in a function called `clickme()`, and the code that responds to the event is inserted into a second function called `showalert()`.

When we use this technique to group the Javascript code together, we not only have to find a way to reference elements from the code but also have to register events handlers for those elements. For this purpose, event attributes are replaced by the `addEventListener()` method to add listeners to the `click` event for the element and the `load` event for the window.

So, let's take a look at the execution of the whole document of Listing 4-37. First, the functions are declared but not executed. Then, the HTML elements, including the `<p>` elements, are created. And finally, when the whole document is loaded, the `load` event for the window is fired and then the `clickme()` function is called.

In this function, the method `getElementsByTagName` is referencing the `<p>` elements. This method belongs to the Document object, so we have to use the `document` property to call it. It returns an array containing a list of the elements found in the document. However, by using the index `[0]` at the end of the method, we indicate that only the first element should be selected. Once this element is identified, an event handler is registered for the `click` event using the `onclick` event property. The `showalert()` function is set as the handler and will be executed every time the event is fired, showing a small window with the message "you clicked me!".

It might look like a lot of code and effort to reproduce the effect achieved by a single attribute in the example in Listing 4-36. However, considering the potential of HTML5 and the complexity achieved by Javascript applications, the concentration of code in one place and proper organization represent a great advantage for our future implementations and make our websites and applications easy to develop and maintain.

> **Review the Basics:** In the last line of the script in Listing 4-37, we do not use parentheses to call the `clickme()` function because we pass the reference of the function to the event property, not the result of the execution of the function.

External File

Javascript codes grow exponentially with the addition of new functions and the application of some of the APIs studied later. Embedded codes make our documents bigger and repetitive. To reduce the time it takes to download our documents, increase our productivity, and distribute and reuse our codes in every document without compromising efficiency, we recommend saving the Javascript codes in one or more external files and call them using the `src` attribute.

```
<!DOCTYPE html>
<html lang="en">
<head>
  <title>Javascript</title>
  <script src="mycode.js"></script>
</head>
<body>
  <section id="main">
    <p>Click Me</p>
    <p>You Can't Click Me</p>
  </section>
</body>
</html>
```

Listing 4-38: Introducing Javascript code from *an external file*

The `<script>` element in Listing 4-38 loads the Javascript code from an external file called `mycode.js`. From now on, we can insert this file in every document of our website and reuse the code any time we want. From the user's perspective, this practice reduces the time to download and access our website; from the programmer's perspective, it simplifies development and maintenance.

> **Do It Yourself:** Copy the code in Listing 4-38 inside the HTML file previously created. Create a new empty file called `mycode.js` and copy the Javascript code of Listing 4-37. Note that only the code between `<script>` tags has to be copied, not including the tags.

It is worth mentioning that there are two more attributes available for the `<script>` element: `async` and `defer`. These are Boolean attributes that indicate how and when the script included by the `src` attribute will be executed. If `async` is declared, the script is executed asynchronously. If the `defer` attribute is declared, the script will be executed when the document has been parsed. And when both attributes are absent, the script is executed immediately (as occurred in our examples).

4.4 New Selectors

HTML elements have to be referenced by Javascript in order to be affected by the code. If you remember from previous chapters, CSS, especially CSS3, has a powerful system for reference and selection that far surpasses the few methods presently provided by Javascript. The `getElementById`, `getElementsByTagName` and `getElementsByClassName` methods are insufficient to support the integration this language needs and the relevance it has in the HTML5 specification. To get Javascript to the level required, better alternatives have been incorporated. We can now select HTML elements applying all kinds of CSS selectors using the new methods `querySelector()`, `querySelectorAll()` and `matchesSelector()`.

QuerySelector()

The `querySelector()` method returns the first element that matches the specified group of CSS selectors within the parentheses. The selectors are declared using quotes and CSS syntax, as in the following example:

```
function clickme(){
  var elem = document.querySelector("#main p:first-child");
  elem.addEventListener('click', showalert);
}
function showalert(){
  alert('you clicked me!');
}
addEventListener('load', clickme);
```

Listing 4-39: Using `querySelector()`

In Listing 4-39, the method `getElementsByTagName` used in the script in Listing 4-37 is replaced by `querySelector()`. The selectors for this particular query reference the first `<p>` element that is a child of the element identified by the `id` attribute with the value `main`.

Because, as we explained, this method only returns the first element found, you may have noticed that the `first-child` pseudo-class is redundant. The method `querySelector()` in our example returns the first `<p>` element inside the `<div>` that is, of course, its first child. The purpose of this example is to show you that `querySelector()` accepts all kinds of valid CSS selectors and now, as well as CSS, Javascript also provides important tools to reference any element in the document.

Several groups of selectors may be declared separated by a comma. The `querySelector()` method will return the first element that matches any one of them.

> **Do It Yourself:** Copy the code in Listing 4-39 into the `mycode.js` file, and open the HTML document of Listing 4-38 in your browser to see the `querySelector()` method in action. Repeat this process for the examples that follow.

QuerySelectorAll()

Instead of one element, `querySelectorAll()` returns *every* element that matches the specified group of selectors within the parentheses. The value returned is an array containing every element found in document order (similar to the effect produced by the `getElementsByTagName` method previously examined, but in this case we are matching CSS selectors).

```
function clickme(){
  var list = document.querySelectorAll("#main p");
  list[0].addEventListener('click', showalert);
}
```

```
function showalert(){
  alert('you clicked me!');
}
addEventListener('load', clickme);
```

Listing 4-40: Using querySelectorAll()

The group of selectors provided in the **querySelectorAll()** method in Listing 4-40 will find every **<p>** element in the HTML document of Listing 4-38 that is a child of the **<section>** element. After the execution of the first line, the array **list** has two values: a reference to the first **<p>** element and a reference to the second **<p>** element. Because the keywords of every array created automatically starts from 0, in the next line the first element found is retrieved using square brackets with the value 0 (**list[0]**).

Notice that this example doesn't show the potential of **querySelectorAll()**. Usually this method will be used to affect several elements and not only one, as in our case. To iterate through the list of elements returned by the method, we can use a **for** loop.

```
function clickme(){
  var list = document.querySelectorAll("#main p");
  for(var f = 0; f < list.length; f++){
    list[f].addEventListener('click', showalert);
  }
}
function showalert(){
  alert('you clicked me!');
}
addEventListener('load', clickme);
```

Listing 4-41: Working with all the elements found by querySelectorAll()

In Listing 4-41, instead of selecting only the first element found, we add a listener to the **click** event for each one using a **for** loop. Now, all the **<p>** elements inside the **<section>** element will pop-up a small window when the user clicks on them.

> **Review the Basics:** The **length** property is available in different objects to set or return their length. In case of arrays, we can use it to get the number of elements available in the array. In the example in Listing 4-41, we use it to get the number of elements found by **querySelectorAll()** and establish the condition for the loop (it will run while **f < list.length**).

The **querySelectorAll()** method, as well as **querySelector()**, may contain one or more groups of selectors separated by a comma. These and previous methods may be combined to reach the elements we want. For example, in Listing 4-42, the same result of the script in Listing 4-41 will be achieved using **querySelectorAll()** and **getElementById()** together.

```
function clickme(){
  var list = document.getElementById("main").querySelectorAll("p");
  list[0].addEventListener('click', showalert);
}
```

```
function showalert(){
  alert('you clicked me!');
}
addEventListener('load', clickme);
```

Listing 4-42: Combining methods

Using this technique, we can see how precise these methods can be. We are able to combine methods in the same line or select a group of elements and then perform a second selection with another method to reach elements inside the first group.

MatchesSelector()

The `MatchesSelector()` method doesn't find elements but instead checks whether the elements we have found are exactly the ones we were looking for. It can also be used to determine if the element will be returned by the selector we are using. The method takes the same CSS selectors as the previous methods but only returns **true** or **false**.

```
function clickme(){
  var elem = document.getElementById('main');
  var pelem;
  if(elem.webkitMatchesSelector("section")){
    pelem = elem.querySelector("p:first-child")
    pelem.addEventListener('click', showalert);
  }
}
function showalert(){
  alert('you clicked me!');
}
addEventListener('load', clickme);
```

Listing 4-43: Controlling the element found using matchesSelector()

> **IMPORTANT:** The method **matchesSelector()** is still experimental. Consequently, we have to use the prefixed methods provided by browser vendors (e.g., **webkitMatchesSelector()** for browsers based on WebKit, like Google Chrome, and **mozMatchesSelector()** for Mozilla Firefox).

In the script in Listing 4-43, the method is used to determine whether the element returned by the `getElementById()` method is a **<section>** element or not. If it is, then the `querySelector()` method is used to get a reference to the first **<p>** element, and a listener is added for the **click** event.

4.5 Interacting with the Document

There are more things we can do with Javascript than reference elements and register events. We can also assign styles, manipulate classes, get information from the elements, change their attributes and content, create new elements or even erase them as we please.

Javascript Styles

Similar to CSS, there is a list of styles we can assign to an element. These styles are provided through properties of the Style object. Because this object is accessible from any element in the document, to apply a new style we get a reference to the element and use its properties.

```
function newstyle(){
  var elem = document.getElementById('main');
  elem.style.background = "#990000";
}
addEventListener('load', newstyle);
```

Listing 4-44: *Assigning styles with Javascript*

Styles' names in Javascript are not the same as in CSS. There was no consensus on this matter, so although we are able to provide the same values for the properties, we have to learn the name of each of them. Here is a list of the most common:

background—This property sets or returns all the background styles. We can also work with each style individually using the associated properties `backgroundColor`, `backgroundImage`, `backgroundRepeat`, `backgroundPosition` and `backgroundAttachment`.

border—This property sets or returns the styles for the whole border. We can affect each border individually using the associated properties `borderTop`, `borderBottom`, `borderLeft` and `borderRight`.

margin—This property sets or returns the margin styles. We can also use the associated properties `marginBottom`, `marginLeft`, `marginRight` and `marginTop`.

padding—This property sets or returns the padding styles. We can also use the associated properties `paddingBottom`, `paddingLeft`, `paddingRight` and `paddingTop`.

width—This property sets or returns the width of the element. There are two associated properties that allow us to set the maximum and minimum width of an element: `maxWidth` and `minWidth`.

height—This property sets or returns the height of the element. There are also two associated properties that allow us to set the maximum and minimum height of the element: `maxHeight` and `minHeight`.

visibility—This property determines whether an element is visible or not. It can take two values, `visible` and `hidden`. Like the rest of the properties, it can also be used to return the current value.

color—This property sets or returns the color of the text.

font—This property sets or returns the font styles all together. We can also set the styles individually using the associated properties `fontFamily`, `fontSize`, `fontSizeAdjust`, `fontStyle`, `fontVariant` and `fontWeight`.

> **IMPORTANT:** These are standard properties available since the first versions of Javascript. For a complete list, please visit our website and follow the links for this chapter.

ClassList

Working with styles individually is not common practice in the real world. Usually, elements are styled by a group of CSS properties assigned through the **class** attribute. As we explained in Chapter 2, these rules are called **classes**. Classes are permanently defined in CSS styles sheets; they can't be changed but they can be replaced. Javascript lets us change the classes assigned to an element by modifying the value of the **class** attribute.

```
<!DOCTYPE html>
<html lang="en">
<head>
  <title>Javascript</title>
  <style>
    .myclass {
      background: #DDDD00;
    }
  </style>
  <script>
    var elem;
    function initiate(){
      elem = document.getElementById('main');
      elem.addEventListener('click', changeclass);
    }
    function changeclass(){
      elem.className = "myclass";
    }
    addEventListener('load', initiate);
  </script>
</head>
<body>
  <section id="main">My content</section>
</body>
</html>
```

Listing 4-45: Changing the class

The **className** property sets or returns the value of the **class** attribute. As shown in Listing 4-45, we declare a new class for an element by assigning the name to the **className** property. In this example, we create the **initiate()** function to get a reference and add a listener for the **click** event to the **<section>** element. When the user clicks on this element, the **changeclass()** function is called and the CSS class **myclass** is assigned to the element changing its background color.

As mentioned in Chapter 2, multiple classes may be assigned to an element. When this is the case, instead of the **className** property it is better to apply the new **classList** object. This object provides the following methods:

add(class)—This method adds another class to the element.

remove(class)—This method removes a class from the element.

toggle(class)—This method adds or removes a class depending on the current status. If the class was already assigned to the element then it is removed. Otherwise, the class is added to the element.

contains(class)—This method detects whether the class was assigned to the element or not and returns **true** or **false** accordingly.

```
<!DOCTYPE html>
<html lang="en">
<head>
  <title>Javascript</title>
  <style>
    .myclass {
      background: #DDDD00;
    }
  </style>
  <script>
    var elem;
    function initiate(){
      elem = document.getElementById('main');
      elem.addEventListener('click', changeclass);
    }
    function changeclass(){
      elem.classList.toggle("myclass");
    }
    addEventListener('load', initiate);
  </script>
</head>
<body>
  <section id="main">My content</section>
</body>
</html>
```

Listing 4-46: Turning classes on and off

The **add()** and **remove()** methods are similar to **className** but are more suitable for work with multiple classes. The **contains()** method is like an **if** statement, useful to check whether a specific class was assigned to an element or not. The most unusual is **toggle()**. This method will check the status of the element and add the class if it wasn't assigned before or remove it otherwise.

The document of Listing 4-46 uses the same source code as the previous example, but the **changeclass()** function is modified. The **className** property was replaced by the **toggle()** method. Now, every time the user clicks on the **<section>** element, the styles of this element will change, switching from having a background color to no color.

> **Do It Yourself:** Replace the **toggle()** method in Listing 4-46 by **add()** or **remove()** to add or remove the class from the element (e.g., **elem.classList. add("myclass")**). Try to create a script to work as **toggle()** but applying the **contains()** method. Using an **if** statement, you can check if the class was assigned to the element and add it or remove it accordingly.

Accessing Attributes

The **className** property and all the methods from the **classList** object we just discussed are specific for the **class** attribute. Javascript provides other methods to work with any attribute, get its value, set a new one or remove it:

> **getAttribute(name)**—This method returns the value of the attribute specified by **name**.
>
> **setAttribute(name, value)**—This method sets a new attribute for an element. The parameters provide the **name** and the **value** of the attribute. If the attribute already exists, the method will only change its value.
>
> **removeAttribute(name)**—This method removes the attribute specified by **name**.

```
<!DOCTYPE html>
<html lang="en">
<head>
  <title>Javascript</title>
  <script>
    var elem;
    function initiate(){
      elem = document.getElementById('main');
      alert(elem.getAttribute("id"));
    }
    addEventListener('load', initiate);
  </script>
</head>
<body>
  <section id="main">My content</section>
</body>
</html>
```

Listing 4-47: *Getting the value of an attribute*

The script in Listing 4-47 uses the **getAttribute()** method to show a pop-up window with the value of the **id** attribute of the **<section>** element. As soon as the document is loaded, the **initiate()** function is called and the **alert()** method shows the message on the screen.

Dataset

So far, we have been working with standard attributes. In Chapter 1, we explained how to customize elements using the **data-*** attribute. This is an important technique to add more information to an element. The information is not visible to the user, but it is accessible for the document and the browser. To read these kinds of attributes, Javascript provides the **dataset** property.

```
<!DOCTYPE html>
<html lang="en">
<head>
  <title>Javascript</title>
```

```
  <script>
    function initiate(){
      var elem = document.getElementById('main');
      alert(elem.dataset.total);
    }
    addEventListener('load', initiate);
  </script>
</head>
<body>
  <section id="main" data-total="3">My content</section>
</body>
</html>
```

Listing 4-48: Reading customized attributes

The **data-*** attribute can take any value we want instead of the * symbol, and we can add all the attributes we need for a single element. The value we choose for the name of each attribute allows us to identify them later using **dataset**. This property returns an object with all the **data-*** attributes defined in the element. To get the value of a specific attribute, we just use its name as a property of **dataset**.

In Listing 4-48, the value of the custom attribute **data-total** is shown on the screen as soon as the document is loaded (**alert(elem.dataset.total)**).

Create and Erase Elements

As with attributes, we can create or erase HTML elements from Javascript. Basically, we use the following three methods for this purpose:

> **createElement(keyword)**—This method creates a new element node of the type specified by **keyword**. It doesn't add the element to the document.

> **appendChild(element)**—This method works along with **createElement()** to insert a new element as the child of an existent element in the document. The specified attribute must be the value returned by the **createElement()** method.

> **removeChild(element)**—This method removes a child from an element. The specified attribute must be a reference to the child to be removed.

```
<!DOCTYPE html>
<html lang="en">
<head>
  <title>Javascript</title>
  <script>
    function initiate(){
      var elem = document.getElementById('main');
      var newelement = document.createElement('p');
      elem.appendChild(newelement);
    }
    addEventListener('load', initiate);
  </script>
</head>
```

```
<body>
  <section id="main">My content</section>
</body>
</html>
```

Listing 4-49: Adding new elements to the document

The `createElement()` method belongs to the Document object. In Listing 4-49, we call it to create a new `<p>` element. This new element is added next as a child of the `<section>` element by the `appendChild()` method.

The `createElement()` method adds a new element to the DOM (Document Object Model) but not to the HTML document. As we mentioned before, the DOM is a tree structure of objects created by the browser to represent the HTML document. When we just need an object to work with, such as an image or a video that will be processed but not shown on the screen, this method is more than sufficient. However, when the element is required as a part of the HTML document, we add it using `appendChild()`.

InnerHTML, OuterHTML and InsertAdjacentHTML

The previous example added a new `<p>` element to the document but nothing was shown on the screen because the element was empty. There are different ways to add content to an element from Javascript. The most flexible (and the new standard in HTML5) is the `innerHTML` property. This property sets or returns the content of an element.

```
<!DOCTYPE html>
<html lang="en">
<head>
  <title>Javascript</title>
  <script>
    function initiate(){
      var elem = document.getElementById('main');
      var newelement = document.createElement('p');
      elem.appendChild(newelement);
      newelement.innerHTML = "Hello World!";
    }
    addEventListener('load', initiate);
  </script>
</head>
<body>
  <section id="main">My content</section>
</body>
</html>
```

Listing 4-50: Adding content to an element

All we need for the addition of new content is a reference to the element we want to modify. In the script in Listing 4-50, the reference is taken from the value returned by the `createElement()` method (`newelement`), but we can use any reference returned by referencing methods such as `getElementById()`, as we will see in later examples.

The value provided to the `innerHTML` property may be text or HTML code. It is usually recommended to add new HTML elements using the combination of `createElement()` and `appendChild()` and apply `innerHTML` (or its brother `textContent`) when we are working only with text. This is because `innerHTML` is more efficient for replacing content but not so much for adding new one.

In the following example, the current content of the `<section>` element will be read and stored in the `content` variable. Then, this value, plus new content, will be assigned back to the element. Using this property we will be able to add elements and content without the application of any method.

```
<!DOCTYPE html>
<html lang="en">
<head>
  <title>Javascript</title>
  <script>
    function initiate(){
      var elem = document.getElementById('main');
      var content = elem.innerHTML;
      elem.innerHTML = content + "<p>Hello World!</p>";
    }
    addEventListener('load', initiate);
  </script>
</head>
<body>
  <section id="main">My content.</section>
</body>
</html>
```

Listing 4-51: *Adding elements with* `innerHTML`

Along with `innerHTML`, HTML5 includes the following properties and methods to work with content:

> **textContent**—This property sets or returns the content of an element as text.
>
> **outerHTML**—This property sets or returns content to the document. Unlike `innerHTML`, this property replaces not only the content but also the element in which it is applied.
>
> **insertAdjacentHTML(location, content)**—This method inserts content in a location according to the value of the first attribute. The values available are `beforebegin`, before the element; `afterbegin`, inside the element, before its first child; `beforeend`, inside the element, after its last child; and `afterend`, after the element.

```
<!DOCTYPE html>
<html lang="en">
<head>
  <title>Javascript</title>
  <script>
    function initiate(){
      var elem = document.getElementById('main');
      elem.insertAdjacentHTML("beforebegin", "<section>Hello
World!</section>");
    }
    addEventListener('load', initiate);
  </script>
```

```
</head>
<body>
  <section id="main">My content</section>
</body>
</html>
```

Listing 4-52: *Adding a new section before* `<section>`

In addition to `innerHTML`, `insertAdjacentHTML()` can insert HTML code into the document. Using this method in Listing 4-52 we are able to add a new element over the previous `<section>` element.

> **IMPORTANT:** When we apply `innerHTML`, the HTML and Javascript codes are interpreted. For security reasons, it is always better to use `textContent` instead. That decision should be made according to the demands of your application and the level of security required.

4.6 APIs

If you have any previous experience programming, or have followed the chapter up to this point, it is easy to see the amount of code necessary to perform simple tasks. Imagine all the work required to build a database system from scratch, to generate complex graphics on the screen, or to create an application for the editing of photographs, for example.

Javascript is as powerful as any other programming language. And for the same reasons that professional programming languages have libraries to create graphic elements, 3D engines for video games or interfaces to access databases, to name a few, Javascript has its own libraries to help programmers deal with complex issues.

Native APIs

Javascript APIs (Application Programming Interfaces) are, in fact, easy to use interfaces to access complex libraries. These APIs, along with their corresponding libraries, are included natively by HTML5 compatible browsers and are ready to use. They provide access to objects with methods, properties and events to take full advantage of the libraries available.

HTML5 introduces several APIs to address common issues such as graphic generation, storage, communication, etc. The potential of these interfaces is so important that shortly they will become our main subject for study.

External APIs

HTML5 was developed to expand the Web with a standard set of technologies that every browser would support and to provide everything a developer needs. In fact, HTML5 was conceptualized to be independent of any third-party technology. But for one reason or another, we often need extra help.

Before the appearance of HTML5, several Javascript libraries were developed to overcome the limitations of the technologies available. Some of those libraries were created with specific purposes—from processing and validation of forms, to generation and manipulation of graphics.

These libraries have become extremely popular, and some of them, such as **Google Maps**, are almost impossible to imitate by independent developers.

Even when future specifications provide better methods or new native APIs, programmers will always find an easier way to deal with complex issues. Libraries that simplify complicated tasks will always be growing and multiplying. These libraries are not part of HTML5 but are an important part of the Web, and some of them have been implemented in today's most successful websites and applications. Along with the rest of the features incorporated by this specification, they enhance Javascript and help disseminate cutting-edge technology.

One of the most popular external libraries is **jQuery**. This library is free and was designed to simplify the creation of modern applications with Javascript. It makes HTML elements easier to select and animations easy to generate as well as handling events and help implement Ajax in our applications.

jQuery has the advantage of providing support for old browsers and making normal tasks simpler and accessible for any developer. It can be used along with HTML5 or as a simple way to replace some basic HTML5 features in browsers not ready for this technology.

This library is only a small file that you can download from www.jquery.com, and then you can include it in your documents using `<script>` tags. It provides a simple API that anyone can learn and immediately apply. Once jQuery is included in our document, we are able to take advantage of simple methods added by the library and turn our static website into a modern and practical application.

> **IMPORTANT:** There are presently dozens of Javascript libraries available. This book doesn't cover the subject, but you can visit our website and follow the links for this chapter to get a list of the most popular libraries in use.

4.7 Errors and Debugging

Browsers always report Javascript errors when they occur, but the system they use to inform the user is not a standard feature. Some browsers deploy a small window containing information about the error and others provide consoles to not only list errors but also inform the user about processing, show custom messages and provide tools for debugging.

Console

The most simple and useful tool to check for errors and debug is probably the Console. Consoles are available in almost every browser but in different forms. Usually, it is composed of several panels detailing information of every aspect of the document, including the HTML source code, CSS styles and, of course, Javascript.

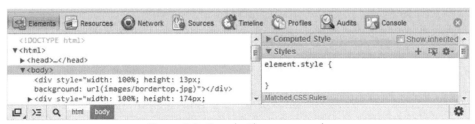

Figure 4-2: Google Chrome console

How to access this console varies from browser to browser, and even among different versions of the same browser, as explained below:

Google Chrome—This browser offers a console with information about the document, the source codes, the network, and also access to resources such as storage space, databases, cache, etc. The Javascript console is shown in the `Console` tab. To open this console, press the F12 key on your keyboard or go to the main menu (a button at the upper-right corner of the window) and select `Tools/Developers Tools` or `Tools/Javascript Console` to get to the Javascript Console tab.

Mozilla Firefox—This browser provides different tools for developers from the `Web Developer` menu. In that menu, you will find two options to check for Javascript errors: the `Web Console` and the `Error Console`. To access these tools, open the main menu (in the latest version using the orange button at the top-left corner of the window) and go to `Web Developer/Web Console` or `Web Developer/Error Console`. There is also a good debugger for Mozilla Firefox called Firebug. For more information and to download this add-on, go to www.getfirebug.com.

Safari—This browser is based on the same engine than Google Chrome and it provides a similar console, but the access to that console has to be activated by the user from the `Preferences` menu. Go to the View menu (click the button at the upper-right corner of the window) and select `Preferences`. Then open the `Advanced` tab and check the box with the title "Show Develop Menu in menu bar". A new submenu called `Develop` will be shown on the menu bar. Select the option `Show Web Inspector` to open the console.

Opera—This browser also offers a full console solution, but to get it open is a little bit tricky. We can right-click on the web page and select the option `Inspect Element` (this option is also available in other browsers) or press the keys `Ctrl + Shift + I`.

Internet Explorer—This browser offers a more simple console with basic options, but it is still useful. It is available pressing the F12 key or selecting the `F12 Developer tools` option from the Tools menu.

console.log()

Sometimes errors are not programming errors but logical errors. The Javascript interpreter can't find any errors in the code, but the application is not doing what we expected. There can be a number of reasons for this, from an operation we forgot to a variable set with the wrong value. Determining what is wrong with our code requires reading the instructions one by one and following the logic until something doesn't make sense. Fortunately, there is a traditional programming technique we can use called **breakpoints**. Breakpoints are stopping points in our code we set to check the current state of the application. In a breakpoint, we show the current values of variables or simply a message letting us know that the interpreter reached that point.

Traditionally, Javascript programmers inserted an **alert()** method in parts of the code to expose some values that could provide information to help them find the bug. But this method was not suitable for most common situations because it stops the execution of the code until the pop-up window is closed. To simplify the process of providing feedback from the code, browsers introduced the **console** object and the **log()** method. This method shows the message between parentheses in the Javascript console.

```
<script>
  var myvariable = 9;
  for(var f = 0; f < myvariable; f++) {
    console.log("The current number is " + f);
  }
</script>
```

Listing 4-53: Showing a message with `console.log()`

The previous example is based on the script in Listing 4-13. The **alert()** method was replaced by the **console.log()** method to show a message in every cycle of the loop. These messages only appear in the Javascript console, allowing developers to check the state of the application without interrupting its execution.

In addition, **console.log()** can print objects into the Javascript console, allowing developers to read the content of an unknown object and identify its properties and methods.

> **IMPORTANT:** In some browsers, the **log()** method allows the inclusion of more parameters between parentheses. Likewise, the **console** object includes other methods besides **log()** for debugging purposes. To learn more about this object and its methods, please visit our website and follow the links for this chapter.

Error Event

At some point, you will find that sometimes errors are not your fault. As your scripts get more complex and incorporate sophisticated APIs, errors will depend on factors out of your control, such as momentarily inaccessible resources or an unexpected change in the device running your application. To help the code detect these errors and correct itself, Javascript provides the **error** event. This event is available for several APIs but also as a general event in the Window object. Taking advantage of this event, we can program our code to respond to the new conditions.

```
<script>
  function showerror(e){
    console.log('Error: ' + e.message);
    console.log('Line: ' + e.lineno);
    console.log('URL: ' + e.filename);
  }
  addEventListener('error', showerror);
  wrongfunction();
</script>
```

Listing 4-54: Responding to script's errors

The **error** event returns an object containing properties with information about the error. In the script in Listing 4-54, we send messages to the console with the values of these properties. The **message** property contains a short text describing the error, the **lineno** property provides the number of the line in the script that produced the error, and the **filename** property offers the full URL pointing to the file that contains the script. In our example, the error is produced by the execution of an nonexistent function called **wrongfunction()**, but it could be any

Javascript error (although sometimes it will be better to use the APIs' specific `error` events instead, as we will see in later chapters).

Chapter 5
Forms and Forms API

5.1 HTML Forms

The Web 2.0 is all about the user. And when the user is the center of attention, it is all about interfaces—how to make them more intuitive, more natural, more practical and, of course, more beautiful. Forms are the most important interface of all; they allow users to insert data, make decisions, communicate information and change an application's behavior. Over the last few years, customized codes and libraries were created to process forms in a user's computer. HTML5 made these features standard, providing new attributes, elements and an entire API. Now, the capacity to process information inserted in forms in real time has been incorporated in browsers and completely standardized.

The <form> Element

Forms haven't changed so much from previous versions of HTML. The structure is still the same, but HTML5 has added new elements, input types and attributes to expand them as far as necessary to provide the features currently implemented in web applications.

```
<!DOCTYPE html>
<html lang="en">
<head>
  <title>Forms</title>
</head>
<body>
  <section>
    <form name="myform" method="get" action="file.php">

    </form>
  </section>
</body>
</html>
```

Listing 5-1: *Using the* `<form>` *element*

The `<form>` element defines the form and its components. It has opening and closing tags to enclose its elements and requires a few attributes to determine how the information is going to be processed and sent:

name—This is the name of the form. This attribute is also available for every other HTML element but is particularly useful for a form's elements, as we will see later.

method—This attribute determines the method used to send the form to the server. There are two possible values: `GET` and `POST`. The `GET` method is used to send limited public information (the data are sent in the URL and are usually no longer than 255 characters). The `POST` method is used to send unlimited private information (the data are not visible for the user).

action—This attribute declares the URL of the file in the server that is going to process the information sent by the form.

target—This attribute determines where the response sent by the server will be shown. The possible values are `_blank` (new window), `_self` (same frame), `_parent` (parent frame) and `_top` (the window containing the frame). The value `_self` is set by default. This attribute and its values are also applicable to the `<a>` element.

enctype—This attribute declares the codification to be applied to the data sent by the form. It takes three values: `application/x-www-form-urlencoded` (characters are encoded), `multipart/form-data` (characters are not encoded), `text/plain` (only spaces are encoded). The first value is the one set by default.

accept-charset—This attribute declares the type of encoding to be applied to the form. The most common values are `UTF-8` and `ISO-8859-1`. The default value is the one set for the document in the `<meta>` tags.

The <input> Element

The most important element in a form is `<input>`. This element generates an input field for the user to insert data. The characteristics of the element and the type of data allowed to be entered depend on the value of the `type` attribute. This attribute determines what kind of input is expected from users. There are several values available for the `type` attribute, the traditional values are:

text—This value generates an input field to insert generic text.

hidden—This value hides the input field. It is usually used to send complementary information.

password—This value generates an input field to insert a password. It masks the characters to hide sensitive information. The characters inserted by the user are usually shown on the screen as star or dot characters, depending on the browser.

checkbox—This value generates a checkbox. This type of input requires the declaration of the `value` attribute to specify the value to be sent. The value is sent only if the checkbox was checked (if no value is specified, the value `on` is sent).

radio—This value generates a radio button to select one option from a group. Using the same value for the `name` attribute, we can group several buttons (options) together. The value of the `value` attribute of the button checked is the value sent when the form is submitted. The `checked` attribute let us declare which button will be checked by default.

file—This value generates an input field to select a file from user's computer.

button—This value generates a button. This button does not perform any action nor submit the form by itself. It is a multipurpose button that has to be controlled from Javascript code (usually through the `click` event. The `value` attribute is used to declare the text to be shown on the button.

submit—This value generates a button to submit the form. This type of input uses the `value` attribute to declare the text to be shown on the button. The form can also be submitted from Javascript using the `submit()` method, as we will see later.

reset—This value generates a button to reset the form.

image—This value loads an image to use as a submit button. The `<input>` element has to include the `src` attribute to specify the URL of the image.

Listing 5-2, below, includes an example of the most common input types. We will see more examples of this in following chapters.

```
<!DOCTYPE html>
<html lang="en">
<head>
  <title>Forms</title>
</head>
<body>
  <section id="form">
    <form name="myform" method="get" action="file.php">
      <br><label for="myname">Text: </label>
      <input type="text" name="myname">
      <br><label for="myoption">Radio Buttons: </label>
      <input type="radio" name="myoption" value="1" checked> 1
      <input type="radio" name="myoption" value="2"> 2
      <input type="radio" name="myoption" value="3"> 3
      <br><label for="mypassword">Password: </label>
      <input type="password" name="mypassword">
      <br><label for="mycheckbox">Checkbox: </label>
      <input type="checkbox" name="mycheckbox" value="123">
      <input type="hidden" value="secret key">
      <input type="submit" value="Send">
    </form>
  </section>
</body>
</html>
```

Listing 5-2: *Creating a simple form with traditional input types*

Text: [ ]
Radio Buttons: ⦿ 1 ○ 2 ○ 3
Password: [ ]
Checkbox: ☐ [Send]

Figure 5-1: *Traditional* `<input>` *elements*

Review the Basics: The `<label>` element declares the label for a form's element. The `for` attribute in this element is used to associate the label with the corresponding element (the value of `for` must be the value of the `name` attribute of the element that label is related to).

More Form Elements

Besides the `<input>` element, there are a few more traditional elements you should know:

<textarea>—This element generates a multi-line text field. The size can be declared in integer numbers using the attributes `rows` and `cols`.

<select>—This element generates a list of options that are declared by the `<option>` element.

<option>—This element declares each option for a `<select>` element.

In the following example, a simple form shows the syntax of these elements. The size for the `<textarea>` element will be set as 5 rows and 30 columns, and three options will be included for the `<select>` element. The name/value pair sent by the form for this element will be composed of the value of the `name` attribute of the `<select>` element (`mylist`) and the value of the `value` attribute of the option selected.

```
<!DOCTYPE html>
<html lang="en">
<head>
  <title>Forms</title>
</head>
<body>
  <section id="form">
    <form name="myform" method="post" action="file.php">
      <label for="mytext">Textarea: </label>
      <textarea name="mytext" rows="5" cols="30"></textarea>
      <br><label for="mylist">Select: </label>
      <select name="mylist">
        <option value="1">One</option>
        <option value="2">Two</option>
        <option value="3">Three</option>
      </select>
      <input type="submit" value="Send">
      <input type="reset" value="Reset">
    </form>
  </section>
</body>
</html>
```

Listing 5-3: *Using* `<textarea>` *and* `<select>`

Figure 5-2: Traditional form elements

Form Submit

When a form is submitted, the data introduced in the form are sent using a name/value pair for each element, where *name* is the value of the `name` attribute of the element and *value* is the value introduced by the user. For example, if we insert the text "Robert" in the first `<input>` element in the form in Listing 5-2, the name/value pair sent will be `myname=Robert`.

These name/value pairs are sent in the URL or hidden, according to the method declared by the `method` attribute of the form: `GET` or `POST`. If you set the method as `GET`, you will see these data in the URL when the form is submitted (e.g., `www.minkbooks.com?myname=Robert`). To retrieve this information from the server, you also have to use a technique according to the method set by the form. Let's see an example in PHP:

```
<?PHP
  print('Your name is: '.$_GET['myname']);
?>
```

Listing 5-4: Processing data in the server with PHP (`file.php`)

The PHP script in Listing 5-4 is a sample of the script that could be part of the `file.php` file declared as the value of the `action` attribute in the form in Listing 5-2. This file is loaded from the server by the browser when the form is submitted. In the server, the PHP code is executed and the result is returned to the browser as an HTML document. The PHP in our example uses a global variable called `$_GET` to capture the information sent to the server and prints the value in the document to be returned. If we change the method of the form to `POST`, then we have to use the `$_POST` variable instead.

> **IMPORTANT:** This is only an example of how the information is processed and how the browser transmits the data entered in a form to the server. PHP is a popular language used to process information in the server but is not the only one available. For more information on this subject, go to our website and follow the links for this chapter.

5.2 New Input Types

HTML5 has increased the number of options for the `type` attribute and enhanced the `<input>` element. Now the types are not only specifying what kind of input is expected, but also telling the browser what to do with the information received. The browser will process the input data according to the value of the `type` attribute and validate the entry or not. This attribute works along with additional attributes to help the browser limit and control the user's input in real time.

Do It Yourself: Create a new HTML file with the document of Listing 5-1. To check how each input type works, place the `<input>` elements you want to test in between the `<form>` tags and open the file in your browser. At present, the way these new input types are processed varies, so we recommend checking the code in every available browser.

Email Type

Almost every form in the world has an input field to insert an email address. But up to this point, the only type available for this kind of data was **text**. The type **text** represents a general text, not specific data, so we had to control the input with Javascript code to ensure that the text entered was a valid email address. Now the browser takes care of this thanks to the new **email** type.

```
<input type="email" name="myemail">
```

Listing 5-5: Declaring the email *type*

The text inserted in the field generated by the code in Listing 5-5 is checked by the browser and validated as an email. If the validation fails, the form won't be sent.

A browser's response to an invalid input is not determined by the HTML5 specification. For example, some browsers will show a red border around the `<input>` element that produced the error, and others will show a blue one. Later, we will study different techniques to customize this procedure.

Search Type

The **search** type doesn't control the entry; it is just an indication for browsers. Some browsers will change the design of this element by default to provide a hint to the user about the purpose of the field.

```
<input type="search" name="mysearch">
```

Listing 5-6: Declaring the search *type*

URL Type

The **url** type works exactly like **email** but for Web addresses. It accepts only absolute URLs and returns an error if the value is invalid.

```
<input type="url" name="myurl">
```

Listing 5-7: Declaring the url *type*

Forms and Forms API

Tel Type

The `tel` type is for telephone numbers. Unlike the `email` and `url` types, the `tel` type doesn't force any particular syntax. It is an indication for the browser in case the application needs to make adjustments according to the device in which it is being executed.

```
<input type="tel" name="myphone">
```

Listing 5-8: Declaring the `tel` type

Number Type

As indicated by its name, the `number` type is only valid when it receives a numeric input. There are a few optional attributes that might be useful to limit this field:

> **min**—The value of this attribute determines the minimum acceptable value for the field.
>
> **max**—The value of this attribute determines the maximum acceptable value for the field.
>
> **step**—The value of this attribute determines the size of the steps by which the value of the field will be increased or decreased. For example, if you set a step of 5 with a minimum value of 0 and a maximum of 10, the browser won't let you specify a value between 0 and 5 or 5 and 10.

```
<input type="number" name="mynumber" min="0" max="10" step="5">
```

Listing 5-9: Declaring the `number` type

Range Type

The `range` makes the browser build a new kind of control that didn't exist before. As its name indicates, this new control lets users pick a value from a range of numbers. Usually it is rendered with a slider or arrows to move the value up and down, but there is no standard design.

The `range` type uses the attributes `min` and `max` to set the limits of the range. It can also have the attribute `step` to declare the amount the value will be increased or decreased in each step of the range.

```
<input type="range" name="mynumbers" min="0" max="10" step="5">
```

Listing 5-10: Declaring the `range` type

You can set the initial value with the old `value` attribute and use Javascript to show numbers on screen for a reference.

Date Type

`Date` is another type that will generate a new kind of control. In this case, it is included to provide a better way for date entry. Browsers implement this feature with a calendar that shows up every time the user clicks on the field. The calendar lets users select a day that will be inserted in the input field along with the rest of the date. An example of this is when a user tries to pick a date for a flight or a ticket; in this case, with the `date` type, the browser will build the calendar for us and we just have to insert the `<input>` element in the document to make it available for our users.

```
<input type="date" name="mydate">
```

Listing 5-11: *Declaring the* date *type*

The interface is not declared in the specification. Every browser is providing its own interface and sometimes adapting the design according to the device in which the application is being executed. Usually, the value generated and expected has the syntax `year-month-day`.

Week Type

The **week** type provides a similar interface as **date** but only for picking entire weeks. The value expected has the syntax `2012-W50`, where 2012 is the year and 50 is the number of the week.

```
<input type="week" name="myweek">
```

Listing 5-12: *Declaring the* week *type*

Month Type

Similar to the previous type, the **month** is for an entire month. The value expected has the syntax `year-month`.

```
<input type="month" name="mymonth">
```

Listing 5-13: *Declaring the* month *type*

Time Type

The **time** type is similar to **date** but rather for the time. It takes the format of hours and minutes, but currently, its behavior also depends on each browser. Usually, the value expected has the syntax `hour:minutes:seconds` but also can be `hour:minutes`.

```
<input type="time" name="mytime">
```

Listing 5-14: Declaring the `time` *type*

Datetime Type

The **datetime** type is for full date and time input, including a time zone.

```
<input type="datetime" name="mydatetime">
```

Listing 5-15: Declaring the `datetime` *type*

Datetime-local Type

The **datetime-local** type is a **datetime** type without a time zone.

```
<input type="datetime-local" name="mylocaldatetime">
```

Listing 5-16: Declaring the `datetime-local` *type*

Color Type

In addition to types for dates and times, there is also a type that provides a predefined interface so that users can pick a color. Usually, the value expected for this field is a hexadecimal number, such as #00FF00.

```
<input type="color" name="mycolor">
```

Listing 5-17: Declaring the `color` *type*

There is no standard interface specified by HTML5 for **color**, but it is possible that a regular grid with a set of basic colors will be adopted by browsers in the future.

5.3 New Attributes

Some input types require the help of attributes—such as **min**, **max** and **step**, examined before—to perform their tasks. Other input types require the assistance of attributes to improve their performance or to determine their importance in the validation process. The following are the new attributes incorporated in HTML5 for this purpose:

Autocomplete Attribute

The **autocomplete** attribute is an old attribute that has become a standard. It can take two values: **on** and **off**. The value by default is **on**. When it is set to **off**, the **<input>** element will have the autocomplete feature disabled, not showing texts from previous entries as possible values. It can also be implemented in the **<form>** element to affect every element in the form.

```
<input type="search" name="mysearch" autocomplete="off">
```

Listing 5-18: *Using the* autocomplete *attribute*

Novalidate and Formnovalidate Attributes

One of the characteristics of forms in HTML5 is a built-in capability for validation. By default, every form will be validated unless the **novalidate** attribute is present. This Boolean attribute is specific for the **<form>** tag. When included, the form is submitted without validation.

Sometimes, the validation process will be required only in some circumstances. For example, when the information inserted has to be saved to resume the work later. In cases like this, we can rely on another Boolean attribute specific for **<input>** elements called **formnovalidate**.

```
<!DOCTYPE html>
<html lang="en">
<head>
  <title>Forms</title>
</head>
<body>
  <section>
    <form name="myform" method="get" action="file.php">
      <input type="email" name="myemail">
      <input type="submit" value="Send">
      <input type="submit" value="Save" formnovalidate>
    </form>
  </section>
</body>
</html>
```

Listing 5-19: *Sending a form without validation with the* formnovalidate *attribute*

In the example in Listing 5-19, the form is going to be validated, but we provide a second submit button with the **formnovalidate** attribute to be able to send the form without going through the validation process. The "Send" button requires a valid value for **myemail**, but the "Save" button doesn't.

Placeholder Attribute

The **placeholder** attribute represents a short hint, a word or phrase, provided to help the user produce the right entry. The value of this attribute is rendered by browsers inside the field, like preview text that disappears when the element is focused.

```
<input type="search" name="mysearch" placeholder="type your seach">
```

Listing 5-20: Using the `placeholder` *attribute*

Required Attribute

The Boolean attribute `required` won't let the form be submitted if the field is empty. For example, when we used the `email` type previously to receive an email address, the browser would check whether the entry is a valid email or not but would validate the input field when it is empty. When the `required` attribute is included, the input will be valid if the field is filled in and if its value complies with the requisites of its type.

```
<input type="email" name="myemail" required>
```

Listing 5-21: Declaring the `email` *input as a required field*

Multiple Attribute

The `multiple` attribute is another Boolean attribute that can be used in some input types (for example, `email` or `file`) to allow multiple entries in the same field. The values inserted have to be separated by a comma to be valid.

```
<input type="email" name="myemail" multiple>
```

Listing 5-22: Declaring the `email` *input as a multiple field*

The code in Listing 5-22 allows the insertion of multiple values separated by comma, and each one of them is validated by the browser as an email address.

Autofocus Attribute

The `autofocus` feature has, so far, been applied by most developers using the Javascript method `focus()`. This method was effective but forced the focus over the selected element, even when the user was already using another one. This behavior was irritating but impossible to avoid, until now. The `autofocus` attribute will focus the web page over the selected element but considering the current situation; it will not move the focus when it has already been set in another element by the user.

```
<input type="search" name="mysearch" autofocus>
```

Listing 5-23: Using the `autofocus` *attribute*

Pattern Attribute

The **pattern** attribute increases the alternatives provided by default for validation. It uses regular expressions to customize validation rules. Some of the input types already mentioned validate specific kinds of strings, but suppose, for example, you want to validate a zip code that consists of 5 numbers. There is no predetermined input type for this kind of entry. The **pattern** attribute will let you create your own to check values like that. You can also include a **title** attribute to customize the error message.

```
<input pattern="[0-9]{5}" name="pcode" title="insert the 5 numbers of
your postal code">
```

Listing 5-24: Customizing types with the pattern *attribute*

> **IMPORTANT:** It is not the purpose of this book to teach Regular Expressions. For more information about this subject, please visit our website and follow the links for this chapter.

Form Attribute

The **form** attribute is a useful addition that lets us declare elements for a form outside the **<form>** tags. Until now, to build a form, you had to write the opening and closing **<form>** tags and then declare every element for the form in between them. In HTML5, we can insert the elements in anywhere we want and then reference the form they belong to by its name using the **form** attribute.

```
<!DOCTYPE html>
<html lang="en">
<head>
  <title>Forms</title>
</head>
<body>
  <nav>
    <input type="search" name="mysearch" form="myform">
  </nav>
  <section>
    <form name="myform" method="get" action="file.php">
      <input type="text" name="myname">
      <input type="submit" value="Send">
    </form>
  </section>
</body>
</html>
```

Listing 5-25: Declaring form elements anywhere

Forms and Forms API

5.4 New Form Elements

We have discussed the new types and also new attributes available for the `<input>` elements in HTML5, now it is time to learn about new HTML elements that were incorporated to improve or expand the possibilities of forms.

The <datalist> Element

The `<datalist>` element prebuilds a list of items that, with the help of the `list` attribute, will be used as a suggestion by an input field later.

```
<datalist id="mydata">
  <option value="123123123" label="Phone 1">
  <option value="456456456" label="Phone 2">
</datalist>
```

Listing 5-26: *Building the list of options*

With the `<datalist>` declared, the next step is to reference the list of items from an `<input>` element using the `list` attribute. The value required for this attribute is the value of the `id` attribute of the `<datalist>` element.

The element in the following example will show possible values for the user to choose from.

```
<input type="tel" name="myphone" list="mydata">
```

Listing 5-27: *Suggesting values with the* `list` *attribute*

The <progress> Element

This element is not a form-specific element, but because it represents the completion progress of a task, and usually tasks are started and processed through forms, it can be included in the group of form elements.

The `<progress>` element uses two attributes to set its status and limits. The `value` attribute indicates how much of the task has been completed, and `max` declares the value needed to be reached for the task to be complete.

```
<progress value="0" max="100">0%</progress>
```

Listing 5-28: *Using the* `<progress>` *element*

The <meter> Element

Similar to `<progress>`, the `<meter>` element is used to show a scale, but not for progression. It is intended to be a representation of a known range—for example, bandwidth usage.

The element **<meter>** has several associated attributes. The attributes **min** and **max** set the bounds of the range, **value** determines the value measured, and **low**, **high** and **optimum** are used to segment the range into differentiated sections and set the position that is optimum.

```
<meter value="60" min="0" max="100" low="40" high="80"
optimum="100">60</meter>
```

Listing 5-29: *Using the* <meter> *element*

The code in Listing 5-29 generates a bar on the screen showing a level of 60 on a scale of 0 to 100 (according to the values declared by the **value**, **min** and **max** attributes). The color of the bar generated by the element on the screen will depend on the levels set by the **low**, **high** and **optimum** attributes (yellow in this case).

The <output> Element

The **output** element represents the result of a calculation. Usually it will help to show the result of values processed by form elements. The **for** attribute will let us associate **<output>** with the element that participates in the calculation, but the element is referenced and modified from Javascript code. The syntax for this element is **<output>value</output>**.

5.5 New Pseudo-Classes

Previously, we mentioned that it is possible to customize the appearance of invalid form elements. CSS3 provides new pseudo-classes that let us declare our own styles not only for invalid but also for valid, required, optional and even range limitation elements, such as **<input>** elements with the **range** type. Now, every time a new condition for an element is established, CSS is responsible for showing the new status on the screen.

Valid and Invalid

These pseudo-classes represent any **<input>** element with a valid or invalid value.

```
<!DOCTYPE html>
<html lang="en">
<head>
  <title>Forms</title>
  <style>
    :valid{
      background: #EEEEFF;
    }
    :invalid{
      background: #FFEEEE;
    }
  </style>
</head>
```

```
<body>
  <section>
    <form name="myform" method="get" action="file.php">
      <input type="email" name="myemail">
      <input type="submit" value="Send">
    </form>
  </section>
</body>
</html>
```

Listing 5-30: *Using the* :valid *and* :invalid *pseudo-classes*

The form in Listing 5-30 includes an **<input>** element for emails. When the content of the element is valid for an **email** type, the **:valid** pseudo-class assigns a blue background to the field. As soon as the content becomes invalid, the **:invalid** pseudo-class changes the background color to red.

Optional and Required

These pseudo-classes represent any form element declared as required or not.

```
<!DOCTYPE html>
<html lang="en">
<head>
  <title>Forms</title>
  <style>
    :required{
      border: 2px solid #990000;
    }
    :optional{
      border: 2px solid #009999;
    }
  </style>
</head>
<body>
  <section>
    <form name="myform" method="get" action="file.php">
      <input type="text" name="myname">
      <input type="text" name="mylastname" required>
      <input type="submit" value="Send">
    </form>
  </section>
</body>
</html>
```

Listing 5-31: *Using the* :required *and* :optional *pseudo-classes*

The example in Listing 5-31 includes two input fields: **myname** and **mylastname**. The first one is optional, but **mylastname** is required. The pseudo-classes color the border of these fields according to their condition.

In-range and Out-of-range

These pseudo-classes represent any element with range limitations with a value inside or outside the specified range (e.g., an **<input>** element with the **number** type).

```
<!DOCTYPE html>
<html lang="en">
<head>
  <title>Forms</title>
  <style>
    :in-range{
      background: #EEEEFF;
    }
    :out-of-range{
      background: #FFEEEE;
    }
  </style>
</head>
<body>
  <section>
    <form name="myform" method="get" action="file.php">
      <input type="number" name="mynumber" min="0" max="10">
      <input type="submit" value="Send">
    </form>
  </section>
</body>
</html>
```

Listing 5-32: *Using the* :in-range *and* :out-of-range *pseudo-classes*

A **number** type input field is inserted in the example above to test these pseudo-classes. When the value entered in the element is less than **0** or greater than **10**, the background turns the color red, but as soon as we enter a value inside the specified range, the background turns blue.

> **IMPORTANT:** Pseudo-classes may be applied only to specific elements using CSS selectors and the **id** or the **class** attributes (e.g., **#myemail:invalid{}**).

5.6 Forms API

As we have seen, there are different ways to take advantage of form validation in HTML5. We can use input types that require validation by default, such as **email**, turn a regular **text** type into a required field with the **required** attribute, or even use special types like **pattern** to customize the validation requisites. However, when it comes to more complex validation mechanisms, such as combining fields or checking for the results of a previous calculation, our only option is to customize the validation process using the new Forms API.

SetCustomValidity()

Browsers that support HTML5 show an error message when the user tries to submit a form that has an invalid field. We can create messages for our own validation requirements using the `setCustomValidity(message)` method. With this method, we set a custom error that will display a message when the form is submitted. When a null message is provided, the error is cleared.

```
<!DOCTYPE html>
<html lang="en">
<head>
  <title>Forms</title>
  <script>
    var name1, name2;
    function initiate(){
      name1 = document.getElementById("firstname");
      name2 = document.getElementById("lastname");
      name1.addEventListener("input", validation);
      name2.addEventListener("input", validation);
      validation();
    }
    function validation(){
      if(name1.value == '' && name2.value == ''){
        name1.setCustomValidity('insert at least one name');
        name1.style.background = '#FFDDDD';
        name2.style.background = '#FFDDDD';
      }else{
        name1.setCustomValidity('');
        name1.style.background = '#FFFFFF';
        name2.style.background = '#FFFFFF';
      }
    }
    addEventListener("load", initiate);
  </script>
</head>
<body>
  <section>
    <form name="registration" method="get" action="file.php">
      <label for="firstname">First Name: </label>
      <input type="text" name="firstname" id="firstname">
      <label for="lastname">Last Name: </label>
      <input type="text" name="lastname" id="lastname">
      <input type="submit" value="Sign Up">
    </form>
  </section>
</body>
</html>
```

Listing 5-33: *Setting custom errors*

> **Review the Basics:** As we have discussed, every HTML element is an object (it is, in fact, reproduced as an object in an internal structure created by the browser). Most of the element's attributes are accessible from Javascript using the name of the attribute as a property of the element (e.g., `name1.value`). In the previous example, the values

from the input fields are retrieved using the `value` property (values inserted in input fields are stored as the value of the `value` attribute).

The document of Listing 5-33 presents a situation of complex validation. Two input fields are created to receive the user's first and last name. However, the form is only invalid when both fields are empty. The user must enter either a first or last name to validate the entry. In a case like this, it is impossible to use the `required` attribute, because we don't know which input field the user will choose to fill. Only by using Javascript code and customized errors will we be able to create an effective validation mechanism for this scenario.

Our code starts running when the `load` event is fired. The `initiate()` function is called to handle the event. This function creates references for the two `<input>` elements and adds listeners for the `input` event to both. The `validation()` function, set as the listener for those events, is executed every time the user types into the fields, adding or erasing characters.

Because the `<input>` elements are empty when the document is loaded, we have to set an invalid condition to stop the user from submitting the form before at least one name is typed. For this reason, the `validation()` function is also called at the end of the `initiate()` function to check this condition. If both names are empty strings, the error is set and the background color for both elements is changed to red. However, if that condition does not hold true later because at least one of the names was inserted, the error is cleared and the backgrounds are set back to white.

It is important to remember that the only change produced during the processing is the modification of the background color. The message declared for the error with `setCustomValidity()` will only be visible when the user tries to submit the form.

> **Review the Basics:** Several variables may be declared in the same line separated by a comma. In Listing 5-33, we declare two global variables `name1` and `name2`. The purpose of this is to be able to access their values from any function. The statement could have been avoided, because, as we mentioned before, variables declared inside functions without the `var` operator have global scope.

> **Do It Yourself:** For testing purposes, we included the Javascript code in the document. To test this example simply copy the code in Listing 5-33 into an empty HTML file and open the file in your browser.

The Invalid Event and the CheckValidity() Method

Every time the user submits a form, an event is fired if an invalid element is detected. The event is called `invalid` and is focused on the element that produces the error. We can register an event handler to customize the response as in the following example:

```
<!DOCTYPE html>
<html lang="en">
<head>
  <title>Forms</title>
  <script>
    var form;
    function initiate(){
      var button = document.getElementById("send");
      button.addEventListener("click", sendit);
```

```
    form = document.querySelector("form[name='information']");
    form.addEventListener("invalid", validation, true);
  }
  function validation(e){
    var elem = e.target;
    elem.style.background = '#FFDDDD';
  }
  function sendit(){
    var valid = form.checkValidity();
    if(valid){
      form.submit();
    }
  }
  addEventListener("load", initiate);
</script>
</head>
<body>
  <section>
    <form name="information" method="get" action="file.php">
      <label for="nickname">Nickname: </label>
      <input pattern="[A-Za-z]{3,}" name="nickname" id="nickname"
maxlength="10" required>
      <label for="myemail">Email: </label>
      <input type="email" name="myemail" id="myemail" required>
      <input type="button" id="send" value="Sign Up">
    </form>
  </section>
</body>
</html>
```

Listing 5-34: *Creating our own validation system*

In Listing 5-34, we create a new form with two input fields to ask for a nickname and an email. The **nickname** input has three validation attributes: the **pattern** attribute that only admits a minimum of 3 characters from A to Z (upper and lower case), the traditional **maxlength** attribute that limits the input to 10 characters maximum and the **required** attribute that invalidates the field if it's empty. The **email** input, on the other hand, has its natural limitation due to its type and a **required** attribute.

What the Javascript code does with this form is simple: when the user clicks on the "Sign Up" button, an **invalid** event will be fired for every invalid field, and the background color of those fields will be changed to red by the **validation()** function.

Let's take a closer look. The scripts starts running when the typical **load** event is fired after the document is completely loaded. The **initiate()** function is executed and two listeners are added to the "Sign Up" button and the **<form>** element. The listener for the **click** event is added to the "Sign Up" button as we did before for other elements, but the listener for the **invalid** event is different. We want to achieve a validation control for the entire form, therefore, the listener has to be added to the **<form>** element not to each element inside the form. Consequently, we have to capture the events down the HTML tree, and that is why the last parameter of the **addEventListener()** method used for the **invalid** event is set to **true**. As a result, even when the listener is added to the **<form>** element, it responds to events fired by the elements inside the form.

When the **invalid** event is fired, the **validation()** function is called to change the background color of the invalid field. This event will be fired by an invalid input when the form is submitted and then captured by the listener of the **<form>** element. To determine which element is invalid, we store a reference to the event in the variable **e** and read the value of its **target** property. This property returns a reference to the element that fired the event. Using that reference, the last instruction of the **validation()** function changes the background color of the corresponding element.

> **IMPORTANT:** The processes to register event handlerss or add event listeners, such as **addEventListener()**, always send an object referencing the event. This object is sent to the handler function as an attribute. Traditionally, the variable **e** is used to store this value, but you can use any name you want. The object provides properties with important information of the event. The **target** property, for example, returns a reference to the element that fired the event. We will see other event properties and more examples throughout the book.

Returning to the **initiate()** function, we still have one more listener to analyze. To have absolute control over the form's submission and the moment of validation, we create a regular button instead of a **submit** button. The **sendit()** function, added before as the handler of the **click** event for this element, is executed when the button is clicked. Using the **checkValidity()** method, we force browser validation and only submit the form using the traditional **submit()** method when there are no more invalid conditions.

With the Javascript code in this document, we took control over the entire process of validation, customizing every aspect and also browser's behavior.

> **Review the Basics:** In the last example we applied the **querySelector()** method to get a reference to the form using a CSS selector. This selector looks for a **<form>** element with the **name** attribute and the value "information". See Chapter 2 for more on CSS selectors and Chapter 4 to review the **querySelector()** method.

Real-Time Validation with ValidityState

When you open the file of the document of Listing 5-34 in the browser, you will notice that there is no real-time validation. The fields are validated only when the form is submitted. To make our customized validation process more practical, we can take advantage of the several properties provided by the ValidityState object.

```
<!DOCTYPE html>
<html lang="en">
<head>
  <title>Forms</title>
  <script>
    var form;
    function initiate(){
      var button = document.getElementById("send");
      button.addEventListener("click", sendit);
      form = document.querySelector("form[name='information']");
      form.addEventListener("invalid", validation, true);
      form.addEventListener("input", checkval);
    }
```

```
     function validation(e){
       var elem = e.target;
       elem.style.background = '#FFDDDD';
     }
     function sendit(){
       var valid = form.checkValidity();
       if(valid){
         form.submit();
       }
     }
     function checkval(e){
       var elem = e.target;
       if(elem.validity.valid){
         elem.style.background = '#FFFFFF';
       }else{
         elem.style.background = '#FFDDDD';
       }
     }
     addEventListener("load", initiate);
   </script>
</head>
<body>
   <section>
     <form name="information" method="get" action="file.php">
       <label for="nickname">Nickname: </label>
       <input pattern="[A-Za-z]{3,}" name="nickname" id="nickname"
maxlength="10" required>
       <label for="myemail">Email: </label>
       <input type="email" name="myemail" id="myemail" required>
       <input type="button" id="send" value="Sign Up">
     </form>
   </section>
</body>
</html>
```

Listing 5-35: Validating in real time

In Listing 5-35, a new listener for the `input` event is added to the form. Every time the user modifies a field, writing or changing its content, the `checkval()` function is executed to handle the event.

The `checkval()` function also takes advantage of the `target` property to create a reference to the element that fired the event and controls its validity by checking the `valid` state with the `validity` property in the construction `elem.validity.valid`. This property is referencing the ValidityState object, as we will see next.

The `valid` state will be `true` if the element is valid and `false` if not. Using this information, we change the color of the background for the element that fired the `input` event. The color will be white for valid and red for invalid.

With that simple addition, now every time the user modifies the value of any element of the form, the element will be validated and its condition will be shown on the screen in real time.

Validity Constraints

In the example in Listing 5-35, we checked the **valid** state. This particular state is a property of the ValidityState object that will return the validity state of an element considering every other possible validity status. If every condition is valid then the **valid** property will return **true**.

There are eight validity statuses for different conditions:

valueMissing—This status is **true** when the **required** attribute was declared and the input field is empty.

typeMismatch—This status is **true** when the entry's syntax doesn't comply with the type specified—for example, if the text inserted for an **email** type input is not an email address.

patternMismatch—This status is **true** when the entry doesn't match the provided pattern.

tooLong—This status is **true** when the **maxlength** attribute was declared and the entry is longer than the value specified for the attribute.

rangeUnderflow—This status is **true** when the **min** attribute was declared and the entry is lower than the value specified for the attribute.

rangeOverflow—This status is **true** when the **max** attribute was declared and the entry is higher than the value specified for the attribute.

stepMismatch—This status is **true** when the **step** attribute was declared and its value doesn't correspond with the value of attributes such as **min**, **max** and **value**.

customError—This status is **true** when we set a custom error—for example, when we use the **setCustomValidity()** method studied earlier.

To access the ValidityState object and check for these validity statuses, we have to use the **validity** property in the syntax **element.validity.status** (where **status** is any of the values listed before). We can take advantage of these properties to know exactly what triggered the error on the form, as in the following example:

```
function sendit(){
  var elem = document.getElementById("nickname");
  var valid = form.checkValidity();
  if(valid){
    form.submit();
  }else if(elem.validity.patternMismatch || elem.validity.valueMissing){
    alert('nickname must have a minimum of 3 characters');
  }
}
```

Listing 5-36: *Using validity status to display a customized error message*

In Listing 5-36, the **sendit()** function is modified to include this kind of control. The form is validated by the **checkValidity()** method, and if it's valid, it is submitted with **submit()**. Otherwise, the validity statuses **patternMismatch** and **valueMissing** for the **nickname** input are checked and an error message is shown when one or both of them return **true**.

Review the Basics: The `if` statement can be concatenated using the `else` `if` construction (with a space in between). In the last example, if the first condition is false, then the `if` after `else` is evaluated. You can continue adding `if` indefinitely to check for more conditions if necessary.

Do It Yourself: Replace the `sendit()` function in the document from Listing 5-35 with the new function in Listing 5-36 and open the HTML file in your browser.

Forms and Forms API

Chapter 6
Video and Audio

6.1 Video with HTML5

One of the most discussed features of HTML5 was video processing. The excitement had nothing to do with the new tools provided by HTML5 for this purpose, but rather because video became the centerpiece of Internet, everybody expected native support from browsers. It was as though everyone knew the importance of videos except those developing technologies for the Web.

But now that we have native support—and even a standard that will let us build cross-browser applications for video processing—we realize that it was more complicated than we had imagined. From codecs to resource consumption issues, the reasons not to implement video before were far more complex than the codes necessary to do so.

Despite the complications, HTML5 finally introduced an element to insert and play video files in an HTML document. The **<video>** element uses opening and closing tags and just a few parameters to accomplish its function. The syntax is extremely simple and only the **src** attribute is mandatory.

```
<!DOCTYPE html>
<html lang="en">
<head>
  <title>Video Player</title>
</head>
<body>
  <section>
    <video src="http://minkbooks.com/content/trailer.mp4" controls>
    </video>
  </section>
</body>
</html>
```

Listing 6-1: *Using the* <video> *element*

In theory, the code in Listing 6-1 should be more than enough—in theory. But as we just described, things get a little more complicated in real life. First, we have to provide at least two files with different video formats. This is because even when the **<video>** element and its attributes are standard, there is no standard video format. The problem is that some browsers support a group of codecs that others don't (and the other way around), and the codec used in the MP4 format (the only one supported by important browsers such as Safari and Internet Explorer) has a commercial license.

The most common options nowadays are OGG and MP4, but WebM is trying to make its way and become standard. These formats are containers for video and audio. OGG contains Theora video and Vorbis audio codecs, MP4 contains H.264 for video and AAC for audio, and WebM uses VP8 video codec and Vorbis audio codec. Presently, OGG and WebM are supported by Mozilla Firefox, Google Chrome and Opera, while MP4 works on Safari, Internet Explorer and Google Chrome.

The <video> Element

Let's try to avoid those complications and enjoy the simplicity of the `<video>` element for a moment. This element has several attributes to set its properties and default configuration. The attributes `width` and `height`, like those for a traditional `<img>` element, declare the dimensions of the element or window's player in pixels. The size of the video will automatically be adjusted to fit into these dimensions, but they are not intended to compress or stretch the video. We may use them to limit the area occupied by the media and preserve consistency in our design. The attribute `src` specifies the source for the video. This attribute can be replaced by the `<source>` element and its own `src` attribute to declare several sources for different video formats.

```
<!DOCTYPE html>
<html lang="en">
<head>
  <title>Video Player</title>
</head>
<body>
  <section>
    <video width="720" height="400" controls>
      <source src="http://minkbooks.com/content/trailer.mp4">
      <source src="http://minkbooks.com/content/trailer.ogg">
    </video>
  </section>
</body>
</html>
```

Listing 6-2: Creating a cross-browser video player with default controls

In Listing 6-2, the `<video>` element is expanded. Now, within the element's tags, there are two `<source>` elements. These elements provide different video sources for the browser to choose from. The browser will read the `<source>` tags and decide which file should be played according to the supported formats (in this case, MP4 or OGG).

> **Do It Yourself:** Create a new empty HTML file with a name and the `.html` extension (e.g., `video.html`), copy the HTML document of Listing 6-2 into this file, and open the file in different browsers to see the `<video>` element at work.

> **IMPORTANT:** Browsers require videos to be sent by the server with the corresponding MIME type. Every file has a MIME type associated to indicate the format of its content. For instance, the MIME type for an HTML file is `text/html`. Servers are already configured for the most common video formats but usually are not for new formats such as OGG or WEBM. How to include this new MIME type depends on which kind of server you have. An easy way to do it is to append a new line to the `.htaccess` file. Most servers provide this configuration file in the root folder of every website. The

corresponding syntax is **Addtype MIME/type extension** (e.g., **AddType video/ogg ogg**).

Attributes for the <video> Element

There is an attribute in the **<video>** tag used in Listings 6-1 and 6-2 that probably caught your attention. The **controls** attribute is one of several specific attributes available for this element. This, in particular, shows video controls provided by browsers. Every browser will activate its own interface, allowing the user to start the video, pause it or jump to a specific frame, among other features.

Along with **controls**, you can also use the following:

autoplay—When this attribute is present, the browser will automatically play the video as soon as it can.

loop—If this attribute is specified, the browser will restart the video upon reaching the end.

poster—This attribute provides a URL of an image that will be shown while waiting for the video to be played.

preload—This attribute can take three values: **none**, **metadata** or **auto**. The first value indicates that the video shouldn't be cached, usually with the purpose of minimizing unnecessary traffic. The second value, **metadata**, will recommend the browser fetch some information about the resource—for example, dimensions, duration, first frame, etc. The third value, **auto**, is the value set by default and will prompt the browser to download the file as soon as possible.

```
<!DOCTYPE html>
<html lang="en">
<head>
  <title>Video Player</title>
</head>
<body>
  <section>
    <video width="720" height="400" preload controls loop
poster="http://minkbooks.com/content/poster.jpg">
      <source src="http://minkbooks.com/content/trailer.mp4">
      <source src="http://minkbooks.com/content/trailer.ogg">
    </video>
  </section>
</body>
</html>
```

Listing 6-3: Taking advantage of <video> *attributes*

The HTML document of Listing 6-3 preloads the right video for the browser, provides default controls, shows an image instead of the video until the video starts playing, and plays the video over and over again.

Video Formats

As we explained before, at present, there is no standard video and audio format for the Web. There are several containers and different codecs available, but none has been widely adopted, and there is no consensus among browser vendors to do so in the near future.

The most common containers are OGG, MP4, FLV and the newest, WEBM, proposed by Google.

- **OGG**—Theora video codec and Vorbis audio codec
- **MP4**—H.264 video codec and AAC audio codec
- **FLV**—VP6 video codec and MP3 audio codec; it also supports H.264 and AAC
- **WEBM**—VP8 video codec and Vorbis audio codec

The codecs used for OGG and WEBM are free, but the codecs used for MP4 and FLV are restricted by patents, which means if you want to use MP4 and FLV for your applications, you will have to pay to do so (some restrictions are revoked for free applications).

A large issue is that, currently, Safari and Internet Explorer do not support free technology and both work only with MP4. Internet Explorer has announced the inclusion of VP8 video codec in the future, though. Here is a list of the codecs browsers support:

- **Mozilla Firefox**—Theora video codec, VP8 video codec and Vorbis audio codec (OGG and WEBM).
- **Google Chrome**—Theora video codec, VP8 video codec and Vorbis audio codec. It also supports H.264 video codec and AAC audio codec (OGG, WEBM and MP4)
- **Opera**—Theora video codec, VP8 video codec and Vorbis audio codec (OGG and WEBM).
- **Safari**—H.264 video codec and AAC audio codec (MP4).
- **Internet Explorer**—H.264 video codec and AAC audio codec (MP4).

In the future, support for open formats such as WEBM will make things easier; but there probably won't be a standard format available for the next two or three years, and we will have to consider different alternatives according to the nature of our application and business.

6.2 Audio with HTML5

Audio is not as popular as video on the Web. We can shoot a video with a personal camera that will generate millions of views on websites such as www.youtube.com but accomplishing the same result with an audio file would be almost impossible. However, audio is still present, growing its market through radio shows and podcasts around the Web.

HTML5 provides a new element to play audio in an HTML document. The element, of course, is **<audio>**, and it shares almost the same characteristics of the **<video>** element.

```
<!DOCTYPE html>
<html lang="en">
<head>
  <title>Audio Player</title>
</head>
```

```
<body>
  <section id="player">
    <audio src="http://minkbooks.com/content/beach.mp3" controls>
    </audio>
  </section>
</body>
</html>
```

Listing 6-4: Using the <audio> element

The <audio> Element

The `<audio>` element works in the same way and shares several attributes with the `<video>` element:

> **src**—This attribute specifies the URL of the file to be played. As with the `<video>` element, `src` will usually be replaced by the `<source>` element to provide different audio formats for the browser to choose from.
>
> **controls**—This attribute activates the interface provided by default by every browser.
>
> **autoplay**—When this attribute is present, the browser will automatically play the audio as soon as it can.
>
> **loop**—If this attribute is specified, the browser will play the audio over and over again.
>
> **preload**—This attribute can take three values: `none`, `metadata` or `auto`. The first value indicates that the audio shouldn't be cached, usually with the goal of minimizing unnecessary traffic. The second value, `metadata`, will recommend the browser fetch some information about the resource (for example, duration). The third value, `auto`, is the value set by default and it prompts the browser to download the file as soon as possible.

Again, we have to talk about codecs, and again, the HTML code in Listing 6-4 should be more than enough, but it's not. MP3 is under commercial license; therefore, it is not supported by browsers such as Mozilla Firefox or Opera. Vorbis (the audio codec in the OGG container) is supported by these browsers but not by Safari and Internet Explorer. So, once again, we have to use the `<source>` element to provide at least two formats for the browser to choose from.

```
<!DOCTYPE html>
<html lang="en">
<head>
  <title>Audio Player</title>
</head>
<body>
  <section id="player">
    <audio id="media" controls>
      <source src="http://minkbooks.com/content/beach.mp3">
      <source src="http://minkbooks.com/content/beach.ogg">
    </audio>
```

```
    </section>
  </body>
</html>
```

Listing 6-5: Creating a cross-browser audio player with default controls

The document of Listing 6-5 plays music in every browser with controls by default. Those that can't play MP3 will play OGG and vice versa. Just remember that MP3, as well as MP4 for video, are restricted by commercial licenses, so we can only use them in specific circumstances according to what is determined by each license.

The support for free audio codecs (such as Vorbis) is expanding, but it will take time to turn an unknown format into a standard.

6.3 Closed Captioning

Closed captioning is a simple method to provide additional information and extend the scope of the media. This feature shows text on the screen while the media is being played. It has been used in television and different forms of video distribution for decades, but it has always been difficult to replicate on the Web. HTML5 has come to the rescue, incorporating a new element and a simple API for this purpose.

The <track> Element

The **<track>** element allows developers to incorporate closed captioning to web media. It works with both the **<video>** and the **<audio>** elements, and it accepts several file formats to show the information (although the specification declares the WebVTT as the official one). As a result of this new element, now, we are able to add subtitles or show additional information for our videos and audio tracks.

```
<!DOCTYPE html>
<html lang="en">
<head>
  <title>Video Subtitles</title>
</head>
<body>
  <section>
    <video width="720" height="400" controls>
      <source src="trailer.mp4">
      <source src="trailer.ogg">
      <track src="subtitles.vtt" srclang="en" default>
    </video>
  </section>
</body>
</html>
```

Listing 6-6: Adding subtitles with the <track> *element*

IMPORTANT: The **<track>** element does not allow the construction of cross-origin applications; therefore, you will have to upload all the files to your own server (using any FTP program such as FileZilla) and run everything under the same domain (including the HTML document, the videos and the subtitles). This situation can be avoided using the CORS technology and the `crossorigin` attribute explained in Chapter 10.

The `<track>` element has to be included as a child of the `<video>` or `<audio>` elements. To specify the source, type, and how the closed captioning is going to be shown on the screen, this element provides the following attributes:

src—This attribute declares the URL of the file containing the text for the closed captioning. The format of this file may be any of those supported by browsers (the specification declares the WebVTT format as the official for this element).

srclang—This attribute declares the human language of the text. It works with the same values as the `lang` attribute of the `<html>` element studied in Chapter 1.

default—Media can include several `<track>` elements for different purposes and languages. The `default` attribute declares which one is shown by default. If only one `<track>` element is provided, this attribute may be used to activate closed captioning.

label—This attribute provides a title for the track. In case multiple `<track>` elements are included, this attribute will help users to find the right one.

kind—This attribute declares the type of content for the track. The possible values are `subtitles` (for subtitles), `captions` (usually for captions representing sound), `descriptions` (intended for audio synthesis), `chapters` (for navigation between chapters) and `metadata` (for additional information, not shown on the screen). The value by default is `subtitles`.

In the example in Listing 6-6, we declared only one `<track>` element. The language for the source was set as English, and the `default` attribute was included to set this track as default and activate closed captioning. The source for this element was declared as a file in the WebVTT format (`subtitles.vtt`). WebVTT stands for Web Video Text Tracks. What WebVTT does is provide a standard format for closed captioning. The `.vtt` file is just a simple text file with a specific structure:

```
WEBVTT

00:02.000 --> 00:07.000
Welcome
to the &lt;track&gt; element!

00:10.000 --> 00:15.000
This is a simple example.

00:17.000 --> 00:22.000
Several tracks can be used simultaneously

00:22.000 --> 00:25.000
to provide text in different languages.

00:27.000 --> 00:30.000
Good bye!
```

Listing 6-7: WebVTT file

Listing 6-7 shows the basic structure of a WebVTT file. The first line with the text **WEBVTT** is mandatory as is the empty line in between declarations. These declarations are called **clues**, and they require the syntax **minutes:seconds.milliseconds** to indicate the start and the end times. This is a rigid format; we always have to respect the structure shown in the example in Listing 6-7 and declare each parameter with the same number of digits (two for minutes, two for seconds and three for milliseconds).

> **Do It Yourself:** Create an HTML file with the code in Listing 6-6. Using your text editor, create a WebVTT file with the declarations in Listing 6-7 and name it **subtitles.vtt**. Upload these files and the video files to your server (using any FTP program such as FileZilla), and open the HTML document in your browser. You can download our videos using the URLs from previous examples, use your own video, or get them from www.minkbooks.com/content/.

> **IMPORTANT:** WebVTT uses UTF-8 encoding. When you save the text file using an editor such as Notepad in Windows, select UTF-8 from the encoding options.

The cues (the lines of text in a closed captioning file) may include special tags, such as **<b>**, **<i>**, **<u>**, **<v>** and **<c>**. The first three, as in HTML, are for emphasis, while the **<v>** tag declares whose voice the text is representing and the **<c>** tag allows us to provide custom styles using CSS.

```
WEBVTT

00:02.000 --> 00:07.000
<i>Welcome</i>
to the &lt;track&gt; element!

00:10.000 --> 00:15.000
<v Robert>This is a simple <c.captions>example</c>.

00:17.000 --> 00:22.000
<v Martin>Several tracks can be used simultaneously

00:22.000 --> 00:25.000
<v Martin>to provide text in different languages.

00:27.000 --> 00:30.000
<b>Good bye!</b>
```

***Listing 6-8:** Including tags in a WebVTT file*

WebVTT uses a pseudo-element for referencing the cues. This element, called **::cue**, can take a selector for a specific class between parentheses. In the example in Listing 6-8, the class is called **captions** (**<c.captions>**), so the CSS selector should be written as **::cue(.captions)**, as in the following example:

```
::cue(.captions){
  color: #990000;
}
```

Listing 6-9: CSS for WebVTT

IMPORTANT: Only a reduced group of CSS properties, such as `color`, `background` and `font`, are available for this pseudo-class; the rest are ignored. At the writing of this book, the `<c>` tag has not yet been implemented in browsers. To check the current status of this specification and find updates for the previous examples, go to www.minkbooks.com/updates/.

WebVTT also provides the ability to align and position each cue using the following parameters and values:

align—This parameter aligns the cue in relation to the center of the space covered by the media. The possible values are `start`, `middle` and `end`.

vertical—This parameter changes the orientation to vertical and orders the cue according to two values: `rl` (right to left) or `lr` (left to right).

position—This parameter sets the position of the cue in columns. The value can be expressed as a percentage or a number from `0` to `9`. The position declared is according to the orientation.

line—This parameter sets the position of the cue in rows. The value can be expressed as a percentage or a number from `0` to `9`. In a horizontal orientation, the position declared is vertical, and vice versa. Positive numbers set the position from one side and negative numbers from the other, depending on the orientation.

size—This parameter sets the size of the cue. The value may be declared as percentage, and it represents the percentage of the width of the media.

These parameters and their corresponding values are declared at the end of the cue separated by a colon. Multiple declarations can be made for the same cue, as shown in the following example:

```
WEBVTT

00:02.000 --> 00:07.000 align:start position:5%
<i>Welcome</i>
to the &lt;track&gt; element!
```

Listing 6-10: Configuring cues

Do It Yourself: Using the WebVTT file created in Listing 6-7, try to combine different parameters in the same cues to see the effects available for this format.

6.4 Programming a Media Player

If you have tested the previous examples in different browsers, you will have noticed that the graphic design for the player's control panel differs in each case. Each browser has its own buttons and progress bars, and even its own features. This situation might be acceptable in some circumstances, but in a professional environment, where every detail counts, it's absolutely necessary to have control over the whole process and provide a consistent design across all devices and applications.

HTML5 provides new events, properties and methods to manipulate and integrate video and audio. From now on, we can create our own video or audio player and provide the features we want using HTML, CSS and Javascript. The media is now part of the document.

> **IMPORTANT:** The events, properties and methods of this API are the same for both video and audio. To apply the scripts studied next for audio, you just have to replace the `<video>` elements by `<audio>` elements in the HTML document and provide the corresponding audio files for the source.

Designing a Video Player

Every video player needs a control panel with some basic features. In the HTML document of Listing 6-11, following, a `<nav>` element will be added after `<video>` to contain two buttons, a slider and a progress bar.

```
<!DOCTYPE html>
<html lang="en">
<head>
  <title>Video Player</title>
  <link rel="stylesheet" href="player.css">
  <script src="player.js"></script>
</head>
<body>
  <section id="player">
    <video id="media" width="720" height="400">
      <source src="http://minkbooks.com/content/trailer.mp4">
      <source src="http://minkbooks.com/content/trailer.ogg">
    </video>
    <nav>
      <div id="buttons">
        <input type="button" id="play" value="Play">
        <input type="button" id="mute" value="Mute">
      </div>
      <div id="bar">
        <div id="progress"></div>
      </div>
      <div id="control">
        <input type="range" id="volume" min="0" max="1" step="0.1"
value="0.6">
      </div>
      <div class="clear"></div>
    </nav>
  </section>
```

```
</body>
</html>
```

Listing 6-11: *HTML document for our video player*

This document also includes resources from two external files. One of those files is **player.css** for the following CSS styles:

```css
body{
  text-align: center;
}
header, section, footer, aside, nav, article, figure, figcaption, hgroup{
  display: block;
}
#player{
  width: 720px;
  margin: 20px auto;
  padding: 10px 5px 5px 5px;
  background: #999999;
  border: 1px solid #666666;
  border-radius: 10px;
}
#play, #mute{
  padding: 2px 10px;
  width: 65px;
  border: 1px solid #000000;
  background: #DDDDDD;
  font-weight: bold;
  border-radius: 10px;
}
nav{
  margin: 5px 0px;
}
#buttons{
  float: left;
  width: 135px;
  height: 20px;
  padding-left: 5px;
}
#bar{
  float: left;
  width: 400px;
  height: 16px;
  padding: 2px;
  margin: 2px 5px;
  border: 1px solid #CCCCCC;
  background: #EEEEEE;
}
#progress{
  width: 0px;
  height: 16px;
  background: rgba(0,0,150,.2);
}
.clear{
  clear: both;
}
```

Listing 6-12: *CSS styles for the player*

The CSS code in Listing 6-12 uses techniques from the Traditional Box Model to create a box that contains every part of the video player. The box is centered in the window using this model. Notice that we also add an extra <div> at the end of the <nav> element to recover the normal flow of the document.

Figure 6-1: *Our video player at work*
© *Copyright 2008, Blender Foundation / www.bigbuckbunny.org*

There are no surprises in the last CSS code; it's just a group of properties (which we already studied) to provide basic styles to the elements. However, there is one property that could be considered unusual: the `width` for the <div> element, identified as `progress`, was initialized to 0. This is because we are going to use this element to simulate a progress bar that will grow while the video is being played.

> **Do It Yourself:** Copy the new document of Listing 6-11 into an empty file (e.g., `video.html`). Create two new empty files for the CSS styles and Javascript codes. These files should be named `player.css` and `player.js`, respectively. Copy the code in Listing 6-12 into the CSS file and then copy every Javascript code listed below into the Javascript file.

Application

There are different ways to program a video player. For the purpose of this book, we are going to present most of the components of this API but only teach you how to use the elemental methods and properties for video processing. We will work with a few simple functions to play the video, pause it, control the volume, show a progress bar while the video is being played, and give the option of clicking on this bar to move forward and backwards in the timeline.

Events

HTML5 incorporates new events that are API specific. For video and audio processing, events were incorporated to inform users about the current situation of the media—such as the progress downloading the file, whether the video has reached the end, or whether the video is paused or playing, among others. We are not going to use them for our example, but they are necessary to build more complex applications. Here are the most common:

progress—This event is fired periodically to provide updates about the progress in downloading the media. The information will be accessible through the `buffered` attribute, as we will see later.

canplaythrough—This event is fired when the entire media can be played without interruption. The status is established considering the current download rate and assuming that it will be the same for the rest of the process. There is another event for this purpose, `canplay`, but it doesn't consider the whole situation and it's fired when there are just a couple of frames available (see the example in Listing 11-8, Chapter 11).

ended—This event is fired when the media reaches the end.

pause—This event is fired when the media is paused.

play—This event is fired when the media starts playing.

error—This event is fired when an error occurs. It's delivered to the `<source>` element corresponding to the media source that produces the error.

Script

Let's start our script defining some variables and adding a few listeners for the events. We are going to declare the variables in the global space to be able to access them from every part of the code. Global variables are good for testing and didactic purposes, but in real applications, you should avoid them and follow the common practice of declaring a global object and then creating your application within this object (see Chapter 10, Listing 10-30 for an example).

```
var maxim, mmedia, play, bar, progress, mute, volume, loop;
function initiate(){
  maxim = 400;
  mmedia = document.getElementById('media');
  play = document.getElementById('play');
  bar = document.getElementById('bar');
  progress = document.getElementById('progress');
  mute = document.getElementById('mute');
  volume = document.getElementById('volume');

  play.addEventListener('click', push);
  mute.addEventListener('click', sound);
  bar.addEventListener('click', move);
  volume.addEventListener('change', level);
}
```

Listing 6-13: Initializing the application

Listing 6-13 introduces the first function for our video player. The function will run the application once the document is loaded. In this function we create a reference to every player's element using the selector `getElementById` and also set the variable `maxim` to always know the maximum size of the progress bar (400 pixels).

There are several actions we have to pay attention to for our player: when the user clicks on the "Play" and "Mute" buttons, changes the volume from the `range` input or clicks on the progress bar to go forward or backward in the timeline. For this purpose, listeners to the `click` event are added for the elements `play`, `mute` and `bar`, and one for the `change` event is added to the `range` input to control the volume. Every time the user clicks on one of these elements or move the slider, the correspondent listener functions are executed: `push()` for the "Play" button, `sound()` for the "Mute" button, `move()` for the progress bar, and `level()` for the `range` input.

Methods

The `push()` function incorporated in Listing 6-14 will be the first function that already performs an action. It will execute the special methods `play()` and `pause()` according to the situation.

```
function push(){
  if(!mmedia.paused && !mmedia.ended) {
    mmedia.pause();
    play.value = 'Play';
    clearInterval(loop);
  }else{
    mmedia.play();
    play.value = 'Pause';
    loop = setInterval(status, 1000);
  }
}
```

Listing 6-14: Playing and pausing the video

The methods `play()` and `pause()` are part of a list of methods incorporated by HTML5 for media processing. Here are the most common:

play()—This method plays the media.

pause()—This method pauses the media.

load()—This method loads the media file. It's useful for loading the media in advance for dynamic applications.

canPlayType(type)—With this method, we are able to know whether a file format is supported by the browser or not. The `type` attribute is a MIME type for the media, such as video/mp4 or video/ogg. The method can return three values depending on how confident it is that it can play the media: empty string (not supported), the string "maybe" and the string "probably".

Properties

The `push()` function also uses a few properties to retrieve information about the media. Here are the most common:

> **paused**—This property returns `true` if the media is currently paused or hasn't started playing.
>
> **ended**—This property returns `true` if the media has finished playing.
>
> **duration**—This property returns the duration of the media in seconds.
>
> **currentTime**—This is a property that can return and receive a value to inform the position in which the media is being played, or it sets a new position to start playing.
>
> **volume**—This property returns or sets the volume of the media. The possible values range from 0.0 to 1.0.
>
> **muted**—This property returns or sets the condition of the audio. The values are `true` (muted) or `false` (not muted).
>
> **error**—This property returns the error value if an error has occurred.
>
> **buffered**—This property offers information about how much of the file has loaded into the buffer. Because users may force the browser to download the media from different positions in the timeline, the information returned by `buffered` is an array containing every part of the media that was downloaded, not just the one that starts from the beginning. The elements of the array are accessible by the attributes `end()` and `start()`. For example, the code `buffered.start(0)` will return the time when the first portion of the media starts, and `buffered.end(0)` will return the time when it ends.

Code at Work

Now that we know all the elements involved in video processing, let's take a look at how the `push()` function works. The function is executed when the user clicks the "Play" button. This button has two purposes: it shows the text "Play" to play the video or "Pause" to pause it, according to the circumstances. So, when the video is paused or it hasn't started, pressing the button will play the video, but the opposite will occur if the video is already being played.

To accomplish this, the code detects the situation of the media checking the properties `paused` and `ended`. This is done by the `if` statement in the first line of the function. If the value of `mmedia.paused` and `mmedia.ended` is `false`, it means that the video is playing, then the `pause()` method is executed to pause the video and the text for the button is changed to "Play". Notice we apply the `!` operator to each property (logical NOT) to achieve this purpose. If the properties return `false`, the operator changes this value to `true`. The `if` statement should be read as "if the media is *not* paused and the media has *not* ended, then do this."

If the video is paused or has finished playing, the condition is `false` and the `play()` method is executed to start or resume the video. In this case, we are also performing an important action which is start the execution of the `status()` function each second with `setInterval()`.

```
function status(){
  if(!mmedia.ended){
    var size = parseInt(mmedia.currentTime * maxim / mmedia.duration);
    progress.style.width = size + 'px';
  }else{
    progress.style.width = '0px';
    play.innerHTML = 'Play';
    clearInterval(loop);
  }
}
```

Listing 6-15: Updating the progress bar

The **status()** function in Listing 6-15 is executed each second while the video is being played. We also have an **if** statement in this function to test the video status. If the property **ended** returns **false**, we calculate how long the progress bar should be in pixels and set the size of the **<div>** that is representing it. If the value of the property is **true** (which means the video has finished), we set the size of the progress bar back to **0** pixels, change the text for the button to "Play" and cancel the loop with **clearInterval()**. After doing this, the **status()** function will no longer be executed.

Let's go back to how we calculated the size of the progress bar. Because the **status()** function is executed each second while the video is being played, the current time changes constantly. For this reason, the **currentTime** property has to be consulted in each cycle. We also have to get the value of the **duration** property for the duration of the video, and the **maxim** variable for the maximum size of the progress bar. With those three values, we can calculate how many pixels long the bar should be to represent the seconds already played. The formula **current-time × maximum / total-duration** transforms the seconds into pixels to change the size of the **<div>** that represents the progress bar.

> **Review the Basics:** The method **parseInt()** is a native Javascript method that parses a string and returns an integer number. It is usually used to ensure we get a number when the source of information is not reliable, may have hidden characters, or we simply want to extract a number from a text. There is also another method for floating numbers called **parseFloat()**.

The function to handle the **click** event for the **play** element (the "Play" button) has already been created, now it's time to do the same for the progress bar.

```
function move(e){
  if(!mmedia.paused && !mmedia.ended){
    var mouseX = e.pageX - bar.offsetLeft;
    var newtime = mouseX * mmedia.duration / maxim;
    mmedia.currentTime = newtime;
    progress.style.width = mouseX + 'px';
  }
}
```

Listing 6-16: Playing from the position selected by the user

In the `initiate()` function, a listener for the `click` event was added to the `bar` element to check every time the user wants to start playing the video from a new position. When the event is fired, the `move()` function is executed to handle it. You can see this function in Listing 6-16. It starts with an `if` statement, like the previous functions, but this time the goal is to perform the action only when the video is being played. If the properties `paused` and `ended` are `false` it means that the video is playing and the code has to be executed.

We have to do several things to calculate the time when the video should start playing. We have to determine the position of the mouse pointer when the `click` event took place, the distance in pixels from that position to the beginning of the progress bar and how many seconds that distance represents in the timeline.

In the function in Listing 6-16, the reference to the event (`e`) is used along with the event property `pageX` to capture the exact position of the mouse pointer when the user clicked on the progress bar. This property returns a value in pixels relative to the page, not to the progress bar or the window. To know how many pixels there are from the beginning of the progress bar to the position of the mouse pointer, we have to subtract the space between the left side of the page and the beginning of the bar. Remember that the progress bar is located inside a box that is centered on the screen. So, let's say that the bar is located 421 pixels from the left side of the page, and the click was made in the middle of the bar. Because the bar is 400 pixels long, the click was made at 200 pixels. However, the property `pageX` won't return 200; it will return the value 621 (421 + 200). To get the exact position on the bar where the click was made, we have to subtract the distance from the left side of the page to the beginning of the bar (in this example, 421 pixels). This distance can be retrieved using the property `offsetLeft`. So, with the formula `e.pageX - bar.offsetLeft` we get the exact position of the mouse pointer relative to the bar. In this example, the end result will be 621 − 421 = 200.

Once we have this value, it has to be converted into seconds. Using the property `duration`, the exact position of the mouse pointer in the bar, and the maximum size of the bar, we build the formula `mouseX × video.duration / maxim` to get the value and store it in the variable `newtime`. The result is the time in seconds that the position of the mouse pointer represents in the timeline.

Now, we have to start playing the video from that new position. The property `currentTime`, as we mentioned before, returns the current time at which the video is being played, but it also moves the video to a specific time if a new value is assign to it. Assigning the value of the variable `newtime` to the `currentTime` property the video is moved to the desired position.

The last step is to change the size of the `progress` element to reflect the new situation on the screen. Using the value in the variable `mouseX`, we can modify the `width` style of the element to make it grow to the exact position where the click was made.

> **Review the Basics:** The `pageX` and `offsetLeft` properties applied in the last example are traditional Javascript properties. The first one, along with `pageY`, returns the position of the mouse pointer relative to the edge of the page, while `offsetLeft`, along with `offsetTop`, returns the position of the element relative to its container.

There are two small functions left we need to introduce to control the volume of the media. The first one is the `sound()` function, included to respond to the `click` event for the "Mute" button.

```
function sound(){
  if(mute.value == 'Mute'){
    mmedia.muted = true;
    mute.value = 'Sound';
  }else{
    mmedia.muted = false;
    mute.value = 'Mute';
  }
}
```

Listing 6-17: Switching to sound or silence with the muted property

The function in Listing 6-17 activates or deactivates the audio of the media depending on the value of the **value** attribute of the "Mute" button. The button will show different texts according to the situation. If the current value is "Mute," the sound is muted and the value of the button is changed to "Sound." Otherwise, the audio is activated and the value of the button is changed to "Mute."

When the sound is active, the volume can be controlled through the **range** input at the end of the progress bar. The element fires the **change** event when its value changes. The event is handles by the **level()** function.

```
function level(){
  mmedia.volume = volume.value;
}
```

Listing 6-18: Controlling the volume

The function in Listing 6-18 simply assigns the value of the **value** attribute of the **<input>** element to the **volume** property of the media. The only thing you have to keep in mind is that this property takes digital values from 0.0 to 1. Numbers out of that range will return an error.

With this small function, the source code for the video player is almost ready. We have all the events, methods, properties and functions we need for our application. There is only one more line, one more event that has to be listened to get this running.

```
addEventListener('load', initiate);
```

Listing 6-19: Listening to the load event to start the application

Do It Yourself: Copy all the Javascript codes since Listing 6-13 into the **player.js** file. Open the **video.html** file with the document of Listing 6-11 in the browser and click the "Play" button. Try the application in different browsers.

Chapter 7
TextTrack API

7.1 TextTrack API

As we mentioned in the previous chapter, HTML5 introduces not only the `<track>` element for closed captioning but also a new API to have access to the content of the tracks from Javascript.

The TextTrack API provides an object called TextTrack to access the content of a track. There are two ways to get this object: from the media or from the `<track>` element.

> **textTracks**—This property contains an array with the TextTrack objects corresponding to each track of the media. TextTrack objects are stored in the array in sequential order starting from index 0. The array, as any other array, provides the `length` property to get the number of objects available.
>
> **track**—This property returns the TextTrack object of the specified track.

If the media (video or audio) has several `<track>` elements, it may be easier to find the track we want accessing the `textTracks` array.

```
<!DOCTYPE html>
<html lang="en">
<head>
  <title>Working with Tracks</title>
  <script>
    function initiate(){
      var video = document.getElementById('media');
      var track1 = video.textTracks[0];
      var mytrack = document.getElementById('mytrack');
      var track2 = mytrack.track;
      console.log(track1);
      console.log(track2);
    }
    addEventListener("load", initiate);
  </script>
</head>
<body>
  <section>
    <video id="media" width="720" height="400" controls>
      <source src="trailer.mp4">
      <source src="trailer.ogg">
      <track id="mytrack" label="English Subtitles" src="subtitles.vtt"
srclang="en" default>
    </video>
```

```
    </section>
  </body>
</html>
```

Listing 7-1: Getting the TextTrack object

The document of Listing 7-1 shows how to access the TextTrack object using both properties. The `initiate()` function first creates a reference to the `<video>` element to get the TextTrack object of the track accessing the `textTracks` array with the index 0. Then, the same object is obtained from the `<track>` element using the `track` property. Finally, the content of both variables is printed in the console.

> **Do It Yourself:** Create a new HTML file with the document of Listing 7-1. You have to upload all the files to your server before testing.

Reading Tracks

Once we get the TextTrack object of the track we want to work with, we are able to access its properties:

kind—This property returns the type of the track, as specified by the `kind` attribute of the `<track>` element (`subtitles`, `captions`, `descriptions`, `chapters` and `metadata`).

label—This property returns the label of the track, as specified by the `label` attribute of the `<track>` element.

language—This property returns the language of the track, as specified by the `srclang` attribute of the `<track>` element.

mode—This property returns or sets the mode of the track. The three possible values are `disabled`, `hidden` and `showing`. It may be used to switch tracks.

cues—This property is an array containing all the cues from the track file.

activeCues—This property returns the cues currently shown on the screen (the previous, current and next cue).

```
<!DOCTYPE html>
<html lang="en">
<head>
  <title>Working with Tracks</title>
  <style>
    #player, #info{
      float: left;
    }
  </style>
  <script>
    function initiate(){
      var list = "";
      var info = document.getElementById('info');
      var mytrack = document.getElementById('mytrack');
      var obj = mytrack.track;
```

```
      list += "<br>Kind: " + obj.kind;
      list += "<br>Label: " + obj.label;
      list += "<br>Language: " + obj.language;
      info.innerHTML = list;
    }
    addEventListener('load', initiate);
  </script>
</head>
<body>
  <section id="player">
    <video id="media" width="720" height="400" controls>
      <source src="trailer.mp4">
      <source src="trailer.ogg">
      <track id="mytrack" label="English Subtitles" src="subtitles.vtt"
srclang="en" default>
    </video>
  </section>
  <aside id="info"></aside>
</body>
</html>
```

Listing 7-2: *Displaying the track's information on the screen*

The document of Listing 7-2 includes styles for the two columns created by the `<section>` and `<aside>` elements and Javascript code to get and show the data from the `<track>` element. As usual, we take advantage of the `load` event to call the `initiate()` function as soon as the document is loaded. In this function, we first define an empty variable (`list`) and get references to the `<aside>` element (`info`) and the `<track>` element (`mytrack`). Using the latter reference, the TextTrack object is retrieved by the `track` property and stored in the `obj` variable. From this variable we get the object's properties and generate the text to be shown on the screen. The text is finally inserted into the `<aside>` element using the `innerHTML` property.

> **Review the Basics:** The `+=` operator is a shorthand for the operation `variable = variable + value`, where `variable` is the variable that uses the operator and `value` is the new value assigned to the variable. The operator just appends the new value to the current variable's value.

Reading Cues

In addition to those applied in the last example, there is an important property called `clues`. This property contains an array with TextTrackCue objects representing each cue of the track file.

```
function initiate(){
  var list = "";
  var info = document.getElementById('info');
  var mytrack = document.getElementById('mytrack');
  var obj = mytrack.track;
  var mycues = obj.cues;
  for(var f = 0; f < mycues.length; f++){
    list += mycues[f].text + "<br>";
  }
```

```
info.innerHTML = list;
}
```

Listing 7-3: Displaying cues on the screen

The new `initiate()` function in Listing 7-3 stores the `cues` array in the `mycues` variable and then accesses every cue using a `for` loop. Because the array was created automatically, the first index is 0. For this reason, to read each one of the cues, the `f` variable in the loop starts at 0 (the initial value) and goes to the number of cues (returned by the `length` property of the array).

TextTrackCue objects provide properties to access the information of the cue. In our example, we showed the content of the `text` property. Here is a list of all the properties available:

text—This property returns the text of the cue.

startTime—This property returns the start time of the cue in seconds.

endTime—This property returns the end time of the cue in seconds.

vertical—This property returns the value of the `vertical` parameter. If the parameter was not defined, the value returned is an empty string.

line—This property returns the value of the `line` parameter. If the parameter was not defined, the default value is returned.

position—This property returns the value of the `position` parameter. If the parameter was not defined, the default value is returned.

size—This property returns the value of the `size` parameter. If the parameter was not defined, the default value is returned.

align—This property returns the value of the `align` parameter. If the parameter was not defined, the default value is returned.

Do It Yourself: Copy the code in Listing 7-2 into an empty HTML file and open the file in your browser. To work with cues, replace the `initiate()` function in Listing 7-2 by the one in Listing 7-3.

Adding New Tracks

The TextTrack object obtained from the tracks not only has properties but also has three important methods to create new tracks and cues from Javascript:

addTextTrack(kind, label, language)—This method creates a new track for the specified media and returns the corresponding TextTrack object. It's useful for creating new tracks programmatically from scratch. The attributes are the values of the attributes for the new track (only `kind` is mandatory).

addCue(object)—This method adds a new cue to the specified track. The `object` attribute is a TextTrackCue object returned by the `TextTrackCue()` constructor.

removeCue(object)— This method removes a cue from the specified track. The `object` attribute is a TextTrackCue object returned by the TextTrack object.

To add cues to the track, we have to provide a TextTrackCue object. The API includes a constructor to create this object from the information of the cue:

TextTrackCue(startTime, endTime, text)—This constructor returns a TextTrackCue object to use with the `addCue()` method. The attributes represent the data for the cue: start time, end time and the text for the caption.

```
<!DOCTYPE html>
<html lang="en">
<head>
  <title>Working with Tracks</title>
  <script>
    function initiate(){
      var cue;
      var cues = [
        { start: 2.000, end: 7.000, text: 'Welcome'},
        { start: 10.000, end: 15.000, text: 'This is an example'},
        { start: 15.001, end: 20.000, text: 'of how to add'},
        { start: 20.001, end: 25.000, text: 'a new track.'},
        { start: 27.000, end: 30.000, text: 'Good bye!'},
      ]
      var video = document.getElementById('media');
      var newtrack = video.addTextTrack('subtitles');
      newtrack.mode = 'showing';
      for(var f = 0; f < cues.length; f++){
        cue = new TextTrackCue(cues[f].start, cues[f].end, cues[f].text);
        newtrack.addCue(cue);
      }
      video.play();
    }
    addEventListener('load', initiate);
  </script>
</head>
<body>
  <section>
    <video id="media" width="720" height="400" controls>
      <source src="trailer.mp4">
      <source src="trailer.ogg">
    </video>
  </section>
</body>
</html>
```

Listing 7-4: Adding tracks and cues from Javascript

We start the `initiate()` function in Listing 7-4 by defining the `cues` array with five cues for our new track. The cues are declared as elements of the array. Each cue is an object with the properties `start`, `end` and `text`. The values for the start and end times don't use the syntax of a WebVTT file; they have to be declared in seconds as decimal numbers.

The cues may be added to an existing track or a new one. In our example, we create a new track as `subtitles` using the `addTextTrack()` method. We also have to declare the `mode` of this track as `showing`, to order the browser to show the track on the screen. When the track is ready, all the cues from the `cues` array are converted into TextTrackCue objects and added to the track using the `addCue()` method. Finally, the video is played with the `play()` method studied in Chapter 6.

> **Do It Yourself:** Copy the document of Listing 7-4 into an empty HTML file and open the file in your browser. Remember to upload the files to your server.

> **IMPORTANT:** At the time of writing, the methods and properties declared by the specification to select and activate tracks were not implemented yet in browsers. For more information and updates on this subject please visit our website.

Chapter 8
Fullscreen API

8.1 No More Windows

When developers say that the Web is changing, it is true. It is greatly advanced from those over hyperlinked-framed web pages with small icons and ugly scroll bars everywhere. Now the Web is a multipurpose and multimedia platform where everything is possible. From social media to a massive storage space, the Web is involved in every aspect of people's lives; for work to entertainment, all our needs are being addressed. In the Web's progression, the browser is becoming irrelevant, like a new form of operating system, in charge of everything but hidden in the background, almost barely noticed. Menus have been omitted and options minimized. Currently, browsers' windows only have a navigation bar to indicate where we want to go. With so many absorbing new applications and the adoption of independent mobile apps, the word *navigation* has almost lost significance. The browser window is not only unnecessary but can sometimes get in the way. For this reason, HTML5 introduces the Fullscreen API.

Going Fullscreen

The Fullscreen API is a multipurpose API that allows us to expand any element in the document to occupy the entire screen. As a result of this new feature, a browser's interface is hidden in the background, focusing user's attention to our videos, pictures, applications, video games, etc.

The API provides a few properties, methods and events to make an element full screen, exit the full screen mode or even retrieve some information from the element and the document:

> **requestFullscreen()**—This method applies to every element in the document. It activates full screen mode for the element.
>
> **exitFullscreen()**—This method applies to the document. If an element is in full screen mode the method cancels the mode and returns the focus back to the browser window.
>
> **fullscreenElement**—This property returns a reference to the element that is in full screen mode. If no element is in full screen, the property returns `null`.
>
> **fullscreenEnabled**—This Boolean property returns `true` when the document is able to go full screen or `false` otherwise.
>
> **fullscreenchange**—This event is fired by the document when an element enters or exits the full screen mode.
>
> **fullscreenerror**—This event is fired by the element in case of failure (the full screen mode is not available for that element or for the document). No data are returned by this event.

The `requestFullscreen()` method and the `fullscreenerror` event are associated with the elements in the document, but the rest of the properties, methods and events are part of the Document object, therefore, they are accessible from the `document` property.

```
<!DOCTYPE html>
<html lang="en">
<head>
  <title>Full Screen</title>
  <script>
    var video;
    function initiate(){
      video = document.getElementById('media');
      video.addEventListener('click', gofullscreen);
    }
    function gofullscreen(){
      if(!document.webkitfullscreenElement){
        video.webkitRequestFullscreen();
        video.play();
      }
    }
    addEventListener('load', initiate);
  </script>
</head>
<body>
  <section>
    <video id="media" width="720" height="400">
      <source src="http://minkbooks.com/content/trailer.mp4">
      <source src="http://minkbooks.com/content/trailer.ogg">
    </video>
  </section>
</body>
</html>
```

Listing 8-1: *Taking a <video> element full screen*

The `initiate()` function in Listing 8-1 adds a listener to the `click` event for the `<video>` element. The `gofullscreen()` function, set as the listener for this event, is executed every time the user clicks on the video. In this function, we use the `fullscreenElement` property to detect whether an element is already in full screen mode or not, and if not, the video is made full screen by the `requestFullscreen()` method. At the same time, the video is played applying the `play()` method.

> **IMPORTANT:** This is an experimental API. The properties, methods and events have been prefixed by browsers until the final specification is implemented. Google Chrome and Mozilla Firefox are presently the browsers that have a working implementation of the Fullscreen API. In the case of Google Chrome, instead of the original names we have to use `webkitRequestFullscreen()`, `webkitExitFullscreen()`, `webkitfull-screenchange`, `webkitfullscreenerror` and `webkitFullscreenElement`. For Mozilla Firefox, the names are `mozRequestFullScreen()`, `mozCancelFull-Screen()`, `mozfullscreenchange`, `mozfullscreenerror` and `mozFullScreen-Element`. This situation may change after publication, so please visit our website for updates.

Fullscreen Styles

Browsers adjust the dimensions of the `<video>` element to the size of the screen automatically, but for any other element, the original dimensions are preserved and the free space on the screen is filled with a black background. For this reason, the specification provides a new pseudo-class called `:full-screen` to modify the styles of the element when it expands to full screen.

> **IMPORTANT:** The last specification declares the name of this pseudo-class without the hyphen (`:fullscreen`), but, at the time of writing, browsers such as Mozilla Firefox and Google Chrome have only implemented the previous specification and work with the name mentioned in this chapter (`:full-screen`). Please visit our website for updates.

```html
<!DOCTYPE html>
<html lang="en">
<head>
  <title>Full Screen</title>
  <style>
    #player:-webkit-full-screen, #player:-webkit-full-screen #media{
      width: 100%;
      height: 100%;
    }
  </style>
  <script>
    var video, player;
    function initiate(){
      video = document.getElementById('media');
      player = document.getElementById('player');
      player.addEventListener('click', gofullscreen);
    }
    function gofullscreen(){
      if(!document.webkitFullscreenElement){
        player.webkitRequestFullscreen();
        video.play();
      }else{
        document.webkitExitFullscreen();
        video.pause();
      }
    }
    addEventListener('load', initiate);
  </script>
</head>
<body>
  <section id="player">
    <video id="media" width="720" height="400">
      <source src="http://minkbooks.com/content/trailer.mp4">
      <source src="http://minkbooks.com/content/trailer.ogg">
    </video>
  </section>
</body>
</html>
```

***Listing 8-2:** Taking any element full screen*

In Listing 8-2, we take the `<section>` element and its content full screen. The `gofullscreen()` function is modified to be able to activate and deactivate the full screen mode for this element. As in the previous example, the video is played when it is in full screen mode, but now it will be paused when the mode is canceled.

These improvements are insufficient to really make our player full screen. In full screen mode, the new container for the elements is the screen, but the original dimensions and styles for the `<section>` and `<video>` elements are preserved intact. Using the `:full-screen` pseudo-class we change the values of the `width` and `height` properties of these elements to 100%, matching the dimensions of the container. Now the elements occupy the whole screen and truly reflect the full screen mode.

> **Do It Yourself:** Create a new HTML file to test the examples in this Chapter. Once the document is opened in the browser, click on the video to activate the full screen mode.

Chapter 9
Stream API

9.1 Capturing Media

The Stream API allows us to access media streams provided by the device. The most common stream sources are the webcam and the microphone, but the API lets us access any other source that produces an audio or video stream.

The API specifies the MediaStream object to reference the media streams and the LocalMediaStream object for media generated by local devices. These objects have an input represented by the device and an output represented by the `<video>` element, the `<audio>` element and also other APIs.

To get the LocalMediaStream object, the API provides the `getUserMedia()` method:

getUserMedia(constraints, success, error)—This method belongs to the navigator object. It generates a LocalMediaStream object. The first attribute is an object with two Boolean properties `video` or `audio` to indicate the type of media to be captured; the second attribute is a function that will receive and process the LocalMediaStream object; and the last attribute is another function to process errors.

The LocalMediaStream object is referencing media streams, but it is not suitable as the source for media elements. To turn this object into an appropriate source for the `<video>` and `<audio>` elements, we have to convert it into an URL. Javascript offers two general methods to get and work with URLs:

createObjectURL(data)—This method belongs to the URL object. It returns an URL that we can use later to reference the data. The `data` attribute may be a file, a blob or, in the case of this API, a MediaStream object.

revokeObjectURL(URL)—This method belongs to the URL object. It deletes an URL created by `createObjectURL()`. It is useful to avoid the use of old URLs by external scripts or by accident from our own code.

Accessing the Webcam

Let's see an example of how to access the webcam and show the stream on the screen.

```
<!DOCTYPE html>
<html lang="en">
```

```
<head>
  <title>Stream API</title>
  <script>
    function initiate(){
      navigator.webkitGetUserMedia({video: true}, success, showerror);
    }
    function success(stream){
      var video = document.getElementById("media");
      video.setAttribute('src', URL.createObjectURL(stream));
      video.play();
    }
    function showerror(e){
      console.log(e.code);
    }
    addEventListener('load', initiate);
  </script>
</head>
<body>
  <section>
    <video id="media"></video>
  </section>
</body>
</html>
```

Listing 9-1: Accessing the webcam

The **initiate()** function in the script in Listing 9-1 gets the media from the webcam using the **getUserMedia()** method. This will prompt a request for the user in the browser window. If the user allows our application to access the webcam, then the **success()** function is executed. This function receives the LocalMediaStream object and stores it in the **stream** variable. Using the **createObjectURL()** method we get the URL representing the stream. The URL is assigned to the **src** attribute of the **<video>** element, and the video is played with the **play()** method studied in Chapter 6 (the **autoplay** attribute may be used instead).

Notice that we didn't have to declare the **src** attribute in the **<video>** tag because the source will be the media stream captured by the Javascript code, but we could have set the **width** and **height** attributes if we wanted to change the size of the video on the screen.

In case of failure, the API returns different types of errors depending on the implementation. The most common is PERMISSION_DENIED, produced when the user denies access to the media or the media is not available for other reasons. When this happens, the **error** property returns the value **1**.

> **IMPORTANT:** The examples in this chapter use the Google Chrome prefixed method **webkitGetUserMedia()**. At the moment, some browsers, such as Opera, have an implementation without prefixes, but others haven't implemented the method at all. We recommend you use the latest version of Google Chrome to test this and the following codes.

> **Review the Basics:** The navigator object is a traditional object that offers methods and properties to access the browser. We are only going to use the object to apply the new methods incorporated by HTML5. For more information on old methods and properties, visit our website and follow the links for this chapter.

MediaStreamTrack objects

MediaStream objects (and therefore LocalMediaStream objects) contain MediaStreamTrack objects that represent each media track (usually one for video and another for audio). These objects are stored in arrays accessible by the properties `videoTracks` and `audioTracks` and provide the following properties:

enabled—This property returns `true` or `false` according to the track's condition. If the track is still associated with the source, the value is `true`.

kind—This property returns the type of source the track represents. It has two possible values: `audio` or `video`.

label—This property returns the name of the source for the track.

```html
<!DOCTYPE html>
<html lang="en">
<head>
  <title>Stream API</title>
  <style>
    section{
      float: left;
    }
  </style>
  <script>
    function initiate(){
      navigator.webkitGetUserMedia({video: true}, success, showerror);
    }
    function success(stream){
      var video = document.getElementById("video");
      video.setAttribute('src', URL.createObjectURL(stream));
      video.play();

      var databox = document.getElementById('databox');
      var track = stream.videoTracks[0];
      databox.innerHTML = '<br> Enabled: ' + track.enabled;
      databox.innerHTML += '<br> Type: ' + track.kind;
      databox.innerHTML += '<br> Device: ' + track.label;
    }
    function showerror(e){
      console.log(e.code);
    }
    addEventListener('load', initiate);
  </script>
</head>
<body>
  <section>
    <video id="video"></video>
  </section>
  <section id="databox"></section>
</body>
</html>
```

Listing 9-2: *Showing stream's information*

The **videoTracks** and **audioTracks** properties are arrays. To access the track generated by the webcam, we have to read the **videoTracks** array with the index 0 (the first track on the list). In case multiple tracks were added to the object, the **length** property may be consulted to get the total number and create a **for** loop to access each one of them.

In the document of Listing 9-2, we use the same code from the previous example to access the stream, but this time the track for the webcam is stored in the **track** variable and then every one of its properties is shown on the screen.

> **IMPORTANT:** The tracks mentioned here are video or audio tracks. These types of tracks have nothing to do with the closed captioning tracks studied in Chapter 6 and 7.

MediaStreamTrack objects also offer events to report the state of the track:

> **muted**—This event is fired when the track is unable to provide data.
>
> **unmuted**—This event is fired as soon as the track starts providing data again.
>
> **ended**—This event is fired when the track can no longer provide data. There may be several reasons for this, from the user denying access to the stream to the use of the **stop()** method, studied next.

These events are meant to be used to control remote streaming, a process studied in Chapter 24.

Stop() Method

A LocalMediaStream object has the **stop()** method to manually stop the stream. Here is an example:

```
<!DOCTYPE html>
<html lang="en">
<head>
  <title>Stream API</title>
  <script>
    function initiate(){
      navigator.webkitGetUserMedia({video: true}, success, showerror);
    }
    function success(stream){
      var button = document.getElementById("button");
      button.addEventListener('click', function(){ stopstream(stream) });
      var video = document.getElementById("video");
      video.setAttribute('src', URL.createObjectURL(stream));
      video.play();
    }
    function showerror(e){
      console.log(e.code);
    }
    function stopstream(stream){
      stream.stop();
      alert('Stream Canceled');
    }
    addEventListener('load', initiate);
  </script>
```

```
</head>
<body>
  <section>
    <video id="video"></video>
  </section>
  <nav>
    <input type="button" id="button" value="Turn Off">
  </nav>
</body>
</html>
```

Listing 9-3: Canceling the stream

In Listing 9-3, we include a button to turn off the camera. The `stopstream()` function is assigned to handle the `click` event for this button. In this function, the `stop()` method is called to stop the stream (the camera is turned off), and the message "Stream Canceled" is shown on the screen.

> **Do It Yourself:** Try to apply to the `<video>` element in any of the examples above the CSS `filter` property with the methods studied in Chapter 3 to get some interesting effects (e.g., `filter: grayscale(1);`).

> **Review the Basics:** The functions declared as attributes for the `getUserMedia()` method, `success()` and `showerror()`, are called **callback functions**. In Javascript, callback functions are widely used to process the result produced by the primary function or method. In this case, the `success()` function receives an object representing the media stream, and the `showerror()` function receives an event with properties whose values correspond to the error generated by the process. Callback functions are part of almost every Javascript API. Don't worry if you don't grasp this concept immediately, after working more with this kind of pattern, it will become familiar.

Stream API

Chapter 10
Canvas API

10.1 Graphics for the Web

At the beginning of the book, we discussed how HTML5 is replacing previous plug-ins, such as Flash or Java applets, for example. There were at least two important things to consider in making the Web independent of third-party technologies: video processing and graphic applications. The **<video>** element and the APIs studied in previous chapters cover the first aspect very well, but they do not deal with graphics. For this purpose, HTML5 introduces the Canvas API. This API handles the graphic aspect and does it in an extremely efficient way. Canvas lets you draw, render graphics, animate, and process images and text, and it works along with the rest of the APIs to create full applications and even 2D and 3D video games for the Web.

The <canvas> Element

The **<canvas>** element generates an empty rectangular space on the web page in which the results of the methods provided by the API will be shown. It produces a white space, like an empty **<div>** element, but for an entirely different purpose.

```
<!DOCTYPE html>
<html lang="en">
<head>
  <title>Canvas API</title>
  <script src="canvas.js"></script>
</head>
<body>
  <section id="canvasbox">
    <canvas id="canvas" width="500" height="300"></canvas>
  </section>
</body>
</html>
```

Listing 10-1: Using the <canvas> element

There are only a few attributes we need to provide for this element, as you can see in Listing 10-1. The **width** and **height** attributes declare the size of the box. These are necessary because everything rendered over the element will have these values for reference.

This is basically the purpose of the **<canvas>** element: it creates an empty box on the screen. It is only through Javascript and the new methods and properties introduced by the API that this surface becomes a practical feature.

IMPORTANT: For compatibility purposes, in case the Canvas API is not available in the browser, the content between <canvas> tags is shown on the screen.

GetContext()

The getContext() method is the first method we have to call for the <canvas> element to be ready to work. It generates a drawing context that will be assigned to the canvas. Through its reference we will be able to apply the rest of the API.

```
function initiate(){
  var elem = document.getElementById('canvas');
  var canvas = elem.getContext('2d');
}
addEventListener("load", initiate);
```

Listing 10-2: Creating the drawing context for the canvas

In Listing 10-2, a reference to the <canvas> element is stored into the elem variable, and the context is created by getContext('2d'). The method can take two values: 2d and webgl. These are for a two-dimensional and three-dimensional environment, respectively. Currently, 2d is available in every HTML5 compatible browser, while webgl is only applicable in browsers that have implemented and enabled the use of the WebGL library for the generation of 3D graphics. We will study WebGL in the next chapter.

The 2D canvas drawing context will be a grid of pixels listed in rows and columns from top to bottom and left to right, with its origin (the pixel 0, 0) located at the top-left corner of the square.

Do It Yourself: Copy the HTML document of Listing 10-1 into a new empty file. Also, create a file named canvas.js and copy every script presented from Listing 10-2 into this file. Each example in this chapter is independent and replaces the previous one.

10.2 Drawing on Canvas

After the <canvas> element and its context are ready, we can finally start creating and manipulating actual graphics. The list of tools provided by this API for this purpose is extensive, allowing the generation of multiple effects, from the creation of simple shapes and draws to text, shadows or complex transformations. In this section of the chapter, we will study these methods one by one.

Drawing Rectangles

Usually the developer must prepare the figure to be drawn before sending it to the context (as we will see soon), but there are a few methods that let us draw directly on the canvas. These methods are specific for rectangular shapes, and they are the only ones that generate a primitive shape. (To get other shapes, we will have to combine other drawing techniques and complex paths.) The methods available are the following:

fillRect(x, y, width, height)—This method draws a solid rectangle. The top-left corner will be located at the position specified by the **x** and **y** attributes. The **width** and **height** attributes declare the size of the rectangle.

strokeRect(x, y, width, height)—Similar to the previous method, this will draw an empty rectangle—in other words, just the outline.

clearRect(x, y, width, height)—This method is used to subtract pixels from the area specified by its attributes. It's like a rectangular eraser.

```
function initiate(){
  var elem = document.getElementById('canvas');
  var canvas = elem.getContext('2d');

  canvas.strokeRect(100, 100, 120, 120);
  canvas.fillRect(110, 110, 100, 100);
  canvas.clearRect(120, 120, 80, 80);
}
addEventListener("load", initiate);
```

Listing 10-3: Drawing rectangles

This is the same function as the one in Listing 10-2 but with a new few methods that will actually draw something on the canvas. As you can see, the context is assigned to the variable **canvas**, and now this variable is used for referencing the context in every method.

The first method, **strokeRect(100, 100, 120, 120)**, draws an empty rectangle with the top-left corner at the position 100, 100 and a size of 120 pixels. The second method, **fillRect(110, 110, 100, 100)**, draws a solid rectangle, this time starting from the position 110, 110 of the canvas. And finally, with the last method, **clearRect(120, 120, 80, 80)**, a square space of 80 pixels is removed from the middle of the previous rectangle.

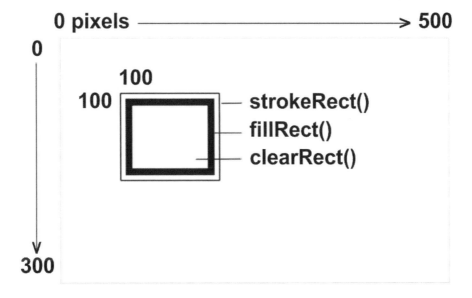

Figure 10-1: Canvas representation and rectangles drawn by the code in Listing 10-3

Figure 10-1 is just a representation of what you will see after the execution of the code in Listing 10-3. The `<canvas>` element is rendered as a grid with its origin at the top-left corner and the size specified in its attributes. The rectangles are drawn on the canvas at the position declared by the attributes **x** and **y** and one on top of another according to the order in the source code. (The first to appear in the source code will be drawn first; the second will be drawn on top of the first; and so on.) There is a method for customizing how the shapes are drawn, but we will see that later.

Colors

So far we have been using the default color: black. We can specify the color we want using CSS syntax and the following properties:

> **strokeStyle**—This property declares the color of the lines of the shape.
>
> **fillStyle**—This property declares the color of the interior of the shape.
>
> **globalAlpha**—This property is not for color but for transparency. It sets the transparency for all the shapes drawn on the canvas.

```
function initiate(){
  var elem = document.getElementById('canvas');
  var canvas = elem.getContext('2d');

  canvas.fillStyle = "#000099";
  canvas.strokeStyle = "#990000";

  canvas.strokeRect(100, 100, 120, 120);
  canvas.fillRect(110, 110, 100, 100);
  canvas.clearRect(120, 120, 80, 80);
}
addEventListener("load", initiate);
```

Listing 10-4: Adding color

The colors in Listing 10-4 are declared using hexadecimal numbers. We can also use functions such as `rgb()` or even specify transparency for the shape by taking advantage of the `rgba()` function. The value for these methods always has to be in quotes—for example, `strokeStyle = "rgba(255, 165, 0, 1)"`.

When a color is specified using these methods, it becomes the default color for the rest of the drawings.

Even when it is possible to use the `rgba()` function, another property can be used to set the level of transparency: `globalAlpha`. Its syntax is `globalAlpha = value`, where `value` is a number between 0.0 (fully opaque) and 1.0 (fully transparent).

Gradients

Gradients are an essential part of every drawing program today, and the Canvas API is no exception. As in CSS3, the gradients on the canvas may be linear or radial, and we can provide stop points to combine colors.

createLinearGradient(x1, y1, x2, y2)—This creates a linear gradient object to apply to the canvas.

createRadialGradient(x1, y1, r1, x2, y2, r2)—This creates a radial gradient object to apply to the canvas using two circles. The values represent the position of the center of each circle and its radius.

addColorStop(position, color)—This specifies the colors to create the gradient. The position is a value between 0.0 and 1.0 to determine where the degradation will start for that particular color.

```
function initiate(){
  var elem = document.getElementById('canvas');
  var canvas = elem.getContext('2d');

  var grad = canvas.createLinearGradient(0, 0, 10, 100);
  grad.addColorStop(0.5, '#00AAFF');
  grad.addColorStop(1, '#000000');
  canvas.fillStyle = grad;

  canvas.fillRect(10, 10, 100, 100);
  canvas.fillRect(150, 10, 200, 100);
}
addEventListener("load", initiate);
```

Listing 10-5: Applying a linear gradient to the canvas

In Listing 10-5, we create the gradient object from the position `0, 0` to `10, 100`, providing a slight angle to the left. The colors are set by the `addColorStop()` methods, and the final gradient is applied to the `fillStyle` property, like a regular color.

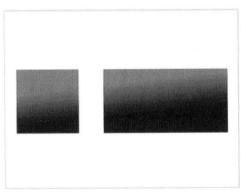

Figure 10-2: Linear gradient for the canvas

Notice that the gradient positions are relative to the canvas, not to the shapes we want to affect. The result is that, if you move the rectangles to a new position on the screen, the gradient for these rectangles will change.

> **Do It Yourself:** The radial gradient is similar to CSS3. Try to replace the linear gradient in the code in Listing 10-5 by a radial gradient using an expression such as `createRadialGradient(0, 0, 30, 0, 0, 300)`. You can also experiment with the location of the rectangles to see how the gradient is applied.

Creating Paths

The methods studied so far draw directly on the canvas, but that's not always the case. Usually we will have to process shapes and images in the background, and once that is done, the result is sent to the context and is drawn. For this purpose, the Canvas API introduces several methods to generate paths.

A path is like a blueprint for a pen to follow. Once we set a path, it is sent to the context and drawn permanently on the canvas. The path may include different kinds of strokes, such as straight lines, arcs, rectangles and others, to create complex shapes.

There are two methods to start and close a path:

beginPath()—This method begins a new shape description.

closePath()—This method closes the path, generating a straight line from the last point to the point of origin. It can be omitted when you want an open path or when you use the `fill()` method to draw the path.

We also have three methods to draw the path on the canvas:

stroke()—This method draws the path as an outlined shape.

fill()—This method draws the path as a solid shape. When you use this method you don't need to close the path with `closePath()`; it is automatically closed with a straight line from the last point to the first one.

clip()—This sets a new clipping area for the context. When the context is initialized, the clipping area is the entire area occupied by the canvas. The `clip()` method will change the clipping area to a new shape thus creating a mask. Everything that falls outside that mask won't be drawn.

```
function initiate(){
  var elem = document.getElementById('canvas');
  var canvas = elem.getContext('2d');

  canvas.beginPath();
  // here goes the path
  canvas.stroke();
}
addEventListener("load", initiate);
```

Listing 10-6: *Starting and ending a path*

Review the Basics: Comments may be inserted into the Javascript code using two slashes for single-line comments (`// comment`) and combining a slash and a star character for multi-line comments (`/* comments */`).

The code in Listing 10-6 does not create anything, it starts the path for the canvas context and draws it with `stroke()`. To set the path and create the real shape, we have several methods available:

moveTo(x, y)—This moves the pen to a specific position. It lets us start or continue the path from different points on the grid, avoiding continuous lines.

lineTo(x, y)—This generates a straight line from the pen's current position to a new one declared by the **x** and **y** attributes.

rect(x, y, width, height)—This generates a rectangle. Unlike the methods studied before, this will generate a rectangle that is part of the path (not directly drawn on the canvas). The attributes have the same functions as previous methods.

arc(x, y, radius, startAngle, endAngle, direction)—This method generates an arc or a circle with the center at the coordinates indicated by **x** and **y** and with the radius and angles declared by the rest of the attributes. The last value has to be declared as `true` or `false` for the direction (clockwise or counterclockwise, respectively).

quadraticCurveTo(cpx, cpy, x, y)—This method generates a quadratic Bézier curve starting from the current position of the pen and ending at the position declared by the **x** and **y** attributes. The **cpx** and **cpy** attributes are a control point that shapes the curve.

bezierCurveTo(cp1x, cp1y, cp2x, cp2y, x, y)—This is similar to the previous method but adds two more attributes to generate a cubic Bézier curve. Now we have two control points in the grid declared by the values **cp1x**, **cp1y**, **cp2x** and **cp2y** to shape the curve.

Let's examine a simple path to understand how they work.

```
function initiate(){
  var elem = document.getElementById('canvas');
  var canvas = elem.getContext('2d');

  canvas.beginPath();
  canvas.moveTo(100, 100);
  canvas.lineTo(200, 200);
  canvas.lineTo(100, 200);
  canvas.stroke();
}
addEventListener("load", initiate);
```

Listing 10-7: Creating a path

It is always recommended to set the initial position of the pen immediately after starting the path. In the script in Listing 10-7, we first move the pen to the position 100, 100 and then generate a line from this point to 200, 200. The position of the pen is now 200, 200, and the next line is drawn from here to the point 100, 200. Finally, the path is drawn as an outline shape by the `stroke()` method.

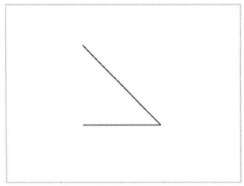

Figure 10-3: Opened path

Figure 10-3 shows a representation of the open triangle produced by the script in Listing 10-7. This triangle may be closed or even filled using different methods, as shown in the following examples:

```
function initiate(){
  var elem = document.getElementById('canvas');
  var canvas = elem.getContext('2d');

  canvas.beginPath();
  canvas.moveTo(100, 100);
  canvas.lineTo(200, 200);
  canvas.lineTo(100, 200);
  canvas.closePath();
  canvas.stroke();
}
addEventListener("load", initiate);
```

Listing 10-8: Completing the triangle

The `closePath()` method simply adds a straight line to the path, from the end point to the start point, closing the shape.

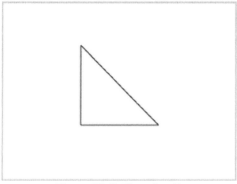

Figure 10-4: Closed path

Using the `stroke()` method at the end of our path, we drew an empty triangle on the canvas. For a solid triangle, the `fill()` method is required.

```
function initiate(){
  var elem = document.getElementById('canvas');
  var canvas = elem.getContext('2d');
  canvas.beginPath();
  canvas.moveTo(100, 100);
  canvas.lineTo(200, 200);
  canvas.lineTo(100, 200);
  canvas.fill();
}
addEventListener("load", initiate);
```

Listing 10-9: Drawing a solid triangle

Now the figure on the screen is a solid triangle. The `fill()` method closes the path automatically, so we don't have to use `closePath()` anymore.

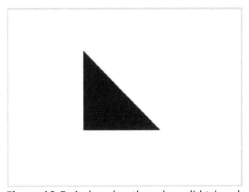

Figure 10-5: A closed path and a solid triangle

One of the methods previously presented to draw a path on the canvas was `clip()`. This method does not draw anything, but it creates a mask with the shape of the path to select what will be drawn and what won't be drawn. Everything that falls out of the mask is not drawn.

```
function initiate(){
  var elem = document.getElementById('canvas');
  var canvas = elem.getContext('2d');
  canvas.beginPath();
  canvas.moveTo(100, 100);
  canvas.lineTo(200, 200);
  canvas.lineTo(100, 200);
  canvas.clip();

  canvas.beginPath();
  for(var f = 0; f < 300; f = f + 10){
    canvas.moveTo(0, f);
    canvas.lineTo(500, f);
  }
  canvas.stroke();
}
addEventListener("load", initiate);
```

Listing 10-10: Using our triangle as a mask

To show how the `clip()` method works, in Listing 10-10 we create a `for` loop to generate horizontal lines every 10 pixels. The lines goes from the left to the right side of the canvas, but only the parts of the lines that fall inside the triangle mask will be shown.

Figure 10-6: *Clipping area*

Now that we know how to draw paths, it is time to look at alternative ways to create shapes. Thus far, we have learned how to generate straight lines and square shapes. For circular shapes, the API provides three methods: `arc()`, `quadraticCurveTo()` and `bezierCurveTo()`. The first one is relatively simple and can generate partial or full circles, as shown in the following example:

```
function initiate(){
  var elem = document.getElementById('canvas');
  var canvas = elem.getContext('2d');

  canvas.beginPath();
  canvas.arc(100, 100, 50, 0, Math.PI * 2, false);
  canvas.stroke();
}
addEventListener("load", initiate);
```

Listing 10-11: *Drawing circles with* `arc()`

The first thing you may notice in the `arc()` method is the use of the value PI. This method uses radians instead of degrees for the angle's values. In radians, the value of PI represents 180 degrees, so the formula `PI × 2` will multiply PI by 2 getting an angle of 360 degrees.

The script in Listing 10-11 generates an arc with a center at the point `100, 100` and a radius of 50 pixels, starting at 0 degrees and ending at `Math.PI * 2` degrees, which represents a full circle. The use of the property `PI` from the Math object lets us get the precise value of PI.

> **Review the Basics:** The Math object is a native Javascript object with properties and methods to perform mathematical operations. The properties return constants such as `PI` or `E`, while the methods perform complex operations such as exponentiation or trigonometry. For a complete list, please visit our website and follow the links for this chapter.

If you need to calculate the value in radians from degrees, use the formula: `Math.PI / 180 × degrees`, as in the next example:

```
function initiate(){
  var elem = document.getElementById('canvas');
  var canvas = elem.getContext('2d');

  canvas.beginPath();
  var radians = Math.PI / 180 * 45;
  canvas.arc(100, 100, 50, 0, radians, false);
  canvas.stroke();
}
addEventListener("load", initiate);
```

Listing 10-12: *Drawing an arc of 45 degrees*

With the script in Listing 10-12, we get an arc that covers 45 degrees of a circle. Try to change the direction value of the method to **true**. In that case, the arc will be generated from 0 degrees to 315, creating an open circle, as shown in the next figure:

Figure 10-7: *Semicircle with the* arc() *method*

An important thing to consider is that if you continue working with this path, the current starting point will be the end of the arc. If you don't want to start at the end of the arc, you will have to use the **moveTo()** method to change the pen's position. However, if the next shape is another arc, always remember that the **moveTo()** method moves the virtual pen to the point in which the circle will start to be drawn, not to the center of the circle. So let's say that the center of the circle is at the point **300, 150**, and its radius is **50**. Then **moveTo()** should move the pen to the position **350, 150** to start drawing the circle.

Besides **arc()**, we have two more methods for drawing more complex curves. The **quadraticCurveTo()** method generates a quadratic Bézier curve, and the **bezierCurveTo()** method generates cubic Bézier curves. The difference between the methods is that the first one has only one point of control and the second one has two, thus creating different types of curves.

```
function initiate(){
  var elem = document.getElementById('canvas');
  var canvas = elem.getContext('2d');

  canvas.beginPath();
  canvas.moveTo(50, 50);
  canvas.quadraticCurveTo(100, 125, 50, 200);
```

```
    canvas.moveTo(250, 50);
    canvas.bezierCurveTo(200, 125, 300, 125, 250, 200);
    canvas.stroke();
}
addEventListener("load", initiate);
```

Listing 10-13: Creating complex curves

For the quadratic curve, we move the virtual pen to the position `50, 50` and finish the curve at the point `50, 200`. The control point for this curve is at the position `100, 125`.

The cubic curve generated by the `bezierCurveTo()` method is a little bit more complicated. There are two control points for this curve, the first one at the position `200, 125` and the second one at the position `300, 125`.

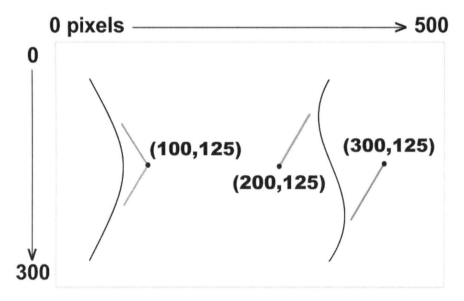

Figure 10-8: Representation of Bézier curves and their control points on the canvas

The values in Figure 10-8 indicate the position of the control points for the curves. Moving those points changes the shape of the curve.

> **Do It Yourself:** You can add as many curves as you need to build your shape. Try to change the values of the control points in Listing 10-13 to see how they affect the curves. Build more complex shapes by combining curves and lines to understand how the construction of the path is made.

Line Styles

Up to this point we have been using the same style for every line drawn on the canvas. The width, ending and other aspects of the line can be manipulated to get exactly the type of line we need for our drawings. There are four properties specifically for this purpose:

lineWidth—This property determines the line thickness. By default the value is 1.0 units.

lineCap—This property determines the shape of the end of the line. There are three possible values: `butt`, `round` or `square`.

lineJoin—This property determines the shape of the connection between two lines. The possible values are `round`, `bevel` or `miter`.

miterLimit—Working along with `lineJoin`, this property determines how far the connections between lines will be extended when the `lineJoin` property is set to `miter`.

These properties affect the entire path. Every time we have to change the characteristics of the lines we have to create a new path with new property values.

```
function initiate(){
  var elem = document.getElementById('canvas');
  var canvas = elem.getContext('2d');

  canvas.beginPath();
  canvas.arc(200, 150, 50, 0, Math.PI * 2, false);
  canvas.stroke();

  canvas.lineWidth = 10;
  canvas.lineCap = "round";
  canvas.beginPath();
  canvas.moveTo(230, 150);
  canvas.arc(200, 150, 30, 0, Math.PI, false);
  canvas.stroke();

  canvas.lineWidth = 5;
  canvas.lineJoin = "miter";
  canvas.beginPath();
  canvas.moveTo(195, 135);
  canvas.lineTo(215, 155);
  canvas.lineTo(195, 155);
  canvas.stroke();
}
addEventListener("load", initiate);
```

Listing 10-14: Testing properties for lines

We start the drawing in the example in Listing 10-14 by creating a path for a full circle with default properties. Then, using `lineWith`, we change the width of the line to `10` and set the `lineCap` to `round`. This makes the path thick with rounded endings, which will help us create a smiling mouth. To create the path, we move the pen to the position `230, 150` and then generate a semicircle. Finally, we add a path created by two lines to form a shape like a nose. Notice that the lines for this path have a width of `5` and are joined with the property `lineJoin` set to the value `miter`. This property makes the nose pointy, expanding the outside edges of the corner until they reach a single point.

Figure 10-9: Different types of lines

Do It Yourself: Experiment with changing the lines for the nose modifying the property `miterLimit`—for example, with the instruction `miterLimit = 2`. Change the value for the property `lineJoin` to `round` or `bevel`. You can also modify the shape of the mouth by trying different values for the property `lineCap`. And finish the face with a pair of eyes!

Text

Writing text on the canvas is as simple as defining a few properties and calling the appropriate method. There are three properties to configure text:

font—This property sets the type of font to be used. It takes the same values as the `font` property from CSS.

textAlign—This property aligns the text horizontally. The alignment can be made to the `start`, `end`, `left`, `right` or `center`.

textBaseline—This property is for vertical alignment. It sets different positions for the text (including Unicode text), and the values can be `top`, `hanging`, `middle`, `alphabetic`, `ideographic` or `bottom`.

Two methods are available to draw text on the canvas:

strokeText(text, x, y)—Similar to the method for a path, this will draw the specified text as an outline shape at the position `x`, `y`. It can also include a fourth value to declare the maximum size. If the text is longer than this value, it will be shrunk to fit into that space.

fillText(text, x, y)—This is similar to the previous method except it will draw a solid text.

```
function initiate(){
  var elem = document.getElementById('canvas');
  var canvas = elem.getContext('2d');

  canvas.font = "bold 24px verdana, sans-serif";
  canvas.textAlign = "start";
```

```
  canvas.fillText("my message", 100, 100);
}
addEventListener("load", initiate);
```

Listing 10-15: Drawing text

As you can see in Listing 10-15, the `font` property can take several values at once using exactly the same syntax as CSS. The `textAling` property forces the drawing of the text to start at the position `100, 100`. (If the value of this property were `end`, for example, the text would end at the position `100, 100`.) Finally, the `fillText` method draws solid text on the canvas.

Besides those already mentioned, the API provides another important method to work with text:

> **measureText(text)**—This method returns information about the size of the text between parentheses. It can be useful to combine text with other shapes on the canvas and calculate positions and even collisions in animation.

```
function initiate(){
  var elem = document.getElementById('canvas');
  var canvas = elem.getContext('2d');

  canvas.font = "bold 24px verdana, sans-serif";
  canvas.textAlign = "start";
  canvas.textBaseline = "bottom";
  canvas.fillText("My message", 100, 124);

  var size = canvas.measureText("My message");
  canvas.strokeRect(100, 100, size.width, 24);
}
addEventListener("load", initiate);
```

Listing 10-16: Measuring text

In this example we start with the same script of Listing 10-15, but a vertical alignment is added. The `textBaseline` is set to `bottom`, which means that the bottom of the text is at the position `124`. This helps us know the exact vertical position of the text on the canvas.

Using the `measureText()` method and its `width` property, we get the horizontal size of the text. With all the measurements taken, we are now able to draw a rectangle that surrounds the text.

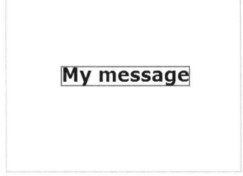

Figure 10-10: Working with text

IMPORTANT: The `measureText()` method returns an object with several properties. The `width` property used in our example is only one of them. For a complete list, read the Canvas API specification. The link is available at www.minkbooks.com.

Do It Yourself: Using the script in Listing 10-16, test different values for the `textAlign` and `textBaseline` properties. Use the rectangle as a reference to see how they work. Write different text to see how the rectangle automatically adapts to every size.

Shadows

Shadows are, of course, also an important part of the Canvas API. We can generate shadows for every path and even for texts. The API provides four properties to do this:

shadowColor—This property declares the color of the shadow using CSS syntax.

shadowOffsetX—This property receives a number to determine how far the shadow will be from the object in the horizontal direction.

shadowOffsetY—This property receives a number to determine how far the shadow will be from the object in the vertical direction.

shadowBlur—This property produces a blurring effect for the shadow.

```
function initiate(){
  var elem = document.getElementById('canvas');
  var canvas = elem.getContext('2d');

  canvas.shadowColor = "rgba(0, 0, 0, 0.5)";
  canvas.shadowOffsetX = 4;
  canvas.shadowOffsetY = 4;
  canvas.shadowBlur = 5;

  canvas.font = "bold 50px verdana, sans-serif";
  canvas.fillText("my message", 100, 100);
}
addEventListener("load", initiate);
```

Listing 10-17: Applying shadows

The shadow created in Listing 10-17 is using the `rgba()` function to get a semi-transparent black color. It is displaced 4 pixels from the object and has a blur value of 5.

Do It Yourself: Apply shadows to another shape instead of text. For example, try shadows on strokes or solid shapes, or using rectangles or circles.

Transformations

Canvas allows complex operations on the graphics and the canvas itself. These operations are made using five different transformation methods, each one with a specific purpose.

translate(x, y)—This transformation method is used to move the origin of the canvas. Every canvas has the point 0, 0 located at the top-left corner, and the values increase in any direction inside the canvas. Negative values are outside the canvas. Sometimes negative values can be useful when creating complex shapes. The `translate()` method lets us move the point 0, 0 to a specific position to use the origin as a reference for our drawings.

rotate(angle)—This transformation method will rotate the canvas around the origin as many radians as specified.

scale(x, y)—This transformation method increases or decreases the units in the canvas to reduce or enlarge everything drawn on it. The scale can be changed independently for horizontal or vertical values using **x** and **y**. The values may be negative, producing a mirror effect. By default the values are set to `1.0`.

transform(m1, m2, m3, m4, dx, dy)—The canvas has a matrix of values that specify its properties. The `transform()` method applies a new matrix over the current one to modify the canvas.

setTransform(m1, m2, m3, m4, dx, dy)—This resets the current transformation and sets a new one from the values provided by its attributes.

```
function initiate(){
  var elem = document.getElementById('canvas');
  var canvas = elem.getContext('2d');

  canvas.font = "bold 20px verdana, sans-serif";
  canvas.fillText("TEST", 50, 20);

  canvas.translate(50, 70);
  canvas.rotate(Math.PI / 180 * 45);
  canvas.fillText("TEST", 0, 0);

  canvas.rotate(-Math.PI / 180 * 45);
  canvas.translate(0, 100);
  canvas.scale(2, 2);
  canvas.fillText("TEST", 0, 0);
}
addEventListener("load", initiate);
```

Listing 10-18: Translating, rotating and scaling

The best way to understand how transformations work is to use them in our code. In Listing 10-18, we apply the `translate()`, `rotate()` and `scale()` methods to the same text. First, we draw a text on the canvas with the default canvas state. The text appears in the position 50, 20 with a size of 20 pixels. Using `translate()`, the canvas origin is moved to the position 50, 70 and the entire canvas is rotated 45 degrees with the `rotate()` method. Then, another text is drawn at the new origin with an inclination of 45 degrees. The transformations applied become the default values, so to test the `scale()` method, we rotate the canvas 45 degrees back to its default position and again translate the origin down 100 pixels. Finally, the canvas' scale is duplicated and another text is drawn, this time doubling the size of the original text.

Figure 10-11: *Applying transformations*

Every transformation is cumulative. If we perform two transformations using `scale()`, for example, the second method will perform the scaling using the current status. A `scale(2,2)` after another `scale(2,2)` will quadruple the scale of the canvas. And the matrix transformation method is no exception. That's why we have two methods to perform transformations directly to the matrix: `transform()` and `setTransform()`.

```
function initiate(){
  var elem = document.getElementById('canvas');
  var canvas = elem.getContext('2d');

  canvas.transform(3, 0, 0, 1, 0, 0);
  canvas.font = "bold 20px verdana, sans-serif";
  canvas.fillText("TEST", 20, 20);

  canvas.transform(1, 0, 0, 10, 0, 0);
  canvas.font = "bold 20px verdana, sans-serif";
  canvas.fillText("TEST", 20, 20);
}
addEventListener("load", initiate);
```

Listing 10-19: *Cumulative transformation of the matrix*

As in the previous script, in Listing 10-19 we apply transformation methods to the same text to compare effects. The default values of the canvas matrix are 1, 0, 0, 1, 0, 0. By changing the first value to 3, in the first transformation in our example above, we stretch the canvas horizontally. The text drawn after this transformation is wider than text drawn in normal conditions.

With the next transformation in the code, the canvas is stretched vertically by changing the fourth value to 10 and preserving the rest as is.

Figure 10-12: Modifying the transformation matrix

One important thing to remember is that transformations are applied over the matrix set by a previous transformation, so the second text shown by the script in Listing 10-19 is stretched horizontally and vertically, as shown in Figure 10-12. To reset the matrix and set new transformation values, we can use the `setTransform()` method.

> **Do It Yourself:** Try to replace the last `transform()` method in the example by the `setTransform()` method and check the results. Using only one text, change every value in the `transform()` method to see the kind of transformation performed on the canvas by each one.

Restoring Status

The accumulation of transformations makes it really difficult to return to previous states. In the script in Listing 10-18, for example, we had to remember the value of the rotation to be able to perform a new rotation to return to the previous situation. Considering this, the Canvas API provides two methods to save and retrieve the canvas state.

> **save()**—This method saves the canvas state including transformations already applied, values of styling properties and the current clipping path (the area created by the `clip()` method, if any).
>
> **restore()**—This restores the last state saved.

```
function initiate(){
  var elem = document.getElementById('canvas');
  var canvas = elem.getContext('2d');

  canvas.save();
  canvas.translate(50, 70);
  canvas.font = "bold 20px verdana, sans-serif";
  canvas.fillText("TEST1", 0, 30);
  canvas.restore();
  canvas.fillText("TEST2", 0, 30);
}
addEventListener("load", initiate);
```

Listing 10-20: Saving canvas state

If you execute the Javascript code in Listing 10-20, you see the text "TEST1" in big letters at the center of the canvas and "TEST2" in smaller letters, close to the origin. What we did was save the canvas state by default and then set a new position for the origin and styles for the text. Before drawing the second text on the canvas, the original state is restored. Because of this, this second text is shown with default styles, not with those declared for the first text.

It doesn't matter how many transformations you perform, the state will return exactly to the previous status when the **restore()** method is called.

GlobalCompositeOperation

When we were talking about paths, we said that there is a property to determine how a shape is positioned and combined with previous shapes on the canvas. This property is **globalCompositeOperation** and its default value is **source-over**, which means that the new shape will be drawn over the ones already on the canvas. There are 11 more values available:

source-in—Only the part of the new shape that overlaps the existing shape is drawn. The rest of the shape and the rest of the existing shape are made transparent.

source-out—Only the part of the new shape that doesn't overlap the existing shape is drawn. The rest of the shape and the rest of the existing shape are made transparent.

source-atop—Only the part of the new shape that overlaps the existing shape is drawn. The existing shape is preserved, but the rest of the new shape is made transparent.

lighter—Both shapes are drawn, but the color of the parts that overlap is determined by adding the color values.

xor—Both shapes are drawn, but the parts that overlap are made transparent.

destination-over—This is the opposite of the value by default (**source-over**). The new shape is drawn behind the existing shapes on the canvas.

destination-in—The parts of the existing shape on the canvas that overlap with the new shape are preserved. The rest, including the new shape, are made transparent.

destination-out—The parts of the existing shape on the canvas do that not overlap with the new shape are preserved. The rest, including the new shape, are made transparent.

destination-atop—The existing shape and the new shape are preserved only where they overlap.

darker—Both shapes are drawn, but the color of the parts that overlap is determined by subtracting the color values.

copy—Only the new shape is drawn and the existing shape is made transparent.

```
function initiate(){
  var elem = document.getElementById('canvas');
  var canvas = elem.getContext('2d');

  canvas.fillStyle = "#666666";
  canvas.fillRect(100, 100, 200, 80);
```

```
    canvas.globalCompositeOperation = "source-atop";

  canvas.fillStyle = "#DDDDDD";
  canvas.font = "bold 60px verdana, sans-serif";
  canvas.textAlign = "center";
  canvas.textBaseline = "middle";
  canvas.fillText("TEST", 200, 100);
}
addEventListener("load", initiate);
```

Listing 10-21: Testing globalCompositeOperation

Only visual representations of each possible value for the **globalCompositeOperation** property will help you understand how they work, so we prepared the example in Listing 10-21 for this reason. When this code is executed, a red rectangle is drawn in the middle of the canvas, but as a result of the value **source-atop**, only the part of the text that overlaps the rectangle is drawn on the screen.

Figure 10-13: Applying globalCompositeOperation

Do It Yourself: Replace the value **source-atop** with any of the other values for this property and check the result in your browser. Test your code in different browsers.

IMPORTANT: At the time of writing, only Mozilla Firefox produces the right effects for every value of this property when using text. To test each value using Google Chrome, replace the text by a path or a figure.

10.3 Processing Images

The Canvas API would be useless without the capacity to process images. But despite the importance of images, only one method exists for this purpose.

DrawImage()

The **drawImage()** method is the only method for drawing images on the canvas. However, this method can take a number of values that produce different results. Let's look at all the possibilities:

drawImage(image, x, y)—This syntax is for drawing an image on the canvas in the position declared by **x** and **y**. The first value is a reference to the image, which can be a reference to an **<img>** element, a **<video>** element or another **<canvas>** element.

drawImage(image, x, y, width, height)—This syntax lets us scale the image before drawing it on the canvas, changing its size by the values of the **width** and **height** attributes

drawImage(image, x1, y1, width1, height1, x2, y2, width2, height2)—This is the most complex syntax. There are two values for every parameter. The purpose is to be able to slice parts of an image and then draw them on the canvas with a customized size and position. The values **x1** and **y1** set the top-left corner of the part of the image that will be sliced. The values **width1** and **height1** indicate the size of the sliced piece of image. The rest of the values (**x2**, **y2**, **width2** and **height2**) declare where the sliced piece will be drawn on the canvas and its size (which can be different from the original).

In every case, the first attribute can be a reference to an image, a video or another canvas in the same document. We can take a reference generated by methods, such as **getElementById()**, or create a new image object using traditional Javascript methods, as we will see in the next example. It is not possible to use an URL or load files from external sources directly with this method. Let's start with a simple example of how to use it.

```
function initiate(){
  var elem = document.getElementById('canvas');
  var canvas=elem.getContext('2d');

  var img = document.createElement('img');
  img.setAttribute('src', 'http://www.minkbooks.com/content/snow.jpg');
  img.addEventListener("load", function(){
    canvas.drawImage(img, 20, 20);
  });
}
addEventListener("load", initiate);
```

Listing 10-22: Drawing an image

The script in Listing 10-22 loads the image and draws it on the canvas. Because the canvas can only receive images that have already loaded, we need to monitor this situation checking the **load** event. We add a listener and declare the **drawImage()** method to handle the event. After the image has loaded, it will be drawn in the position **20, 20**.

Methods like **addEventListener()** require a function as an attribute. To be able to execute a method, we first have to include an anonymous function. The anonymous function is called when the event is fired, and then the right methods are executed from inside the function.

```
function initiate(){
  var elem = document.getElementById('canvas');
  var canvas = elem.getContext('2d');

  var img = document.createElement('img');
  img.setAttribute('src', 'http://www.minkbooks.com/content/snow.jpg');
```

```
  img.addEventListener("load", function(){
    canvas.drawImage(img, 0, 0, elem.width, elem.height);
  });
}
addEventListener("load", initiate);
```

Listing 10-23: *Adjusting the image to canvas size*

In Listing 10-23, we add two values to the previous `drawImage()` method to resize the image. The properties `width` and `height` return the canvas measures, so the image will be stretched by the method to cover the entire canvas.

```
function initiate(){
  var elem = document.getElementById('canvas');
  var canvas = elem.getContext('2d');

  var img = document.createElement('img');
  img.setAttribute('src', 'http://www.minkbooks.com/content/snow.jpg');
  img.addEventListener("load", function(){
    canvas.drawImage(img, 135, 30, 50, 50, 0, 0, 200, 200);
  });
}
addEventListener("load", initiate);
```

Listing 10-24: *Extracting, resizing and drawing*

The example in Listing 10-24 presents the most complex syntax of `drawImage()`. Nine values are provided to take a portion of the original image, resize it and then draw it on the canvas. We take a square of the original image starting from the position `135, 50`, with a size of `50, 50` pixels. The block is resized to `200, 200` pixels and, finally, is drawn on the canvas at the position `0, 0`.

Image Data

Earlier, we stated that `drawImage()` was the only method available to draw images on the canvas, but that isn't entirely correct. There are a few powerful methods to process images that can also draw them on the canvas; however, these methods work with data not images. So why would we want to process data instead of images?

Every image can be described as a sequence of integers representing rgba values. These are four values for each pixel representing the colors red, green, blue and alpha (transparency). This information will result in a one-dimensional array that can be used to generate an image. The Canvas API offers three methods to manipulate this data and process images this way.

> **getImageData(x, y, width, height)**—This method takes a rectangle of the canvas of the size declared by its attributes and converts it to data. It returns an object with the properties `width`, `height` and `data`.
>
> **putImageData(imagedata, x, y)**—This method turns the data declared by the `imagedata` attribute into an image and draws the image on the canvas in the position specified by `x` and `y`. It is the opposite of `getImageData()`.

createImageData(width, height)—This method creates data for an empty image. All the pixels of the returned image will be transparent black. It can also receive image data as an attribute (instead of the `width` and `height` attributes) and use the image dimensions taken from that data.

The position of every value in the array is calculated by the formula `(width × 4 × y)` + `(x × 4)` + n, where **n** is an index number for the values of the pixel, starting at 0. The formula for red, the first value, is `(width × 4 × y)` + `(x × 4)` + 0; for green is `(width × 4 × y)` + `(x × 4)` + 1; for blue is `(width × 4 × y)` + `(x × 4)` + 2; and for the alpha value is `(width × 4 × y)` + `(x × 4)` + 3. Let's see this in an example:

```
var canvas, img;
function initiate(){
  var elem = document.getElementById('canvas');
  canvas = elem.getContext('2d');

  img = document.createElement('img');
  img.setAttribute('src', 'snow.jpg');
  img.addEventListener("load", modimage);
}
function modimage(){
  canvas.drawImage(img, 0, 0);
  var info = canvas.getImageData(0, 0, 175, 262);
  var pos;
  for(var x = 0; x < 175; x++){
    for(var y = 0; y < 262; y++){
      pos = (info.width * 4 * y) + (x * 4);
      info.data[pos] = 255 - info.data[pos];
      info.data[pos+1] = 255 - info.data[pos+1];
      info.data[pos+2] = 255 - info.data[pos+2];
    }
  }
  canvas.putImageData(info, 0, 0);
}
addEventListener("load", initiate);
```

Listing 10-25: Generating a negative for the image

IMPORTANT: These methods present limitations for cross-origin access. The files for this example have to be uploaded to a server to work properly (including the `snow.jpg` image that you can get at www.minkbooks.com/content/). We will study cross-origin access next.

In the example in Listing 10-25, we create a new function to process the image after it has loaded. The `modimage()` function draws the image on the canvas at the position `0, 0` using the `drawImage()` method. There is nothing unusual in this part of the code, but that's going to change.

The image from our example is 350 pixels wide by 262 pixels tall. Using the `getImageData()` method with the values `0, 0` for the top-left corner and `175, 262` for the horizontal and vertical dimensions, we extract the left half of the original image. The data obtained are stored in the `info` variable and then processed to get the desired effect. For our example, we are going to create a negative of this piece of image.

Because every color is declared by a value between 0 and 255, the negative value is obtained by subtracting the original value from 255 using the formula `color = 255 - color`. To do this for every pixel in our image, we create two `for` loops, one for columns and other for rows. Notice that the `for` loop for **x** values ranges from 0 to 174 (the width of the part of the image we cut from the canvas), and the `for` loop for **y** values ranges from 0 to 261 (the total number of vertical and horizontal pixels of the image we are processing).

After every pixel is processed, the `info` variable with the image data is put on the canvas using the `putImageData()` method. This new image is located in the same position as the original, replacing the left half of our original image with the negative we just created.

Figure 10-14: *Processing image data*

Cross-Origin

A cross-origin application is an application that is allocated in one domain and accessing resources from another. For instance, when you tested the examples for the `<video>` or `<audio>` elements in earlier chapters, you used a cross-domain application: the file with the HTML document was in your computer (or your server), while the video and audio files were stored in MinkBooks' servers. Because of security concerns, some APIs restrict cross-origin access. In the case of the Canvas API, no information can be retrieved from the `<canvas>` element after an image from another domain has been drawn.

These restrictions may be avoided using a new technology called CORS (Cross-Origin Resource Sharing). CORS defines a protocol for servers to share their resources and allow requests from other origins. According to this technology specification, the access from one origin to another must be authorized by the server. The authorization is made by declaring the origins (domains) allowed to access the resources. This is done in the header sent by the server that allocates the file processing the request.

For example, if our application is located at www.domain1.com and is accessing resources from www.domain2.com, this second server must be configured to declare the origin www.domain1.com as a valid origin for the request.

CORS provides several headers to be included as part of the HTTP header sent by the server, but the only one required is `Access-Control-Allow-Origin`. This header indicates what origins (domains) are able to access the server's resources. The * character may be declared to allow requests from any origin.

> **IMPORTANT:** Your server must be configured to send CORS HTTP headers with every request. An easy way to do this is to append a new line to the `.htaccess` file. Most servers provide this configuration file in the root folder of every website. The corresponding syntax is `Header set CORS-Header value` (e.g., `Header set Access-Control-Allow-Origin *`). For more information on how to add HTTP headers to your server, please visit our website and follow the links for this chapter.

Adding the HTTP headers to the server's configuration is only one of the steps we have to take to turn our script into a cross-origin application. We also have to declare the resource as a cross-origin resource using the `crossOrigin` attribute.

```
var canvas, img;
function initiate(){
  var elem = document.getElementById('canvas');
  canvas = elem.getContext('2d');

  img = document.createElement('img');
  img.setAttribute('crossOrigin', 'anonymous');
  img.setAttribute('src', 'http://www.minkbooks.com/content/snow.jpg');
  img.addEventListener("load", modimage);
}
function modimage(){
  canvas.drawImage(img, 0, 0);
  var info = canvas.getImageData(0, 0, 175, 262);
  var pos;
  for(var x = 0; x < 175; x++){
    for(var y = 0; y < 262; y++){
      pos = (info.width * 4 * y) + (x * 4);
      info.data[pos] = 255 - info.data[pos];
      info.data[pos+1] = 255 - info.data[pos+1];
      info.data[pos+2] = 255 - info.data[pos+2];
    }
  }
  canvas.putImageData(info, 0, 0);
}
addEventListener("load", initiate);
```

Listing 10-26: *Cross-origin access*

The `crossOrigin` attribute can take two values: `anonymous` or `use-credentials`. The first value ignores credentials while the second value requires credentials to be sent in the request. Credentials are shared automatically by the client and the server using cookies. To be able to use credentials, we have to include a second header to the server called `Access-Control-Allow-Credentials` with the value `true`.

In Listing 10-26, only one modification was made from the previous example: we added the `crossOrigin` attribute to the `img` element to declare the image as a cross-origin resource. Now you can run the script on your server and use the image from MinkBooks' server without violating the same-origin policy (CORS headers were already added to our server).

IMPORTANT: The `crossOrigin` attribute has to be declared before the `src` attribute to set the source as cross-origin before the file is downloaded by the browser. Of course, the attribute may also be declared in the opening tag of `<img>`, `<video>` and `<audio>` elements, as any other HTML attribute.

Extracting Data

The `getImageData()` method previously studied returns an object that can be processed through its properties (`width`, `height` and `data`) or can be used as is by the `putImageData()` method. The purpose of these methods is to provide access to the data contained in the canvas and return that data to the same or another canvas after being processed. Sometimes we may require the information for other purposes, such using it for the source of an HTML element like `<img>`, sending the canvas content to a server or storing the data in a file. To accomplish these tasks, the Canvas API includes the following methods:

toDataURL(type)—This method returns a data:url containing a representation of the canvas' content in the format specified by the `type` attribute and a resolution of 96dpi. If no type was declared, the data are returned as PNG. The possible values for the attribute are `image/jpeg` and `image/png`.

toDataURLHD(type)—This is similar to the previous method but the data:url returned has the original resolution of the canvas.

toBlob(function, type)— This method returns an object with a blob containing a representation of the canvas' content in the format specified by the `type` attribute and a resolution of 96dpi. The first attribute is the function in charge of processing the object. If no type was declared, the blob is returned as PNG. The possible values for the `type` attribute are `image/jpeg` and `image/png`.

toBlobHD(type)— This is similar to the previous method but the blob returned has the original resolution of the canvas

Because these methods are intended to be used with other APIs, we will see some examples later in this book.

Review the Basics: Data:url and blobs are two different formats for data distribution. The data:url format is officially called Data URI Scheme. This scheme is a way to include data in a document to imitate external resources, such as an image for the `<img>` element (see Chapter 16, Listing 16-4 for an example). This format is just a string of text representing the data to create the resource. Blobs, on the other hand, are blocks containing raw data. We will study blobs in Chapter 16.

Patterns

Patterns are a simple addition that can improve our paths. Patterns let us add a texture to the shapes we create using an image. The procedure is similar to gradients; the pattern is created by the `createPattern()` method and then applied to the path as a color with the `fillStyle` property.

createPattern(image, type)—The `image` attribute is a reference to the image, and `type` can take one of four values: `repeat`, `repeat-x`, `repeat-y` or `no-repeat`.

```
var canvas, img;
function initiate(){
  var elem = document.getElementById('canvas');
  canvas = elem.getContext('2d');

  img = document.createElement('img');
  img.setAttribute('src', 'http://www.minkbooks.com/content/bricks.jpg');
  img.addEventListener("load", modimage);
}
function modimage(){
  var pattern = canvas.createPattern(img, 'repeat');
  canvas.fillStyle = pattern;
  canvas.fillRect(0, 0, 500, 300);
}
addEventListener("load", initiate);
```

Listing 10-27: Adding a pattern for our paths

Do It Yourself: Experiment with the different values available for `createPattern()` and assign patterns to other shapes.

10.4 Animations on Canvas

Animations are created by regular Javascript code. There is no method to help animate things on the canvas, and there is no predetermined procedure for doing it. We basically have to erase the area of the canvas we want to animate, draw the shapes on it and repeat the process again and again. Once the shapes are drawn, they can't be moved, and we are only able to construct an animation by erasing the area and drawing the shapes again. For this reason, in games or applications that require a large number of objects to be animated, it is better to use images instead of shapes built by complex paths (for example, games usually use PNG images).

Elemental Animations

There are many techniques for animation in the programming world. Some are simple, and others are as complex as the applications the animations were created for. We are going to show you the basics of animation using the `clearRect()` method to clear the canvas and draw the shape again.

```
var canvas;
function initiate(){
  var elem = document.getElementById('canvas');
  canvas = elem.getContext('2d');
  addEventListener('mousemove', animation);
}
```

```
function animation(e){
  canvas.clearRect(0, 0, 300, 500);

  var xmouse = e.clientX;
  var ymouse = e.clientY;
  var xcenter = 220;
  var ycenter = 150;
  var ang = Math.atan2(xmouse - xcenter, ymouse - ycenter);
  var x = xcenter + Math.round(Math.sin(ang) * 10);
  var y = ycenter + Math.round(Math.cos(ang) * 10);

  canvas.beginPath();
  canvas.arc(xcenter, ycenter, 20, 0, Math.PI * 2, false);
  canvas.moveTo(xcenter + 70, 150);
  canvas.arc(xcenter + 50, 150, 20, 0, Math.PI * 2, false);
  canvas.stroke();

  canvas.beginPath();
  canvas.moveTo(x + 10, y);
  canvas.arc(x, y, 10, 0, Math.PI * 2, false);
  canvas.moveTo(x + 60, y);
  canvas.arc(x + 50, y, 10, 0, Math.PI * 2, false);
  canvas.fill();
}
addEventListener("load", initiate);
```

Listing 10-28: Creating our first animation

The script in Listing 10-28 shows two eyes that look at the mouse pointer all the time. To move the eyes, we have to update their position every time the mouse is moved. To accomplish this, a listener for the **mousemove** event is added in the **initiate()** function. Now, when the event is fired, the **animation()** function is called. First, this function clears the canvas with the instruction **clearRect(0, 0, 300, 500)** and then initializes the variables. The position of the mouse pointer is captured by the properties **clientX** and **clientY** and the coordinates for the first eye are stored in the variables **xcenter** and **ycenter**.

After the initial values are ready, it is time to do the math. Using the values of the position of the mouse pointer and the center of the left eye, we calculate the angle of the invisible line from one point to the other using the predefined Javascript method **atan2** (this method belongs to the Math object explained before). Next, this angle is used to calculate the exact point of the center of the iris with the formula **xcenter + Math.round(Math.sin(ang)** × **10)**. The number 10 in the formula represents the distance from the center of the eye to the center of the iris (because the iris is not at the center of the eye, it's around the edge).

With these values, we can start drawing the eyes on the canvas. The first path is two circles representing the eyes. The first **arc()** method for the first eye is positioned at the values of **xcenter** and **ycenter**, and the circle for the second eye is generated 50 pixels to the right using the instruction **arc(xcenter + 50, 150, 20, 0, Math.PI * 2, false)**.

Then, the animated part of the graphic is created by the second path. This path uses the **x** and **y** variables with the position previously calculated from the angle. Both irises are drawn as solid black circles using the **fill()** method.

The process is repeated and the values recalculated every time the **mousemove** event is fired (i.e., every time the user moves the mouse).

Review the Basics: The properties `clientX` and `clientY` are traditional event properties that return the position of the mouse pointer related to the screen at the time the event took place.

IMPORTANT: In this example, the distance was calculated without accounting for the position of the canvas on the screen. This is because the `<canvas>` element was created at the top-left corner of the page (top-left corner of the canvas and top-left corner of the document were the same). In the next example, a professional animation, the canvas is centered in the window and the formula for the distance is expanded to consider this new location.

Do It Yourself: Copy the script in Listing 10-28 into the Javascript file called `canvas.js` and open the HTML file with the document of Listing 10-1 in your browser.

Professional Animations

The loop for the animation in the previous example was generated by the `mousemove` event. In a professional animation, loops are running all the time, independent of the user's response. In these complex animations loops are controlled by the code. Javascript offers traditional methods to run a loop such as `setInterval()` and `setTimeout()`. These methods execute a function after a specific period of time. This produces decent animations, but they are not synchronized with the browser, causing glitches that are not tolerated in a professional application. To solve this problem, HTML5 introduces a small API with just two methods: one to generate a new cycle for the loop and another to cancel it.

> **requestAnimationFrame(function)**—This method sends a signal to the browser that the function between parentheses should be executed. The browser calls the function when it is ready to refresh the window, synchronizing the animation with the browser window and the computer's display. We can assign this method to a variable and then cancel the process using `cancelAnimationFrame()` with the name of the variable between the parentheses.

The `requestAnimationFrame()` method works like `setTimeout()`, we have to call it for every cycle of the loop. The implementation is simple, but the code for a professional animation requires a certain organization that can only be achieve with advanced programming. For our example we are going to use a global object and distribute the tasks among several methods.

But first, let's create an HTML document to provide the `<canvas>` element and some styles.

```
<!DOCTYPE html>
<html lang="en">
<head>
  <title>Video Game</title>
  <style>
    body{
      text-align: center;
    }
    #canvasbox{
      margin: 100px auto;
    }
```

```
    #canvas{
      border: 1px solid #999999;
    }
  </style>
  <script src="videogame.js"></script>
</head>
<body>
  <section id="canvasbox">
    <canvas id="canvas" width="600" height="400"></canvas>
  </section>
</body>
</html>
```

Listing 10-29: *HTML document for our video game*

The CSS styles in the document of Listing 10-29 have the purpose to center the canvas on the screen and provide a border to identify its limits. The document also loads a Javascript file for the following code:

```
var mygame = {
  canvas: {
    ctx: '',
    offsetx: 0,
    offsety: 0
  },
  ship:{
    x: 300,
    y: 200,
    movex: 0,
    movey: 0,
    speed: 1
  },
  initiate: function(){
    var elem = document.getElementById('canvas');
    mygame.canvas.ctx = elem.getContext('2d');
    mygame.canvas.offsetx = elem.offsetLeft;
    mygame.canvas.offsety = elem.offsetTop;
    document.addEventListener('click', function(e){ mygame.control(e);});
    mygame.loop();
  },
  loop: function(){
    if(mygame.ship.speed){
      mygame.process();
      mygame.detect();
      mygame.draw();
      webkitRequestAnimationFrame(function(){ mygame.loop() });
    }else{
      mygame.canvas.ctx.font = "bold 36px verdana, sans-serif";
      mygame.canvas.ctx.fillText('GAME OVER', 182, 210);
    }
  },
  control: function(e){
    var distancex = e.clientX - (mygame.canvas.offsetx + mygame.ship.x);
    var distancey = e.clientY - (mygame.canvas.offsety + mygame.ship.y);
    var ang = Math.atan2(distancex, distancey);
```

```
    mygame.ship.movex = Math.sin(ang);
    mygame.ship.movey = Math.cos(ang);
    mygame.ship.speed += 1;
  },
  draw: function(){
    mygame.canvas.ctx.clearRect(0, 0, 600, 400);
    mygame.canvas.ctx.beginPath();
    mygame.canvas.ctx.arc(mygame.ship.x, mygame.ship.y, 20, 0,
Math.PI/180*360, false);
    mygame.canvas.ctx.fill();
  },
  process: function(){
    mygame.ship.x += mygame.ship.movex * mygame.ship.speed;
    mygame.ship.y += mygame.ship.movey * mygame.ship.speed;
  },
  detect: function(){
    if(mygame.ship.x < 0 || mygame.ship.x > 600 || mygame.ship.y < 0 ||
mygame.ship.y > 400){
      mygame.ship.speed = 0;
    }
  }
};
addEventListener('load', function(){ mygame.initiate(); });
```

Listing 10-30: *Creating a 2D video game*

IMPORTANT: This is an experimental API. The methods have been prefixed by browsers until the final specification is implemented. At the moment, Google Chrome and Mozilla Firefox are the browsers that have a working implementation of the `requestAnimationFrame()` method. Google Chrome has it implemented as `webkitRequestAnimationFrame()`, and Mozilla Firefox has it prefixed as `mozRequestAnimationFrame()`. The last example applies the experimental version for Google Chrome. To run this script in a different browser, you have to declare the method using the corresponding prefix.

A professional application should avoid global variables and functions and concentrate the code inside a unique global object. In the example in Listing 10-30, we call this object **mygame**. All the properties and methods necessary to create a small video game are declared inside this object.

Our game is about a black spaceship that moves in the direction indicated by the click of the mouse. The goal is to change the direction of the ship to avoid the walls. Every time the direction is changed, the speed of the ship increases, making it more and more difficult to keep the ship inside the canvas.

The organization required to create this kind of application has some essential elements. We have to declare basic values, initialize them, control the animation loop and distribute tasks. In the example in Listing 10-30, this organization is achieved with the declaration of essential properties and the creation of six methods: `initiate()`, `loop()`, `control()`, `draw()`, `process()` and `detect()`.

We start by declaring the **canvas** and **ship** properties. These properties contain objects with essential information for the game. The **canvas** object has three properties: **ctx** for the context of the canvas, and **offsetx** and **offsety** for the position of the <canvas> element related to the page. The **ship** object, on the other hand, has five properties: **x** and **y** for the coordinates of the ship, **movex** and **movey** for direction, and **speed** for the speed of the ship.

Those are important properties required in almost every section of the code, but some of their values have to be yet initialized. This is done by an important method called `initiate()`. The `initiate()` method is called by the `load` event when the document has loaded, and it is responsible for assigning all the essential values necessary to start the application. First, we get the context of the canvas and the position of the element in the window using the `offsetLeft` and `offsetTop` properties. Then, a listener is added to the `click` event for the entire document with the purpose of getting the user's feedback. At the end, the `loop()` method is called to start the animation loop.

The `loop()` method is the second most important method in the basic organization of a professional application. This method will call itself again and again while the application is running; creating a loop that goes through every part of the process. In our example, this process is divided into three methods: `process()`, `detect()` and `draw()`. The `process()` method calculates the new position of the ship according to the current direction and speed; the `detect()` method compares the coordinates of the ship with the limits of the canvas to determine if the ship has crashed into the walls; and the `draw()` method draws the ship on the canvas. The loop executes these methods one by one and then calls itself with the `requestAnimationFrame()` method, starting all over again.

The only thing left to do to finish the basic structure of our application is to check the user's feedback. In our game, this is done by the `control()` method. When the user clicks on any part of the document, this method is called to calculate the direction of the ship. The formula is similar to the previous example: first, we calculate the distance from the ship to the place where the event occurred, then we get the angle of the invisible line between those two points, and finally, the direction in coordinates obtained by the `sin()` and `cos()` methods is stored in the `movex` and `movey` properties. The last instruction in the `control()` method is simply increasing the speed of the ship to make our game a little more interesting.

The game starts as soon as the document has loaded and finishes when the ship crashes into a wall. To make this small application look more like a video game, we add an `if` statement in the loop to check the condition of the ship. This condition is determined by the value of the speed. When the `detect()` method determines that the coordinates of the ship are out of the limits of the canvas, the speed is reduced to 0. This value turns false the condition for the loop and the message "GAME OVER" is shown on the screen.

> **IMPORTANT:** As we explained before, methods like `requestAnimationFrame()` and `addEventListener()` require a function to be declared as attribute. In our last example, we had to use an anonymous function to call the methods of the game. The anonymous function is called first and then the right methods are called from inside the function.

10.5 Processing Video on Canvas

As in animations, there is no special method to show video on a `<canvas>` element. The only way to do it is by taking every frame from the `<video>` element and drawing it as an image on the canvas using the `drawImage()` method. So basically, processing video on the canvas is done by combining techniques already studied.

Video on Canvas

Let's see how the process works with a simple example. The following document includes a short Javascript code to turn the canvas into a mirror.

```html
<!DOCTYPE html>
<html lang="en">
<head>
  <title>Video on Canvas</title>
  <style>
    section{
      float: left;
    }
  </style>
  <script>
    var canvas, video;
    function initiate(){
      var elem = document.getElementById('canvas');
      canvas = elem.getContext('2d');
      video = document.getElementById('media');

      canvas.translate(483, 0);
      canvas.scale(-1, 1);

      setInterval(processFrames, 33);
    }
    function processFrames(){
      canvas.drawImage(video, 0, 0);
    }
    addEventListener("load", initiate);
  </script>
</head>
<body>
  <section>
    <video id="media" width="483" height="272" autoplay>
      <source src="http://www.minkbooks.com/content/trailer2.mp4">
      <source src="http://www.minkbooks.com/content/trailer2.ogg">
    </video>
  </section>
  <section>
    <canvas id="canvas" width="483" height="272"></canvas>
  </section>
</body>
</html>
```

Listing 10-31: *Showing video on canvas*

As explained before, the `drawImage()` method can take three types of sources: an image, a video or another canvas. Therefore, to show video on the canvas, we provide a reference to the `<video>` element as the first attribute of the method.

However, there is something to consider: videos are composed of multiple frames and the `drawImage()` method is only able to take one frame at a time. Consequently, to show the entire video on the canvas, we have to repeat the process for every frame. In the script in Listing 10-31, a `setInterval()` method is used to call the `processFrames()` function every 33 milliseconds.

This function executes the **drawImage()** method with the video as its source. The time set by **setInterval()** is approximately the time it takes every frame to be shown on the screen.

Once the image of the frame is on the canvas, it is bound to the canvas' properties and can be processed as canvas content. In our example, the image is inverted to create a mirror effect. The effect is produced by the application of the **scale()** method to the canvas context (everything drawn on the canvas is inverted).

Real-Life Application

There are a million things to do with the canvas, but it is always facinating to see how far we can go combining simple methods from different APIs. The following example explains how to take a snapshot with the webcam and show it on the screen using **<canvas>**.

```
<!DOCTYPE html>
<html lang="en">
<head>
  <title>Snapshot Application</title>
  <style>
    section{
      float: left;
      width: 320px;
      height: 240px;
      border: 1px solid #000000;
    }
  </style>
  <script>
    var video, canvas;
    function initiate(){
      navigator.webkitGetUserMedia({video: true}, success, showerror);
    }
    function success(stream){
      var elem = document.getElementById('canvas');
      canvas = elem.getContext('2d');
      var player = document.getElementById("player");
      player.addEventListener('click', snapshot);

      video = document.getElementById("media");
      video.setAttribute('src', URL.createObjectURL(stream));
      video.play();
    }
    function showerror(e){
      console.log(e);
    }
    function snapshot(){
      canvas.drawImage(video, 0, 0, 320, 240);
    }
    addEventListener('load', initiate);
  </script>
</head>
<body>
  <section id="player">
    <video id="media" width="320" height="240"></video>
  </section>
```

```
<section>
  <canvas id="canvas" width="320" height="240"></canvas>
</section>
</body>
</html>
```

Listing 10-32: Programming a snapshot application

The document provides some CSS styles, the Javascript code and a few HTML elements, including the necessary **<video>** and **<canvas>** elements. The **<canvas>** is declared as usual, but we didn't specify the source for the **<video>** element because we are going to use it to show an image from the webcam. To organize both elements on the screen, the **<section>** elements were styled to generate two boxes side by side.

The script is as simple as it is powerful. Our standard **initiate()** function calls the **getUserMedia()** method as soon as the document has loaded to get access to the webcam. In the case of success, the **success()** function is called. Most of the work is done by this function. The context for the canvas is created, a listener for the **click** event is added to the box corresponding to the video, and the video from the webcam is assigned to the **<video>** element. At the end, the video is played using the **play()** method.

So far, we have the video from the webcam displayed in the box to the left. To take a snapshot of that video in the right box, we create the **snapshot()** function. This function responds to the **click** event. When the user clicks on the video, the function is called. Here we call the canvas' method **drawImage()** with a reference to the video and the values corresponding to the size of the **<canvas>** element. The method takes the current video frame and draws it on the canvas, taking a snapshot.

> **IMPORTANT:** This example uses the **webkitGetUserMedia()** method, specific for Google Chrome. This is one of the browsers with an implementation of the Stream API (Chapter 9), but the method is still experimental so it has to be prefixed. To test this example in a different browser you will have to use the corresponding prefix.

> **Do It Yourself:** Create an HTML file with the document of Listing 10-32. To test the example, you must upload the file to your server.

Chapter 11
WebGL and Three.js

11.1 Canvas in 3D

WebGL is an extremely low-level API that works with the `<canvas>` element to create 3D graphics for the Web. It utilizes the GPU (graphic processing unit) of the video card to perform some operations and relieves the CPU (central processing unit) of the hard work. It is based on OpenGL, a well-known library developed by Silicon Graphics Inc. that has been applied for the creation of successful 3D video games and applications since 1992. These characteristics make WebGL very reliable and efficient, and that's probably the reason why it became the standard 3D API for the Web; although it hasn't been officially declared as part of the HTML5 specification.

WebGL has been implemented in almost every HTML5 compatible browser, but its complexity forced developers to work with Javascript libraries built on top of it, instead of the API itself. This complexity goes beyond the fact that WebGL does not incorporate native methods to perform basic 3D operations but requires the inclusion of external scripts programmed in a language called GLSL (OpenGL Shading Language) to provide essential features in the production of the image on the screen. For these reasons, developing an application with WebGL always requires the use of external libraries, from glMatrix for matrix and vectors operations (github.com/toji/gl-matrix), to more general purpose libraries such as Three.js (www.threejs.org), GLGE (www.glge.org), SceneJS (www.scenejs.org), among others.

> **IMPORTANT:** Because of the characteristics of WebGL, and also the extensity of the subject, we will not study and apply WebGL itself. In this chapter, you will learn how to generate and work with 3D graphics using a simple external library called Three.js.

11.2 Three.js

Three.js is probably the most popular and powerful library available for the generation of 3D graphics using WebGL. This library works on top of WebGL, simplifying most tasks and providing all the tools we need for the control of cameras, lights, objects, textures and more. Like other external libraries, it is easy to install; we just have to download the package at www.threejs.org and include the `three.min.js` file in our HTML documents.

Several constructors were included in the library to generate the basic objects required to work with 3D graphics. These objects provide the necessary methods and properties to set the scene, the camera and the meshes representing the physical objects and also to work on these elements to construct and animate the three-dimensional world on the Web. But first, let's see where everything is going to be rendered.

IMPORTANT: This chapter is not intended to be a manual for Three.js. For a complete reference, check the library's documentation available at www.threejs.org.

Renderer

The renderer is the surface where the graphics are drawn. Three.js uses a `<canvas>` element with a WebGL context to render 3D scenes in the browser (it takes care of creating the context with the `webgl` parameter). To configure this renderer, the library provides the `WebGLRenderer()` constructor:

> **WebGLRenderer(parameters)**—This constructor returns an object with the properties and methods to configure the drawing surface and render the graphics on the screen. The `parameters` attribute has to be specified as an object with specific properties. The properties currently available are `canvas` (canvas element), `precision` (values `highp`, `mediump`, `lowp`), `alpha` (Boolean value), `premultipliedAlpha` (Boolean value), `antialias` (Boolean value), `stencil` (Boolean value), `preserveDrawingBuffer` (Boolean value), `clearColor` (integer value), and `clearAlpha` (decimal value). In the examples in this chapter, we will configure our renderer using some of these properties.

A WebGLRenderer object provides multiple methods and properties to set and get information from the renderer. The most common and widely used are:

> **setSize(width, height)**—This method resizes the canvas to the values of `width` and `height`.

> **setViewport(x, y, width, height)**—This method determines the area of the canvas that will be used to render the scene. The size of the area used by WebGL doesn't necessarily have to be the same as the drawing surface. The `x` and `y` attributes indicate the starting coordinates for the viewport, and `width` and `height` indicate its size.

> **setClearColorHex(color, alpha)**—This method sets a color for the surface in hexadecimal values. The `alpha` attribute declares the opacity (from `0.0` to `1.0`).

> **render(scene, camera, target, clear)**—This method renders the scene using a camera. The attributes `scene` and `camera` are objects representing the scene and the camera. The `target` attribute declares where the render will be done (it's not necessary if we want to use the canvas set by the renderer constructor), and the Boolean attribute `clear` determines whether the canvas has to be cleared before rendering or not.

> **IMPORTANT:** The library also includes the `CanvasRenderer()` constructor. This constructor returns an object to work with a 2D canvas context when the browser doesn't have support for WebGL. The canvas renderer doesn't work with the GPU and is not recommended for high-level applications.

Scene

The scene is a global object that contains the rest of the objects representing each element of the 3D world, such as the camera, lights, meshes, etc. Three.js provides a simple constructor to generate a scene:

> **scene()**—This constructor returns an object that represents the scene. A Scene object provides the `add()` and `remove()` methods to add and remove elements from the scene.

The scene establishes a three-dimensional space that helps allocate every element in the virtual world. The coordinates for this space are identified with **x**, **y** and **z**. Each element will have its own coordinate values and position in the 3D world, as represented in the next figure.

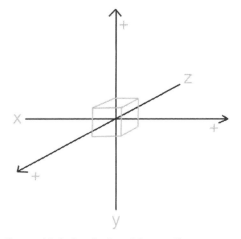

Figure 11-1: A cube in a 3D coordinate system

If we increase the value of the **x** coordinate for an element, that element will be displaced to a new position on the **x** axis, keeping the same position on the rest of the axes, as shown in Figure 11-2.

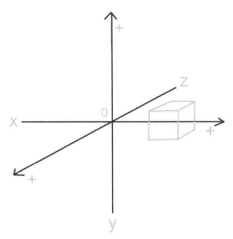

Figure 11-2: Moving elements on the x axis

For every new element of the world, such as the camera, lights and physical objects, we have to set the values of the three coordinates to establish its position in the scene. When these coordinates are not declared, the element is positioned at the origin (the coordinates 0, 0, 0).

Because there is no parameter to determine the size or the scale of a standard 3D world, the units have no specific values; the values used are just decimal numbers. The scale is established by the relation between the elements already defined.

Camera

The camera is an essential part of the 3D scene. It determines the point of view of the viewer (the user) and provides the necessary perspective to make our world look realistic. Three.js includes constructors to create two different types of cameras:

PerspectiveCamera(fov, aspect, near, far)—This constructor returns an object representing a camera with perspective projection. The **fov** attribute determines the vertical field of view, **aspect** declares the aspect ratio, and the **near** and **far** attributes limit what the camera sees (the closest and farthest points).

OrthographicCamera(left, right, top, bottom, near, far)—This constructor returns an object representing a camera with orthographic projection. The attributes **left**, **right**, **top**, and **bottom** declare the corresponding frustum plane. The **near** and **far** attributes limit what the camera sees (the closest and farthest points).

Perspective and orthographic projections are just different ways to project the three-dimensional world onto a two-dimensional surface like canvas. The perspective projection is more realistic in terms of the imitation of the real world and is the one recommended for animations, but the orthographic projection is useful for the visualization of structures and drawings that require access to details because it ignores some effects produced by the human eye.

The Camera object returned by these constructors includes a method to set the vector to which the camera has to look at:

lookAt(vector)—This method allows us to orient the camera towards a specific point in the scene. The **vector** attribute is a Vector object containing the properties of the values for the three coordinates **x**, **y**, and **z** (e.g., **{x: 10, y: 10, z: 20}**). By default, the camera looks at the origin (the coordinates 0, 0, 0).

Meshes

In a 3D world, physical objects are represented through meshes. A mesh is a collection of vertices that define a shape. Each vertex of the mesh is a node in the three-dimensional space. Nodes are joined by invisible lines that generate small faces all around the shape. The group of faces obtained by the intersection of all the vertices of a mesh constitutes the surface of the shape.

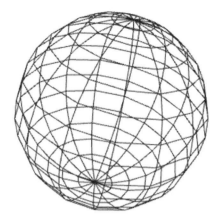

Figure 11-3: Mesh to build a sphere

Figure 11-3 shows a mesh representing a sphere. To create this particular mesh we had to define 256 vertices that generated 225 faces. That means that we had to declare the **x**, **y**, and **z** coordinates 256 times to create all the necessary nodes for the definition of a single sphere. This example shows how hard it is to define three-dimensional shapes, even basic shapes like this one. Because of this complexity, designers work with modeling applications to generate 3D graphics. Software like Blender (www.blender.org), for example, exports the entire mesh in special formats that other applications can read. We will come back to this later.

Meshes, as any other elements, have to be enclosed in an object before they can be introduced into the scene. The library provides a general method for this purpose:

> **Mesh(geometry, material)**—This constructor returns an object representing the mesh. The `geometry` and `material` attributes are objects returned by geometry and material constructors, as we will see next.

Geometric Primitives

A sphere, like the one shown in Figure 11-3, is called **primitive** or **geometric primitive**. Primitives are basic geometric shapes that have a defined structure but can be modified through specific parameters, such as size, dimensions, etc. For some applications, including small video games, primitives are extremely useful and simplify the work for designers and developers. Three.js offers several constructors to create the most common geometric primitives:

> **SphereGeometry(radius, horizontal_segments, vertical_segments, phiStart, phiLength, thetaStart, thetaLength)**—This constructor returns an object containing the mesh to build a sphere. The `radius` attribute defines the radius of the sphere; the `horizontal_segments` and `vertical_segments` attributes declare the number of segments included horizontally and vertically to create the shape; and the combination of `phiStart`, `phiLength`, `thetaStart` and `thetaLength` allow us to generate incomplete spheres. Most attributes are optional and have values by default.

> **CubeGeometry(width, height, depth, horizontal_segments, vertical_segments, depth_segments, materials, sides)**—This constructor returns an object containing the mesh to build a cube. The `width`, `height` and `depth` attributes determine the size

of each side of the cube; the `horizontal_segments`, `vertical_segments` and `depth_segments` attributes determine the number of segments use to create the cube's faces; the `materials` attribute is an array containing different materials for each face; and the `sides` attribute contains six Boolean values to specify whether or not each face will be generated. Most attributes are optional and have values by default.

CylinderGeometry(top_radius, bottom_radius, height, horizontal_segments, vertical_segments)—This constructor returns an object containing the mesh to build a cylinder. The `top-radius` and `bottom_radius` attributes specify the radius for the top and bottom of the cylinder (different radiuses build a cone); the `height` declares the height of the cylinder; and the `horizontal_segments` and `vertical_segments` attributes declare the number of horizontal and vertical segments to be used to create the mesh.

IcosahedronGeometry(radius, detail)—This constructor returns an object containing the mesh to build an icosahedron. The `radius` attribute declares the radius, and `detail` specifies the level of detail. Higher levels require more segments to be used. Usually, the value for this attribute ranges from 0 to no more than 5, depending on the size of the shape and the level of detail needed.

OctahedronGeometry(radius, detail)—This constructor returns an object containing the mesh to build an octahedron. The `radius` attribute declares the radius, and `detail` specifies the level of detail. Higher levels require more segments to be used. Usually, the value for this attribute ranges from 0 to no more than 5, depending on the size of the shape and the level of detail needed.

TetrahedronGeometry(radius, detail)—This constructor returns an object containing the mesh to build a tetrahedron. The `radius` attribute declares the radius, and `detail` specifies the level of detail. Higher levels require more segments to be used. Usually, the value for this attribute ranges from 0 to no more than 5, depending on the size of the shape and the level of detail needed.

PlaneGeometry(width, height, horizontal_segments, vertical_segments)—This constructor returns an object containing the mesh to build a flat plane. The `width` and `height` attributes declare the corresponding width and height for the plane, while `horizontal_segments` and `vertical_segments` specify how many segments will be used to build it.

CircleGeometry(radius, segments, starting_angle, ending_angle)—This constructor returns an object containing the mesh to build a flat circle. The `radius` attribute declares the radius of the circle; the `segments` attribute specifies the number of segments to use to build the shape; and the `starting_angle` and `ending_angle` attributes declare the angles in radians where the circle starts and ends (for a full circle, the values should be 0 and `Math.PI * 2`).

Materials

WebGL uses shaders to represent 3D graphics on the screen. Shaders are scripts programmed in the GLSL language (OpenGL Shading Language) that work directly with the GPU to produce the image on the screen. They provide the right level of light and dark for each pixel of the image to generate the perception of a three-dimensional world. This complex concept is hidden by Three.js behind materials and lights. Defining materials and lights, Three.js determines how the

3D world will be shown on the screen using preprogrammed shaders that are of common implementation in 3D animations.

Three.js defines a few types of materials that have to be applied according to the requirements of the application and the resources available. More realistic materials require more processing power. The material chosen for your projects will have to balance the level of reality your application needs and the amount of processing required. Different materials may be applied to different objects in the same world. The following constructors are provided for their definition:

LineBasicMaterial(parameters)—This material is used to render meshes composed by single lines (for example, a grid). The `parameters` attribute is an object containing properties for the configuration of the material. The properties available are `color` (hexadecimal value), `opacity` (decimal value), `blending` (constant), `depthTest` (Boolean value), `linewidth` (decimal value), `linecap` (values `butt`, `round` or `square`), `linejoin` (values `round`, `bevel` or `miter`), `vertexColors` (Boolean value) and `fog` (Boolean value).

MeshBasicMaterial(parameters)—This material renders the mesh with a single color, without emulating the reflection of lights. It is unrealistic but useful in some circumstances. The `parameters` attribute is an object containing properties for the configuration of the material. The properties available are `color` (hexadecimal value), `opacity` (decimal value), `map` (Texture object), `lightMap` (Texture object), `specularMap` (Texture object), `envMap` (TextureCube object), `combine` (constant), `reflectivity` (decimal value), `refractionRatio` (decimal value), `shading` (constant), `blending` (constant), `depthTest` (Boolean value), `wireframe` (Boolean value), `wireframelinewidth` (decimal value), `vertexColors` (constant), `skinning` (Boolean value), `morphTargets` (Boolean value) and `fog` (Boolean value).

MeshNormalMaterial(parameters)—This material defines one shade of color for each face of the mesh. The effect is unrealistic because the faces are distinguishable from one another, but it is particularly useful when the hardware required for the calculation of a more realistic material is not available. The `parameters` attribute is an object containing properties for the configuration of the material. The properties available are `opacity` (decimal value), `shading` (constant), `blending` (constant), `depthTest` (Boolean value), `wireframe` (Boolean value) and `wireframelinewidth` (decimal value).

MeshLambertMaterial(parameters)—This material generates a smooth shading on the surface of the mesh, producing the effect of light reflection. The effect is independent of the observer's point of view. The `parameters` attribute is an object containing properties for the configuration of the material. The properties available are `color` (hexadecimal value), `ambient` (hexadecimal value), `emissive` (hexadecimal value), `opacity` (decimal value), `map` (Texture object), `lightMap` (Texture object), `specularMap` (Texture object), `envMap` (TextureCube object), `combine` (constant), `reflectivity` (decimal value), `refractionRatio` (decimal value), `shading` (constant), `blending` (constant), `depthTest` (Boolean value), `wireframe` (Boolean value), `wireframelinewidth` (decimal value), `vertexColors` (constant), `skinning` (Boolean value), `morphTargets` (Boolean value), `morphNormals` (Boolean value) and `fog` (Boolean value).

MeshPhongMaterial(parameters)—This material produces a realistic effect with a smooth shading over the whole surface of the mesh. The `parameters` attribute is an object containing properties for the configuration of the material. The properties available are `color` (hexadecimal value), `ambient` (hexadecimal value), `emissive` (hexadecimal value), `specular` (hexadecimal value), `shininess` (decimal value), `opacity` (decimal value), `map` (Texture object), `lightMap` (Texture object), `bumpMap` (Texture object), `bumpScale` (decimal value), `normalMap` (Texture object), `normalScale` (Vector object), `specularMap` (Texture object), `envMap` (TextureCube object), `combine` (constant), `reflectivity` (decimal value), `refractionRatio` (decimal value), `shading` (constant), `blending` (constant), `depthTest` (Boolean value), `wireframe` (Boolean value), `wireframelinewidth` (decimal value), `vertexColors` (constant), `skinning` (Boolean value), `morphTargets` (Boolean value), `morphNormals` (Boolean value) and `fog` (Boolean value).

MeshFaceMaterial()—This constructor is applied when different materials and textures were declared for each face of the geometry.

ParticleBasicMaterial(parameters)—This material is specific for rendering particles (e.g., smoke, explosion, etc.). The `parameters` attribute is an object containing properties for the configuration of the material. The properties available are `color` (hexadecimal value), `opacity` (decimal value), `map` (Texture object), `size` (decimal value), `sizeAttenuation` (Boolean value) `blending` (constant), `depthTest` (Boolean value), `vertexColors` (Boolean value) and `fog` (Boolean value)

ShaderMaterial(parameters)—This constructor allows us to provide our own shaders. The `parameters` attribute is an object containing properties for the configuration of the material. The properties available are: `fragmentShader` (string), `vertexShader` (string), `uniforms` (object), `defines` (object), `shading` (constant), `blending` (constant), `depthTest` (Boolean value), `wireframe` (Boolean value), `wireframelinewidth` (decimal value), `lights` (Boolean value), `vertexColors` (constant), `skinning` (Boolean value), `morphTargets` (Boolean value), `morphNormals` (Boolean value) and `fog` (Boolean value).

IMPORTANT: Most of the parameters for material constructors have default values that are what developers and designers usually require. We are going to show you how to set some of them, but for a complete reference, see the official documentation and examples at www.threejs.org.

These materials' constructors share common properties that may be added as parameters for basic configuration:

name—This property defines the name of the material. An empty string is set by default.

opacity—This property defines material's opacity. It takes values from `0.0` to `1`. The value `1` is set by default (fully opaque).

transparent—This is a Boolean property that defines material's transparency. The default value is `false`.

visible—This property defines whether the material is visible or not. The default value is `true`.

side—This property defines which side of the mesh will be rendered. It can take three possible constants: `THREE.FrontSide`, `THREE.BackSide` or `THREE.DoubleSide`.

Implementation

All this theory may be daunting, but the implementation is quite simple. Let's see an example of how to create a sphere like the one in Figure 11-3. We are going to use a **<canvas>** element of 500 by 400 pixels, a perspective camera and a basic material to render the wireframe on the screen.

```
<!DOCTYPE html>
<html lang="en">
<head>
  <title>Three.js</title>
  <script src="three.min.js"></script>
  <script src="webgl.js"></script>
</head>
<body>
  <section>
    <canvas id="canvas" width="500" height="400"></canvas>
  </section>
</body>
</html>
```

Listing 11-1: Including the Three.js library in the HTML document

The most important step in any Three.js application is loading the library. In Listing 11-1, the **three.min.js** file is included by one of the **<script>** elements in the document. The second **<script>** is for our own Javascript code.

```
function initiate(){
  var canvas = document.getElementById('canvas');
  var width = canvas.width;
  var height = canvas.height;

  var renderer = new THREE.WebGLRenderer({canvas: canvas});
  var scene = new THREE.Scene();
  var camera = new THREE.PerspectiveCamera(75, width / height, 0.1,
1000);
  camera.position.set(0, 0, 150);

  var geometry = new THREE.SphereGeometry(80, 15, 15);
  var material = new THREE.MeshBasicMaterial({color: 0x000000, wireframe:
true});
  var mesh = new THREE.Mesh(geometry, material);
  scene.add(mesh);

  renderer.render(scene, camera);
}
addEventListener('load', initiate);
```

Listing 11-2: Creating a wireframe sphere

As always, our script includes the `initiate()` function to start running the application. In this function, we go through the process of creating a 3D world: set the renderer, the scene, the camera and a mesh.

First, the renderer is set by the `WebGLRenderer()` constructor. Notice that all the properties, methods and constructors offered by Three.js are part of the THREE object. The `WebGLRenderer()` constructor is called from this object as shown in Listing 11-2 (`THREE.WebGLRenderer()`). The constructor receives the `canvas` property to set the `<canvas>` element in the document as the rendering surface and returns an object to represent the renderer.

Next, we create the scene using the `Scene()` constructor. No parameters are required for this constructor. The Scene object returned is stored in the `scene` variable for later use.

Once we have the scene, the next step is to create the camera. Using the `PerspectiveCamera()` constructor we get a camera with perspective projection (the one recommended for animations). The first attribute declares a width for the point of view of 75. This value is appropriate for our scene but may be changed according to the scale of the world. The second parameter sets the ratio of the camera as the same as the rendering surface. To get this value the width is divided by the height of the canvas, using the `width` and `height` variables defined at the beginning of the code. Finally, the closest limit is set to 0.1 and the farthest limit is set to 1000. These values also depend on the scale we are using for the rest of the elements in the world. Our objects are not going to be bigger than 100 or 150 units, so the limit of 1000 is enough for this small scene. The objects that go far from that limit are not going to be drawn on the screen.

The camera, as any other element of the world, is initially located at the origin (the coordinates 0, 0, 0). To be able to visualize the mesh created next, the camera has to be moved to a new position. This is done by the `position` property and the `set()` method. We are going to explain this later. For now, all you need to know is that the `set()` method establishes the camera's coordinates as 0 for `x`, 0 for `y` and 150 for `z`, effectively displacing the camera 150 units on the `z` axis.

The last thing we need to add to our scene is the mesh. The mesh and the corresponding material are first defined by the constructors `SphereGeometry()` and `MeshBasicMaterial()` and then used as the attributes for the `Mesh()` constructor to get the final object. The material is defined with the `wireframe` property set to `true` to get a wireframe sphere on the screen instead of a solid object. The mesh is finally added to the scene by the `add()` method, and the scene is rendered on the canvas at the end of the `initiate()` function using the `render()` method from the `renderer` object.

> **IMPORTANT:** Colors in this library are represented by hexadecimal numbers using the prefix 0x (e.g., 0xFF00FF).

> **Do It Yourself:** Go to www.threejs.org and download the library package. Extract the files and copy the `three.min.js` file from the `build` folder to your working folder. This is the file you have to include in your projects. Create a new HTML file with the document of Listing 11-1, and a Javascript file called `webgl.js` with the code of Listing 11-2. Open the document in your browser. The result should be similar to Figure 11-3.

Transformations

Every element of the 3D world, including camera and lights, has attributes assigned by default. They are positioned at the origin of the scene (the coordinates 0, 0, 0), and their size and orientation are determined by the coordinates of each of their vertices. Modifications for cameras and lights are easy to perform, but meshes require a recalculation of each vertex. To avoid this high resource consumption task, Three.js offers a group of properties and methods to perform the most common transformations. Using a few properties we can translate, rotate or scale an element of the world without having to recalculate thousands of vertices.

> **position**—This property returns an object containing a vertex that we can use to get or set an element's position in the world. The object provides the **x**, **y** and **z** properties to read or change each coordinate independently.
>
> **rotation**— This property returns an object containing a vertex that we can use to get or set the angle of the element in radians. The object provides the **x**, **y** and **z** properties to read or change the angle of each coordinate independently.
>
> **scale**— This property returns an object containing a vertex that we can use to get or set the scale of an element. The object provides the **x**, **y** and **z** properties to read or change the scale in each coordinate independently. By default, the values are set to **1**.

Usually, the values of the three coordinates have to be modified at the same time. Three.js provides the `set()` method to simplify this process. The method is applicable to each transformation property, and the values are declared separated by a comma, as shown in the script of Listing 11-2 (`camera.position.set(0, 0, 150)`).

```
var renderer, scene, camera, mesh;
function initiate(){
  var canvas = document.getElementById('canvas');
  var width = canvas.width;
  var height = canvas.height;

  renderer = new THREE.WebGLRenderer({canvas: canvas});
  scene = new THREE.Scene();
  camera = new THREE.PerspectiveCamera(45, width / height, 0.1, 1000);
  camera.position.set(0, 0, 150);
  var geometry = new THREE.CubeGeometry(50, 50, 50);
  var material = new THREE.MeshBasicMaterial({color: 0x000000, wireframe:
true});
  mesh = new THREE.Mesh(geometry, material);
  scene.add(mesh);

  canvas.addEventListener('mousemove', move);
}
function move(e){
  mesh.rotation.x = e.pageY * 0.01;
  mesh.rotation.z = -e.pageX * 0.01;
  renderer.render(scene, camera);
}
addEventListener('load', initiate);
```

Listing 11-3: *Rotating a cube with the mouse*

The example in Listing 11-3 demonstrates how to dynamically transform a mesh. For better visualization, we generate a cube with the `CubeGeometry()` constructor. The rest of the script is similar to the previous example, but a listener to the `mousemove` event is added at the end of the `initiate()` function to create a simple animation. Now, every time the mouse pointer moves over the `<canvas>` element, the `move()` function is called and the mesh is rotated in the `x` and `z` axes according to the position of the mouse pointer.

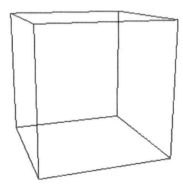

Figure 11-4: *Animated wireframe cube*

Do It Yourself: Copy the Javascript code of Listing 11-3 into the `webgl.js` file created for the previous example, and open the document of Listing 11-1 in your browser.

Lights

To create meshes with material that can emulate light reflection, we need some light. Three.js offers the following constructors to generate light:

AmbientLight(color)—This is a global light that is not attributed to any specific light source. This light is formed by a general light reflected by every object in the scene. It affects all objects alike. The `color` attribute is the color of the light in hexadecimal value.

DirectionalLight(color, intensity, distance)—This type of light is located far away from the 3D world and affects the objects from only one direction. The possible attributes are `color` (hexadecimal value), `intensity` (decimal value) and `distance` (decimal value).

PointLight(color, intensity, distance)—This constructor creates a light source in a specific location in the world. It affects objects in every direction. The possible attributes are `color` (hexadecimal value), `intensity` (decimal value) and `distance` (decimal value).

SpotLight(color, intensity, distance, castShadow)—This constructor creates a light source in a specific location and with a specific direction. The possible attributes are `color` (hexadecimal value), `intensity` (decimal value), `distance` (decimal value) and `castShadow` (Boolean value).

```
function initiate(){
  var canvas = document.getElementById('canvas');
  var width = canvas.width;
  var height = canvas.height;

  var renderer = new THREE.WebGLRenderer({canvas: canvas, antialias:
true});
  var scene = new THREE.Scene();
  var camera = new THREE.PerspectiveCamera(45, width / height, 0.1,
1000);
  camera.position.set(0, 0, 150);

  var geometry = new THREE.CubeGeometry(50, 50, 50);
  var material = new THREE.MeshPhongMaterial({color: 0x0000FF});
  var mesh = new THREE.Mesh(geometry, material);
  scene.add(mesh);

  mesh.rotation.set(10, 10, 0);

  var light = new THREE.SpotLight(0xFFFFFF);
  light.position.set(50, 50, 150);
  scene.add(light);

  renderer.render(scene, camera);
}
addEventListener('load', initiate);
```

***Listing 11-4:** Adding light to our scene*

In addition to the spot light added at the end, there are a few more changes in the script of Listing 11-4 from the previous one. The configuration of the renderer now includes a second property called `antialias` with the value `true`. This smoothes the image on the screen, creating a more realistic effect. The geometric primitive is also replaced by a cube. This new mesh is built by the `CubeGeometry()` constructor and the material is defined as `MeshPhongMaterial()`, in the color blue. The Phong material is probably the most realistic material but also the most computationally demanding. It is perfect for our example, but you should always consider the possibility of alternative materials to achieve a balance between performance and quality.

The cube is created at the origin of the world (the coordinates 0, 0, 0) and faces the camera at one side. If we render the mesh in this position, we will only be able to see a square on the screen. To make the cube more appealing, we apply a transformation using the `rotation` property and the `set()` method.

For the light, we used the `SpotLight()` constructor with the color white. Because this light has a specific location, we have to move it to the right position. This is done by the `position` property and the `set()` method.

Figure 11-5: Light reflecting on a cube

Do It Yourself: Copy the Javascript code of Listing 11-4 into the `webgl.js` file created for the previous example, and open the document of Listing 11-1 in your browser.

Textures

Colors and light reflection produce a very realistic effect, but the level of detail in reality is much higher than that. Reproducing the real world on a computer screen is not as easy as taking a picture that records an image on a camera. Protuberances, particles, fabrics and even small molecules on a surface can produce millions of visual effects. The details in the real world are usually so complex that reproducing a realistic object would require resources not available in computers nowadays. To solve this problem, 3D engines offer the possibility of adding textures to meshes. Textures are images that are drawn on the surface of a shape to simulate complex details.

Textures in Three.js are created by a specific constructor and then declared as part of the material for the mesh. The library provides the `Texture()` constructor for this purpose:

> **Texture(image, mapping, wrapS, wrapT, magFilter, minFilter)**—This constructor returns an object representing the texture to be applied to the material for the mesh. The `image` attribute is the image for the texture. It may be declared as an image, a canvas element or a video. The `mapping` attribute defines how the texture will be mapped on the surface of the mesh; the `wrapS` and `wrapT` attributes determine how the image will be distributed on the surface; and the `magFilter` and `minFilter` attributes set the filters to be applied to the texture in order to smooth the image and produce a more realistic effect.

```
var canvas, img, renderer, scene, camera, mesh;
function initiate(){
  canvas = document.getElementById('canvas');

  img = document.createElement('img');
  img.setAttribute('src', 'crate.jpg');
```

```
  img.addEventListener('load', createworld);
}
function createworld(){
  var width = canvas.width;
  var height = canvas.height;

  renderer = new THREE.WebGLRenderer({canvas: canvas, antialias: true});
  scene = new THREE.Scene();
  camera = new THREE.PerspectiveCamera(45, width / height, 0.1, 1000);
  camera.position.set(0, 0, 150);

  var geometry = new THREE.CubeGeometry(50, 50, 50);
  var texture = new THREE.Texture(img);
  texture.needsUpdate = true;
  var material = new THREE.MeshPhongMaterial({map: texture});
  mesh = new THREE.Mesh(geometry, material);
  scene.add(mesh);

  var light = new THREE.SpotLight(0xFFFFFF, 1);
  light.position.set(0, 100, 250);
  scene.add(light);

  canvas.addEventListener('mousemove', move);
}
function move(e){
  mesh.rotation.z = -e.pageX * 0.01;
  mesh.rotation.x = e.pageY * 0.01;
  renderer.render(scene, camera);
}
addEventListener('load', initiate);
```

Listing 11-5: Adding texture to our object

The file containing the image for the texture has to be completely downloaded from the server before it can be applied to the material. In most applications, a script is designed to download the resources and indicate the progress to the user. In the example in Listing 11-5, we separate this process from the creation of the world to provide a perspective of how the script should be organized. Later on this chapter, we will study better alternatives.

The `initiate()` function creates an Image object, declares the source for that image as the `crate.jpg` file and adds the `createworld()` function as the listener for the `load` event to continue the process when the file has loaded.

The `createworld()` function follows the same procedure we have used before to create the 3D world and all its elements, but in this example, the texture is defined before the material is applied to the mesh. The Texture object was generated by the `Texture()` constructor using the reference to the image previously downloaded. Once the texture is ready, it is stored in the `texture` variable and assigned to the material as one of its attributes. This whole process is usually called **texture mapping**, and for that reason the property in charge of assigning the texture to the material is called `map`.

> **Do It Yourself:** Copy the Javascript code of Listing 11-5 into the `webgl.js` file, upload this file, the image for the texture and the document of Listing 11-1 to your server, and open the HTML document in your browser. The image for this example is available from www.minkbooks.com/content/.

IMPORTANT: Due to cross-origin restrictions, the files for the textures have to be located at the same server as the application. Visit www.minkbooks.com/content/ to download the resources for this book.

Figure 11-6: *Our simple cube now looks like a wooden box*

The Texture object provides some properties to help define and configure the texture:

needsUpdate—This property informs the renderer that an update for the texture is necessary. It is required every time a new texture is defined or changes to an existing texture are made (see example in Listing 11-5).

repeat—This property defines how many times the image of the texture has to be repeated on the same side of the mesh. It returns or sets a vertex with two coordinates, **x** and **y** (for each axis of the side). This property requires the **wrapS** and **wrapT** attributes of the texture constructor to be set as **THREE.RepeatWrapping**, and the image used for the texture has to be of a size power of 2 (e.g., 128 x 128, 256 x 256, 512 x 512, 1024 x 1024, etc).

offset—This property displaces the image on the surface, allowing, among others effects, the creation of a simple but effective animation. It returns and sets a vertex with two coordinates, **x** and **y** (for each axis of the face). This property requires the **wrapS** and **wrapT** attributes of the texture constructor to be set as **THREE.RepeatWrapping**, and the image used for the texture has to be of a size power of 2 (e.g., 128 x 128, 256 x 256, 512 x 512, 1024 x 1024, etc).

UV Mapping

UV Mapping is a process in which specific points of the image for the texture are associated with vertices of the mesh to draw the image in the exact position. The name derives from the names assigned to the axes of the image, U corresponding to **x** and V corresponding to **y** (**x** and **y** are already used to describe the axes for the vertices of the mesh).

Fortunately, Three.js takes care of most of the calculations and provides easier alternatives for the application of textures in most common circumstances. For basic geometric primitives, the library is even configured with default values to distribute the image in the way expected, as we can see from the wooden box in the last example. This preprogrammed logic allows us to simply compose (or map) the image according to the shape of the mesh we want to apply it to and leaves the rest of the work to the library.

One important effect achieved by UV Mapping is the application of different materials, and therefore textures, to the same geometry. The procedure is usually reserved for complex meshes created by 3D software, but in the case of cube geometry, Three.js provides an easy way to do this:

```
var renderer, scene, camera, mesh;
function initiate(){
  canvas = document.getElementById('canvas');
  var width = canvas.width;
  var height = canvas.height;

  renderer = new THREE.WebGLRenderer({canvas: canvas, antialias: true});
  scene = new THREE.Scene();
  camera = new THREE.PerspectiveCamera(45, width / height, 0.1, 1000);
  camera.position.set(0, 0, 150);

  var materials = [
    new THREE.MeshPhongMaterial({map:
THREE.ImageUtils.loadTexture('dice3.jpg')}),
    new THREE.MeshPhongMaterial({map:
THREE.ImageUtils.loadTexture('dice4.jpg')}),
    new THREE.MeshPhongMaterial({map:
THREE.ImageUtils.loadTexture('dice5.jpg')}),
    new THREE.MeshPhongMaterial({map:
THREE.ImageUtils.loadTexture('dice2.jpg')}),
    new THREE.MeshPhongMaterial({map:
THREE.ImageUtils.loadTexture('dice1.jpg')}),
    new THREE.MeshPhongMaterial({map:
THREE.ImageUtils.loadTexture('dice6.jpg')})
  ];
  var geometry = new THREE.CubeGeometry(50, 50, 50, 1, 1, 1, materials);
  mesh = new THREE.Mesh(geometry, new THREE.MeshFaceMaterial());
  scene.add(mesh);

  var light = new THREE.SpotLight(0xFFFFFF, 2);
  light.position.set(0, 100, 250);
  scene.add(light);

  canvas.addEventListener('mousemove', move);
}
function move(e){
  mesh.rotation.x = e.pageY * 0.01;
  mesh.rotation.z = -e.pageX * 0.01;
  renderer.render(scene, camera);
}
addEventListener('load', initiate);
```

Listing 11-6: Using a different image for every side of the cube

In this example, we take advantage of the `loadTexture()` method of the ImageUtils object provided by the library to download the files and assign the textures to the material without disrupting the rest of the process. The meshes and the entire 3D world are generated and the textures applied later when the images have downloaded. This is an easy way to work with textures in simple applications. The `loadTexture()` method downloads the image and returns the corresponding Texture object, all in one step. It saves us from creating a script to download the resources, but because it doesn't provide good control of the process, it is not recommended for professional developing; we included the method here to simplify the example.

Using `loadTexture()` and the `MeshPhongMaterial()` constructor we create an array with six different Material objects, each one with its corresponding texture. This array is later assigned as an attribute to the `CubeGeometry()` constructor. Because all the definitions were already made by this constructor, the `Mesh()` constructor only requires the Geometry object; but we also have to use the `MeshFaceMaterial()` constructor as the second attribute to indicate the types of materials included by the geometry. This is a constructor that returns a composite material type for the application of different materials to the same mesh.

The order of the materials and textures declared in the array are important. It determines the exact location in which the images will be drawn on the surface of the mesh.

> **Do It Yourself:** Copy the Javascript code of Listing 11-6 into the `webgl.js` file, upload this file, the images and the document of Listing 11-1 to your server, and open the HTML document in your browser. Visit www.minkbooks.com/content/ to download the images for this example.

Figure 11-7: Making the cube into a die

> **IMPORTANT:** Applying texture to complex shapes requires a deep knowledge of UV Mapping and texture mapping in general. For more information, please visit our website and follow the links for this chapter.

Canvas Textures

There are different combinations of techniques we can apply to create impressive effects using textures, but probably one of the most interesting is the use of an extra `<canvas>` element. This alternative gives us access to a variety of methods provided by the Canvas API to dynamically generate a texture. But one of the greatest things about using a `<canvas>` element as the source of the texture is how easy it is to include 3D text in our scene.

```
var renderer, scene, camera, mesh;
function initiate(){
  canvas = document.getElementById('canvas');
  var width = canvas.width;
  var height = canvas.height;

  renderer = new THREE.WebGLRenderer({canvas: canvas, antialias:true});
  renderer.setClearColorHex(0xCCFFFF);

  scene = new THREE.Scene();
  camera = new THREE.PerspectiveCamera(45, width / height, 0.1, 1000);
  camera.position.set(0, 0, 150);

  var textcanvas = document.createElement('canvas');
  textcanvas.setAttribute('width', '400');
  textcanvas.setAttribute('height', '200');
  var context = textcanvas.getContext('2d');
  context.fillStyle = "rgba(255,0,0,0.95)";
  context.font = "bold 70px verdana, sans-serif";
  context.fillText("Text in 3D", 0, 60);

  var geometry = new THREE.PlaneGeometry(100, 40);
  var texture = new THREE.Texture(textcanvas);
  texture.needsUpdate = true;
  var material = new THREE.MeshPhongMaterial({map: texture, side:
THREE.DoubleSide});
  mesh = new THREE.Mesh(geometry, material);
  scene.add(mesh);

  var light = new THREE.PointLight(0xffffff);
  light.position.set(0, 100, 250);
  scene.add(light);

  canvas.addEventListener('mousemove', move);
}
function move(e){
  mesh.rotation.y = e.pageX * 0.02;
  renderer.render(scene, camera);
}
addEventListener('load', initiate);
```

Listing 11-7: Including 3D text in our scene

The canvas for the texture is a second **<canvas>** element that won't be shown on the screen. Its only purpose is to generate the image for the texture. We could have declared this element in the HTML document and used CSS to change its **visibility** property, but the best way is to create the object for the DOM (Document Object Model) dynamically with the **createElement()** method and work with this object instead.

In Listing 11-7, the second **<canvas>** element is created and its **width** and **height** attributes defined. The process to draw a text on the canvas is the same one explained in the previous chapter: the 2D context is created, the style for the text defined, and the string is drawn by the **fillText()** method.

One of the advantages of using the **<canvas>** element as the source for the texture is its capacity to make the parts of the drawing surface that are not in use transparent. To show this effect, we declare a background color for the renderer with the **setClearColorHex()** method and apply the texture to a plane geometry. This is a plane mesh with only two sides, like a three-dimensional square. The geometry is created by the `PlaneGeometry()` constructor.

The rest of the process is the same, but we add a new parameter to the `MeshPhongMaterial()` constructor to declare the material as double sided. This means that the texture will be shown on the front and the back of the mesh, producing an effect like the screen of a movie theater.

Figure 11-8: 3D text on a plane geometry

Do It Yourself: Copy the Javascript code of Listing 11-7 into the `webgl.js` file, and open the document of Listing 11-1 in your browser. Move the mouse pointer over the canvas to rotate the mesh and see the texture from both sides.

Video Textures

Speaking of movie theaters, what about using a video as the source for the texture? This is almost as simple as applying the reference to a `<video>` element as the attribute of the `Texture()` constructor.

```
var canvas, video, renderer, scene, camera, mesh;
function initiate(){
  canvas = document.getElementById('canvas');
  video = document.createElement('video');
  video.setAttribute('src', 'trailer.ogg');
  video.addEventListener('canplaythrough', createworld);
}
function createworld(){
  var width = canvas.width;
  var height = canvas.height;
  renderer = new THREE.WebGLRenderer({canvas: canvas, antialias:true});
  scene = new THREE.Scene();
  camera = new THREE.PerspectiveCamera( 45, width / height, 0.1, 1000);
  camera.position.set(0, 0, 250);

  texture = new THREE.Texture(video);
  texture.minFilter = THREE.LinearFilter;
  texture.magFilter = THREE.LinearFilter;
  texture.generateMipmaps = false;
```

```
  var material = new THREE.MeshPhongMaterial({map: texture, side:
THREE.DoubleSide});
  var geometry = new THREE.PlaneGeometry(240, 135);
  mesh = new THREE.Mesh(geometry, material);
  scene.add(mesh);

  var light = new THREE.PointLight(0xffffff);
  light.position.set(0, 100, 250);
  scene.add(light);

  canvas.addEventListener('mousemove', move);
  video.play();
  render();
}
function move(e){
  mesh.rotation.y = e.pageX * 0.02;
}
function render(){
  texture.needsUpdate = true;
  renderer.render(scene, camera);
  webkitRequestAnimationFrame(render);
}
addEventListener('load', initiate);
```

Listing 11-8: *Introducing video in a 3D world*

We used "almost as simple" in our description of this procedure because, as you can see in Listing 11-8, playing a video on the surface of a mesh requires some configuration and also the creation of a loop to update the texture which each video frame.

The script starts with the creation of the **<video>** element. The source for the element is declared as **trailer.ogg**, the same file used in the examples of Chapter 6. To know when the video is ready to be played, a listener to the **canplaythrough** event is added. Once the browser considers there is enough data to start playing the video, the event is fired and the **createworld()** function is executed.

The procedure for the creation of the world follows previous examples, but this time we have to configure the Texture object to be able to use the video as a texture. By default, Three.js applies a mipmap filter to the textures. This filter produces an antialias effect to smooth the texture and make it look more realistic, but video textures don't support this filter. After the creation of the Texture object, we set the **minFilter** and **magFilter** properties to **THREE.LinearFilter** (a simple filter) and deactivate the generation of mipmaps.

But our work doesn't stop there. We still have to create the loop to update the texture for every frame and render the scene. This is done by the **render()** function. In this function, the **needsUpdate** property for the texture is set to **true**, and the scene is rendered again.

> **IMPORTANT:** The script uses the **requestAnimationFrame()** method to run the loop, but in our example it is declared as the experimental version for Google Chrome. To run this application in a different browser, you have to declare the method using the corresponding prefix. This will no longer be necessary once this API becomes standard.

At the end of the **createworld()** function, a listener to the **mousemove** event is added to provide some interaction with the mesh. We also start playing the video with the **play()** method and call the **render()** function for the first time to start the rendering loop.

Figure 11-9: *Video texture*
© Copyright 2008, Blender Foundation / www.bigbuckbunny.org

Do It Yourself: Copy the Javascript code of Listing 11-8 into the `webgl.js` file, upload this file, the video and the document of Listing 11-1 to your server, and open the HTML document in your browser. Visit www.minkbooks.com/content/ to download the video for this example.

IMPORTANT: An OGG video only plays in browsers that support the OGG format, such as Google Chrome, Mozilla Firefox or Opera. See Chapter 6 for more information.

Loading 3D Models

Complex meshes are almost impossible to develop declaring the vertices individually or even using the constructors for basic geometric primitives. The work requires professional 3D software capable of constructing elaborate models that can later be loaded and implemented by 3D applications. One of the most popular softwares on the market is Blender (www.blender.org), created by the Blender Foundation and distributed for free. This program offers all the tools necessary to create professional 3D models and also several formats in which the models can be exported. Developers and collaborators of the Three.js library have built external scripts to help programmers load files in these formats and adapt them to what Three.js can understand and process.

Loaders are already available for the COLLADA format, OBJ format, UTF8 format and JSON format, among others. The loaders are Javascript files that have to be included in the document along with the Three.js file. Let's see an example using the COLLADA format and the `ColladaLoader.js` file:

```
<!DOCTYPE html>
<html lang="en">
<head>
  <title>Three.js</title>
  <script src="three.min.js"></script>
  <script src="ColladaLoader.js"></script>
  <script>
    var canvas, video, renderer, scene, camera, mesh;
    function initiate(){
      canvas = document.getElementById('canvas');
      var loader = new THREE.ColladaLoader();
      loader.load('police.dae', createworld);
    }
    function createworld(collada){
      var width = canvas.width;
      var height = canvas.height;

      renderer = new THREE.WebGLRenderer({canvas: canvas,
antialias:true});
      scene = new THREE.Scene();
      camera = new THREE.PerspectiveCamera(45, width / height, 0.1,
1000);
      camera.position.set(0, 0, 150);

      mesh = collada.scene;
      mesh.scale.set(20, 20, 20);
      mesh.rotation.set(-Math.PI / 2, 0, 0);
      scene.add(mesh);
      var light = new THREE.PointLight(0xffffff);
      light.position.set(0, 100, 250);
      scene.add(light);

      canvas.addEventListener('mousemove', move);
    }
    function move(e){
      mesh.rotation.z = -e.pageX * 0.01;
      renderer.render(scene, camera);
    }
    addEventListener('load', initiate);
  </script>
</head>
<body>
  <section>
    <canvas id="canvas" width="500" height="400"></canvas>
  </section>
</body>
</html>
```

Listing 11-9: Loading 3D models

The models exported as COLLADA are stored in a group of files. Basically, after exporting the model, we will have one text file with the .**dae** extension containing all the specifications for the model and one or more image files for the textures. The model of our example is stored in the **police.dae** file, and two files are created for the textures (**SFERIFF.JPG** and **SFERIFFI.JPG**). We are going to load this model to add an old police car to our scene.

Model files have to be downloaded as any other resource we previously used, but the COLLADA loader provides its own method to do so. In the `initiate()` function in Listing 11-9, the `ColladaLoader()` constructor is used to create the Loader object, and the `load()` method provided by the object is called to download the `.dae` file (only the `.dae` file has to be declared in the method, the files for the textures are downloaded automatically). The `load()` method has two attributes, the `file` attribute to indicate the path of the file to be downloaded and the `callback` attribute to declare a function to be called when the file has downloaded. The `load()` method sends a Scene object to this function that we can process to insert the model in our own scene.

In our example, the function that processes the Scene object is `createworld()`. After following the standard procedure of creating the renderer, the scene and the camera, the Scene object representing the model is stored in the `mesh` variable, scaled to the dimensions of our world, rotated to the right angle for the camera and finally added to our scene.

The model is now part of our 3D world and is rendered as soon as we move the mouse pointer over the `<canvas>` element.

Figure 11-10: *COLLADA model*
Model provided by TurboSquid Inc. (www.turbosquid.com)

Do It Yourself: The file for the COLLADA loader is available in the Three.js package in the `examples` folder. Follow the path `examples/js/loaders/` and copy the file `ColladaLoader.js` to your project's folder. This file has to be included in the document as we did in Listing 11-9 to have access to the methods that will allow us to read and process files in this format. Create a new HTML file with the document of Listing 11-9, upload this file, the HTML document and the three files for the model to your server, and open the document in your browser.

IMPORTANT: The model used in this example is accompanied by two files containing the images for the textures (`SFERIFF.JPG` and `SFERIFFI.JPG`). The three files for this model are available at www.minkbooks.com/content/.

3D Animations

Animations in 3D only differ from 2D animations in how the frames are constructed. In WebGL, the renderer does most of the hard work and the whole process looks almost automatic, while in a 2D canvas context, we have to take care of clearing the surface ourselves. Despite minor differences, the requirements of the codes for a professional application are always the same. The greater the complexity, the greater the need for proper organization, and the best way to establish this organization is by working with properties and methods declared inside a common global object.

To provide an example of 3D animation, we are going to create a small video game. The organization of the Javascript code is going to be similar to the one generated for the 2D animation in Chapter 10. In the game, we will drive a car around a big area surrounded by walls. The purpose is to capture the green spheres floating around.

Let's start with the construction of the HTML document:

```
<!DOCTYPE html>
<html lang="en">
<head>
  <title>Three.js</title>
  <style>
    body{
      margin: 0px;
      overflow: hidden;
    }
  </style>
  <script src="three.min.js"></script>
  <script src="ColladaLoader.js"></script>
  <script src="webgl.js"></script>
</head>
<body></body>
</html>
```

Listing 11-10: HTML document for our 3D video game

The HTML document is as basic as it can get. Only the CSS styles for the **<body>** element may look strange. We are going to use the browser's entire window for the renderer, so these properties are required to make sure no margins or scroll bars take space from our application.

The Javascript files included are the **three.min.js** file for the Three.js library, the **ColladaLoader.js** file to bring the scene back to our lovely police car and the **webgl.js** file for the application itself.

> **Do It Yourself:** Create a file for the document of Listing 11-10 with a name and the **.html** extension. Copy the Javascript codes presented in this part of the chapter into an empty file called **webgl.js**. All the scripts studied from here on are necessary to run the application.

> **Review the Basics:** The **overflow** property is a traditional CSS property that determines how the browser responds when the content exceeds the limits of its parent box. It can take four possible values: **visible**, **hidden**, **scroll** or **auto**. In our example, we assigned the value **hidden** to hide the content beyond the limits of the body and avoid the scroll bars shown automatically by the browser when there is more content available outside the limits of the element.

The script for a 3D application is usually more extensive than the Javascript code required for other purposes. To simplify this example, we are going to present the global object with the elemental properties first and add the rest of the properties and methods required by the game in later listings.

```
var mygame = {
  renderer: '',
  scene: '',
  camera: '',
  light: '',
  car: {
    mesh: '',
    speed: 0,
    speedUP: false,
    left: false,
    right: false,
    wheelangle: 0
  },
  walls: [{x: 0, y: 100, z: -1000},
          {x: -1000, y: 100, z: 0},
          {x: 0, y: 100, z: 1000},
          {x: 1000, y: 100, z:0}],
  textures: {
    car: '',
    floor: '',
    walls: ''
  },
  targets: {
    mesh: '',
    edges: [],
  },
  input: []
}
```

Listing 11-11: Defining basic properties

The global object for the application is called **mygame**. We start the definition of **mygame** by declaring properties necessary to control and modify the status of the game. The **renderer**, **scene**, **camera** and **light** properties store the references to the elements of our 3D world. The **car** property contains an object with the car's basic data, such as a reference to the mesh and the value of the current speed. The **walls** property is an array containing four vertices for the definition of the position of the walls. The **textures** property is an object with properties to reference the textures for the car, the floor and the walls. The **targets** property is also an object to store the mesh and the edges of the green spheres (the targets in our game). And the **input** property is an empty array to store user's input.

Some of these properties are initialized with null values. The next step is to declare the right values and define the basic elements for our scene. This is done using the **initiate()** method.

```
mygame.initiate = function(){
  var width = window.innerWidth;
  var height = window.innerHeight;
  var canvas = document.createElement('canvas');
  canvas.setAttribute('width', width);
  canvas.setAttribute('height', height);
  document.body.appendChild(canvas);
```

```
  mygame.renderer = new THREE.WebGLRenderer({canvas: canvas,
antialias:true});
  mygame.renderer.setClearColorHex(0x000000);
  mygame.scene = new THREE.Scene();
  mygame.camera = new THREE.PerspectiveCamera(45, width / height, 0.1,
10000);
  mygame.camera.position.set(0, 50, 150);

  mygame.light = new THREE.PointLight(0xFFFFFF);
  mygame.light.position.set(0, 50, 150);
  mygame.scene.add(mygame.light);

  addEventListener('keydown', function(e){mygame.input.push({type:
'keydown', key: e.keyCode});});
  addEventListener('keyup', function(e){mygame.input.push({type: 'keyup',
key: e.keyCode});});

  mygame.loading();
  mygame.create();
};
```

Listing 11-12: Defining the `initiate()` *method*

We want to use the browser's entire window for our game, but the dimensions of this space always vary according to the device running the application, the browser used to load the document and even the current window's size set by the user or the system. To create a **<canvas>** element as big as the window, we first have to get the current window's dimensions by consulting the traditional **innerWidth** and **innerHeight** properties of the Window object. Using these values, the canvas is dynamically created, sized and added to the body by the **appendChild()** method.

After the usual definitions of the renderer, the scene, the camera and the light, two listeners are added for the **keydown** and **keyup** events. These listeners are necessary to control the user's input. The **keydown** event is fired when a key is pressed, and the **keyup** event is fired when a key is released. Both return the **keyCode** property containing a value identifying the key that fired the event. Anonymous functions are set to listen to the events and store the **keyCode** values in the **input** array when they are fired. We will process this input later.

At the end of the **initiate()** method, the **loading()** method is called to download the files with the description of the model and the textures.

```
mygame.loading = function(){
  var loader = new THREE.ColladaLoader();
  loader.load('police.dae', function(collada){ mygame.textures.car =
collada; });

  var img = document.createElement('img');
  img.setAttribute('src', 'wet_asphalt.jpg');
  img.addEventListener('load', function(e){ mygame.textures.floor =
e.target; });

  var img = document.createElement('img');
  img.setAttribute('src', 'wall.jpg');
  img.addEventListener('load', function(e){ mygame.textures.walls =
e.target; });
```

```
  var controlloop = function(){
    if(mygame.textures.car && mygame.textures.floor &&
mygame.textures.walls){
      mygame.create();
    }else{
      setTimeout(controlloop, 200);
    }
  };
  controlloop();
};
```

Listing 11-13: *Defining the* loading() *method*

This method is a small but practical loader script. It starts the downloading process for each of the files (the COLLADA model, the texture for the floor and the texture for the walls) and defines a small internal function to check the situation. When the files are completely downloaded, the resulting objects are stored in the corresponding properties (**textures.car**, **textures.floor** and **textures.walls**). The **controlloop()** function calls itself generating a loop to constantly check for the value of these properties and execute the **create()** method only when the model and both textures have already loaded.

```
mygame.create = function(){
  var geometry, material, texture, mesh;
  mesh = mygame.textures.car.scene;
  mesh.scale.set(20, 20, 20);
  mesh.rotation.set(-Math.PI / 2, 0, Math.PI);
  mesh.position.y += 14;
  mygame.scene.add(mesh);
  mygame.car.mesh = mesh;
  geometry = new THREE.PlaneGeometry(2000, 2000, 10, 10);
  texture = new THREE.Texture(mygame.textures.floor, THREE.UVMapping,
THREE.RepeatWrapping, THREE.RepeatWrapping);
  texture.repeat.set(20, 20);
  texture.needsUpdate = true;
  material = new THREE.MeshPhongMaterial({map: texture});
  mesh = new THREE.Mesh(geometry, material);
  mesh.rotation.x = Math.PI * 1.5;
  mygame.scene.add(mesh);

  for(var f = 0; f < 4; f++){
    geometry = new THREE.PlaneGeometry(2000, 200, 10, 10);
    texture = new THREE.Texture(mygame.textures.walls, THREE.UVMapping,
THREE.RepeatWrapping, THREE.RepeatWrapping);
    texture.repeat.set(10, 1);
    texture.needsUpdate = true;

    material = new THREE.MeshPhongMaterial({map: texture});
    mesh = new THREE.Mesh(geometry, material);
    mesh.position.set(mygame.walls[f].x, mygame.walls[f].y,
mygame.walls[f].z);
    mesh.rotation.y = Math.PI / 2 * f;
    mygame.scene.add(mesh);
  }
  mygame.loop();
};
```

Listing 11-14: *Defining the* create() *method*

In the `create()` method, the meshes for the car, the floor and the four walls are created. There is nothing new in this method except for the use of the `repeat` property. This property declares how many times the image has to be repeated on the side of the mesh to create the texture. For example, the image of the texture for the walls is a perfect square, but the walls are 10 times longer than they are tall. Setting the values for the `repeat` property as `10`, `1` (`texture.repeat.set(10, 1);`), the image is drawn on the wall in the right proportions.

As we mentioned before, for the `repeat` property to work properly a few conditions have to be established. The size of the image for the texture has to be a power of 2 (e.g., 128 x 128, 256 x 256, 512 x 512, 1024 x 1024, etc.); more than one segment has to be declared for the side of the plane geometry; and the `wrapS` and `wrapT` attributes of the `Texture()` constructor have to be set to `THREE.RepeatWrapping`. These attributes are set by default to `THREE.ClampToEdgeWrapping`, which means the image is scaled to occupy the whole size of the side of the mesh (as we have seen in previous examples). The `THREE.RepeatWrapping` constant cancels this effect and allows us to distribute the image the way we want.

The definition of the 3D world is complete; now it's time to program the core of the application, the methods that will handle the main processing. We need a method to control the user's input, another method to calculate new positions for dynamic elements, a third method to detect collisions and one more to update the renderer.

```
mygame.control = function(e){
  var action;
  while(mygame.input.length){
    action = mygame.input.shift();
    switch(action.type){
      case 'keydown':
        switch(action.key){
          case 38:
            mygame.car.speedUP = true;
            break;
          case 37:
            mygame.car.left = true;
            break;
          case 39:
            mygame.car.right = true;
            break;
        }
        break;
      case 'keyup':
        switch(action.key){
          case 38:
            mygame.car.speedUP = false;
            break;
          case 37:
            mygame.car.left = false;
            break;
          case 39:
            mygame.car.right = false;
            break;
        }
        break;
    }
  }
};
```

Listing 11-15: Defining the `control()` *method*

The `control()` method in Listing 11-15 processes the values stored in the `input` array by the handlers of the `keydown` and `keyup` events. This is part of a technique used to avoid the delay produced by the system every time a key is pressed. When the user presses or releases a key, the action is detected by those events and the new condition is stored in the `speedUP`, `left` or `right` properties accordingly. These properties will return `true` from the moment the key is pressed until it is released. Using this procedure, there is no delay and the keys to control the car respond instantly.

To identify which key was pressed or released by the user, the value of the `keyCode` taken from the `input` array is compared to the numbers **38**, **37** and **39**. These codes correspond to the up arrow, the left arrow and the right arrow, respectively. According to these values and the event we are responding to, the `speedUP`, `left` and `right` properties are set to `true` or `false` to indicate the current condition to the rest of the methods in the script.

> **Review the Basics:** Each key in the keyboard is associated with a unique value. Using these values we are able to identify the exact key pressed or released. For a complete list of values, visit our website and follow the links for this chapter.

> **IMPORTANT:** An input system similar to the one programmed for this application may be used to store any kind of input, not only keys. We can store custom values for mouse events in the `input` array and then respond to those values from the `control()` method the same way we did in this example for the arrow keys.

The `speedUP`, `left` and `right` properties are extremely relevant. They help us define the speed and the rotation of the car. Everything else is calculated using this information, from the position of the camera to the detection of collisions against the walls or the spheres. A big part of this work is done by the `process()` method.

```
mygame.process = function(){
  if(mygame.car.speedUP){
    if(mygame.car.speed < 8){
      mygame.car.speed += 0.1;
    }
  }else{
    if(mygame.car.speed > 0){
      mygame.car.speed -= 0.1;
    }else{
      mygame.car.speed += 0.1;
    }
  }
  if(mygame.car.left && mygame.car.wheelangle > - 0.5){
    mygame.car.wheelangle -= 0.01;
  }
  if(!mygame.car.left && mygame.car.wheelangle < 0){
    mygame.car.wheelangle += 0.02;
  }
  if(mygame.car.right && mygame.car.wheelangle < 0.5){
    mygame.car.wheelangle += 0.01;
  }
  if(!mygame.car.right && mygame.car.wheelangle > 0){
    mygame.car.wheelangle -= 0.02;
  }
```

```
  var angle = mygame.car.mesh.rotation.z;
  angle -= mygame.car.wheelangle * mygame.car.speed / 100;
  mygame.car.mesh.rotation.z = angle;

  mygame.car.mesh.position.x += Math.sin(angle) * mygame.car.speed;
  mygame.car.mesh.position.z += Math.cos(angle) * mygame.car.speed;

  var deviation = mygame.car.wheelangle / 3;
  posx = mygame.car.mesh.position.x -
(Math.sin(mygame.car.mesh.rotation.z + deviation) * 150);
  posz = mygame.car.mesh.position.z -
(Math.cos(mygame.car.mesh.rotation.z + deviation) * 150);
  mygame.camera.position.set(posx, 50, posz);
  mygame.camera.lookAt(mygame.car.mesh.position);
  mygame.light.position.set(posx, 50, posz);
};
```

Listing 11-16: *Defining the* `process()` *method*

There are two important values we have to recalculate in each cycle of the loop to process the user's input: the speed and the angle of the car. The speed increases while the user keeps the up arrow pressed and decreases when the key is released. The first **if else** statement in the **process()** method in Listing 11-16 controls this situation. If the value of **speedUP** is **true**, the car's speed is increased by **0.1**, to a maximum of **8**. Otherwise, the speed is gradually reduced to **0**.

The next four **if** statements control the angle of the wheels. This angle is added to or subtracted from the angle of the car to steer to the left or the right according to the values of the **left** and **right** properties. As for the statements for the speed, the **if** statements for the angle of the wheels establish limits for the possible value (from **-0.5** to **0.5**).

Once the values for the speed and the angle of the wheels are set, the calculation to determine the new position of every element of the scene starts. First, the current angle of the car is stored in the **angle** variable (this is the angle of the **z** axis). Next, the angle of the wheels is subtracted from the value of the angle of the car, and this new value is assigned back to the **rotation** property of the car to rotate the mesh (**mygame.car.mesh.rotation.z = angle**).

With the angle set, it is time to determine the new position of the car. The values for the **x** and **z** coordinates are calculated from the angle and the speed using the formula **Math.sin(angle)** × **speed** and **Math.cos(angle)** × **speed**. The results are immediately assigned to the **position.x** and **position.z** properties of the car, effectively moving the mesh to the new position, but we still have to translate the camera and the light along the axes or our vehicle will soon disappear in the shadows. Using the values for the new position of the car, its angle and the permanent distance between the camera and the car (**150**), the values for the coordinates of the camera are calculated. These values are stored in the **posx** and **posy** variables and assigned to the **position** property of the camera and the light (camera and light always have the same coordinates). With this formula, the camera looks as if it is attached to the back of the car. To achieve a more realistic effect, a small deviation value is calculated from the angle of the wheels and added to the angle of the car in the last formula to move the camera slightly to one side or another (**deviation = mygame.car.wheelangle / 3**).

At the end of the **process()** method, we point the camera to the new position of the car using the **lookAt()** method and the vertex returned by the **position** property (**mygame.car.mesh.position**). No matter how much the value of this property changes, the camera always aims to the car.

Review the Basics: The mathematic formulas implemented in this example are simple trigonometric functions used to obtain the values of coordinates from angles and specific points in a two-dimensional coordinate system. For more examples, go to Listing 10-28, Chapter 10.

With the positions of the car, camera and light defined, we are ready to render the scene. There is only one element left. The green spheres that our car has to chase are positioned randomly all over the scene, one at a time. When we pass through the current sphere, the mesh is removed and a new one is created in a different position. Because this operation may occur at any time during the animation, we decided to include it along with the rendering process in the `draw()` method:

```
mygame.draw = function(){
  if(!mygame.targets.mesh){
    var geometry = new THREE.SphereGeometry(20, 10, 10);
    var material = new THREE.MeshBasicMaterial({color: 0x00FF00,
wireframe: true});
    var mesh = new THREE.Mesh(geometry, material);
    var posx = (Math.random() * 1800) - 900;
    var posz = (Math.random() * 1800) - 900;
    mesh.position.set(posx, 30, posz);
    mygame.scene.add(mesh);

    mygame.targets.mesh = mesh;
    mygame.targets.edges[0] = posx - 30;
    mygame.targets.edges[1] = posx + 30;
    mygame.targets.edges[2] = posz - 30;
    mygame.targets.edges[3] = posz + 30;
  }else{
    mygame.targets.mesh.rotation.y += 0.02;
  }
  mygame.renderer.render(mygame.scene, mygame.camera);
};
```

Listing 11-17: Defining the draw() *method*

If no sphere is yet created, the **draw()** method generates a new one. The material is set as a green wireframe, and the position is determined randomly by the **random()** method. After the mesh is added to the scene, an area around the sphere is calculated to be able to detect its position later. The position of every element in the scene is determined by only one vertex. It would be almost impossible to detect a collision between elements comparing these single coordinates. By adding and subtracting 30 units to each coordinate of the sphere and storing those values in the **targets.edges** array, we generate a virtual area of 60 units wide containing the sphere (see Figure 11-11). When the vertex for the position of the car is inside this area, the collision is confirmed.

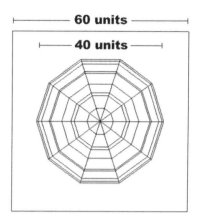

Figure 11-11: Expanding the edges of the sphere

Review the Basics: The `random()` method belongs to the native Math object. It returns a random number between 0 and 1. The limits may be customized with the formula `Math.random() * (max - min) + min`, where `min` is the smaller value we want to get and `max` is the greater. For example, the formula `Math.random() * (50 - 20) + 20` returns a random number between 20 and 50.

The last operation of the `draw()` method in Listing 11-17 renders the scene on the canvas. Although this is important, it is not the last thing we have to do. We still have to improve the collision detection system. The car in our game can crash against any of the four walls and the green spheres. To detect and respond to these situations, we created the `detect()` method.

```
mygame.detect = function(){
  var posx = mygame.car.mesh.position.x;
  var posz = mygame.car.mesh.position.z;

  if(posx < -980 || posx > 980 || posz < -980 || posz > 980){
    mygame.car.speed = -7;
  }

  if(posx > mygame.targets.edges[0] && posx < mygame.targets.edges[1] &&
posz > mygame.targets.edges[2] && posz < mygame.targets.edges[3]){
    mygame.scene.remove(mygame.targets.mesh);
    mygame.targets.mesh = '';
  }
};
```

Listing 11-18: Defining the `detect()` *method*

Comparing the current coordinates of the car by the position of the walls and the edges of the area surrounded the sphere, we determine the possible collisions. If the vertex for the position of the car falls outside the area of the game (beyond the walls), the value of the **speed** property is set to negative 7, making the car bounce off the wall. In the case where this vertex falls inside the area of the sphere, the mesh is removed from the 3D world by the **remove()** method and the **targets.mesh** property is set to null. When this happens, the **draw()** function of Listing 11-17 detects the absence of a sphere and draws a new one.

The detection is the last feature necessary for our game. But as people often say, "It's not over till it's over." We still have to build a loop that calls the methods over and over again and add the listener for the **load** event to start running the application.

```
mygame.loop = function(){
  mygame.control();
  mygame.process();
  mygame.detect();
  mygame.draw();

  webkitRequestAnimationFrame(function(){ mygame.loop() });
};
addEventListener('load', function(){ mygame.initiate() });
```

Listing 11-19: Defining the loop() *method*

The Javascript code for this example is extremely simplified. There is no game over, no points to celebrate, no lives to lose. The good news is that you already know all you need to know to add those features, customize the game and make it your own.

Figure 11-12: 3D video game for the Web
Model and textures provided by TurboSquid Inc. (www.turbosquid.com)

IMPORTANT: The meshes, textures and models in the examples of this chapter are not royalty free and do not include the rights for free distribution. Please consult TurboSquid Inc. (www.turbosquid.com) or the Blender Foundation (www.blender.org) before using this material for your own projects.

Do It Yourself: All the codes presented in this part of the chapter work together to create the video game, including the HTML document of Listing 11-10. Try to apply the Fullscreen API to this example to take your video game full screen.

Chapter 12
Pointer Lock API

12.1 New Mouse Pointer

Visual applications, like those created with the `<canvas>` element or WebGL, sometimes demand the use of an alternative method to express the movement of the mouse. There are countless reasons for this, from having to replace the image of the mouse pointer to the need to modify the camera's position in a 3D scene so there isn't an arrow moving around. Some applications may need to hide the mouse pointer to avoid affecting the graphic design or distracting the user from an image or video when the use of the mouse is not necessary. To accommodate these requirements, HTML5 introduces the Pointer Lock API.

Mouse Capture

The API is a small group of properties, methods and events that help the application assume control over the mouse pointer. Two methods are provided to lock and unlock the mouse:

> **requestPointerLock()**—This method locks the mouse and binds it to a specific element.

> **exitPointerLock()**—This method unlocks the mouse and makes the mouse pointer visible again.

When the `requestPointerLock()` method is called, the graphic representing the pointer (usually a small arrow) is hidden, and the code becomes responsible for providing the visual clues for the user to be able to continue interacting with the application through the mouse.

```
<!DOCTYPE html>
<html lang="en">
<head>
  <title>Pointer Lock API</title>
  <script>
    function initiate(){
      var element = document.getElementById('application');
      element.addEventListener('click', lockmouse);
    }
    function lockmouse(e){
      var element = e.target;
      element.webkitRequestPointerLock();
    }
    addEventListener('load', initiate);
  </script>
```

```
</head>
<body>
  <section id="application">
    Click here to lock the mouse
  </section>
</body>
</html>
```

Listing 12-1: *Taking control of the mouse pointer*

Unless the element requesting control of the mouse is in full screen mode, the `requestPointerLock()` method will return an error when it is called without user intervention. A user gesture, such as the `click` of the mouse, must precede the action. Considering this, the script of Listing 12-1 adds a listener to the `click` event for the `<section>` element. When the user clicks on this element, the `lockmouse()` function is called and the `requestPointerLock()` method is used to lock the mouse. At that moment, the mouse pointer disappears from the screen and is not shown again unless the user switches to another window or cancels the mode pressing the escape key on the keyboard.

When the mouse is locked for an element, the rest of the elements don't fire any mouse event until the mouse is unlocked by the application or the mode is canceled by the user. The API includes an event to inform when an element has locked the mouse, and also to report errors.

pointerlockchange—This event is fired when an element locks or unlocks the mouse.

pointerlockerror—This event is fired when the attempt to lock the mouse fails. No data are returned by this event.

IMPORTANT: The examples in this chapter apply the properties, methods and events specific for Google Chrome. Pointer Lock is an experimental API and is being implemented in browsers at the time of writing. The browsers in which this API is available are Google Chrome and Mozilla Firefox. For Mozilla Firefox, the properties, methods and events are `mozRequestPointerLock()`, `mozExitPointerLock()`, `mozpointerlockchange`, `mozpointerlockerror` and `mozFullscreenElement`.

PointerLockElement

The API includes the `pointerLockElement` property to inform which element locked the mouse. If no element has current control over the mouse, the value `null` is returned.

```
<!DOCTYPE html>
<html lang="en">
<head>
  <title>Pointer Lock API</title>
  <script>
    var canvas;
    function initiate(){
      var element = document.getElementById('canvas');
      canvas = element.getContext('2d');

      element.addEventListener('click', lockmouse);
      element.addEventListener('mousemove', draw);
    }
```

```
  function draw(e){
    canvas.clearRect(0, 0, 500, 400);
    var posx = e.clientX;
    var posy = e.clientY;
    canvas.beginPath();
    canvas.moveTo(posx, posy - 20);
    canvas.lineTo(posx, posy + 20);
    canvas.moveTo(posx - 20, posy);
    canvas.lineTo(posx + 20, posy);
    canvas.moveTo(posx + 20, posy);
    canvas.arc(posx, posy, 20, 0, Math.PI * 2);
    canvas.stroke();
  }
  function lockmouse(e){
    var element = e.target;
    if(!document.webkitPointerLockElement){
      element.webkitRequestPointerLock();
    }else{
      document.webkitExitPointerLock();
    }
  }
  addEventListener('load', initiate);
 </script>
</head>
<body>
  <section id="application">
    <canvas id="canvas" width="500" height="400"></canvas>
  </section>
</body>
</html>
```

Listing 12-2: Locking and unlocking the mouse

In this example, we create a small application to show a more realistic approach of the use of this API. We use the **pointerLockElement** property to determine whether the canvas is in control of the mouse or not. Every time the user clicks on the **<canvas>** element, we check this condition and lock or unlock the mouse with **requestPointerLock()** or **exitPointerLock()** accordingly.

When the mouse is locked, the browser assigns control of the mouse to the element that made the request. All the mouse events, such as **mousemove**, **click** or **mousewheel**, are only fired for this element, but events that are related to the mouse pointer, such as **mouseover** or **mouseout**, are no longer fired. As a result, to interact with the mouse and detect its movements, we have to listen to the **mousemove** event. The script of Listing 12-2 adds a listener to the **mousemove** event to draw a gun sight on the canvas in the position returned by the **clientX** and **clientY** properties. These are traditional event properties that return the coordinates of the mouse pointer in pixels relative to the top-left corner of the window. While this is useful in some circumstances, it limits the action and control of the mouse pointer to the boundaries of the element or the window. The API offers two new properties for the **mousemove** event that will let us calculate the movement of the mouse no matter how far it is displaced.

MovementX and MovementY

The **movementX** and **movementY** properties differ from their sisters, **clientX** and **clientY**, in the type of value returned. While **clientX** and **clientY** return the position of the mouse pointer considering a grid of pixels that starts from the coordinates 0, 0 at the top-left corner of the window, the `movementX` and `movementY` properties provide values that represent only the change in position (the difference between the previous and the current positions). The focus is on the amount of displacement and not on a specific position. This approach has the advantage of being able to constantly process mouse moves in the same way, no matter where the mouse is located or how much it has moved in one direction or another.

In the example in Listing 12-2, the gun sight moves along with the mouse pointer, but as soon as the mouse is locked, the sight is frozen on the screen. This is because when the mouse is locked, only the values of `movementX` and `movementY` are updated (the rest of the event properties keep the last values stored prior to the activation of the mode). To be able to work with the mouse when it is locked and take advantage of the level of control provided by these properties, we must implement them as in the following example:

```html
<!DOCTYPE html>
<html lang="en">
<head>
  <title>Pointer Lock API</title>
  <script>
    var canvas, posx, posy;
    function initiate(){
      var element = document.getElementById('canvas');
      canvas = element.getContext('2d');

      element.addEventListener('click', lockmouse);
      startmessage();
    }
    function draw(e){
      canvas.clearRect(0, 0, 500, 400);

      var test1, test2;
      test1 = posx + e.webkitMovementX;
      test2 = posy + e.webkitMovementY;
      if(test1 > 0 && test1 < 500){
        posx = test1;
      }
      if(test2 > 0 && test2 < 400){
        posy = test2;
      }
      canvas.beginPath();
      canvas.moveTo(posx, posy - 20);
      canvas.lineTo(posx, posy + 20);
      canvas.moveTo(posx - 20, posy);
      canvas.lineTo(posx + 20, posy);
      canvas.moveTo(posx + 20, posy);
      canvas.arc(posx, posy, 20, 0, Math.PI * 2);
      canvas.stroke();
    }
    function lockmouse(e){
      var element = e.target;
      if(!document.webkitPointerLockElement){
        element.webkitRequestPointerLock();
        posx = e.clientX;
        posy = e.clientY;
        element.addEventListener('mousemove', draw);
      }else{
```

```
      document.webkitExitPointerLock();
      element.removeEventListener('mousemove', draw);
      startmessage();
    }
  }
  function startmessage(){
    canvas.clearRect(0, 0, 500, 400);
    canvas.font = "bold 36px verdana, sans-serif";
    canvas.fillText('Click to Start', 120, 180);
  }
  addEventListener('load', initiate);
 </script>
</head>
<body>
  <section id="application">
    <canvas id="canvas" width="500" height="400"></canvas>
  </section>
</body>
</html>
```

Listing 12-3: Calculating the position of the mouse pointer with `movementX` *and* `movementY`

We make a few changes in this script to increase the level of control and show you how to take advantage of this API in certain phases of the application. The `initiate()` function sets the canvas, adds the listener to the `click` event to lock the mouse and calls the `startmessage()` function to show a welcome message on the screen, but it doesn't add a listener for the `mousemove` event. This listener is added in the `lockmouse()` function after the mouse is locked and is removed in the same function after the mouse is unlocked. Following this procedure, the `<canvas>` element gets control of the mouse only after the first stage of the application is executed (where we ask the user to click on the screen). If the user returns to this first stage, the mouse is unlocked again, and the listener for the `mousemove` event is removed by the `removeEventListener()` method.

The values returned by the `movementX` and `movementY` properties reflect the change in the position. Before the mouse is locked, we capture its coordinates with the `clientX` and `clientY` properties to set the initial position of the gun sight. Usually this is not necessary, but in an application like this, where the mouse is constantly locked and unlocked, it helps produce a better transition from one state to another. This initial position is stored in the variables `posx` and `posy` and is only modified by the value of the displacement when they don't exceed the limits established by the `<canvas>` element (check the `if` statements in the `draw()` function). Unless we are just checking for the direction of the mouse, this control is necessary to avoid storing values that our application can't process.

> **IMPORTANT:** At the time of writing, the `movementX` and `movementY` properties are prefixed in Google Chrome and Mozilla Firefox (`webkitMovementX`, `webkit-MovementY`, `mozMovementX`, `mozMovementY`).

> **Do It Yourself:** Create an HTML file and copy any of the examples you want to try from this chapter.

Pointer Lock API

Chapter 13
Drag and Drop API

13.1 Drag and Drop for the Web

Dragging and dropping elements from one place to another is something that we do all the time in desktop applications, but we don't expect to do it on the Web. This is not because web applications are different but because developers never had a standard technology available to offer this feature. Now, with the Drag and Drop API introduced by HTML5, we finally have the opportunity to create software for the Web that will behave exactly like desktop applications.

Events

One of the most important aspects of this API is a set of seven specific events introduced for different situations. Some of these events are fired by the source (the element being dragged), and others are fired by the target (the element into which the source is being dropped). For example, when a user performs a drag and drop operation, the source fires these three events:

> **dragstart**—This event is fired the moment the drag operation starts. The data associated with the source element are set in the system at this moment.
>
> **drag**—This event is similar to the `mousemove` event, except that it's fired during a drag operation by the source element.
>
> **dragend**—When the drag operation is over, whether it was successful or not, this event is fired from the source.

And here are the events fired by the target during the same operation:

> **dragenter**—This event is fired when the mouse pointer enters the area of a possible target element during a drag operation.
>
> **dragover**—This event is similar to the `mouseover` event, except that it's fired during a drag operation by possible target elements.
>
> **drop**—This event is fired when the element is dropped.
>
> **dragleave**—This event is fired when the mouse pointer leaves an element during a drag operation. It is used along with `dragenter` to provide feedback and help users identify the target element.

Before working with this feature, there is an important aspect that has to be considered. Browsers perform actions by default during a drag and drop operation. To get the results we want, we might have to prevent the default behavior and customize the response. For some events, like **dragenter, dragover** and **drop**, the prevention is necessary even when a customized action was specified. Let's see how we must proceed with a simple example:

```
<!DOCTYPE html>
<html lang="en">
<head>
  <title>Drag and Drop</title>
  <link rel="stylesheet" href="dragdrop.css">
  <script src="dragdrop.js"></script>
</head>
<body>
  <section id="dropbox">
    Drag and drop the image here
  </section>
  <section id="picturesbox">
    <img id="image" src="http://www.minkbooks.com/content/monster1.gif">
  </section>
</body>
</html>
```

Listing 13-1: HTML document to test the Drag and Drop API

The HTML document of Listing 13-1 includes a **<section>** element identified as **dropbox** to be used as a target and an image to be used as the source. It also includes two files for CSS styles and the Javascript code that will control the operation.

```
#dropbox{
  float: left;
  width: 500px;
  height: 300px;
  margin: 10px;
  border: 1px solid #999999;
}
#picturesbox{
  float: left;
  width: 320px;
  margin: 10px;
  border: 1px solid #999999;
}
#picturesbox > img{
  float: left;
  padding: 5px;
}
```

*Listing 13-2: Styles for the boxes (*dragdrop.css*)*

The rules in Listing 13-2 simply style the boxes that will let us identify the source and the drop box. Here is the Javascript code that will control the whole operation:

```
var source1, drop;
function initiate(){
  source1 = document.getElementById('image');
  source1.addEventListener('dragstart', dragged);

  drop = document.getElementById('dropbox');
  drop.addEventListener('dragenter', function(e){ e.preventDefault(); });
  drop.addEventListener('dragover', function(e){ e.preventDefault(); });
  drop.addEventListener('drop', dropped);
}
function dragged(e){
  var code = '<img src="' + source1.getAttribute('src') + '">';
  e.dataTransfer.setData('Text', code);
}
function dropped(e){
  e.preventDefault();
  drop.innerHTML = e.dataTransfer.getData('Text');
}
addEventListener('load', initiate);
```

Listing 13-3: *Creating an elemental script for a drag and drop operation*

In Listing 13-3, we have three functions. The `initiate()` function adds the event listeners for this operation, and the `dragged()` and `dropped()` functions generate and receive the information to be transmitted in the process.

For a regular drag and drop operation to take place, we must prepare the information that will be shared between the source and the target elements. To do this, a listener for the `dragstart` event is added. The `dragged()` function, set as the listener for this event, prepares the information to be sent using the API's specific method `setData()`.

The drop action is usually not allowed in most elements of the document by default. Therefore, to make this operation available for our drop box, we must prevent the default behavior. This is done by adding a listener for the `dragenter` and `dragover` events and executing the `preventDefault()` method with an anonymous function.

In addition, a listener for the `drop` event is added. When the event is fired, the `dropped()` function is called. This function receives and processes the data sent by the source.

> **Review the Basics:** For the `dragenter` and `dragover` events, we use an anonymous function to apply the `preventDefault()` method and cancel the behavior by default. The variable **e** is sent as an attribute to the anonymous function to be able to reference the event from inside the function.

When the user starts dragging the element, the `dragstart` event is fired and the `dragged()` function is called. In this function, we get the value of the `src` attribute of the element being dragged and set the data to be transferred using the `setData()` method of the dataTransfer object. From the other side, when an element is dropped over our drop box, the `drop` event is fired and the `dropped()` function is called. This function modifies the content of the drop box with the information obtained by the `getData()` method. Browsers also perform actions by default when this event takes place (for example, open a link or refresh the window to show the image that was dropped), so we have to prevent this behavior using the `preventDefault()` method, as we did for the other events before.

Do It Yourself: Create an HTML file with the document of Listing 13-1, a CSS file called `dragdrop.css` with the styles of Listing 13-2 and a Javascript file called `dragdrop.js` with the source code of Listing 13-3. To test the example, open the HTML file in your browser.

IMPORTANT: Most elements, such as images, are draggable by default, but in case we want to drag and drop an element such as `<div>`, for example, the API provides an attribute called `draggable`. We just have to add this attribute to the element with the value `true` to allow users to drag it (e.g., `<div draggable="true">`).

DataTransfer

This is the object that will hold the information in a drag and drop operation. The dataTransfer object includes several methods and properties. We already used `setData()` and `getData()` in our example in Listing 13-3. Along with `clearData()`, these are the methods in charge of the information being transferred:

setData(type, data)—This method is used to declare the data to be sent and its type. The method receives regular MIME types (like `text/plain`, `text/html` or `text/uri-list`), special types (like `URL` or `Text`) or even personalized types. A `setData()` method must be called for every type of data that we want to send in the same operation.

getData(type)—This method returns the data of the specified type sent by the source element.

clearData()—This method removes the data of the specified type.

In the `dragged()` function of Listing 13-3, we created HTML code including the value of the `src` attribute of the element that fired the `dragstart` event, stored this code in the variable `code` and then sent the variable as data through the `setData()` method. Because we are sending text, we declared the `Text` type for this data.

IMPORTANT: We could have used a more appropriate type in our example, such as `text/html` or even a customized type, but several browsers only admit a few types at present, so `Text` makes our application more compatible and our examples ready to be tested.

When we retrieved the data in the `dropped()` function using the `getData()` method, we had to specify the type of data to be read. This is because different kinds of data can be sent at the same time by the same element. For example, an image might send the image itself, the URL and the text declaring what the image is about. All this information may be sent using several `setData()` methods with different type values and then retrieved by `getData()` specifying those same types.

IMPORTANT: To get more information about data types for the drag and drop operation, visit our website and follow the links for this chapter.

The dataTransfer object has a few more methods and properties that might be useful for our applications:

setDragImage(element, x, y)—This method is used to customize the thumbnail of the element being dragged and select its position relative to the mouse pointer with the **x** and **y** attributes.

types—This property returns an array containing the types that were set in the `dragstart` event (by the code or the browser). You can store this array in a variable (e.g., `list = dataTransfer.types`) and then read it with a `for` loop.

files—This property returns an array containing information about the files that are being dragged.

dropEffect—This property returns the type of operation currently selected. It can also be set to change the selected operation. The possible values are `none`, `copy`, `link` and `move`.

effectAllowed—This property returns or sets the types of operations that are allowed. The possible values are `none`, `copy`, `copyLink`, `copyMove`, `link`, `linkMove`, `move`, `all` and `uninitialized`.

We will apply some of these properties and methods in the following examples.

Dragenter, Dragleave and Dragend

So far, we have only used the `dragenter` event to cancel the browser's default behavior. And we haven't taken advantage of the `dragleave` and `dragend` events either. These are important events that let us provide feedback that will guide users while moving elements all over the screen.

```
var source1, drop;
function initiate(){
  source1 = document.getElementById('image');
  source1.addEventListener('dragstart', dragged);
  source1.addEventListener('dragend', ending);

  drop = document.getElementById('dropbox');
  drop.addEventListener('dragenter', entering);
  drop.addEventListener('dragleave', leaving);
  drop.addEventListener('dragover', function(e){ e.preventDefault(); });
  drop.addEventListener('drop', dropped);
}
function entering(e){
  e.preventDefault();
  drop.style.background = 'rgba(0, 150, 0, .2)';
}
function leaving(e){
  e.preventDefault();
  drop.style.background = '#FFFFFF';
}
function ending(e){
  elem = e.target;
  elem.style.visibility = 'hidden';
}
```

```
function dragged(e){
  var code = '<img src="' + source1.getAttribute('src') + '">';
  e.dataTransfer.setData('Text', code);
}
function dropped(e){
  e.preventDefault();
  drop.style.background = '#FFFFFF';
  drop.innerHTML = e.dataTransfer.getData('Text');
}
addEventListener('load', initiate);
```

Listing 13-4: *Controlling the whole drag and drop process*

The Javascript code in Listing 13-4 replaces the code in Listing 13-3. In this new code, we add two functions for the drop box and one for the source. The functions **entering()** and **leaving()** change the background color of our drop box every time the mouse drags something and enters or leaves the area occupied by the element. (These actions fire the **dragenter** and **dragleave** events.) In addition, the **ending()** function is called when the **dragend** event is fired (when the element is dropped). Notice that this event and function do not control whether the process was successful or not; you have to do this yourself.

As a result of these functions, every time the mouse drags something and enters the drop box area, the box will turn green, and when the element is dropped, the source image will be hidden. These visible changes do not affect the drag or drop process but rather provide feedback to guide users during the operation.

Again, to prevent default actions, we have to use the **preventDefault()** method in every function, even when customized actions are declared.

> **Do It Yourself:** Replace the source code in the Javascript file by the script of Listing 13-4, open the HTML document of Listing 13-1 in your browser, and drag the image into the drop box.

Selecting a Valid Source

There is no specific method to detect whether the source is valid or not. We can't rely on the information returned by the **getData()** method because even when we only get the data of the type specified in the attribute, other sources might use the same type and provide data we didn't expect. There is a property of the dataTransfer object called **types** that returns an array with a list of the types set by the **dragstart** event, but it's also useless for validation purposes.

For this reason, the techniques for selecting and validating data transferred in a drag and drop operation varies, and the procedure can be as simple or as complex as our application requires.

```
<!DOCTYPE html>
<html lang="en">
<head>
  <title>Drag and Drop</title>
  <link rel="stylesheet" href="dragdrop.css">
  <script src="dragdrop.js"></script>
</head>
```

```
<body>
  <section id="dropbox">
    Drag and drop images here
  </section>
  <section id="picturesbox">
    <img id="image1" src="http://www.minkbooks.com/content/monster1.gif">
    <img id="image2" src="http://www.minkbooks.com/content/monster2.gif">
    <img id="image3" src="http://www.minkbooks.com/content/monster3.gif">
    <img id="image4" src="http://www.minkbooks.com/content/monster4.gif">
  </section>
</body>
</html>
```

Listing 13-5: HTML document with multiple sources

Using the new HTML document in Listing 13-5, we are going to filter sources by checking the image's **id** attribute. The following Javascript code will indicate which image can be dropped and which cannot:

```
var drop;
function initiate(){
  var images = document.querySelectorAll('#picturesbox > img');
  for(var i = 0; i < images.length; i++){
    images[i].addEventListener('dragstart', dragged);
  }
  drop = document.getElementById('dropbox');
  drop.addEventListener('dragenter', function(e){ e.preventDefault(); });
  drop.addEventListener('dragover', function(e){ e.preventDefault(); });
  drop.addEventListener('drop', dropped);
}
function dragged(e){
  elem = e.target;
  e.dataTransfer.setData('Text', elem.getAttribute('id'));
}
function dropped(e){
  e.preventDefault();
  var id = e.dataTransfer.getData('Text');
  if(id != "image4"){
    var src = document.getElementById(id).src;
    drop.innerHTML = '<img src="' + src + '">';
  }else{
    drop.innerHTML = 'not admitted';
  }
}
addEventListener('load', initiate);
```

Listing 13-6: Sending the id *attribute*

Not too many things changed in Listing 13-6 from previous scripts. We are using the **querySelectorAll()** method to add a listener for the **dragstart** event to every image in the **picturesbox** element, send the **id** attribute with **setData()** every time an image is dragged and check the value of this **id** in the **dropped()** function to prevent the user from dropping the image with the **id = "image4"** . (The "not admitted" message is shown in the drop box when the user tries to drop this particular image.)

This is a simple filter. You can use the `querySelectorAll()` method in the `dropped()` function to check that the image received is in the `picturesbox` element, for example, or use properties from the dataTransfer object (like `types` or `files`), but it is always a customized process. In other words, you have to take care of it yourself.

SetDragImage()

Changing the image that is dragged with the mouse pointer in a drag and drop operation may sound pointless, but sometimes it avoids headaches. The `setDragImage()` method not only lets us change the image but also uses two attributes, **x** and **y**, to set the position of that image relative to the mouse pointer. Usually the browser generates a thumbnail with the source, but the position of this thumbnail relative to the mouse pointer is set according to the position of the mouse pointer when the drag started. The `setDragImage()` method provides a specific position that will be the same for every drag and drop operation.

```
<!DOCTYPE html>
<html lang="en">
<head>
  <title>Drag and Drop</title>
  <link rel="stylesheet" href="dragdrop.css">
  <script src="dragdrop.js"></script>
</head>
<body>
  <section id="dropbox">
    <canvas id="canvas" width="500" height="300"></canvas>
  </section>
  <section id="picturesbox">
    <img id="image1" src="http://www.minkbooks.com/content/monster1.gif">
    <img id="image2" src="http://www.minkbooks.com/content/monster2.gif">
    <img id="image3" src="http://www.minkbooks.com/content/monster3.gif">
    <img id="image4" src="http://www.minkbooks.com/content/monster4.gif">
  </section>
</body>
</html>
```

Listing 13-7: *Using a* `<canvas>` *element as a drop box*

With the new HTML document of Listing 13-7, we will show the importance of the `setDragImage()` method using a **<canvas>** element as the drop box.

```
var drop, canvas;
function initiate(){
  var images = document.querySelectorAll('#picturesbox > img');
  for(var i = 0; i < images.length; i++){
    images[i].addEventListener('dragstart', dragged);
    images[i].addEventListener('dragend', ending);
  }
  drop = document.getElementById('canvas');
  canvas = drop.getContext('2d');
```

```
    drop.addEventListener('dragenter', function(e){ e.preventDefault(); });
    drop.addEventListener('dragover', function(e){ e.preventDefault(); });
    drop.addEventListener('drop', dropped);
}
function ending(e){
  elem = e.target;
  elem.style.visibility = 'hidden';
}
function dragged(e){
  elem = e.target;
  e.dataTransfer.setData('Text', elem.getAttribute('id'));
  e.dataTransfer.setDragImage(elem, 0, 0);
}
function dropped(e){
  e.preventDefault();
  var id = e.dataTransfer.getData('Text');
  var elem = document.getElementById(id);
  var posx = e.pageX - drop.offsetLeft;
  var posy = e.pageY - drop.offsetTop;
  canvas.drawImage(elem, posx, posy);
}
addEventListener('load', initiate);
```

Listing 13-8: Programming a small drag and drop application

With this example, we are probably getting close to a real-life application. The script in Listing 13-8 controls three different aspects of the process. The **dragged()** function is called when the image is dragged and sets a customized drag image with the **setDragImage()** method. The script also gets the context to work with the canvas and draws the dropped image using the **drawImage()** method and the reference to the source. Finally, the source is hidden with the **ending()** function.

For the custom thumbnail, we use the same element that is being dragged. We didn't change anything about this aspect, but we set the position as **0, 0**. This means that now we know exactly where the thumbnail is positioned relative to the mouse pointer. We utilized this information in the **dropped()** function. Using the same technique introduced in previous chapters, we calculate exactly where the source was dropped on the canvas and draw the image in that precise location. If you test this example in browsers that support the **setDragImage()** method (e.g., Mozilla Firefox), you will see that the image is drawn on the canvas exactly where the thumbnail was located, making it easy for users to find the right place to drop the image.

> **IMPORTANT:** The script in Listing 13-8 uses the **dragend** event to hide the original image when the operation is over. This event is fired by the source when a drag operation is finished, either in success or failure. In our example, the image is hidden in both cases. You will have to create the proper controls to proceed only in case of success.

Files

Possibly the most interesting characteristic of the Drag and Drop API is the ability to work with files. The API is not only available within the document but also integrated with the system, allowing users to drag elements from the browser to other applications and vice versa. And usually files are the most required elements from external applications.

As we saw before, there is a special property for this purpose in the dataTransfer object that will return an array containing the list of files that have been dragged. We can use this information to build complex scripts to help users work with files or upload them to the server.

```html
<!DOCTYPE html>
<html lang="en">
<head>
  <title>Drag and Drop</title>
  <link rel="stylesheet" href="dragdrop.css">
  <script src="dragdrop.js"></script>
</head>
<body>
  <section id="dropbox">
    Drag and drop FILES here
  </section>
</body>
</html>
```

Listing 13-9: Simple HTML document to drop files

The HTML document of Listing 13-9 provides a drop box. The files will be dragged into this box from an external application (for example, File Explorer). The data from the files is processed by the following script:

```javascript
var drop;
function initiate(){
  drop = document.getElementById('dropbox');
  drop.addEventListener('dragenter', function(e){ e.preventDefault(); });
  drop.addEventListener('dragover', function(e){ e.preventDefault(); });
  drop.addEventListener('drop', dropped);
}
function dropped(e){
  e.preventDefault();
  var files = e.dataTransfer.files;
  var list = '';
  for(var f = 0; f < files.length; f++){
    list += 'File: ' + files[f].name + ' ' + files[f].size + '<br>';
  }
  drop.innerHTML = list;
}
addEventListener('load', initiate);
```

Listing 13-10: Processing the data contained in the files *property*

The information returned by the **files** property can be stored in a variable and then read by a **for** loop. The script of Listing 13-10 shows the name and size of every file in the drop box. To use this information to build more complex applications, we need to implement the Drag and Drop API along with other APIs, as we will see later in this book.

> **Do It Yourself:** Create new files with the document and the script of Listings 13-9 and 14-10, and open the HTML document in your browser. Drag files from the File Explorer

Drag and Drop API

or any other similar program to the drop box. You should see a list with the name and size of every file dropped inside this box.

Drag and Drop API

Chapter 14
Web Storage API

14.1 Two Storage Systems

The Web was first thought of as a way to display static information. The processing of that information started later, first with applications in servers and then inefficiently with short scripts and plug-ins on users' computers. However, the essence of the Web was basically still the same: the information was cooked on the server and then shown to users. The hard work was always done on the server side because the system wasn't taking advantage of the high resources available in users' computers.

HTML5 balanced this situation. Motivated by the particular characteristics of mobile devices, the emergence of cloud computing, and the need to standardize technologies and innovations incorporated by plug-ins over the years, HTML5 included features that make it possible to run full and completely functional applications on the client side.

One of the most necessary features for any application is the ability to store data and make it available when needed, but there was no effective mechanism that allowed this. Cookies were used to store small pieces of information on the client side, but due to their nature, they were limited to short strings and only useful in specific circumstances.

The Web Storage API is an improvement on cookies. The API lets us store data in the user's hard drive and use it later as a desktop application would. The storage process provided by this API may be used in two particular situations: when the information has to be available only during a session and when it has to be preserved as long as is determined by the user. To make this clear for developers, the API was divided into two parts called `sessionStorage` and `localStorage`.

> **sessionStorage**—This is a storage mechanism that will keep data available only for the duration of a page session. Actually, unlike real sessions, the information stored through this mechanism is only accessible from a single window or tab and lasts until the window is closed. The specification still talks about "sessions" because the information is preserved even when the window is refreshed or a new page from the same website is loaded.

> **localStorage**—This mechanism works similarly to a storage system for a desktop application. The data stored is permanently preserved and always available from the application that created it.

Both mechanisms work with a similar interface, sharing the same methods and properties. And both are origin dependent, which means the information is available only for the website that created it. Every website will have its own storage space that will last until the window is closed or will be permanent, according to the mechanism applied.

The API clearly differentiates temporary data from permanent data, facilitating the construction of small applications that need to preserve just a few strings as temporary reference (for example, shopping carts) or large, more complex ones that have to store entire documents for as much time as needed.

> **IMPORTANT:** Most browsers only work properly with this API when the source is a real server. To test the following examples, we recommend you first upload the files to your server.

14.2 sessionStorage

The `sessionStorage` is like a substitute for session cookies. Cookies, as well as `sessionStorage`, keep the data available during a specific period of time, but while cookies use the browser as reference, `sessionStorage` uses a single window or tab. This means that cookies created for a session are available as long as any browser window is still open, but the data created by `sessionStorage` are only available until the window is closed (and only for that particular window or tab).

Data Storage Implementation

Because both systems, `sessionStorage` and `localStorage`, work with the same interface, we are only going to need one HTML document and a simple form to test the codes and experiment with this API:

```
<!DOCTYPE html>
<html lang="en">
<head>
  <title>Web Storage API</title>
  <link rel="stylesheet" href="storage.css">
  <script src="storage.js"></script>
</head>
<body>
  <section id="formbox">
    <form name="form">
      <label for="keyword">Keyword: </label><br>
      <input type="text" name="keyword" id="keyword"><br>
      <label for="text">Value: </label><br>
      <textarea name="text" id="text"></textarea><br>
      <input type="button" id="save" value="Save">
    </form>
  </section>
  <section id="databox">
    No Information available
  </section>
</body>
</html>
```

Listing 14-1: *HTML document for the Storage API*

We will also create a simple set of styles to shape the page and differentiate the form area from the box where the data will be shown and listed:

```css
#formbox{
  float: left;
  padding: 20px;
  border: 1px solid #999999;
}
#databox{
  float: left;
  width: 400px;
  margin-left: 20px;
  padding: 20px;
  border: 1px solid #999999;
}
#keyword, #text{
  width: 200px;
}
#databox > div{
  padding: 5px;
  border-bottom: 1px solid #999999;
}
```

Listing 14-2: Styles for the boxes

Do It Yourself: Create an HTML file with the document of Listing 14-1 and a CSS file called `storage.css` with the styles in Listing 14-2. You will also need a file named `storage.js` to save and test the Javascript codes presented next.

Creating Data

Both `sessionStorage` and `localStorage` store data as items. The items are formed by a keyword/value pair, and every value will be converted to a string before being stored. Think of items as variables, each with a name and a value that can be created, modified or deleted.

The API provides specific methods to create and get an item from the storage space:

setItem(key, value)—This is the method we must call to create an item. The item will be created with a keyword and a value according to the specified attributes. If there is already an item with the same keyword, it will be updated with the new value, so this method may be also used to modify data previously stored.

getItem(key)—To retrieve the value of an item, we must call this method by specifying the keyword of the item we want. The keyword in this case is the same as the keyword declared when the item was created by `setItem()`.

```javascript
function initiate(){
  var button = document.getElementById('save');
  button.addEventListener('click', newitem);
}
```

```
function newitem(){
  var keyword = document.getElementById('keyword').value;
  var value = document.getElementById('text').value;
  sessionStorage.setItem(keyword, value);

  show(keyword);
}
function show(keyword){
  var databox = document.getElementById('databox');
  var value = sessionStorage.getItem(keyword);
  databox.innerHTML = '<div>' + keyword + ' - ' + value + '</div>';
}
addEventListener('load', initiate);
```

Listing 14-3: Storing and retrieving data

The process is extremely simple. The methods are part of `sessionStorage` and called with the syntax `sessionStorage.method()`. In the script of Listing 14-3, the `newitem()` function is executed every time the user clicks the "Save" button from the form. This function creates an item with the information inserted in the input fields and then calls the `show()` function. In this second function, the item is retrieved using the `getItem()` method and the value of the `keyword` attribute, and then the content of the item is inserted in the `databox` element and shown on the screen.

In addition to these methods, the API also provides a shortcut to create and get an item from the storage space. We can use the keyword of the item as a property of `sessionStorage` and get the values of the item this way. As for any other property, there are two syntaxes available: we can enclose a variable for the keyword in square brackets (for example, `sessionStorage[keyword] = value`), or we can use the dot notation (for example, `sessionStorage.myitem = value`).

```
function initiate(){
  var button = document.getElementById('save');
  button.addEventListener('click', newitem);
}
function newitem(){
  var keyword = document.getElementById('keyword').value;
  var value = document.getElementById('text').value;
  sessionStorage[keyword] = value;

  show(keyword);
}
function show(keyword){
  var databox = document.getElementById('databox');
  var value = sessionStorage[keyword];
  databox.innerHTML = '<div>' + keyword + ' - ' + value + '</div>';
}
addEventListener('load', initiate);
```

Listing 14-4: Using a shortcut to work with items

Reading Data

The previous examples only retrieve the last item stored. We are going to improve the script to make it more useful by taking advantage of more methods and properties provided by the API to manipulate items.

> **length**—This property returns the number of items accumulated in the storage space for this application. It works exactly like the `length` property used regularly in Javascript for arrays. It is useful for sequential readings.

> **key(index)**—The items are stored sequentially, enumerated with an automatic index that starts from 0. With this method, we can retrieve a specific item or create a loop to retrieve all the information stored.

```
function initiate(){
  var button = document.getElementById('save');
  button.addEventListener('click', newitem);
  show();
}
function newitem(){
  var keyword = document.getElementById('keyword').value;
  var value = document.getElementById('text').value;

  sessionStorage.setItem(keyword, value);
  document.getElementById('keyword').value = '';
  document.getElementById('text').value = '';
  show();
}
function show(){
  var databox = document.getElementById('databox');
  databox.innerHTML = '';
  for(var f = 0; f < sessionStorage.length; f++){
    var keyword = sessionStorage.key(f);
    var value = sessionStorage.getItem(keyword);
    databox.innerHTML += '<div>' + keyword + ' - ' + value + '</div>';
  }
}
addEventListener('load', initiate);
```

***Listing 14-5:** Listing the items in the storage space*

The purpose of this example is to get a complete list of items in the right box on the screen. The `show()` function was improved using the `length` property and the `key()` method. Inside a `for` loop, the `key()` method is called to return the corresponding keyword for each item. For example, if the item in the position 0 of the storage space was created with the keyword `myitem`, the instruction `sessionStorage.key(0)` will return the value `myitem`. Calling this method from a loop allows us to list all the items on the screen, each with its corresponding keyword and value.

The `show()` function is also called at the end of the `initiate()` function to show the items already stored in the storage space as soon as the application has loaded.

Do It Yourself: You can take advantage of the Forms API studied in Chapter 5 to check the validity of the input fields and not allow the insertion of invalid or empty items.

Deleting Data

The items can be created, read and, of course, deleted. There are two methods incorporated for this last purpose:

removeItem(key)—This method will delete a single item. The keyword to identify the item must be the same declared when it was created with the `setItem()` method.

clear()—This method will empty the storage space. Every item will be erased.

```
function initiate(){
  var button = document.getElementById('save');
  button.addEventListener('click', newitem);
  show();
}
function newitem(){
  var keyword = document.getElementById('keyword').value;
  var value = document.getElementById('text').value;

  sessionStorage.setItem(keyword, value);
  document.getElementById('keyword').value = '';
  document.getElementById('text').value = '';
  show();
}
function show(){
  var databox = document.getElementById('databox');
  databox.innerHTML = '<div><input type="button" onclick="removeAll()"
value="Erase Everything"></div>';
  for(var f = 0; f < sessionStorage.length; f++){
    var keyword = sessionStorage.key(f);
    var value = sessionStorage.getItem(keyword);
    databox.innerHTML += '<div>' + keyword + ' - ' + value + '<br><input
type="button" onclick="removeItem(\'' + keyword + '\')"
value="Remove"></div>';
  }
}
function removeItem(keyword){
  if(confirm('Are you sure?')){
    sessionStorage.removeItem(keyword);
    show();
  }
}
function removeAll(){
  if(confirm('Are you sure?')){
    sessionStorage.clear();
    show();
  }
}
addEventListener('load', initiate);
```

Listing 14-6: Deleting items in the storage space

The `initiate()` and `newitem()` functions in Listing 14-6 are the same as the previous script. Only the `show()` function changed to incorporate buttons with the `onclick` event attribute to call the functions that will delete an individual item or all of them. The code creates a "Remove" button for each item on the list and also a unique button at the top of the list to erase the entire storage space.

The `removeItem()` and `removeAll()` functions are responsible for deleting the selected item or clearing the storage space, respectively. Each function calls the `show()` function at the end to update the list of items on the screen.

> **Do It Yourself:** With the script of Listing 14-6, you will be able to test how the information is processed by `sessionStorage`. Open the HTML document of Listing 14-1 in your browser, create new items and then open the same document in a new window. The information in each window is different: the old window will keep its data available, but the storage space for the new window will be empty. Unlike other systems (like cookies), with `sessionStorage`, every window is considered an independent instance of the application and the information of the session is not shared between them.

The `sessionStorage` system preserves the data created in a window only until the window is closed. It is useful for controlling shopping carts or any other application that requires short-term data access.

14.3 localStorage

Having a reliable system to store data during a window session may be extremely useful in some circumstances, but when you try to emulate powerful desktop applications on the Web, a temporary data storage system is insufficient. To account for this, the Storage API provides a second system that will reserve storage space for every origin and keep the information permanently available. With `localStorage`, we can finally store large amounts of data and let the user decide whether the information is still useful and must be preserved or not.

This system uses the same interface as `sessionStorage`; therefore, every method and property studied so far in this chapter is available for `localStorage` as well. Only the substitution of the prefix `session` by `local` is required to prepare the codes.

```
function initiate(){
  var button = document.getElementById('save');
  button.addEventListener('click', newitem);
  show();
}
function newitem(){
  var keyword = document.getElementById('keyword').value;
  var value = document.getElementById('text').value;

  localStorage.setItem(keyword, value);
  show();
  document.getElementById('keyword').value = '';
  document.getElementById('text').value = '';
}
```

```
function show(){
  var databox = document.getElementById('databox');
  databox.innerHTML = '';
  for(var f = 0; f < localStorage.length; f++){
    var keyword = localStorage.key(f);
    var value = localStorage.getItem(keyword);
    databox.innerHTML += '<div>' + keyword + ' - ' + value + '</div>';
  }
}
addEventListener('load', initiate);
```

Listing 14-7: *Using* localStorage

In Listing 14-7, we take a previous script and replace **sessionStorage** with **localStorage**. Now every item created will be preserved through different windows or even after the browser is completely closed.

> **Do It Yourself:** Using the HTML document of Listing 14-1, test the script of Listing 14-7. This code will create a new item with the information from the form and automatically list every item available in the storage space reserved for the application. Close the browser and open the HTML file again. You will still be able to see all the items on the list.

Storage Event

Because **localStorage** makes the information available in every window where the same application is loaded, at least two problems arise: how these windows will communicate and how we will update the information in a window that is not active or focused. To solve both problems, the **storage** event was included in the specification.

> **storage**—This event will be fired by the window every time a change occurs in the storage space. It can be used to inform to every window opened with the same application that a change was made to the storage space and that something needs to be done about it.

```
function initiate(){
  var button = document.getElementById('save');
  button.addEventListener('click', newitem);
  addEventListener('storage', show);
  show();
}
function newitem(){
  var keyword = document.getElementById('keyword').value;
  var value = document.getElementById('text').value;

  localStorage.setItem(keyword, value);
  document.getElementById('keyword').value = '';
  document.getElementById('text').value = '';
  show();
}
```

Web Storage API

```
function show(){
  var databox = document.getElementById('databox');
  databox.innerHTML = '';
  for(var f = 0; f < localStorage.length; f++){
    var keyword = localStorage.key(f);
    var value = localStorage.getItem(keyword);
    databox.innerHTML += '<div>' + keyword + ' - ' + value + '</div>';
  }
}
addEventListener('load', initiate);
```

Listing 14-8: Listening to the `storage` *event to keep the list of items updated*

In this example, the **show()** function listens to the **storage** event and is executed every time an item is created, updated or erased. Now, if something changes in one window, it will be automatically shown in the other windows that are running the same application.

> **Do It Yourself:** Using the HTML document of Listing 14-1, test the script of Listing 14-8. Remember to upload the files to your server first. Open the document in two different windows. Insert or update an item in one window and move to the other window to see the **storage** event at work.

The **storage** event returns an object with several properties to provide information about the modification produced to the storage space:

> **key**—This property returns the key of the affected item.
>
> **oldValue**—This property returns the previous value of the affected item.
>
> **newValue**—This property returns the new value assigned to the item.
>
> **url**—This property returns the URL of the document that produced the modification. Remember that the storage space is reserved for the entire domain, so different documents have access to it.
>
> **storageArea**—This property returns an array containing all the keyword/value pairs in the storage space after the modification.

```
function initiate(){
  var button = document.getElementById('save');
  button.addEventListener('click', newitem);
  addEventListener('storage', storagechange);
  show();
}
function newitem(){
  var keyword = document.getElementById('keyword').value;
  var value = document.getElementById('text').value;
  localStorage.setItem(keyword, value);
  document.getElementById('keyword').value = '';
  document.getElementById('text').value = '';
  show();
}
```

```
function storagechange(e){
  console.log(e.key);
  console.log(e.oldValue);
  console.log(e.newValue);
  console.log(e.url);
  console.log(e.storageArea);
  show();
}
function show(){
  var databox = document.getElementById('databox');
  databox.innerHTML = '';
  for(var f = 0; f < localStorage.length; f++){
    var keyword = localStorage.key(f);
    var value = localStorage.getItem(keyword);
    databox.innerHTML += '<div>' + keyword + ' - ' + value + '</div>';
  }
}
addEventListener('load', initiate);
```

Listing 14-9: *Accessing the event properties*

In Listing 14-9, we add a new function to handle the **storage** event. The **storagechange()** function is called by the event when the storage space is modified by another window. It prints the values of the properties one by one in the browser's console and calls the **show()** function at the end to update the information on the screen.

Chapter 15
IndexedDB API

15.1 Structuring Data

The Storage API studied in the previous chapter is useful for storing small amounts of data, but when it comes to large amounts of structured data, we must resort to a database system. HTML5 provides the IndexedDB API to solve this issue.

IndexedDB is a database system capable of storing indexed information in users' computers. It was developed as a low-level API with the intention of allowing a wide range of uses. This turned it not only into a powerful API, but also into one of the most complex. The goal was to provide the most basic infrastructure possible to allow developers build things on top of it and create high-level interfaces for very specific needs. In a low-level API like this one, we have to take care of everything and control the condition of every process in every operation performed. The result is an API that most developers will take time to get used to and probably apply indirectly through third-party libraries such as jQuery, or others that will come out in the future.

The structure proposed by IndexedDB is also different from SQL or other popular database systems that developers are used to. The information is stored in the database as objects (records) inside what is called Object Stores (tables). The Object Stores have no specific structure, simply a name and indexes to find the objects inside. These objects don't have a predefined structure either; they can be different from one another and as complex as we want. The only condition for objects is that they have at least one property declared as the index so the Object Store is able to find them.

Database

The database itself is simple. Because every database is associated with one computer and one website or application, there are no users to assign or any other access restrictions to manage. We simply specify the name and the version, and the database is ready.

The API includes the **indexedDB** property to have access to the database. This property provides an object with the following methods:

> **open(name, version)**—This method creates or opens the database with the name and version specified by its attributes. The version may be ignored when the database is created, but it is required to set a new version for an existing database. The method returns an object that fires two events (**error** and **success**) to indicate an error or the success in creating or accessing the database.
>
> **deleteDatabase(name)**—This method deletes the database with the name specified in its attribute.

The API provides the opportunity to assign a version to the database to be able to update its structure. When you have to update the structure of a database on the server side to add more tables or indexes, you usually create a second database with the new structure and then move data from the old database to the new one. This process requires full access to the server and even the ability to turn it off. However, you can't turn off the user's computer to repeat this process in a browser. As a result, a version number has to be declared in the `open()` method to be able to migrate the information from the old version to the new one.

To work with database versions, the API also provides the `upgradeneeded` event. This event is fired when the `open()` method tries to open a non-existent database or a new version for the current database was specified.

Objects and Object Stores

What we used to call records are called objects in IndexedDB. These objects include properties to store and identify values. The number of properties and how the objects are structured is irrelevant. They just have to include at least one property declared as the index for the Object Store to be able to find them.

The Object Stores (tables) don't have a specific structure either. Only the name and one or more indexes must be declared when they are created in order to be able to find objects inside.

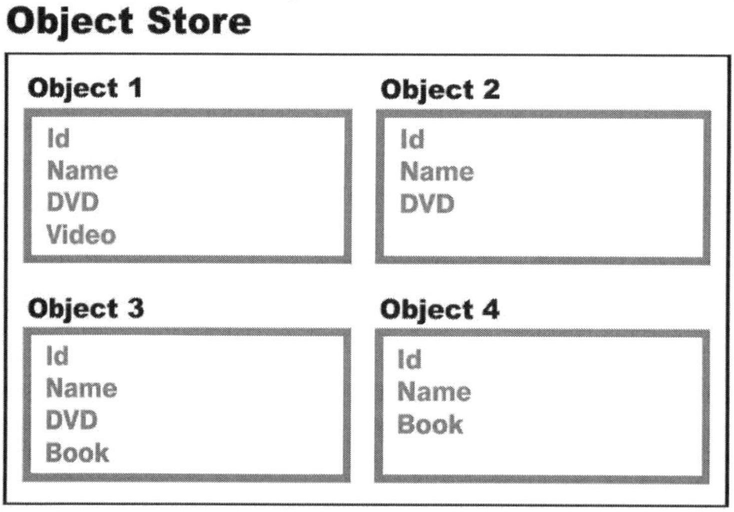

Figure 15-1: Objects with different properties stored in an Object Store

As you can see in Figure 15-1, an Object Store contains diverse objects with different properties. In this example, some objects have the DVD property, others have the Book property, etc. Each one has its own structure, but they must have at least one property selected as the index for the Object Store to be able to find them (in Figure 15-1's example, the property assigned for this purpose could be Id).

To work with objects and Object Stores, we need to create the Object Store, declare the properties that will be used as indexes and then start storing objects in it. We don't have to think about the structure and content of the objects right now, but only consider the indexes we are going to need to be able to find them later. The API provides several methods to manipulate Object Stores:

createObjectStore(name, object)—This method creates a new Object Store with the name and configuration set by its attributes. The attribute `name` is mandatory. The `object` attribute is an object that may include the properties `keyPath` and `autoIncrement`. The `keyPath` property declares a common index for every object, and the `autoIncrement` property is a Boolean property that determines whether or not the Object Store will have a key generator.

deleteObjectStore(name)—This method will destroy the Object Store with the name declared by the `name` attribute.

objectStore(name)—To access the objects in an Object Store, a transaction must be started, and the Object Store has to be opened for that transaction. This method will open the Object Store with the name declared by the `name` attribute.

The `createObjectStore()` and `deleteObjectStore()` methods, as well as other methods responsible for the configuration of the database, can only be applied when the database is created or upgraded to a new version.

Indexes

To find objects in an Object Store, we need to set some properties of these objects as indexes. An easy way to do this is to declare the `keyPath` property in the `createObjectStore()` method. The property declared as `keyPath` will be a common index for every object stored in that particular Object Store. When we set a `keyPath`, the property declared as the index must be present in every object.

Besides the `keyPath`, we can set all the indexes we want for an Object Store using special methods provided for this purpose:

createIndex(name, property, object)—This method creates an index for a specific object. The `name` attribute is a name to identify the index, and the `property` attribute is the object's property used for the index. The `object` attribute is an object that may include the properties `unique` or `multiEntry`. The `unique` property indicates whether the index value has to be unique or multiple objects can share the same index value. The `multiEntry` property determines how the keys for an object will be generated when the index is an array.

deleteIndex(name)—If we no longer need an index, we can delete it using this method. This method can only be called from a `versionchange` transaction.

index(name)—To use an index we first have to create a reference to the index and then assign this reference to the transaction. The `index()` method creates a reference to the index declared by the `name` attribute.

Transactions

A database system working on a browser must consider some unique circumstances that are not present in other platforms. For example, the browser could fail, it could be closed abruptly, the process could be stopped by the user, or another website could be loaded in the same window. There are many situations in which working directly with the database can cause a malfunction or even data corruption. To prevent this from happening, every action is performed through transactions.

The method for generating a transaction is called `transaction()`, and several attributes set the type of the transaction:

readonly—This attribute sets a read-only transaction. Modifications are not allowed.

readwrite—Using this type of transaction, we can read and write the database. Modifications are allowed, but we can't add or remove Object Stores and indexes.

versionchange—This type of transaction is used for updating the version of the database as well as adding or removing Object Stores and indexes.

The most common transactions are `readwrite`. However, to prevent misuse, the `readonly` type is set by default, so when we need to just get information from the database, the only thing we have to do is specify the scope of the transaction (usually the name of the Object Store we are going to get the information from) and the type of transaction is set automatically.

Object Stores' Methods

To interact with Object Stores, read and store information, the API provides several methods:

add(object)—This method receives a keyword/value pair or an object containing several keyword/value pairs, and with this information, it adds an object to the selected Object Store. If an object with the same index already exist, the `add()` method returns an error.

put(object)—This method is similar to the previous one except it overwrites an existing object with the same index. This method is useful to update an object already stored in the selected Object Store.

get(key)—We can retrieve a specific object from an Object Store using this method. The `key` attribute is the value of the index of the object we want to read.

delete(key)—To delete an object from the selected Object Store, we simply call this method with the value of the index as attribute.

15.2 Implementing IndexedDB

Enough with theory! Let's create our first database and apply some of the methods already mentioned in this chapter. We are going to simulate an application to store information about movies. You can add your own information, but for our examples, we are going to use the following:

id: tt0068646 **name:** The Godfather **date:** 1972
id: tt0086567 **name:** WarGames **date:** 1983
id: tt0111161 **name:** The Shawshank Redemption **date:** 1994
id: tt1285016 **name:** The Social Network **date:** 2010

IMPORTANT: The names of these properties (`id`, `name` and `date`) are going to be used for our examples in the rest of the chapter. The information was collected from the website www.imdb.com, but you can make your own list or use random information to test the codes.

HTML Document

As usual, we need an HTML document and some CSS styles to get the boxes for a form and to show the information retrieved. The form will let us add new movies to the database by asking for a keyword, the title of the movie and the year when it was made.

```
<!DOCTYPE html>
<html lang="en">
<head>
  <title>IndexedDB API</title>
  <link rel="stylesheet" href="indexed.css">
  <script src="indexed.js"></script>
</head>
<body>
  <section id="formbox">
    <form name="form">
      <label for="keyword">Keyword: </label><br>
      <input type="text" name="keyword" id="keyword"><br>
      <label for="text">Title: </label><br>
      <input type="text" name="text" id="text"><br>
      <label for="year">Year: </label><br>
      <input type="text" name="year" id="year"><br>
      <input type="button" id="save" value="Save">
    </form>
  </section>
  <section id="databox">
    No Information available
  </section>
</body>
</html>
```

Listing 15-1: HTML document for the IndexedDB API

The CSS styles define the boxes for the form and how to render the information on the screen.

```
#formbox{
  float: left;
  padding: 20px;
  border: 1px solid #999999;
}
#databox{
  float: left;
  width: 400px;
  margin-left: 20px;
  padding: 20px;
  border: 1px solid #999999;
}
#keyword, #text{
  width: 200px;
}
```

```
#databox > div{
  padding: 5px;
  border-bottom: 1px solid #999999;
}
```

Listing 15-2: Styles for the boxes

Do It Yourself: You will need an HTML file for the document in Listing 15-1, a CSS file called `indexed.css` for the styles in Listing 15-2 and a Javascript file called `indexed.js` for all the codes studied next.

Opening the Database

The first step in the Javascript code is to open the database. The `open()` method of the indexedDB object opens the database with the given name or creates a new one if it doesn't exist.

```
var databox, db;
function initiate(){
  databox = document.getElementById('databox');
  var button = document.getElementById('save');
  button.addEventListener('click', addobject);

  var request = indexedDB.open('mydatabase');
  request.addEventListener('error', showerror);
  request.addEventListener('success', start);
  request.addEventListener('upgradeneeded', createdb);
}
```

Listing 15-3: Opening the database

The `initiate()` function in Listing 15-3 prepares the elements of the document and opens the database. The `indexedDB.open()` instruction tries to open a database with the name `mydatabase` and returns the request object with the result of the operation. The `error`, `success` and `upgradeneeded` events are fired from this object according to the result of the operation.

Events are an important part of this API. IndexedDB is both a synchronous and asynchronous API. The synchronous part is currently being developed, and it's intended to work with the Web Workers API. In contrast, the purpose of the asynchronous API is to be used in the document as any other script and is already available. An asynchronous system performs tasks in the background and returns the results later. For this purpose, this API fires different events for every operation. Any action over the database and its content is processed in the background (while the system is executing other codes), and events are fired later to inform the results.

After the API processes the request for the database, an `error` or `success` event is fired, and the `showerror()` or the `start()` function in our code is executed to control the errors or continue with the definition of the database.

```
function showerror(e){
  alert('Error: ' + e.code + ' ' + e.message);
}
function start(e){
  db = e.target.result;
}
```

Listing 15-4: Reporting errors and getting a reference to the database

Our **showerror()** and **start()** functions are simple (we don't need to process errors or do anything other than get a reference to the database for this small application). Error information is shown using the **code** and **message** properties of the event; and a reference to the database is captured by the **result** property and then is stored in the global variable **db**. This variable will be used to represent the database in the rest of the code.

The **result** property is part of the IDBRequest interface. An object based on this interface is sent by the events in every operation. The object provides the following properties:

> **result**—This property returns an object with the result of the request—for example, an object representing the database or an object representing the object retrieved from the Object Store.
>
> **source**—This property returns an object with information about the source of the request.
>
> **transaction**—This property returns an object with information about the transaction.
>
> **readyState**—This property returns the current condition of the transaction. The possible values are **pending** or **done**.
>
> **error**—This property returns the error of the request.

In our examples, we are only going to use the **result** property to get a reference to the database and the objects from the Object Store.

Object Stores and Indexes

In case a new version for the database is declared by the **open()** method, or the database doesn't yet exist, the **upgradeneeded** event is fired and the **createdb()** function is called to handle the event. At this point, you have to think about what kind of objects you need to store in the database and how you are going to get this information from the Object Stores later. If the structure is incorrect or you want to add something to the configuration of your database in the future, you will have to set a new version and migrate the data from the previous one or modify the structure through a **versionchange** transaction.

```
function createdb(e){
  var datababase = e.target.result;
  var mystore = datababase.createObjectStore('movies', {keyPath: 'id'});
  mystore.createIndex('SearchYear', 'date', {unique: false});
}
```

Listing 15-5: Declaring Object Stores and indexes

For our example, we only need one Object Store (to store the movies) and two indexes. The first index, `id`, is set as the `keyPath` attribute for the `createObjectStore()` method when the Object Store is created. The second index is assigned to the Object Store using the `createIndex()` method. This index is identified with the name `SearchYear` and declared for the `date` property. We are going to use this index to order the movies by year.

Notice that in this function we had to take the reference to the database from the `result` property again. When the `createdb()` function is called, the `success` event hasn't been fired yet and the reference to the database hasn't been created (the value for the `db` variable hasn't been defined yet).

Adding Objects

So far, we have a database named `mydatabase` and one Object Store named `movies` with two indexes: `id` and `date`. Now, it's time to start adding objects to this Object Store.

```
function addobject(){
  var keyword = document.getElementById('keyword').value;
  var title = document.getElementById('text').value;
  var year = document.getElementById('year').value;

  var mytransaction = db.transaction(['movies'], "readwrite");
  var mystore = mytransaction.objectStore('movies');
  var request = mystore.add({id: keyword, name: title, date: year});
  request.addEventListener('success', function(){ show(keyword) });
  document.getElementById('keyword').value = '';
  document.getElementById('text').value = '';
  document.getElementById('year').value = '';
}
```

Listing 15-6: *Adding objects to our Object Store*

At the beginning of the `initiate()` function, we added a listener for the `click` event to the button in the form. This `addobject()` function is executed when this event is fired. This function takes the values from the form (`keyword`, `text` and `year`) and generates a transaction to store a new object using this information.

To start a transaction, we have to use the `transaction()` method and specify the Object Stores involved in the transaction and the type of transaction. In this case, the only Object Store is `movies` and the type is set as `readwrite`.

The next step is to select the Object Store we are going to use. Because the transaction can be started for several Object Stores, we have to declare which one corresponds to the operation we want to perform. Using the `objectStore()` method, we open the Object Store and assign it to the transaction with the following line: `mytransaction.objectStore('movies')`.

Now, it's time to add the object to the Object Store. In this example, we use the `add()` method because we want to create new objects, but we could have used the `put()` method if we wanted to modify or replace old objects. The `add()` method takes the properties `id`, `name` and `date` and the variables `keyword`, `title` and `year` and creates the object using these values as keyword/value pairs.

Finally, the `show()` function listens to the `success` event fired by this request and is executed in case of success. There is also an `error` event, of course, but since the answer depends on the requirements of the application, we are not considering this possibility in our example.

Getting Objects

If the object is stored correctly, the **success** event is fired and the **show()** function is executed. In the code in Listing 15-6, this function was declared inside an anonymous function to be able to pass the variable **keyword**. Now we are going to take this value to read the object previously stored.

```
function show(keyword){
  var mytransaction = db.transaction(['movies']);
  var mystore = mytransaction.objectStore('movies');
  var request = mystore.get(keyword);
  request.addEventListener('success', showlist);
}
function showlist(e){
  var result = e.target.result;
  databox.innerHTML = '<div>' + result.id + ' - ' + result.name + ' - ' +
result.date + '</div>';
}
```

Listing 15-7: Showing the new object

The script of Listing 15-7 generates a **readonly** transaction and uses the **get()** method to retrieve the object with the keyword received. We don't have to declare the transaction type because **readonly** is set by default.

The **get()** method returns the object stored with the property **id** = **keyword**. If, for example, we inserted the movie *The Godfather* from our list, the variable **keyword** would have the value "tt0068646". This value is received by the **show()** function and used by the **get()** method to retrieve the movie *The Godfather*. As you can see, this code is just for demonstration purposes because it returns the same movie we just added.

Because every operation is asynchronous, we need two functions to show this information. The **show()** function generates the transaction, and the **showlist()** function shows the value of the properties on the screen in the case of success. Again, we are only listening to the **success** event, but an **error** event is also fired from this operation in case something went wrong.

The **showlist()** function takes the object returned by the **result** property and stores its value in the **result** variable. The value is the object retrieved from the Object Store, so to access its content, we write the variable representing the object and the name of the property (for example, **result.id**). The variable **result** represents the object and **id** is one of its properties.

Finishing the Code and Testing

As in any previous script, to end this example we must add the **initiate()** function as the listener for the **load** event.

```
addEventListener('load', initiate);
```

> **Do It Yourself:** Copy all the Javascript codes from Listings 15-3 to 15-8 in the `indexed.js` file, and open the HTML document of Listing 15-1 in your browser. Using the form on the screen, insert the movie information listed at the beginning of this chapter. Every time a new movie is inserted, the same information will be shown in the right box on the screen.

15.3 Listing Data

The `get()` method implemented in the script of Listing 15-7 returns only one object at a time (the last movie inserted). In the next example, we are going to use a cursor to generate a list that includes all the movies stored in the `movies` Object Store.

Cursors

Cursors are the alternative provided by the API to retrieve and navigate through a group of objects returned by the database in a transaction. A cursor gets a specific list of objects from the Object Store and starts a pointer that points to one object of the list at a time.

The API provides the `openCursor()` method to generate a cursor. This method extracts information from the selected Object Store and returns an IDBCursor object that has its own methods to manipulate the cursor:

> **continue(index)**—This method moves the pointer of the cursor one position, and the **success** event of the cursor is fired again. When the pointer reaches the end of the list, the **success** event is also fired but the object returned is empty. The pointer can be moved to a specific position by providing an index value between the parentheses.
>
> **delete()**—This method deletes the object in the current cursor position.
>
> **update(value)**—This method is similar to `put()` but updates the value of the object in the current cursor position.

The `openCursor()` method also has properties to specify the type and order of objects returned. The values by default return all the objects available in the selected Object Store in ascending order. We will see more on this later.

```
var databox, db;
function initiate(){
  databox = document.getElementById('databox');
  var button = document.getElementById('save');
  button.addEventListener('click', addobject);
```

```
  var request = indexedDB.open('mydatabase');
  request.addEventListener('error', showerror);
  request.addEventListener('success', start);
  request.addEventListener('upgradeneeded', createdb);
}
function showerror(e){
  alert('Error: ' + e.code + ' ' + e.message);
}
function start(e){
  db = e.target.result;
  show();
}
function createdb(e){
  var datababase = e.target.result;
  var mystore = datababase.createObjectStore('movies', {keyPath: 'id'});
  mystore.createIndex('SearchYear', 'date', {unique: false});
}
function addobject(){
  var keyword = document.getElementById('keyword').value;
  var title = document.getElementById('text').value;
  var year = document.getElementById('year').value;

  var mytransaction = db.transaction(['movies'], "readwrite");
  var mystore = mytransaction.objectStore('movies');
  var request = mystore.add({id: keyword, name: title, date: year});
  request.addEventListener('success', show);
  document.getElementById('keyword').value = '';
  document.getElementById('text').value = '';
  document.getElementById('year').value = '';
}
function show(){
  databox.innerHTML = '';
  var mytransaction = db.transaction(['movies']);
  var mystore = mytransaction.objectStore('movies');
  var newcursor = mystore.openCursor();
  newcursor.addEventListener('success', showlist);
}
function showlist(e){
  var cursor = e.target.result;
  if(cursor){
    databox.innerHTML += '<div>' + cursor.value.id + ' - ' +
cursor.value.name + ' - ' + cursor.value.date + '</div>';
    cursor.continue();
  }
}
addEventListener('load', initiate);
```

Listing 15-9: *Listing objects*

Listing 15-9 shows the full Javascript code necessary for this example. Of all the functions used to initialize and configure the database, only **start()** presents a small change. Now the **show()** function is called at the end of **start()** to show the list of objects in the Object Store on the screen as soon as the document has loaded.

The big changes in this script are in the **show()** and **showlist()** functions. Here, we are working with cursors for the first time.

Reading information from the database with a cursor is also an operation that has to be made through a transaction. So, the first step in the **show()** function is to generate a **readonly** transaction for the **movies** Object Store. This Object Store is selected for this transaction, and then the cursor is open for this Object Store with the **openCursor()** method.

If the operation is successful, an object is returned with all the information retrieved from the Object Store; a **success** event is fired from this object; and the **showlist()** function is executed.

To read the information, the object returned by the operation provides several properties:

> **key**—This property returns the value of the key for the object in the current cursor position.
>
> **value**—This property returns an object with the values of the properties of the object in the current cursor position. To read these values we have to access the properties from the **value** property using the dot notation (e.g., **value.year**).
>
> **direction**—The objects can be read in ascending or descending order; this property returns the current condition.
>
> **count**—This property returns the approximate number of objects in the cursor.

In the **showlist()** function of Listing 15-9, we used the **if** statement to test the content of the cursor. If no objects are returned or the pointer reaches the end of the list, then the value of the **cursor** variable will be **null** and the loop will be over. However, when the pointer is pointing to a valid object, the information is shown on the screen, and the pointer is moved to the next position with **continue()**.

It's important to mention that we don't have to use a **while** loop here because the **continue()** method fires the **success** event again, and the whole function is executed again until the cursor returns **null**.

> **Do It Yourself:** The script of Listing 15-9 replaces all the previous Javascript codes in this chapter. Copy this script into the **indexed.js** file. Open the document of Listing 15-1 and, if you haven't yet, insert all the movies listed at the beginning of this chapter. You will see the complete list of the movies in the right box in ascending order according to the value of the **id** property.

Changing Order

There are two things we probably need to modify to finally get the list we want. All the movies in our example are listed in ascending order, and the property used to organize the objects is **id**. This property is the **keyPath** for the **movies** Object Store, but it is not likely the value that will interest our users.

Considering this situation, in the **createdb()** function in Listing 15-9 we added another index to our store. The name of this additional index is **SearchYear**, and the property assigned to the index is **date**. This index will let us order the movies according to the value of the year in which they were made.

```
function show(){
  databox.innerHTML = '';
  var mytransaction = db.transaction(['movies']);
  var mystore = mytransaction.objectStore('movies');
  var myindex = mystore.index('SearchYear');
```

```
var newcursor = myindex.openCursor(null, "prev");
newcursor.addEventListener('success', showlist);
}
```

Listing 15-10: Listing objects by year in d*escending order*

The function in Listing 15-10 replaces the `show()` function of the script in Listing 15-9. This new function generates a transaction, then assigns the index `SearchYear` to the Object Store used in the transaction, and finally uses `openCursor()` to get the objects that have the property corresponding to that index (in this case, `date`).

There are two attributes we can provide to select and order the information returned by the cursor. The first attribute specifies the range to select the objects, and the second is one of the following constants:

> **next**—The order of the objects returned will be ascending (which is the value by default).
>
> **nextunique**—The order of the objects returned will be ascending, and duplicated objects will be ignored. (Only the first object is returned if a duplicated keyword is found.)
>
> **prev**—The order of the objects returned will be descending.
>
> **prevunique**—The order of the objects returned will be descending, and duplicated objects will be ignored. (Only the first object is returned if a duplicated keyword is found.)

With the `openCursor()` method applied in the `show()` function of Listing 15-10, we retrieved the objects in descending order and declared the range attribute as `null`. We are going to see how to build a range at the end of this chapter.

> **Do It Yourself:** Take the previous script of Listing 15-9 and replace the `show()` function with the new function of Listing 15-10. This new function lists the movies on the screen by year in descending order (the newest first). The result should be the following:
>
> **id:** tt1285016 **name:** The Social Network **date:** 2010
> **id:** tt0111161 **name:** The Shawshank Redemption **date:** 1994
> **id:** tt0086567 **name:** WarGames **date:** 1983
> **id:** tt0068646 **name:** The Godfather **date:** 1972

15.4 Deleting Data

We have learned how to add, get and list data. It's time to provide the possibility to delete objects from the Object Store. As we mentioned previously, the `delete()` method provided by the API receives a value and deletes the object with the keyword corresponding to that value.

The script is simple; it only needs to create a button for every object listed on the screen and generate a `readwrite` transaction to be able to perform the delete operation.

```
function showlist(e){
  var cursor = e.target.result;
  if(cursor){
    databox.innerHTML += '<div>' + cursor.value.id + ' - ' +
cursor.value.name + ' - ' + cursor.value.date + ' <input type="button"
onclick="removeobject(\'' + cursor.value.id + '\')"
value="remove"></div>';

    cursor.continue();
  }
}
function removeobject(keyword){
  if(confirm('Are you sure?')){
    var mytransaction = db.transaction(['movies'], "readwrite");
    var mystore = mytransaction.objectStore('movies');
    var request = mystore.delete(keyword);
    request.addEventListener('success', show);
  }
}
```

Listing 15-11: Deleting objects

The button added for every object in the `showlist()` function in Listing 15-11 has an event attribute. Every time the user clicks on one of these buttons, the `removeobject()` function is executed with the value of the `id` property as its attribute. This function first generates the `readwrite` transaction, and then, using the value of the `keyword` variable, proceeds to delete the corresponding object from the `movies` Object Store.

At the end, if the operation is successful, the `success` event is fired and the `show()` function is executed to update the list of movies on the screen.

> **Do It Yourself:** Take the previous script of Listing 15-9, replace the `showlist()` function and add the `remove()` function of Listing 15-11. Finally, open the HTML document of Listing 15-1 to test the application. You will see the list of movies, but now, every line includes a button to delete the movie from the Object Store.

15.5 Searching Data

The most important operation performed in a database system is probably search. The purpose of this kind of system is to index information to make it easier to find. As we studied earlier in this chapter, the `get()` method is useful to return one object at a time when we know the value of its keyword, but a search operation is usually more complex than that.

In order to get a specific list of objects from an Object Store, we have to pass a range as the first argument for the `openCursor()` method. The API provides the IDBKeyRange interface with several methods and properties to declare a range and limit the objects returned:

> **only(value)**—Only the objects with the keyword equal to `value` are returned. For example, if we search movies by year using `only("1972")`, the movie *The Godfather* will be the only one returned from our list.

bound(lower, upper, lowerOpen, upperOpen)—To really create a range, we must have starting and ending values and also specify whether or not those values will be included in the list. The value of the attribute `lower` specifies the starting point of the list. The `upper` attribute specifies the ending point. `LowerOpen` and `upperOpen` are Boolean values to declare if the objects that exactly match the values of the `lower` and `upper` attributes will be ignored. For example, `bound("1972", "2010", false, true)` will return the list of the movies made from the year 1972 to the year 2010 but not include those made in 2010, because the Boolean value is `true` for the ending point and the movies made that year are not included.

lowerBound(value, open)—This method creates an open range that will start from `value` and go to the end of the list. For example, `lowerBound("1983", true)` will return all the movies made after 1983 not including the ones made that year.

upperBound(value, open)—This method is the opposite of the previous. It will create an open range, but the objects returned will be from the beginning of the list to `value`. For example, `upperBound("1983", false)` will return the movies made before 1983 including those made that year.

Let's first prepare a new document to provide a form for searching movies:

```
<!DOCTYPE html>
<html lang="en">
<head>
  <title>IndexedDB API</title>
  <link rel="stylesheet" href="indexed.css">
  <script src="indexed.js"></script>
</head>
<body>
  <section id="formbox">
    <form name="form">
      <label for="year">Find Movie by Year: </label><br>
      <input type="text" name="year" id="year"><br>
      <input type="button" id="find" value="Find">
    </form>
  </section>
  <section id="databox">
    No Information available
  </section>
</body>
</html>
```

Listing 15-12: HTML document with a *search form*

This new HTML document provides a button and a text input field to let us type the year and find movies according to the range specified in the script below:

```
var databox, db;
function initiate(){
  databox = document.getElementById('databox');
  var button = document.getElementById('find');
  button.addEventListener('click', findobjects);
```

```
  var request = indexedDB.open('mydatabase');
  request.addEventListener('error', showerror);
  request.addEventListener('success', start);
  request.addEventListener('upgradeneeded', createdb);
}
function showerror(e){
  alert('Error: ' + e.code + ' ' + e.message);
}
function start(e){
  db = e.target.result;
}
function createdb(e){
  var datababase = e.target.result;
  var mystore = datababase.createObjectStore('movies', {keyPath: 'id'});
  mystore.createIndex('SearchYear', 'date', {unique: false});
}
function findobjects(){
  databox.innerHTML = '';
  var find = document.getElementById('year').value;

  var mytransaction = db.transaction(['movies']);
  var mystore = mytransaction.objectStore('movies');
  var myindex = mystore.index('SearchYear');
  var myrange = IDBKeyRange.only(find);

  var newcursor = myindex.openCursor(myrange);
  newcursor.addEventListener('success', showlist);
}
function showlist(e){
  var cursor = e.target.result;
  if(cursor){
    databox.innerHTML += '<div>' + cursor.value.id + ' - ' +
cursor.value.name + ' - ' + cursor.value.date + '</div>';
    cursor.continue();
  }
}
addEventListener('load', initiate);
```

Listing 15-13: Searching for movies

The **findobjects()** function is a new addition to Listing 15-13. In this function, we generate
a **readonly** transaction for the **movies** Object Store, open the index **SearchYear** to use the
date property as index and create a range that will only involve the objects with a keyword
equal to the value of the variable **find** (the year inserted in the form). The method used for the
range is **only()**, but you can test any other mentioned before. This range is passed as an
attribute of the **openCursor()** method. After a successful operation, the **showlist()** function
will print the list of the movies on the screen that match the selected year.

The **only()** method returns only movies that exactly match the value of the variable **find**.
To test other methods, you can provide your own values for the attributes—for example,
bound(find, "2012", false, true).

The **openCursor()** method can take the two possible attributes at the same time.
Therefore, an instruction like **openCursor(range, "prev")** is valid and will get the objects
inside the range in descending order (using the same index as a reference).

Chapter 16

File API

16.1 File Storage

Files are units of information that users can easily share with others. Users can't share the value of a variable, but they can make copies of their files and share them on a DVD, on portable hard drives, through the Internet, etc. Files can store a large amount of data and be moved, duplicated or transmitted independently of the nature of their content.

Files have always been an essential part of every application, but until now there was no possible way to work with them on the Web. The options were basically limited to downloading or uploading pre-existing files in servers' or users' computers. There was no file creation, duplication nor processing on the Web until HTML5 arrived. This new technology was developed considering every aspect of the construction and operability of web applications. From design to elemental data structure, everything has been included; and files, of course, couldn't be ignored. For this reason, HTML5 introduces the File API.

The File API shares characteristics with some of the APIs studied in previous chapters. The File API has a low-level infrastructure, although not as complex as IndexedDB, and it can work synchronously or asynchronously. The synchronous part was developed to be used with the Web Workers API, like IndexedDB and other APIs, and the asynchronous part was made to run in the document as a common script. These characteristics mean that we will have to manage each aspect of the process, check for success or failure and probably adopt (or develop ourselves) simpler APIs built on the top of it.

The File API is an old API that has been improved and expanded. At this point, it is composed of three specifications—File API, File API: Directories & System, and File API: Writer—but this situation might change in the months following publication with the incorporation of new specifications or even the unification of some. Basically, the File API lets us interact with local files and process their content in our application; the File API: Directories & System extension provides the tools to work with a small file system created specifically for each application; and the File API: Writer extension is used for writing content within files that were created or downloaded by the application.

16.2 Processing the User's Files

Working with local files from a web application can be dangerous. Browsers have to consider security measures before even contemplating the possibility of letting applications have access to the user's files. Considering this, the File API provides only two loading methods: the `<input>` tag and the drag and drop operation.

In Chapter 13, we learned how to use the Drag and Drop API to drag files from desktop applications and drop them into a space on our web page. The `<input>` tag with the `file` type shares similar characteristics. Both this tag and the Drag and Drop API transmit files through the `files` property. Just as before, we can explore the value of this property to get every file that was selected or dropped.

> **IMPORTANT:** This API and its extensions do not work from a local host, and only Google Chrome and Mozilla Firefox have implementations available. To run the examples in this chapter, you will have to upload every file to your server.

HTML Document

In this part of the chapter, we are going to use the `<input>` tag to select files, but you can always utilize the information in Chapter 13 to integrate these codes with the Drag and Drop API.

```
<!DOCTYPE html>
<html lang="en">
<head>
  <title>File API</title>
  <link rel="stylesheet" href="file.css">
  <script src="file.js"></script>
</head>
<body>
  <section id="formbox">
    <form name="form">
      <label for="myfiles">File: </label><br>
      <input type="file" name="myfiles" id="myfiles">
    </form>
  </section>
  <section id="databox">
    No File Selected
  </section>
</body>
</html>
```

Listing 16-1: *Working with user's files*

The CSS file includes styles for this document and others we are going to use later:

```
#formbox{
  float: left;
  padding: 20px;
  border: 1px solid #999999;
}
#databox{
  float: left;
  width: 500px;
  margin-left: 20px;
  padding: 20px;
  border: 1px solid #999999;
}
```

```
.directory{
  color: #0000FF;
  font-weight: bold;
  cursor: pointer;
}
```

Listing 16-2: Styles for the form and the `databox`

Reading Files

The API provides a constructor to get the FileReader object. This object includes properties, methods and events to read users' files from their computer.

FileReader()—This constructor returns a FileReader object. The object must be created before reading the files. The process is asynchronous and the result is informed through events.

To get file's content, the FileReader object includes the following methods:

readAsText(file, encoding)—This method processes the file's content as text. The content is returned decoded as UTF-8 text unless the **encoding** attribute is specified. This method will try to interpret every byte or multi-byte sequences as text characters.

readAsBinaryString(file)—The information is read by this method as a succession of integers in the range of 0 to 255. This method ensures that each byte is read as it is, without any attempt to interpret it. It's useful to process binary content like images or videos.

readAsDataURL(file)—This method generates a base64 encoded data:url representing the file's data.

readAsArrayBuffer(file)—This method generates data as an ArrayBuffer from the file's data.

```
var databox;
function initiate(){
  databox = document.getElementById('databox');
  var myfiles = document.getElementById('myfiles');
  myfiles.addEventListener('change', process);
}
function process(e){
  var files = e.target.files;
  var myfile = files[0];
  var reader = new FileReader();
  reader.addEventListener('load', show);
  reader.readAsText(myfile);
}
function show(e){
  var result = e.target.result;
  databox.innerHTML = result;
}
addEventListener('load', initiate);
```

Listing 16-3: Reading a text file

The input field in the HTML document of Listing 16-1 let the user select the file to be processed. To detect the selection, in the `initiate()` function of Listing 16-3 a listener for the `change` event is added to the `<input>` element, and the `process()` function is prepared to handle the event.

The `files` property sent by the `<input>` element (and the Drag and Drop API, as well) is an array containing all the files selected. When the `multiple` attribute is not present in the `<input>` element, it is not possible to select multiple files, so the first element of the array will be the only one available. At the beginning of the `process()` function, we take the content of the `files` property, put it into the `files` variable and then select the first element of this array with the instruction `var myfile = files[0]`.

> **IMPORTANT:** To learn more about the `multiple` attribute, see Listing 5-22 in Chapter 5. You can also find an example of how to work with multiple files in the script of Listing 13-10 in Chapter 13.

The first thing we have to do to process the file is to use the `FileReader()` constructor to get a FileReader object. In the `process()` function in Listing 16-3, we call this object `reader`. Next, we must add a listener for the `load` event to detect when the file has loaded and is ready to be processed. Finally, the `readAsText()` method reads the file and gets its content as text.

When the `readAsText()` method finishes reading the file, the `load` event is fired and the `show()` function is called. This function takes the content of the file from the `result` property of the `reader` object and shows it on the screen.

This script, of course, expects text files, but the `readAsText()` method takes everything and interprets it as text, including files with binary content (for example, images). You will see a lot of crazy characters on the screen when a non-text file is selected.

> **Do It Yourself:** Create files with the codes in Listings 16-1, 16-2 and 16-3. The names for the CSS and Javascript files were declared in the HTML document as `file.css` and `file.js`, respectively. Open the document in your browser, and use the form to select a file from your computer. Try with text files as well as images to see how the content of these files is rendered on the screen.

File Properties

In a real application, information such as the name of the file, its size or its type are necessary to inform the user about the files being processed or even to control user's input. The File object sent by the `<input>` tag provides several properties for this purpose:

> **name**—This property returns the full name of the file (name and extension).
>
> **size**—This property returns the size of the file in bytes.
>
> **type**—This property returns the type of the file as a MIME type.

```
var databox;
function initiate(){
  databox = document.getElementById('databox');
  var myfiles = document.getElementById('myfiles');
```

```
  myfiles.addEventListener('change', process);
}
function process(e){
  var files = e.target.files;
  databox.innerHTML = '';
  var myfile = files[0];
  if(!myfile.type.match(/image.*/i)){
    alert('insert an image');
  }else{
    databox.innerHTML += 'Name: ' + myfile.name + '<br>';
    databox.innerHTML += 'Size: ' + myfile.size + ' bytes<br>';

    var reader = new FileReader();
    reader.addEventListener('load', show);
    reader.readAsDataURL(myfile);
  }
}
function show(e){
  var result = e.target.result;
  databox.innerHTML += '<img src="' + result + '">';
}
addEventListener('load', initiate);
```

Listing 16-4: *Loading images*

The example in Listing 16-4 is similar to the previous one except this time we use the **readAsDataURL()** method to read the file. This method returns the file's content in data:url format that can later be used as the source for an **<img>** element to show the selected image on the screen.

When we want to process a particular type of file, the first step is to check the file's **type** property. In the **process()** function of Listing 16-4, we check this by applying the old **match()** method. If the file is not an image, the **alert()** method shows an error message. Otherwise, the name and size of the image file are shown on the screen, and the file is opened.

Despite the use of **readAsDataURL()**, the opening process is exactly the same. The FileReader object is created, a listener is added to the **load** event, and the file is loaded. Once the process is over, the **show()** function uses the content of the **result** property as source for an **<img>** tag, and the image is shown on the screen.

> **Review the Basics:** To build the filter, we used Regular Expressions and the old Javascript method **match()**. This method searches for a match between the regular expression and the string, returning an array of matches or null. The MIME type for images is something like **image/jpeg** for JPG images, or **image/gif** for GIF images, so the expression **/image.*/i** allows only images to be read. For more information on Regular Expressions or MIME types, visit our website and follow the links for this chapter.

Blobs

In addition to data:url, the API works with another type of format called **blobs**. A blob is an object representing raw data. It was created with the purpose of overcoming Javascript limitations to work with binary data. A blob is usually generated from a file, but not necessarily. It's a good alternative to work with data without loading the entire file into memory, and it provides the possibility of processing binary information in small pieces.

A blob has multiple purposes, but it is focused on providing better ways to process big pieces of raw data or large files. To generate blobs from a previous blob or file, the API offers the `slice()` method:

> **slice(start, length, type)**—This method returns a new blob generated from another blob or a file. The first attribute indicates the starting point; the second specifies the length of the new blob; and the third is an optional attribute to specify the type of data.

```
var databox;
function initiate(){
  databox = document.getElementById('databox');
  var myfiles = document.getElementById('myfiles');
  myfiles.addEventListener('change', process);
}
function process(e){
  databox.innerHTML = '';
  var files = e.target.files;
  var myfile = files[0];
  var reader = new FileReader();
  reader.addEventListener('load', function(e){ show(e, myfile) });
  var blob = myfile.slice(0,1000);
  reader.readAsBinaryString(blob);
}
function show(e, myfile){
  var result = e.target.result;
  databox.innerHTML = 'Name: ' + myfile.name + '<br>';
  databox.innerHTML += 'Type: ' + myfile.type + '<br>';
  databox.innerHTML += 'Size: ' + myfile.size + ' bytes<br>';
  databox.innerHTML += 'Blob size: ' + result.length + ' bytes<br>';
  databox.innerHTML += 'Blob: ' + result;
}
addEventListener('load', initiate);
```

Listing 16-5: *Working with blobs and the* `slice()` *method*

In the script of Listing 16-5, we do exactly what we have done before, but this time, instead of reading the entire file, we create a blob with the `slice()` method. The blob is 1000 bytes long and starts from byte 0 of the file. If the loaded file is smaller than 1000 bytes, the blob will be as long as the file (from the starting point to the EOF, or End of File).

To show the information retrieved by this process, we use an anonymous function to handle the **load** event. This function calls the **show()** function with a reference to the **myfile** object as its attribute. This reference is received by the **show()** function, and the values of **myfile**'s properties are shown on the screen.

The advantages offered by blobs are countless. You can create a loop to generate several blobs from a file, for example, and then process this information part by part, creating asynchronous uploaders or image-processing applications, among others. Blobs provide new possibilities for Javascript applications.

Events

The time it takes for a file to be loaded into memory depends on its size. For small files, the process looks like an instant operation, but large files can take several minutes to load. In addition to the `load` event already studied, the API provides special events to inform every instance of the process.

loadstart—This event is fired by the FileReader object when the reading starts.

progress—This event is fired periodically while the file or blob is being read.

abort—This event is fired when the process is aborted.

error—This event is fired when the reading has failed.

loadend—This event is similar to `load` but is fired either in success or failure.

```
var databox;
function initiate(){
  databox = document.getElementById('databox');
  var myfiles = document.getElementById('myfiles');
  myfiles.addEventListener('change', process);
}
function process(e){
  databox.innerHTML = '';
  var files = e.target.files;
  var myfile = files[0];
  var reader = new FileReader();
  reader.addEventListener('loadstart', start);
  reader.addEventListener('progress', status);
  reader.addEventListener('loadend', function(){ show(myfile); });
  reader.readAsBinaryString(myfile);
}
function start(e){
  databox.innerHTML = '<progress value="0" max="100">0%</progress>';
}
function status(e){
  var per = parseInt(e.loaded / e.total * 100);
  databox.innerHTML = '<progress value="' + per + '" max="100">' + per +
'%</progress>';
}
function show(myfile){
  databox.innerHTML = 'Name: ' + myfile.name + '<br>';
  databox.innerHTML += 'Type: ' + myfile.type + '<br>';
  databox.innerHTML += 'Size: ' + myfile.size + ' bytes<br>';
}
addEventListener('load', initiate);
```

Listing 16-6: *Using events to control the process*

In this example, we create an application that loads a file and shows the progress of the operation through a progress bar. Three listeners are added for the FileReader object to control the reading process. The functions to handle the events are: `start()` and `status()`. The `start()` function initiates the progress bar at 0% and shows it on the screen. This progress bar can use any value or range, but we decided to use percentages to make it easier for the user to understand. In the `status()` function, the percentage is calculated from the properties `loaded` and `total` returned by the `progress` event. The progress bar is recreated on the screen every time the `progress` event is fired.

> **IMPORTANT:** We used `innerHTML` to add a new `<progress>` element to the document. This is not the recommended practice, but it is useful and convenient for our example. Usually elements are added to the DOM using the Javascript method `createElement()` along with `appendChild()`, as explained in Chapter 4.

> **Do It Yourself:** Using the document in Listing 16-1 and the Javascript code in Listing 16-6, try to load a large file such as a video or an image to test the progress bar. If the browser doesn't recognize the `<progress>` element, the content of this element will be shown instead.

The `progress` event is declared by the specification in the ProgressEvent interface. This interface is common for every API and includes three valuable properties to return information about the process that is being monitoring by the event:

> **lengthComputable**—This is a Boolean value that returns `true` when the length of the progress is computable or `false` otherwise. It is used sometimes to ensure the values in the rest of the properties are valid.

> **loaded**—This property returns the total number of bytes already downloaded or uploaded.

> **total**—This property returns the total size in bytes of the data to be downloaded or uploaded.

We will see more applications of the `progress` event in later examples.

16.3 Creating Files

The main File API is useful for loading and processing files from the user's computer, but it works with files that already exist in the hard drive. It doesn't consider the possibility of creating new files or directories. An extension of this API called File API: Directories and System takes care of this issue. The API reserves a specific space in the hard drive, a special storage space in which the web application can create and process files and directories just as a desktop application would. The space is unique and only accessible by the application that created it.

HTML Document

To test this part of the API, we are going to need a new form with an input field and a button to create and process files and directories.

```
<!DOCTYPE html>
<html lang="en">
```

```
<head>
  <title>File API</title>
  <link rel="stylesheet" href="file.css">
  <script src="file.js"></script>
</head>
<body>
  <section id="formbox">
    <form name="form">
      <label for="myentry">Name:</label><br>
      <input type="text" name="myentry" id="myentry">
      <input type="button" id="fbutton" value="Save">
    </form>
  </section>
  <section id="databox">
    No entries available
  </section>
</body>
</html>
```

Listing 16-7: HTML document forFile API: Directories and System

Do It Yourself: The new HTML document provides a new form but preserves the same structure and CSS styles. You just replace the previous HTML code with this one and copy the Javascript codes into the file `file.js` to test the following examples.

The Hard Drive

The space reserved for the application is like a sandbox, a small hard drive unit with its own root directory and configuration. To start working with it, we first have to request a `FileSystem` to be initialized for our application.

> **requestFileSystem(type, size, success, error)**—This method creates the File System of the size and type specified in its attributes. The value of the `type` attribute can be either **PERSISTENT** or **TEMPORARY** according to how long the data should be preserved. The `size` attribute determines the space reserved in the hard drive for this File System in bytes. In the case of error or success, this method will call the corresponding callback functions (`success` and `error` attributes).

> **IMPORTANT:** Google Chrome is the only browser at the moment with a working implementation of this part of the API. Because the implementation is experimental, we have to replace the `requestFileSystem()` method by the Google Chrome experimental method `webkitRequestFileSystem()`. Using this method you will be able to test the following examples in your browser.

The `requestFileSystem()` method returns a File System object with two properties:

> **root**—The value of this property is a reference to the root directory of the File System. It returns a DirectoryEntry object with important methods for working with files and directories, as we will see later.

> **name**—This property returns information about the File System, such as the name assigned by the browser and its condition.

```
var databox, hd;
function initiate(){
  databox = document.getElementById('databox');
  var button = document.getElementById('fbutton');
  button.addEventListener('click', create);

  webkitRequestFileSystem(TEMPORARY, 5*1024*1024, createhd, showerror);
}
function createhd(fs) {
  hd = fs.root;
}
function create(){
  var name = document.getElementById('myentry').value;
  if(name != ''){
    hd.getFile(name, {create: true, exclusive: false}, show, showerror);
  }
}
function show(entry){
  document.getElementById('myentry').value = '';
  databox.innerHTML = 'Entry created!<br>';
  databox.innerHTML += 'Name: ' + entry.name + '<br>';
  databox.innerHTML += 'Path: ' + entry.fullPath + '<br>';
  databox.innerHTML += 'FileSystem: ' + entry.filesystem.name;
}
function showerror(e){
  alert('Error: ' + e.code);
}
addEventListener('load', initiate);
```

Listing 16-8: *Setting our own File System*

By using the HTML document in Listing 16-7 and the script in Listing 16-8, we finish our first application for working with new files in the user's computer. The script calls the `requestFileSystem()` method to create or get a reference to our File System. If this is the first visit, the File System will be created as **TEMPORARY** with a size of 5 megabytes (5*1024*1024). If the operation is successful, the `createhd()` function is executed, continuing with the initialization process. For errors, we use the simple `showerror()` function, as we did before for other APIs.

When the File System is created or opened, the `createhd()` function receives a FileSystem object and stores a reference in the `hd` variable with the value of the `root` property.

> **IMPORTANT:** Persistent storage demands a request to the browser for space. This request is made through the Quota Management API. At the time of writing, the specification for this API is under development, and there is no implementation available in browsers yet. Consequently, in this and later examples we declare the **TEMPORARY** attribute to set a temporary file system. To check the state of the specification for the Quota Management API or get more information about this subject, visit our website and follow the links for this chapter.

Creating Files

The starting process for the File System is finished. The rest of the functions in the script of Listing 16-8 create a new file and show the entry's data on the screen. When the "Save" button is pressed on the form, the `create()` function is called. This function assigns the text inserted in the `<input>` element to the variable `name` and then creates a file with that name using the `getFile()` method. This method is part of the DirectoryEntry interface included in the API. The interface provides a total of four methods to create and handle files and directories:

> **getFile(path, options, success, error)**—This method creates or opens a file. The `path` attribute must include the name of the file and the path to where the file is located (from the root of the File System). There are two flags we can use to set the options for this method: `create` and `exclusive`. Both receive Boolean values. The `create` flag indicates whether or not the file will be created, and the `exclusive` flag, when it is set to `true`, forces the `getFile()` method to return an error if we are trying to create a file that already exists. This method also receives two callback functions to respond to success or failure.

> **getDirectory(path, options, success, error)**—This method has exactly the same characteristics as the previous method but used exclusively for directories.

> **createReader()**—This method returns a DirectoryReader object to read entries from the specified directory.

> **removeRecursively()**—This is a specific method to delete a directory and all of its content.

In the script of Listing 16-8, the `getFile()` method uses the value of the `name` variable to create or get the file. The file will be created if it doesn't already exist (`create: true`) or will be fetched otherwise (`exclusive: false`). The `create()` function also checks the value of the `name` variable before executing `getFile()`.

The `getFile()` method uses two functions, `show()` and `showerror()`, to respond to success or failure. The `show()` function receives an Entry object and shows the value of its properties on the screen. This type of object has several methods and properties associated that we will study later. For now, we are just using the `name`, `fullPath` and `filesystem` properties.

Creating Directories

The `getFile()` method (specific for files) and the `getDirectory()` method (specific for directories) are exactly the same. To create a directory from the document in Listing 16-7, we just replace the name of `getFile()` with `getDirectory()`, as shown in the following example:

```
function create(){
  var name = document.getElementById('myentry').value;
  if(name != ''){
    hd.getDirectory(name, {create: true, exclusive: false}, show,
showerror);
  }
}
```

Listing 16-9: Using getDirectory() *to create a directory*

Notice that both methods are part of the DirectoryEntry object called **root** that we are representing with the **hd** variable, so we always have to use this variable to call the methods and create files and directories in the File System of our application.

> **Do It Yourself:** Use the function in Listing 16-9 to replace the **create()** function in Listing 16-8 in order to create directories instead of files. Upload the files to your server, open the HTML document of Listing 16-7 in your browser, and create a directory using the form on the screen.

Listing Files

As we mentioned before, the **createReader()** method allows us to get a list of entries (files and directories) from a specific path. This method returns a DirectoryReader object that contains the **readEntries()** method to read entries from a specific directory:

> **readEntries(success, error)**—This method reads the next block of entries from the selected directory. Every time the method is called, the success function returns an object with the list of entries or null when no entries were found.

The **readEntries()** method reads the list of entries by blocks. As a result, there is no guarantee that all the entries will be returned in one call. We will have to call this method until the object returned is empty.

There is another consideration we have to make before writing our next script. The **createReader()** method returns a DirectoryReader object for a specific directory. To get the files we want, we have to first get the Entry object for the directory we want to read.

```
var databox, hd, path;
function initiate(){
  databox = document.getElementById('databox');
  var button = document.getElementById('fbutton');
  button.addEventListener('click', create);

  webkitRequestFileSystem(TEMPORARY, 5*1024*1024, createhd, showerror);
}
function createhd(fs) {
  hd = fs.root;
  path = '';
  show();
}
```

```
function showerror(e){
  alert('Error: ' + e.code);
}
function create(){
  var name = document.getElementById('myentry').value;
  if(name != ''){
    name = path + name;
    hd.getFile(name, {create: true, exclusive: false}, show, showerror);
  }
}
function show(){
  document.getElementById('myentry').value='';
  databox.innerHTML = '';
  hd.getDirectory(path, null, readdir, showerror);
}
function readdir(dir){
  var reader = dir.createReader();
  var read = function(){
    reader.readEntries(function(files){
        if(files.length){
          list(files);
          read();
        }
      }, showerror);
  }
  read();
}
function list(files){
  for(var i = 0; i < files.length; i++) {
    if(files[i].isFile) {
      databox.innerHTML += files[i].name + '<br>';
    }else if(files[i].isDirectory){
      databox.innerHTML += '<span onclick="changedir(\'' + files[i].name
+ '\')" class="directory">' + files[i].name + '</span><br>';
    }
  }
}
function changedir(newpath){
  path = path + newpath + '/';
  show();
}
addEventListener('load', initiate);
```

Listing 16-10: Programming a File System

This script doesn't replace Windows File Explorer but at least provides all the information you need to understand how to build a useful File System in your browser. Let's analyze it step by step:

The **initiate()** function does the same as in previous examples: it starts or creates the File System and calls the **createhd()** function when successful. Along with declaring the **hd** variable to reference the File System, the **createhd()** function also initializes the **path** variable with an empty string (to represent the root) and calls the **show()** function to show the list of files on the screen as soon as the application has loaded.

The **path** variable will be used in the rest of the application to store the current path in which the user is working. For instance, you can see how the **create()** function is modified in the script of Listing 16-10 to use this value. Now, every time a new name is sent from the form, the name is added to the path and the file is created in the current directory.

As we said before, to show the list of entries we first have to open the directory to be read. Using the `getDirectory()` method in the `show()` function, the current directory is opened according to the value of `path`, and a reference to that directory is sent to the `readdir()` function when successful. This function keeps this reference in the `dir` variable, creates a new DirectoryReader object for the current directory and retrieves the list of entries with the `readEntries()` method.

In `readdir()`, anonymous functions are used to keep everything organized and within the same scope. First, `createReader()` creates a DirectoryReader object for the directory represented by `dir`. Next, a new function called `read()` is created dynamically to read the entries using the `readEntries()` method (this function was created assigning an anonymous function to the `read` variable). The `readEntries()` method reads entries by blocks, which means that the method has to be called several times to ensure every entry available in the directory is retrieved. The `read()` function helps us accomplish this. The process is as follows: at the end of the `readdir()` function, the `read()` function is called for the first time. Inside the `read()` function, we call the `readEntries()` method. This method uses another anonymous function as the success callback function to receive the `files` object and check its contents. If this object is not empty, the `list()` function is called to show on the screen the entries already read, and the `read()` function is executed again to check for the next block of entries. The `read()` function calls itself until no more entries are returned.

The `list()` function, called by `read()`, is in charge of rendering the list of entries (files and directories) on the screen. It takes the `files` object and checks for the characteristic of each entry using two other important properties of the Entry interface: `isFile` and `isDirectory`. As their names indicate, these properties contain Boolean values to inform whether the entry is a file or a directory. After the condition of the entry is checked, the `name` property is used to show the information on the screen.

There is a difference in how a file or a directory is shown on the screen by the application. When a directory is detected, it is shown through a `<span>` element with an `onclick` event attribute that calls the `changedir()` function when the element is clicked. The purpose of this function is to set the new current path. It receives the name of the directory, adds the directory to the path and calls the `show()` function to update the list of entries on the screen. This feature lets us open directories and see the contents with just a click of the mouse, exactly as a normal file explorer would.

This example doesn't consider the possibility of going up the tree. To do that, we have to use another method provided by the Entry interface:

> **getParent(success, error)**—This method returns an Entry object of the directory containing the selected entry. Once you get the Entry object, you can read its properties to obtain all the information needed about the parent of that particular entry.

How the `getParent()` method works is simple: let's suppose a directory tree such as `pictures/myvacations` was created, and the user is listing the content of `myvacations` at this moment. To go back to `pictures`, you could provide a link in the HTML document with an `onclick` event attribute to call a function that moves the current path to the new position. The function called by this event attribute might be something like this:

```
function goback(){
  hd.getDirectory(path, null, function(dir){
    dir.getParent(function(parent){
        path = parent.fullPath;
        show();
      }, showerror);
  },showerror);
}
```

Listing 16-11: *Moving back to the parent*

The **goback()** function in Listing 16-11 changes the value of the **path** variable to point to the parent of the current directory. The first step is to get a reference to the current directory using the **getDirectory()** method. If that is successful, an anonymous function is executed by this method. In the function, the **getParent()** method is used to find the parent of the directory referenced by **dir** (the current directory). If that is successful, this method executes another anonymous function to take the parent object and set the value of the current path to the value of its **fullPath** property. The **show()** function is also called at the end to update the information on the screen (showing the entries in the new path).

Of course, this application can be greatly improved, but that's your homework.

> **Do It Yourself:** Append the function in Listing 16-11 to the script of Listing 16-10, and create a link in the HTML document to call this function (e.g., **<span onclick="goback()">go back</span>**).

Handling Files

We already mentioned that the Entry interface provides a set of properties and methods to get information and operate with files. You will find most of the properties available applied in previous examples. We already took advantage of the **isFile** and **isDirectory** properties to check the condition of an entry, and we used the values of **name**, **fullPath** and **filesystem** to display information on the screen. The **getParent()** method studied in the previous example is also part of this interface. However, there are still a few more methods that are useful to perform regular operations for files and directories. Using these methods, we will be able to move, copy and delete entries as in any desktop application.

> **moveTo(parent, name, success, error)**—This method moves an entry to a different location in the File System. If the **name** attribute is different than null, the name of the entry will change to this value.
>
> **copyTo(parent, name, success, error)**—This method makes a copy of an entry in another location of the File System. If the **name** attribute is different than null, the name of the new entry will change to this value.
>
> **remove(success, error)**—This method deletes a file or an empty directory. (To delete a directory with content, we have to use the **removeRecursively()** method mentioned before.)

A new HTML document will be necessary to test these methods. To simplify the codes, we will provide two input fields for the origin and destination of every operation.

```
<!DOCTYPE html>
<html lang="en">
<head>
  <title>File API</title>
  <link rel="stylesheet" href="file.css">
  <script src="file.js"></script>
</head>
<body>
  <section id="formbox">
    <form name="form">
      <label for="origin">Origin: </label>
      <input type="text" name="origin" id="origin" required><br>
      <label for="destination">Destination: </label>
      <input type="text" name="destination" id="destination" required>
      <br><input type="button" id="fbutton" value="Save">
    </form>
  </section>
  <section id="databox"></section>
</body>
</html>
```

Listing 16-12: *HTML document to handle files*

Moving

The **moveTo()** method requires an Entry object for the file and another for the directory to which the file will be moved. We first have to create a reference to the file using **getFile()**, then get the reference to the directory of destination using **getDirectory()** and finally apply **moveTo()** using this information.

```
var databox, hd, path;
function initiate(){
  databox = document.getElementById('databox');
  var button = document.getElementById('fbutton');
  button.addEventListener('click', modify);

  webkitRequestFileSystem(TEMPORARY, 5*1024*1024, createhd, showerror);
}
function createhd(fs){
  hd = fs.root;
  path = '';
  show();
}
function showerror(e){
  alert('Error: ' + e.code);
}
function modify(){
  var origin = document.getElementById('origin').value;
  var destination = document.getElementById('destination').value;
```

```
    hd.getFile(origin, null, function(file){
       hd.getDirectory(destination, null, function(dir){
          file.moveTo(dir, null, success, showerror);
       },showerror);
    },showerror);
}
function success(){
   document.getElementById('origin').value = '';
   document.getElementById('destination').value = '';
   show();
}
function show(){
   databox.innerHTML = '';
   hd.getDirectory(path, null, readdir, showerror);
}
function readdir(dir){
   var reader = dir.createReader();
   var read = function(){
      reader.readEntries(function(files){
         if(files.length){
            list(files);
            read();
         }
      }, showerror);
   }
   read();
}
function list(files){
   for(var i = 0; i < files.length; i++) {
      if(files[i].isFile) {
         databox.innerHTML += files[i].name + '<br>';
      }else if(files[i].isDirectory){
         databox.innerHTML += '<span onclick="changedir(\'' + files[i].name
+ '\')" class="directory">' + files[i].name + '</span><br>';
      }
   }
}
function changedir(newpath){
   path = path + newpath + '/';
   show();
}
addEventListener('load', initiate);
```

Listing 16-13: Moving files between directories

We use functions from previous examples to create or open our file system and show the list of entries on the screen. The only new function in the script of Listing 16-13 is modify(). This function takes the values of the origin and destination fields from the form and uses them to open the file from the origin first, and if that is successful, the directory of destination later. If both operations are successful, the moveTo() method is applied to the file object, and this file is moved to the directory represented by dir. If that's successful, the success() function is called to clear the form fields and run the show() function again to update the list of entries on the screen.

Do It Yourself: To test this example, you need an HTML file with the document in Listing 16-12, the CSS file used since the beginning of this chapter, and a file called file.js with the code in Listing 16-13. (Remember to upload the files to your server before testing.) Create files and directories in your File System so you have something to work with (you can use previous scripts for this purpose). Use the form from the last HTML document to insert the values of the file to be moved (with the entire path from the root) and the directory to which the file will be moved. (If the directory is in the root of the File System, you don't need slashes, only its name.) For example, let's say you have a file called **balance.txt** and want to move it to the **statements** directory. Write the name of the file in the Origin field (**balance.txt**), the name of the directory in the Destination field (**statements**), and press the "Save" button to complete the process.

Copying

Of course, the only difference between the **moveTo()** method and the **copyTo()** method is that the latter preserves the original file. To try the **copyTo()** method, you simply change the name of the method in the script of Listing 16-13. The **modify()** function will end up like this:

```
function modify(){
  var origin = document.getElementById('origin').value;
  var destination = document.getElementById('destination').value;

  hd.getFile(origin, null, function(file){
    hd.getDirectory(destination, null, function(dir){
      file.copyTo(dir, null, success, showerror);
    },showerror);
  },showerror);
}
```

Listing 16-14: Copying files in a directory

Do It Yourself: Replace the **modify()** function in Listing 16-13 with this one, and open the document in Listing 16-12 to test the code. You must repeat the same procedure used to move a file in order to copy it. Insert the path and name of the file to be copied in the **origin** field and the path of the directory into the **destination** field.

Deleting

Deleting files and directories is even simpler than moving and copying. All we have to do is get the Entry object for the file or directory we want to delete and apply the **remove()** method with that reference.

```
function modify(){
  var origin = document.getElementById('origin').value;
  var origin = path+origin;
  hd.getFile(origin, null, function(entry){
    entry.remove(success, showerror);
  },showerror);
}
```

Listing 16-15: Deleting files and directories

The Javascript code in Listing 16-15 only processes the value of the **origin** field from the form. This value, along with the value of the **path** variable, represents the path of the file we want to delete. So, using the **getFile()** method, we create the Entry object for that file and then apply **remove()** to remove it.

> **Do It Yourself:** Replace the **modify()** function in the script of Listing 16-13 with the new one in Listing 16-15. This time you only have to provide the value of the **origin** field to specify the file to be deleted.

To delete a directory instead of a file, the Entry object must be created for the directory using **getDirectory()**, but the **remove()** method works exactly the same way. There is one situation we have to consider for directories though: if the directory is not empty, the **remove()** method will return an error. To delete both a directory and its content, we have to use another method, mentioned previously in this chapter, called **removeRecursively()**.

```
function modify(){
  var destination = document.getElementById('destination').value;
  hd.getDirectory(destination, null, function(entry){
    entry.removeRecursively(success, showerror);
  },showerror);
}
```

Listing 16-16: Deleting non-empty directories

In the function in Listing 16-16, we use the value of the **destination** field to indicate the directory to be deleted. The **removeRecursively()** method erases the directory and its content in just one execution and calls the **success()** function when successful.

> **Do It Yourself:** The **modify()** functions presented in Listings 16-14, 16-15 and 16-16 were made to replace the same function in Listing 16-13. To test these examples, take the script in Listing 16-13, replace the **modify()** function with the one you want to try, and open the document of Listing 16-12 in your browser. Depending on the method you are testing, you will have to provide one or two values from the form.

16.4 File Content

In addition to the main File API and the File API's extension we just studied, there is another important extension called File API: Writer. This specification declares new interfaces for writing and adding content to files. It works along with the rest of the API by combining methods and sharing objects to achieve its goal.

Writing Content

To write content into a file, we have to create a FileWriter object. These objects are returned by the **createWriter()** method of the FileEntry interface. This interface is an addition to the Entry interface and provides two methods to work with files:

createWriter(success, error)—This method returns a FileWriter object associated with the selected entry.

file(success, error)—This is a method we will use later to read the file's content. It creates a File object (like the one returned by the `<input>` element or a drag and drop operation) associated with the selected entry.

The FileWriter object returned by the `createWriter()` method has its own methods, properties and events to facilitate the process of adding content to a file:

write(data)—This is the method that actually writes content into the file. The content is provided by the `data` attribute as a blob.

seek(offset)—This method sets the position inside the file in which the content will be added. The value of the `offset` attribute must be declared in bytes.

truncate(size)—This method changes the length of the file according to the value of the `size` attribute (in bytes).

position—This property returns the actual position where the next writing will occur. The position will be 0 for a new file or different from 0 if some content was written into the file or the `seek()` method was applied previously.

length—This property returns the length of the file.

writestart—This event is fired when the process starts.

progress—This event is fired periodically to report progress.

write—This event is fired when the data have been fully written.

abort—This event is fired if the process is aborted.

error—This event is fired if an error occurs.

writeend—This event is fired when the process is over.

There is one thing we have to do prior to writing content into the file. The `write()` method only takes blobs as an attribute. To create a blob, the API offers the `Blob()` constructor:

Blob(array, properties)—This constructor takes an array with information for the blob and returns a blob. The array may contain strings, other blobs or data in the format of ArrayBuffer. The `properties` attribute is optional. This is an object with two possible properties: `type` and `endings`. The `type` property defines the MIME type of the data in the array. The `endings` property defines the codification of the data with two values: `transparent` (the data are used as is) or `native` (the codification of the data is adapted to the configuration of the operative system).

The following HTML document incorporates a second field to insert a text that will represent the content of the file. We are going to use this document for the rest of the examples in this part of the chapter.

```
<!DOCTYPE html>
<html lang="en">
<head>
  <title>File API</title>
  <link rel="stylesheet" href="file.css">
  <script src="file.js"></script>
</head>
<body>
  <section id="formbox">
    <form name="form">
      <label for="myentry">File: </label>
      <input type="text" name="myentry" id="myentry" required><br>
      <label for="mytext">Text: </label><br>
      <textarea name="mytext" id="mytext" required></textarea><br>
      <input type="button" id="fbutton" value="Save">
    </form>
  </section>
  <section id="databox">
    No information available
  </section>
</body>
</html>
```

Listing 16-17: *Form to insert the file name and content*

For the writing, we are going to open the File System, get or create the file with `getFile()`, and insert content into the opened file with the values provided from the form.

```
var databox, hd;
function initiate(){
  databox = document.getElementById('databox');
  var button = document.getElementById('fbutton');
  button.addEventListener('click', writefile);
  webkitRequestFileSystem(TEMPORARY, 5*1024*1024, createhd, showerror);
}
function createhd(fs){
  hd = fs.root;
}
function showerror(e){
  alert('Error: ' + e.code);
}
function writefile(){
  var name = document.getElementById('myentry').value;
  hd.getFile(name, {create: true, exclusive: false}, function(entry){
    entry.createWriter(writecontent, showerror);
  }, showerror);
}
function writecontent(fileWriter) {
  var text = document.getElementById('mytext').value;
  fileWriter.addEventListener('writeend', success);
  var blob = new Blob([text]);
  fileWriter.write(blob);
}
```

```
function success(){
  document.getElementById('myentry').value = '';
  document.getElementById('mytext').value = '';
  databox.innerHTML = 'Done!';
}
addEventListener('load', initiate);
```

Listing 16-18: Writing content

When the "Save" button is clicked, the information in the fields is processed by the functions `writefile()` and `writecontent()`. The `writefile()` function takes the value of `myentry` and uses `getFile()` to open or create the file. The Entry object returned is used by `createWriter()` to create a FileWriter object. If the operation is successful, the `writecontent()` function is called.

The `writecontent()` function receives the FileWriter object and, using the value of the `mytext` field, writes content into the file. The text must be converted into a blob to be able to add it as content for the file. For this purpose, the `Blob()` constructor is used to create a blob with the text as its attribute (notice the square brackets between the parentheses to turn the text into an array). Now, the information is in the appropriate format to be written into the file using the `write()` method.

The whole process is asynchronous, which means the status of the operation is constantly informed by events. In the `writecontent()` function, we only listen to the `writeend` event to call the `success()` function and write "Done!" on the screen when the operation is successful. However, you can control the progress or check for errors by watching the rest of the events fired by the FileWriter object.

> **Do It Yourself:** Copy the document of Listing 16-17 into a new HTML file. (This document uses the same CSS styles of Listing 16-2.) Create a Javascript file called `file.js` with the script of Listing 16-18, open the HTML document in your browser, and insert the name and the content of the file you want to create. If the string "Done!" appears on the screen, the process was successful.

Adding Content

Because we didn't specify the position where the content had to be written, the previous script will simply write the blob from the beginning of the file. To select a specific position or to append content at the end of an existing file, we have to use the `seek()` method.

```
function writecontent(fileWriter) {
  var text = document.getElementById('mytext').value;
  fileWriter.seek(fileWriter.length);
  fileWriter.addEventListener('writeend', success);
  var blob = new Blob([text]);
  fileWriter.write(blob);
}
```

Listing 16-19: Adding more content to the file

The function in Listing 16-19 improves the previous `writecontent()` function by incorporating a `seek()` method to move the writing position to the end of the file.

Consequently, the content written by the **write()** method won't overwrite the existing content of the file.

To calculate the position of the end of the file in bytes, we use the **length** property. The rest of the code is exactly the same as in Listing 16-18.

> **Do It Yourself:** Replace the **writecontent()** function in Listing 16-18 with the function in Listing 16-19, and open the HTML file in your browser. In the form, insert the name of the file you created previously and the content you want to add at the end of this file.

Reading Content

It's time to read what we just wrote. The reading process uses techniques of the main File API specification, which we studied at the beginning of this chapter. We are going to use the **FileReader()** constructor and the reading method **readAsText()** to get and read the content of the file.

```
var databox, hd;
function initiate(){
  databox = document.getElementById('databox');
  var button = document.getElementById('fbutton');
  button.addEventListener('click', readfile);
  webkitRequestFileSystem(TEMPORARY, 5*1024*1024, createhd, showerror);
}
function createhd(fs){
  hd = fs.root;
}
function showerror(e){
  alert('Error: ' + e.code);
}
function readfile(){
  var name = document.getElementById('myentry').value;
  hd.getFile(name, {create: false}, function(entry) {
    entry.file(readcontent, showerror);
  }, showerror);
}
function readcontent(file){
  databox.innerHTML = 'Name: ' + file.name + '<br>';
  databox.innerHTML += 'Type: ' + file.type + '<br>';
  databox.innerHTML += 'Size: ' + file.size + ' bytes<br>';

  var reader = new FileReader();
  reader.addEventListener('load', success);
  reader.readAsText(file);
}
function success(e){
  var result = e.target.result;
  databox.innerHTML += 'Content: ' + result;
  document.getElementById('myentry').value = '';
}
addEventListener('load', initiate);
```

Listing 16-20: Reading a file from the File System

The methods provided by the FileReader interface to read the content of a file, such as `readAsText()`, take a blob or a File object as an attribute. The File object represents the file to be read and is generated by the `<input>` element or a drag and drop operation. As we mentioned before, the FileEntry interface provides the option to create this kind of object using a method called `file()`.

When the "Save" button is clicked, the `readfile()` function takes the value of the `myentry` field and opens the file with that name using `getFile()`. The Entry object returned by this method, when successful, is represented by the `entry` variable and is used to generate the File object with the `file()` method.

Because the File object is exactly the same object generated by the `<input>` element or a drag and drop operation, all the same properties used before are available, and we are able to show basic information about the file even before the reading process is started. In the `readcontent()` function, the values of these properties are shown on the screen and the content of the file is read.

The reading process is an exact copy of the code in Listing 16-3. The FileReader object is created with the `FileReader()` constructor; the `success()` function, set as the listener for the `load` event, is executed when the process is over; and the file's content is read by the `readAsText()` method.

In the `success()` function, instead of printing a string as we did before, the file's content is shown on the screen. To do this, we take the `result` property's value of the FileReader object and insert it in the `databox`.

> **Do It Yourself:** The script of Listing 16-20 only processes the value of the `myentry` input field. Open the HTML file with the last document in your browser, and insert the name of the file you want to read. It has to be a file you have already created or the system will return an error message (`create: false`). If the file's name is correct, the information and content of the file will be shown on the screen.

16.5 Access to Files

The File System we have been using all this time is just a space reserved in the hard drive for our application. We can't access the files and directories from outside the browser, and we can't move the entries to another place in the hard drive. To solve this problem, HTML5 introduces two elements: a method and an attribute.

> **toURL()**—This method is similar to the `createObjectURL()` method studied in Chapter 9 but is specific for a file entry. It creates an URL pointing to the file that we can use later as any other URL.

> **download**—This is a new Boolean attribute for `<a>` elements. It allows us to inform to the browser that the resource must be downloaded.

```
var databox, hd, path;
function initiate(){
  databox = document.getElementById('databox');
  var button = document.getElementById('fbutton');
  button.addEventListener('click', create);
```

```
    webkitRequestFileSystem(TEMPORARY, 5*1024*1024, createhd, showerror);
}
function createhd(fs) {
  hd = fs.root;
  path = '';
  show();
}
function showerror(e){
  alert('Error: ' + e.code);
}
function create(){
  var name = document.getElementById('myentry').value;
  if(name != ''){
    name = path + name;
    hd.getFile(name, {create: true, exclusive: false}, show, showerror);
  }
}
function show(){
  document.getElementById('myentry').value='';
  databox.innerHTML = '';
  hd.getDirectory(path, null, readdir, showerror);
}
function readdir(dir){
  var reader = dir.createReader();
  var read = function(){
    reader.readEntries(function(files){
      if(files.length){
        list(files);
        read();
      }
    }, showerror);
  }
  read();
}
function list(files){
  var url;
  for(var i = 0; i < files.length; i++) {
    if(files[i].isFile) {
      url = files[i].toURL();
      databox.innerHTML += '<a href="' + url + '" download>' +
files[i].name + '</a><br>';
    }else if(files[i].isDirectory){
      databox.innerHTML += '<span onclick="changedir(\'' + files[i].name
+ '\')" class="directory">' + files[i].name + '</span><br>';
    }
  }
}
function changedir(newpath){
  path = path + newpath + '/';
  show();
}
addEventListener('load', initiate);
```

Listing 16-21: *Downloading files from the File System to the user's hard drive*

In this example, we take the script of Listing 16-10 and slightly modify the list() function to
generate a link for every file. The function gets the URL of the file applying the toURL() method

to each element of the **files** array and creates a link with the **download** attribute to let users download the files with a click.

> **IMPORTANT:** You are not required to apply the **download** attribute all the time. There may be cases in which you just want the browser to show the content of the file in the window, and for that purpose, the **download** attribute may be ignored.

> **Do It Yourself:** The script of Listing 16-21 may work with the HTML document of Listing 16-7. Upload both files along with the CSS styles to your server, and open the document in your browser. The files will be downloaded to your hard drive when you click on the links.

16.6 File System in Real Life

It's always good to see a real-life example that allows us to understand the potential of the concepts already studied. To close this chapter, we are going to create an application that combines several techniques of the File API with the capabilities of image manipulation provided by the Canvas API.

This example takes multiple image files and draws the images on the canvas in a random position. Every change in the **<canvas>** element is saved in a file for future reading, so every time you access the application, the last work is shown on the screen.

The HTML document for this example is similar to the first document presented in this chapter. However, this time it includes a **<canvas>** element inside the **databox**.

```
<!DOCTYPE html>
<html lang="en">
<head>
  <title>File API</title>
  <link rel="stylesheet" href="file.css">
  <script src="file.js"></script>
</head>
<body>
  <section id="formbox">
    <form name="form">
      <label for="myfiles">Images: </label>
      <input type="file" name="myfiles" id="myfiles" multiple>
    </form>
  </section>
  <section id="databox">
    <canvas id="canvas" width="500" height="350"></canvas>
  </section>
</body>
</html>
```

Listing 16-22: *HTML document with a* <canvas> *element*

The script for our example includes methods and programming techniques you are already familiar with, but the combination of APIs may be confusing at first. Let's list the entire Javascript code and analyze everything later step by step.

```
var canvas, hd;
function initiate(){
  var elem = document.getElementById('canvas');
  canvas = elem.getContext('2d');
  var myfiles = document.getElementById('myfiles');
  myfiles.addEventListener('change', process);
  webkitRequestFileSystem(TEMPORARY, 5*1024*1024, createhd, showerror);
}
function createhd(fs){
  hd = fs.root;
  loadcanvas();
}
function showerror(e){
  alert('Error: ' + e.code);
}
function process(e){
  var files = e.target.files;
  for(var f = 0; f < files.length; f++){
    var file = files[f];
    if(file.type.match(/image.*/i)){
      var reader = new FileReader();
      reader.addEventListener('load', show);
      reader.readAsDataURL(file);
    }
  }
}
function show(e){
  var result = e.target.result;
  var image = document.createElement('img');
  image.setAttribute('src', result);
  image.addEventListener("load", function(){
    var x = Math.floor(Math.random() * 451);
    var y = Math.floor(Math.random() * 301);
    canvas.drawImage(image, x, y, 100, 100);
    savecanvas();
  });
}
function loadcanvas(){
  hd.getFile('canvas.dat', {create: false}, function(entry) {
    entry.file(function(file){
        var reader = new FileReader();
        reader.addEventListener('load', function(e){
          var image = document.createElement('img');
          image.setAttribute('src', e.target.result);;
          image.addEventListener("load", function(){
            canvas.drawImage(image, 0, 0);
          });
        });
        reader.readAsBinaryString(file);
    }, showerror);
  }, showerror);
}
function savecanvas(){
  var elem = document.getElementById('canvas');
  var info = elem.toDataURL();
  hd.getFile('canvas.dat', {create: true, exclusive: false},
    function(entry) {
      entry.createWriter(function(fileWriter){
```

```
      var blob = new Blob([info]);
      fileWriter.write(blob);
    }, showerror);
  }, showerror);
}
addEventListener('load', initiate);
```

Listing 16-23: *Combining the File API with the Canvas API*

In this example, we are working with two APIs: the File API (with its extensions) and the Canvas API. In the **initiate()** function, both APIs are initialized. The drawing context for the canvas is generated first using **getContext()**, and the File System is requested later by **requestFileSystem()**.

As usual, once the File System is ready, the **createhd()** function is called, and the **hd** variable is initialized in this function with a reference to the root of the File System. This time, a call for a new function is added at the end of **createhd()** with the purpose of loading the file containing the image generated the last time the application was executed. But let's first see how this image is generated.

When the user selects new image files from the form provided by the HTML document, the **change** event is fired by the **<input>** element and the **process()** function is called. This function takes the files sent by the input, extracts every File object from this array, checks whether or not the file is an image, and reads the content of every entry with the **readAsDataURL()** method, returning a value in the data:url format.

As you can see, every file is read by the **process()** function, one at a time. If it is successful, the **load** event is fired and the **show()** function is called for each one. As a result, this function will process every image the user has selected.

The **show()** function takes the data from the **reader** object, creates a new Image object with the **createElement()** method and assigns the data as the value of the **src** attribute for that image.

When working with images, you always have to consider the time the image takes to load. For this reason, after declaring the new source for the Image object, we add a listener for the **load** event to ensure the image has fully loaded before being processed. Once the **load** event is fired (the image has loaded), the anonymous function declared as the listener for this event is executed. This function calculates a random position for the image and draws it on the canvas using the **drawImage()** method and a fixed size of 100 x 100 pixels (read the **show()** function in Listing 16-23 and follow the process).

> **Review the Basics:** The **floor()** method belongs to the native Math object. It rounds the number between parentheses and returns an integer.

After the image is drawn, the **savecanvas()** function is called. This function saves the canvas' status whenever it is modified, allowing the application to recover the last work every time it is opened. A method from the Canvas API called **toDataURL()** is used to return the canvas content as data:url. A series of operations are performed in the **savecanvas()** function to process this data. First, the data:url generated from the canvas is stored in the **info** variable. Then, the **canvas.dat** file is created (in case it doesn't exist) and opened with **getFile()**. If **getFile()** is successful, the entry is used by an anonymous function to create a FileWriter object with the **createWriter()** method. If the creation is successful, the method calls an anonymous function where the value of the **info** variable is converted into a blob and written into the file with the **write()** method.

IMPORTANT: In this example, we had to get the information as data:url and convert it into a blob with the `Blob()` constructor before it could be used as the content for the file. This process could have been simplified by applying the `toBlob()` method instead of the `toDataURL()` method. The `toBlob()` method returns a blob instead of data:url; but at the time of writing, it hasn't yet been implemented by browsers.

Okay, it is time to get back to `loadcanvas()`. We already mentioned that this function is called in the `createhd()` function as soon as the application is started. It has the purpose of loading the file with the previous work and drawing it on the canvas. At this point, you already know which file we are talking about and how it was generated, so let's see the work performed by this function.

The `loadcanvas()` function is called from `createhd()` as soon as the File System is ready. Its purpose (as its name indicates) is to load the `canvas.dat` file and draw its content on the canvas. If the file doesn't exist, the `getFile()` method will return an error, but when the file is found, the method calls an anonymous function that will take the entry and use the `file()` method to generate a File object from it. This method, if successful, also calls an anonymous function to read the file and return its content as a binary string using `readAsBinaryString()`. The content we get from this file is a data:url string that has to be assigned as the source of an image before it can be drawn on the canvas. So, inside the anonymous function called by the `load` event, we create the Image object, declare the data:url from the file as the source of the image and (when the image has loaded) draw it on the canvas with `drawImage()`.

The resulting effect produced by the script is simple: the images selected from the `<input>` element are drawn on the canvas in random positions, and this work is preserved in a file. If the browser is closed, the file is loaded, the canvas is restored, and our work is still there. It's an oversimplified example, but you can see the potential, right?

Do It Yourself: Using the Drag and Drop API, you can drag and drop image files onto the canvas instead of loading the images from an `<input>` element. Try combining the script in Listing 16-23 with some codes from Chapter 13 to practice integrating these APIs.

File API

Chapter 17
Geolocation API

17.1 Finding Your Location

The Geolocation API was designed to provide a standard detection mechanism for browsers to let developers determine the user's geographic location. Previously, we only had the option of building a large database with IP addresses and programming resource-consuming scripts into the server that would only give us an approximate idea of the user's location (usually as vague as their country).

This API takes advantage of new systems, such as network triangulation or GPS, to return an accurate location of the device running the application. The valuable information returned may be used to create applications that adapt themselves according to the user's location or provide localized information automatically. Three specific methods are provided by the API for this purpose:

> **getCurrentPosition(location, error, configuration)**—This is the method used for single requests. It can have three attributes: a function to process the location returned, a function to process the errors returned and an object to configure how the information will be acquired. Only the first attribute is required.

> **watchPosition(location, error, configuration)**—This is similar to the previous method except it will start a watch process to detect and inform new locations. It works in a similar way to the `setInterval()` method, repeating the process automatically in a period of time according to the values set by default or the configuration specified in its attributes.

> **clearWatch(id)**—The `watchPosition()` method returns a value that can be stored in a variable and then used as an id by the `clearWatch()` method to stop the watch. This is similar to the `clearInterval()` method used to stop the process started by `setInterval()`.

HTML Document

The following is going to be our document for this chapter. It is as simple as possible, with just a button inside the `<section>` element that we are going to use to show the information retrieved by the location system.

```
<!DOCTYPE html>
<html lang="en">
<head>
  <title>Geolocation</title>
  <script src="geolocation.js"></script>
</head>
<body>
  <section id="location">
    <input type="button" id="getlocation" value="Get my location">
  </section>
</body>
</html>
```

Listing 17-1: HTML document for Geolocation

GetCurrentPosition(location)

As we mentioned above, only the first attribute is required for the `getCurrentPosition()` method to work properly. This attribute is a callback function that receives an object called Position that holds all the information retrieved by the geolocation systems. The Position object has two properties:

> **coords**—This property contains another object with a set of properties to provide the position of the device and other important information. The properties available are **latitude**, **longitude**, **altitude** (in meters), **accuracy** (in meters), **altitudeAccuracy** (in meters), **heading** (in degrees) and **speed** (in meters per second).
>
> **timestamp**—This property indicates the time when the information was acquired.

```
function initiate(){
  var get = document.getElementById('getlocation');
  get.addEventListener('click', getlocation);
}
function getlocation(){
  navigator.geolocation.getCurrentPosition(showinfo);
}
function showinfo(position){
  var location = document.getElementById('location');
  var data = '';
  data += 'Latitude: ' + position.coords.latitude + '<br>';
  data += 'Longitude: ' + position.coords.longitude + '<br>';
  data += 'Accuracy: ' + position.coords.accuracy + 'mts.<br>';
  location.innerHTML = data;
}
addEventListener('load', initiate);
```

Listing 17-2: Getting location information

Implementing the Geolocation API is simple: we use the `getCurrentPosition()` method and create a function that will show the values returned. The `getCurrentPosition()` method is a method of the **geolocation** object. This is a new object that is part of the **navigator** object, a Javascript object that was previously implemented to return information about the browser and the system. So to access the **getCurrentPosition()** method, the syntax is the following: **navigator.geolocation.getCurrentPosition(function)**, where **function** is a custom function that will receive the Position object returned and process the information.

In the script of Listing 17-2, we call this function **showinfo()**. When the **getCurrentPosition()** method is called, a new Position object is created with the information and is sent to the **showinfo()** function. We reference that object inside the function with the **position** variable and then use this variable to show the data.

The Position object has two important properties: **coords** and **timestamp**. In our example, we use **coords** to access the information we want (latitude, longitude and accuracy). These values are stored in the **data** variable and then shown on the screen as the new content of the **location** element.

> **Do It Yourself:** Create files with the codes of Listings 17-1 and 17-2, upload the files to your server, and then open the HTML document in your browser. When you click the button, the browser asks you whether or not to activate the location system for this application. If you allow the application to access this information, then your latitude, longitude and the accuracy of the data will be shown on the screen.

GetCurrentPosition(location, error)

What happens if you don't allow the browser to access information about your location? By adding a second attribute (another function), we are able to capture errors produced in the process, such as the user denying access to the location system.

Along with the Position object, the **getCurrentPosition()** method returns the PositionError object if an error is detected. The object has two properties, **error** and **message**, to provide the value and a description of the error. The three possible errors are represented by constants:

> **PERMISSION_DENIED**—Value 1. This error occurs when the user denies the Geolocation API access to his or her location information.
>
> **POSITION_UNAVAILABLE**—Value 2. This error occurs when the position of the device couldn't be determined.
>
> **TIMEOUT**—Value 3. This error occurs when the position couldn't be determined in the period of time declared in the configuration.

```
function initiate(){
  var get = document.getElementById('getlocation');
  get.addEventListener('click', getlocation);
}
function getlocation(){
  navigator.geolocation.getCurrentPosition(showinfo, showerror);
}
function showinfo(position){
  var location = document.getElementById('location');
  var data = '';
  data += 'Latitude: ' + position.coords.latitude + '<br>';
  data += 'Longitude: ' + position.coords.longitude + '<br>';
```

```
    data += 'Accuracy: ' + position.coords.accuracy + 'mts.<br>';
    location.innerHTML = data;
}
function showerror(error){
    alert('Error: ' + error.code + ' ' + error.message);
}
addEventListener('load', initiate);
```

Listing 17-3: Showing error messages for Geolocation

The error messages are intended for internal use. The purpose is to provide a mechanism for the application to acknowledge the situation and proceed accordingly. In the code in Listing 17-3, we add the second parameter to the `getCurrentPosition()` method (another callback function) and create the `showerror()` function to show the information of the properties `code` and `message`. The value of `code` will be an integer between 0 and 3 according to the number of the error (listed above).

The PositionError object is sent to the `showerror()` function and is represented by the variable `error`. We could also check for the errors individually (`error.PERMISSION_DENIED`, for example) and show an alert only if that particular condition is `true`.

GetCurrentPosition(location, error, configuration)

The third possible value of the `getCurrentPosition()` method is an object containing up to three possible properties:

enableHighAccuracy—This is a Boolean property to inform the system that the most accurate possible location is required. The browser will try to get information through systems like GPS, for example, to provide the exact location of the device. These are high resource-consuming systems, and their use should be limited to specific circumstances. For this reason, the default value of this property is `false`.

timeout—This property indicates the maximum time for the operation to take place. If the information is not acquired within the time limit, the `TIMEOUT` error is returned. Its value is in milliseconds.

maximumAge—The previous positions are cached in the system. If we consider it appropriate to get the last information saved instead of retrieving a new location (to avoid resource consumption or for a quick response), this property can be set with a specific time limit. If the last cached location is older than the value of this property, then a new location will be retrieved from the system. Its value is in milliseconds.

```
function initiate(){
    var get = document.getElementById('getlocation');
    get.addEventListener('click', getlocation);
}
function getlocation(){
    var geoconfig = {
        enableHighAccuracy: true,
        timeout: 10000,
        maximumAge: 60000
    };
```

```
  navigator.geolocation.getCurrentPosition(showinfo, showerror,
geoconfig);
}
function showinfo(position){
  var location = document.getElementById('location');
  var data = '';
  data += 'Latitude: ' + position.coords.latitude + '<br>';
  data += 'Longitude: ' + position.coords.longitude + '<br>';
  data += 'Accuracy: ' + position.coords.accuracy + 'mts.<br>';
  location.innerHTML = data;
}
function showerror(error){
  alert('Error: ' + error.code + ' ' + error.message);
}
addEventListener('load', initiate);
```

Listing 17-4: Configuring the Geolocation system

The script of Listing 17-4 tries to get the most accurate location for the device in no more than 10 seconds, but only if there is no previous location in the cache captured less than 60 seconds ago. (If there is, this will be the Position object returned.)

The object containing the configuration values is stored in the **geoconfig** variable, and this variable is declared as the third attribute of the **getCurrentPosition()** method. Nothing else changed in the rest of the code from the previous example. The **showinfo()** function will show the information on the screen independently of its origin (i.e., if it is cached or new).

In this script, we start to see the real purpose of the Geolocation API and what the API was intended for. The most effective and useful features are geared towards mobile devices. The value **true** for the **enableHighAccuracy** attribute, for example, will suggest the browser use systems like GPS to get the most accurate location. The methods **watchPosition()** and **clearWatch()**, which we will see next, work with location updates, and this is only possible, of course, when the device accessing the application is mobile (and moving).

This brings up two important subjects. First, most of our codes will have to be tested in a mobile device to know exactly how they will perform in a real situation. And second, we have to be responsible with the use of this API. GPS and other location systems consume a lot of resources, and in most cases, devices will run out of battery if we are not careful. Regarding the first issue, we have an alternative: visit http://dev.w3.org/geo/api/test-suite/ and check the test suite for the Geolocation API. Regarding the second issue, here is a piece of advice: set the **enableHighAccuracy** attribute to **true** only when it is strictly necessary, and don't abuse this feature.

WatchPosition(location, error, configuration)

Similar to **getCurrentPosition()**, the **watchPosition()** method takes three attributes and performs the same task: the method gets the location of the device that is accessing the application. The only difference is that **getCurrentPosition()** is a one-time operation while **watchPosition()** automatically offers new data every time the location changes. The method will be watching all the time and sending information to the callback function when there is a new location to show, unless we cancel this process with the **clearWatch()** method.

Here is an example of how to implement the **watchPosition()** method based on previous scripts:

```
function initiate(){
  var get = document.getElementById('getlocation');
  get.addEventListener('click', getlocation);
}
function getlocation(){
  var geoconfig = {
    enableHighAccuracy: true,
    maximumAge: 60000
  };
  control = navigator.geolocation.watchPosition(showinfo, showerror,
geoconfig);
}
function showinfo(position){
  var location = document.getElementById('location');
  var data = '';
  data += 'Latitude: ' + position.coords.latitude + '<br>';
  data += 'Longitude: ' + position.coords.longitude + '<br>';
  data += 'Accuracy: ' + position.coords.accuracy + 'mts.<br>';
  location.innerHTML = data;
}
function showerror(error){
  alert('Error: ' + error.code + ' ' + error.message);
}
addEventListener('load', initiate);
```

Listing 17-5: *Testing the* watchPosition() *method*

You won't notice anything running this example on a static desktop computer, but on a mobile device, new information will be shown every time there is a change in the device's location. The **maximumAge** attribute determines how often this information is sent to the **showinfo()** function. If the new location is retrieved 60 seconds (60000 milliseconds) after the previous one, then it is shown; otherwise the **showinfo()** function won't be called.

Notice that the value returned by the **watchPosition()** method is stored in the **control** variable. This variable is like the id for this operation. If later we want to cancel the processing of this method, we just execute the line **clearWatch(control)** and **watchPosition()** will stop updating the information.

Practical Uses with Google Maps

So far we have shown the location data on the screen exactly the way we receive it. However, these values usually mean nothing to regular people. We cannot immediately state our current locations' latitude and longitude, let alone identify a different location in the world from these values. We have two alternatives: use this information internally to calculate position, distance and other variables that will let us offer specific results to users (such as products or restaurants in the area) or directly show the information retrieved by the Geolocation API in a more comprehensible way. And what can be better for representing a geographic location than a map?

Earlier in this book, we mentioned the Google Maps API. This is an external Javascript API provided by Google that has nothing to do with HTML5 but is widely used in modern websites and applications. It offers a variety of alternatives to work with interactive maps and even real views of very specific locations through the StreetView technology.

We are going to show you a simple example using one part of the API called Static Maps API. With this specific API, we build a URL with the information of the location, and an image of the selected area in a map is returned.

```
function initiate(){
  var get = document.getElementById('getlocation');
  get.addEventListener('click', getlocation);
}
function getlocation(){
  navigator.geolocation.getCurrentPosition(showinfo, showerror);
}
function showinfo(position){
  var location = document.getElementById('location');
  var mapurl = 'http://maps.google.com/maps/api/staticmap?center=' +
position.coords.latitude + ',' + position.coords.longitude +
'&zoom=12&size=400x400&sensor=false&markers=' + position.coords.latitude
+ ',' + position.coords.longitude;
  location.innerHTML = '<img src="' + mapurl + '">';
}
function showerror(error){
  alert('Error: ' + error.code + ' ' + error.message);
}
addEventListener('load', initiate);
```

Listing 17-6: *Representing the location on a map using the Google Maps API*

The application is simple. We use the **getCurrentPosition()** method and send the information to **showinfo()** as usual, but now in this function, the values of the Position object are added to a Google URL, and then the address is inserted as the source of an **<img>** element to show the image returned on the screen.

> **Do It Yourself:** Test the script of Listing 17-6 in your browser using the document of Listing 17-1. Remember to upload the files to your server. Go to the Google Maps API web page to check other alternatives: https://developers.google.com/maps/. Change the values of the attributes **zoom** and **size** in the URL to modify the map returned by the API.

Geolocation API

Chapter 18

History API

18.1 History Interface

The History API in HTML5 is in fact an improvement of an old API that never had an official implementation but was supported by browsers for years. This old API was a little group of methods and properties, a part of which was the History object. The new History API is an improvement on this object and was included in the official HTML5 specification as the History interface. This interface combines all the old methods and properties with a few new ones to use and modify browser history according to our needs.

Navigating the Web

A browser history is a list of all the web pages (URLs) visited by the user in one single session. It is what makes navigation possible. Using the navigation buttons at the left of the navigation bar in every browser, we can go back and forward in this list and see previous documents. This list is built with real URLs generated by websites and included in every hyperlink inside their documents. With browser arrows, we can load a web page we visited before or go back to the last one.

Despite the practicality of browser buttons, sometimes it is useful to be able to navigate through the history list from inside the document. To emulate browser navigation arrows from Javascript, we always had the following methods and properties available:

> **back()**—This method takes the browser one step back in the session history (emulating the left arrow).
>
> **forward()**—This method takes the browser one step forward in the session history (emulating the right arrow).
>
> **go(steps)**—This method takes the browser back or forward the specified steps in the session history. The **steps** attribute may be a negative or positive value according to the direction we choose.
>
> **length**—This property returns the number of entries in the session history (the total of URLs on the list).

These methods and properties belong to the History object that is part of the Window object. We have to declare them as part of the History object with an expression like `history.back()`. We can also mention the Window object but, as we explained before, this is not necessary. For example, if we want to go back to the previous web page, we can use the line `window.history.back()` or `window.history.go(-1)`.

IMPORTANT: This part of the API is already known and used by most web designers and programmers nowadays. We are not going to see any example of these methods, but you can always visit our website and follow the links for this chapter to find more information.

New Methods

By the time using the XMLHttpRequest object became standard and Ajax applications became an extraordinary success, the way people navigated and accessed documents on the Web had changed forever. Now, it is common practice to program small scripts to retrieve information from servers and show it within the current document without refreshing the page or loading a new one. Users interact with modern websites and applications from the same URL, receiving information, entering data and getting processing results from the same page. The Web has begun to emulate desktop applications.

However, the way browsers keep track of the user's activity is through URLs. URLs are, in fact, the data inside the navigation list, the addresses that indicate where the user is currently located. Because new web applications avoided the use of URLs to point to the user's location on the Web, it soon became evident that important steps were lost in the process. Users could update data on a web page dozens of times and yet left no trace in the History list to indicate the steps followed and help them go back or forward.

New methods and properties were incorporated to the existing History API with the intention of manually modifying the URL in the Location bar as well as the history list using Javascript code. From now on, we have the ability to add fake URLs to the history list and keep an eye on the user's activity.

> **pushState(state, title, url)**—This method creates a new entry in the session history. The `state` attribute declares a value for the state of the entry. It is useful to identify the entry later, and it may be specified as a string or a JSON object. The `title` attribute is the title of the entry, and the `url` attribute is the URL for the entry we are generating. (This value will replace the current URL in the Location bar.)

> **replaceState(state, title, url)**—This method works exactly like `pushState()`, but it doesn't generate a new entry. Instead, it replaces the information for the current one.

> **state**—This property returns the value of the state for the current entry. This value will be `null` unless it was declared by one of the previous methods through the `state` attribute.

Fake URLs

The URLs generated using methods such as `pushState()` are fake URLs in the sense that browsers never check for the validity of these addresses and the existence of the document that they are pointing to. It falls on us to make sure that these fake URLs are in fact valid and useful.

To create a new entry in the browser history and change the URL inside the Location bar, we have to use the `pushState()` method. Let's see an example of how this works:

```
<!DOCTYPE html>
<html lang="en">
<head>
  <title>History API</title>
  <link rel="stylesheet" href="history.css">
  <script src="history.js"></script>
</head>
<body>
  <section id="maincontent">
    This content is never refreshed<br>
    <span id="url">page 2</span>
  </section>
  <aside id="databox"></aside>
</body>
</html>
```

Listing 18-1: Basic HTML document to test the History API

In Listing 18-1, we have the HTML code with the basic elements necessary to test the History API. There is permanent content inside a **<section>** element identified as **maincontent**, a text that we will turn into a link to generate the virtual second page of the website and the usual **databox** for the alternative content.

Let's include the styles for the document:

```
#maincontent{
  float: left;
  padding: 20px;
  border: 1px solid #999999;
}
#databox{
  float: left;
  width: 500px;
  margin-left: 20px;
  padding: 20px;
  border: 1px solid #999999;
}
#maincontent span{
  color: #0000FF;
  cursor: pointer;
}
```

Listing 18-2: Styles for the boxes and the <span> *elements (*history.css*)*

Review the Basics: The **cursor** property is a traditional CSS property used to specify the graphic to be displayed to represent the mouse pointer. The system changes this cursor automatically according to the content the mouse pointer is over. For general content, for example, the mouse pointer is represented as an arrow, for text as a vertical bar and for links as a little hand pointing at the link. In Listing 18-2, we change the cursor to the latter to show the user that the content is clickable. There are several values available for this property. For more information, visit our website and follow the links for this chapter.

What we are going to do in this example is add a new entry with the **pushState()** method and update the content without refreshing the page or loading another document.

```
function initiate(){
  databox = document.getElementById('databox');
  url = document.getElementById('url');
  url.addEventListener('click', changepage);
}
function changepage(){
  databox.innerHTML = 'the url is page2';
  history.pushState(null, null, 'page2.html');
}
addEventListener('load', initiate);
```

Listing 18-3: *Generating a new URL and content (*history.js*)*

In the **initiate()** function in Listing 18-3, we create the proper reference to the **databox** and add a listener for the **click** event to the **<span>** element. Every time the user clicks on the text inside **<span>**, the **changepage()** function is called.

The **changepage()** function performs two tasks: it updates the content of the page with new information and inserts a new URL in the history list. After the function is executed, the **databox** shows the text "the url is page2", and the URL of the main document is replaced in the Location bar by the fake URL "page2.html".

The **state** and **title** attributes for the **pushState()** method are declared as **null** this time. The **title** attribute is not used at the moment by any browser and will always be declared as **null**, but we will apply and use the **state** attribute in the examples following.

> **Do It Yourself:** Copy the document of Listing 18-1 into an HTML file, create a CSS file called **history.css** with the styles in Listing 18-2, and a Javascript file called **history.js** with the codes in Listing 18-3. Upload them to your server and open the HTML file in your browser. Click on the text "page 2" and check how the URL in the Location bar changes to the one generated by the code.

State Property

What we have done so far is manipulate the session history. We made the browser believe that the user visited a URL that, at this point, doesn't exist. After you clicked on the "page 2" link, the fake URL "page2.html" was shown in the Location bar and new content inserted in the **databox**, everything without refreshing or loading another page. It's a nice trick but is not complete. The browser doesn't consider the new URL a real document yet. If you go back and forward in the session history using the navigation buttons, the URL changes from the new one to the one of the main document, but the content of the document doesn't change at all. We need to detect when the fake URLs are revisited and perform the right modifications in the document to show the corresponding state.

We mentioned before the existence of the **state** property. The value of this property may be set during the generation of a new URL, and this is the way we can later identify what the current web address is. To work with this property, the API provides a new event:

popstate—This event is fired in certain circumstances when a URL is revisited or the document has loaded. It provides the **state** property with the value of the state declared when the URL was generated with the **pushState()** or **replaceState()** methods. This value is **null** when the URL is real unless we changed it before using **replaceState()**, as we will see next.

In the following script, we will improve the previous example by implementing the **popstate** event and the **replaceState()** method to detect which URL the user is currently requesting.

```
function initiate(){
  databox = document.getElementById('databox');
  url = document.getElementById('url');
  url.addEventListener('click', changepage);
  addEventListener('popstate', newurl);
  history.replaceState(1, null);
}
function changepage(){
  showpage(2);
  history.pushState(2, null, 'page2.html');
}
function newurl(e){
  showpage(e.state);
}
function showpage(current){
  databox.innerHTML = 'the url is page ' + current;
}
addEventListener('load', initiate);
```

Listing 18-4: Keeping track of the user's position (`history.js`*)*

There are two things we have to do in our application to have full control over the situation. First, we must declare a state value for every URL we are going to use, the fake and the real ones. And second, we must update the content of the document according to the current URL.

In the **initiate()** function in Listing 18-4, a listener is added for the **popstate** event. Every time a URL is revisited, the **newurl()** function is executed. This function simply updates the content of the **databox** according to the current URL. It takes the value of the **state** property and sends it to the **showpage()** function to be shown on the screen.

This will work for every fake URL, but as we said before, the real URLs don't have a state value by default. By using the **replaceState()** method at the end of the **initiate()** function, we change the information of the current entry (the real URL for the main document) and declare the value 1 for its state. Now, every time the user revisits the main document, we will be able to detect it, checking this value.

The **changepage()** function is the same, except this time it uses the **showpage()** function to update the document's content and declare the value 2 for the state of the fake URL.

The application works as follows: when the user clicks on the "page 2" link, the message "the url is page 2" is shown on the screen, and the URL in the Location bar is changed to "page2.html" (including the full path, of course). This is what we had done so far, but here is where things get interesting. If the user hits the left arrow in the browser's navigation bar, the URL in the Location bar will change to the previous in the history list (that is the real URL of our document), and the **popstate** event will be fired. This event calls the **newurl()** function that reads the value of the **state** property and sends it to the **showpage()** function. Now the state's value is 1 (the value we declared for this URL using the `replaceState()` method), and the message shown on the screen will be "the url is page 1". If the user goes back to the fake URL using the right arrow in the navigation bar, the state's value will be 2, and the message shown on the screen will again be "the url is page 2".

As you can see, the value of the `state` property is any value you want to control which URL is the current one and to adapt the document's content to this situation.

> **Do It Yourself:** Use the files with the codes of Listings 18-1 and 18-2 for the HTML document and CSS styles. Copy the script of Listing 18-4 into the `history.js` file, and upload the files to your server. Open the HTML document in your browser and click on the text "page 2". The URL and the content of the `databox` will change according to the corresponding URL. Click the back and forward buttons on the navigation bar several times to see the URL changing and the content associated with that URL updated on the screen.

> **IMPORTANT:** The URL "page2.html" generated with the `pushState()` method in previous examples is considered fake, but it should be real. The purpose of this API is not to create fake URLs but to provide the alternative for programmers to preserve the user's activity in the browser history to be able to go back to a previous state anytime that is required (even after the browser is closed). You will have to ensure that the code in your server is returning this state and providing the proper content for every URL requested (the real and the fake ones).

Real-Life Example

The following is a more practical application. We are going to use the History API and all the methods previously studied to load a set of four images from the same document. Each image is associated with a fake URL that can be used to return a specific image from the server later.

The main document is loaded with an image by default. This image will be associated with the first of four links that are part of the permanent content. All these links will point to fake URLs referencing a state, not a real document, including the link for the main document that will be changed to "page1.html". This will make sense soon.

```
<!DOCTYPE html>
<html lang="en">
<head>
  <title>History API</title>
  <link rel="stylesheet" href="history.css">
  <script src="history.js"></script>
</head>
<body>
  <section id="maincontent">
    This content is never refreshed<br>
    <span id="url1">image 1</span> -
    <span id="url2">image 2</span> -
    <span id="url3">image 3</span> -
    <span id="url4">image 4</span> -
  </section>
```

```
<aside id="databox">
  <img id="image" src="http://www.minkbooks.com/content/monster1.gif">
</aside>
</body>
</html>
```

Listing 18-5: HTML document for a real-life application

The only difference between this new application and the previous one is the number of links and new URLs we are generating. In the script of Listing 18-4, there were two states, state 1 corresponding to the main document and state 2 for the fake URL (page2.html) generated by the `pushState()` method. In this case, we have to automate the process and generate a total of four fake URLs corresponding to each image available.

```
function initiate(){
  for(var f = 1; f < 5; f++){
    url = document.getElementById('url'+f);
    url.addEventListener('click', function(x){
      return function(){ changepage(x); }
    }(f));
  }
  addEventListener('popstate', newurl);
  history.replaceState(1, null, 'page1.html');
}
function changepage(page){
  showpage(page);
  history.pushState(page, null, 'page'+page+'.html');
}
function newurl(e){
  showpage(e.state);
}
function showpage(current){
  if(current != null){
    image = document.getElementById('image');
    image.src = 'http://www.minkbooks.com/content/monster' + current +
'.gif';
  }
}
addEventListener('load', initiate);
```

Listing 18-6: Manipulating history (`history.js`*)*

As you can see, we are using the same functions, but with a few obvious changes. First, the `replaceState()` method in the `initiate()` function has the `url` attribute set to "page1.html". We decided to program our application this way, declaring the state of the main document as **1** and the URL as `page1.html` (independently of the real URL of the document). This makes it simple to jump from one URL to another, always using the same name and the values of the `state` property to build each URL. You can see this in practice in the `changepage()` function. Every time the user clicks on one of the links in the document, this function is executed and the fake URL is constructed with the value of the `page` variable and added to the history list. The value received by the function was previously set in the `for` loop at the beginning of the `initiate()` function. This value is set to 1 for the "page 1" link, **2** for the "page 2" link, and so on.

Every time a URL is visited, the `showpage()` function is executed to update the content (image) according to that URL. Because the `popstate` event sometimes is fired when the `state` property is `null` (such as after the main document is loaded for the first time), we check the value received by the `showpage()` function before doing anything else. If the value is different from `null`, it means the `state` property is defined for that URL and the image corresponding to that state is shown on the screen.

The images used for this example are named `monster1.gif`, `monster2.gif`, `monster3.gif` and `monster4.gif`, following the same order as the values of the `state` property. Thus, using this value, we can select the image to be shown. However, always remember that the value can be anyone you want, and the process to create the fake URLs and content associated with them will have to be set according to the needs of your application.

Also, remember that users should be able to return to any of the URLs generated by the application and see the proper content on the screen anytime they want. You must prepare your server to process these URLs in order to make states always available and accessible. For example, if a user opens a new window and types the URL "page2.html", the server should return the main document with the image "monster2.gif" and not just the document of Listing 18-5. The main idea behind this API is to provide an alternative for users to come back to any previous state any time they want, and we can only achieve this by turning the fake URLs into valid ones.

Review the Basics: The `for` loop we used in the script of Listing 18-6, to add a listener for the `click` event to every `<span>` element in the document, takes advantage of a Javascript technique available to send real values to a function. To send a value to a callback function in an `addEventListener()` method, we have to specify the real value. If we send a variable instead, what is really sent is not the value of the variable but its reference. So, in this case, to send the current value of the `f` variable of the `for` loop, we have to use two anonymous functions. The first function is executed when the `addEventListener()` method is called. It receives the current value of the `f` variable (check the parentheses at the end) and puts that value in the `x` variable. Then, the function returns a second anonymous function with the value of the variable `x`. This second function is what will be executed when the event is fired.

Do It Yourself: To test the last example, use the HTML document of Listing 18-5 with the CSS code of Listing 18-2. Copy the script of Listing 18-6 in the `history.js` file, and upload the files to your server. Open the document in your browser and click on the links. Navigate through the URLs you selected using the navigation buttons. The images on the screen should change according to the URL in the Location bar.

Chapter 19
Offline API

19.1 Cache Manifest

The days of working offline are over. Because this chapter is about the Offline API, that statement might sound contradictory, but just think about it. You have been working offline almost all your life. Desktop applications were your primary production tools, and now, suddenly, the Web has emerged as the new working platform. Online applications are getting more and more complex, and HTML5 is making things harder in the offline versus online battle. Databases, file access and storage, graphic tools, image and video editing, and multiprocessing are, among others, a set of essential features now available on the Web. Our daily activities are turning towards the Web, and our productivity depends on it. The offline days are over.

However, as the transition continues, web applications become more sophisticated, requiring bigger files and more time to download. By the time applications on the Web replace desktop applications, working online will be impossible. Users won't be able to download several megabytes of files every time they need to use each application and won't be able to count on having Internet access available 100% of the time. Offline applications will soon disappear, but under the current conditions online applications are destined to fail.

The Offline API was created to avoid this problem. Basically, this API provides an alternative to store applications and web files in the user's computer for future use. Accessing an application once is sufficient to download all the files required to run and use it with or without being connected to the network. Once the files are downloaded, the application runs in the browser but uses these files, like a desktop application would, independently of what happens with the server or the connection.

The Manifest File

A web application or a sophisticated website will consist of several files, but not all of them are necessary to run the application, and not all of them have to be stored in the user's computer. The API assigns a specific file to declare the list of files that are needed to work offline. This is a text file called **manifest**, containing a list of URLs pointing to the location of the required files. The manifest may be created with any text editor. It has to be saved with the **.appcache** extension and begin with the line **CACHE MANIFEST** as in the following example:

```
CACHE MANIFEST
cache.html
cache.css
cache.js
```

Listing 19-1: Creating the cache manifest file

The files listed under **CACHE MANIFEST** are all the files the application needs to run on the user's computer without requesting any external resources. In the example of Listing 19-1, we have the `cache.html` file as the main document for the application, the `cache.css` file with CSS styles and the `cache.js` file for the Javascript codes.

Categories

In the same way that we need to specify the files required for the application to run offline, we could also need to declare specific files available only online. This could be the case for part of the application only useful when connected—for example, a chat room.

To identify the type of files listed in the manifest file, the API introduces three categories:

CACHE—This is the category by default. All the files in this category will be saved in the user's computer for future use.

NETWORK—This category is considered a whitelist; all the files in it are only available online.

FALLBACK—This category is for files that might be useful to get from the server while online, but they may be replaced by an offline version. If the browser detects a connection, it will try to use the original file. Otherwise, the replacement will be loaded from the user's computer.

Using categories, our manifest file could be something like this:

```
CACHE MANIFEST

CACHE:
cache.html
cache.css
cache.js

NETWORK:
chat.html

FALLBACK:
newslist.html nonews.html
```

Listing 19-2: Declaring files by category

In the new manifest file of Listing 19-2, files are listed under the corresponding categories. The three files in the **CACHE** category will be downloaded, stored in the user's computer and used for this application from now on (unless we specify something different later). The `chat.html` file specified in the **NETWORK** category will only be available when the browser is online. The `newslist.html` file under the **FALLBACK** category will also be used when the user is online; however, if it cannot be accessed, it will be replaced by the `nonews.html` file. As well as the files under the **CACHE** category, the `nonews.html` file is cached and saved in user's computer to be available when it is required.

The **FALLBACK** category is useful not only to replace individual files, but also to indicate full directories. For example, the line `/ noconnection.html` will replace any file not available in the cache by the file `noconnection.html`. This is a nice way to divert users to a document that recommends they go online when they try to access the part of the application that is not available for offline use.

Comments

Comments may be added in a manifest file using the **#** symbol (one per line). Because files are ordered by category, comments may appear useless but are important for updates. The manifest file not only declares which files must be cached, but when. Every time the application files are updated, there is no way for the browser to know except through the manifest file. If the updated files are the same and no new ones were added to the list, the manifest file will look the same, and the browser won't be able to recognize the difference and will continue using the old files already cached. However, to force the browser to download the application files again, we can indicate the update using comments. Usually one comment with the date of the last update will be enough, as shown in the following example:

```
CACHE MANIFEST

CACHE:
cache.html
cache.css
cache.js

NETWORK:
chat.html

FALLBACK:
/ noconnection.html

# date 2012/08/10
```

Listing 19-3: Inserting comments to inform about updates

Let's suppose you add more code to the current functions of the **cache.js** file. Users will already have the file cached in their computers, and browsers will use this old version instead of the new one. Changing the date at the end of the manifest file or adding new comments will inform browsers about the update, and all the files will be downloaded again, including the improved version of the **cache.js** file. After the cache is updated, the new copies of the files will be used by the browser to run the application.

Using the Manifest File

After selecting all the files necessary to run the application offline and preparing the full list of URLs pointing to those files, we have to include the manifest file in our documents. HTML5 provides a new attribute for the **<html>** element to indicate the location of this file.

```
<!DOCTYPE html>
<html lang="en" manifest="mycache.appcache">
```

```
<head>
  <title>Offline API</title>
  <link rel="stylesheet" href="cache.css">
  <script src="cache.js"></script>
</head>
<body>
  <section id="databox">
    Offline Application
  </section>
</body>
</html>
```

Listing 19-4: Loading the manifest file

Listing 19-4 shows a short HTML document that includes the `manifest` attribute for the `<html>` element. The `manifest` attribute indicates the location of the manifest file necessary to generate the cache for the application. As you can see, nothing changes in the rest of the document: the files for CSS styles and Javascript codes are included as usual, independent of the content of the manifest file.

The CSS file has to include styles for the `<section>` element of our document. You can create your own styles or use the following:

```
#databox{
  width: 500px;
  height: 300px;
  margin: 10px;
  padding: 10px;
  border: 1px solid #999999;
}
```

Listing 19-5: CSS rule for the `databox`

The manifest file has to be saved with the `.appcache` extension and a name (in our example, `mycache`). Every time the browser finds the `manifest` attribute in a document, it will try to first download the manifest file and then all the resources listed inside. The `manifest` attribute must be included in every HTML document that has to be part of the cache for the application. The process is transparent for users and may be controlled through programming using the API, as we will see soon.

As well as the extension and the internal structure of the manifest file, there is another important requirement to consider. The manifest file must be served by servers with the proper MIME type. Every file has a MIME type associated to indicate the format of its content. For instance, the MIME type for an HTML file is `text/html`. A manifest file must be served using the `text/cache-manifest` MIME type or the browser will return an error.

> **IMPORTANT:** The `text/cache-manifest` MIME type is not currently part of the configuration by default of any server. You must add it to your server manually. How to include this new file type depends on the type of server you have. For some versions of Apache, for example, the addition of the following line in the `httpd.conf` file is enough to start serving these files with the proper type: `AddType text/cache-manifest .appcache`. An easy way to do this is to append a new line to the `.htaccess` file. Most servers provide this configuration file in the root folder of every website. The

corresponding syntax is **Addtype MIME/type extension** (e.g., **AddType text/cache-manifest .appcache**).

19.2 Offline API

The manifest file by itself should be sufficient to generate a cache for small websites or simple codes, but complex applications demand more control. The manifest file declares the files necessary to be cached, but it can't inform how many of those files are already downloaded, the errors found in the process or when an update is ready to be used, among other critical situations. Considering these possibilities, the API provides the new ApplicationCache object with methods, properties and events to manage the whole process.

Errors

The most important event of the ApplicationCache object is probably **error**. If an error occurs during the process of reading files on the server, the application won't be cached or the cache won't be updated. It's extremely important to be aware of these situations and act accordingly.

Using the HTML document presented in Listing 19-4, we are going to build a small application to see how the **error** event works.

```
function initiate(){
  var cache = applicationCache;
  cache.addEventListener('error', showerror);
}
function showerror(){
  alert('error');
}
addEventListener('load', initiate);
```

Listing 19-6: Checking for errors

The Window property **applicationCache** used in the script of Listing 19-6 returns the ApplicationCache object for this document. After storing a reference to the object in the **cache** variable, a listener for the **error** event is added to the object. When the event is fired, the **showerror()** function is called and a message is shown on the screen informing the error.

> **Do It Yourself:** Create an HTML file with the code of Listing 19-4, a Javascript file called **cache.js** with the script of Listing 19-6 and a manifest file called **mycache.appcache**. As we saw before, you have to include the list of the files to be cached under the **CACHE** category in the manifest file. For our example, these files are the HTML file, the **cache.js** file and the **cache.css** file with the styles for the document. Upload the files to your server and open the HTML file in your browser. If you erase the manifest file or forget to add the corresponding MIME type for this file on the server's configuration, the **error** event will be fired. You can also interrupt Internet access or use the Work Offline option in Mozilla Firefox to see the application running offline from the new cache.

Online and Offline

There is a new property for the Navigator object called **onLine** that indicates the current status of the connection. This property is associated with two events that will be fired when its value changes. The property and the events are not part of the ApplicationCache object but are useful for this API.

> **online**—This event is fired when the value of the **onLine** property changes to **true**.
>
> **offline**—This event is fired when the value of the **onLine** property changes to **false**.

Here is an example of how to use them:

```
var databox;
function initiate(){
  databox = document.getElementById('databox');

  addEventListener('online', function(){ state(1); });
  addEventListener('offline', function(){ state(2); });
}
function state(value){
  switch(value){
    case 1:
      databox.innerHTML += '<br>We are ONline';
      break;
    case 2:
      databox.innerHTML += '<br>We are OFFline';
      break;
  }
}
addEventListener('load', initiate);
```

Listing 19-7: *Checking the connection status using the* onLine *property*

In the script of Listing 19-7, we use anonymous functions to handle the events and send a value to the **state()** function to show the corresponding message in the **databox**. The events will be fired every time the value of the **onLine** property changes.

> **IMPORTANT:** There is no guarantee that the property will always have the proper value. Listening to these events on a desktop computer will probably produce no effect, even when the computer is completely disconnected from the Internet. To test this example on a PC, we recommend you use the Work Offline option provided by Mozilla Firefox.

> **Do It Yourself:** Use the same HTML and CSS files from the previous example. Copy the script of Listing 19-7 in the **cache.js** file. Using Mozilla Firefox, erase the cache for your website and load this application. To test the events, you can use the Work Offline option in the Mozilla Firefox menu. Every time you click this option, the condition changes and a new message is appended to the **databox**.

Cache Process

Creating or updating a cache could take anywhere from a few seconds to several minutes, depending on the size of the files that must be downloaded. The entire process goes through different stages according to what the browser is able to do at each moment. In a regular update, for example, browsers will try to read the manifest file to first check for possible updates, download all the files listed in the manifest if an update exists and inform when the process is finished. To inform the current step in the process, the API offers the **status** property. This property may take the following values:

UNCACHED (value 0)—This value indicates that no cache has been created yet for this application.

IDLE (value 1)—This value indicates the cache for the application is the newest and is not obsolete.

CHECKING (value 2)—This value indicates the browser is checking for new updates.

DOWNLOADING (value 3)—This value indicates the files for the cache are being downloaded.

UPDATEREADY (value 4)—This value indicates the cache for the application is available and not obsolete, but it is not the newest; an update is ready to replace it.

OBSOLETE (value 5)—This value indicates the current cache is obsolete.

You can check the value of the **status** property any time, but it's better to use the events provided by the ApplicationCache object to check the state of the process and the cache. The following events are usually fired in sequence, and some of them are associated with a specific application cache status:

checking—This event is fired when the browser is checking for updates.

noupdate—This event is fired when no changes are found in the manifest file.

downloading—This event is fired when the browser finds a new update and starts downloading the files.

cached—This event is fired when the cache is ready.

updateready—This event is fired when the downloading process for an update is complete.

obsolete—This event is fired when the manifest file is no longer available and the cache is being deleted.

The following example will help you understand the process. In this script, every time an event is fired, a message is added to the **databox** with the value of the event and the **status** property:

```
var databox;
function initiate(){
  databox = document.getElementById('databox');
  var cache = applicationCache;
```

```
   cache.addEventListener('checking', function(){ show(1); });
   cache.addEventListener('downloading', function(){ show(2); });
   cache.addEventListener('cached', function(){ show(3); });
   cache.addEventListener('updateready', function(){ show(4); });
   cache.addEventListener('obsolete', function(){ show(5); });
}
function show(value){
  databox.innerHTML += '<br>Status: ' + cache.status;
  databox.innerHTML += ' | Event: ' + value;
}
addEventListener('load', initiate);
```

Listing 19-8: *Checking the connection*

We use anonymous functions for every event to send a different value to identify each event in the **show()** function. This value and the value of the **status** property are shown on the screen every time the browser reaches a new step in generating the cache.

> **Do It Yourself:** Use the HTML and CSS files from previous examples. Copy the script of Listing 19-8 into the **cache.js** file. Upload the application to your server, and see how different steps of the process are shown on the screen according to the status of the cache every time the document is loaded.

> **IMPORTANT:** If the cache was already created, it is important to follow a few steps to clear the cache and load a new version. Modifying the manifest file is one step, but it is not the only one. Browsers keep a copy of the files for a few hours before even considering checking for updates again, so no matter how many new comments or files were added to the manifest file, the browser will run the old cache version for a while. To test each example in this chapter, we recommend you change the name of every file. For instance, adding a number at the end of the name (such as **cache2.js**) will make the browser consider this as a new application and create a new cache. This works only for testing purposes, of course.

Progress

Applications that include images, several script files, information for databases, videos or any other big file may take a long time to download. To monitor this process, the API provides the already known **progress** event. This event is the same we used in previous chapters for other APIs.

The **progress** event is only fired while the files are being downloaded. In the following example, we are going to use the **noupdate** event along with the **cached** and **updateready** events to inform when the process has finished.

```
var databox;
function initiate(){
  databox = document.getElementById('databox');
  databox.innerHTML = '<progress value="0" max="100">0%</progress>';
```

```
  var cache = applicationCache;
  cache.addEventListener('progress', progress);
  cache.addEventListener('cached', show);
  cache.addEventListener('updateready', show);
  cache.addEventListener('noupdate', show);
}
function progress(e){
  if(e.lengthComputable){
    var per = parseInt(e.loaded / e.total * 100);
    var progressbar = databox.querySelector("progress");
    progressbar.value = per;
    progressbar.innerHTML = per + '%';
  }
}
function show(){
  databox.innerHTML = 'Done';
}
addEventListener('load', initiate);
```

Listing 19-9: Download progress

As always, the **progress** event is fired periodically to inform about the state of the process. In the script of Listing 19-9, every time **progress** is fired, the **progress()** function is called and the information on the screen is updated using a **<progress>** element.

There are different possibilities at the end of the process. The application could have been cached for the first time, so the **cached** event would be fired. It could be that the cache already existed and an update was available, so when the files have finally downloaded, the **updateready** event would be fired instead. And a third possibility is that a cache was already in use and no update was available, so the **noupdate** event would be fired. We listen to events for every one of these situations and call the **show()** function in each case to print the message "Done" on the screen, thus indicating the process is complete. You can find an explanation of the **progress** event and its properties in Chapter 16.

> **Do It Yourself:** Use the HTML and CSS files from previous examples. Copy the code in Listing 19-8 into the **cache.js** file. Upload the application to your server, and open the main document. You have to include a large file in the manifest file to be able to see the progress bar working. (At present, browsers have limitations on the size of the cache. We recommend you to try with files of a few megabytes, but no more than five.) For example, using the **trailer.ogg** video introduced in Chapter 6, the manifest file should look like this:
>
> ```
> CACHE MANIFEST
> cache.html
> cache.css
> cache.js
> trailer.ogg
>
> # date 2012/06/27
> ```

IMPORTANT: We used **innerHTML** to add a new **<progress>** element to the document. This is not a recommended practice, but it's useful and convenient for our example. Usually elements are added to the DOM using the Javascript method `createElement()` along with `appendChild()`, as explained in Chapter 4.

Updating the Cache

So far we have seen how to create a cache for our application, how to inform the browser when an update is available and how to control the process every time a user accesses the application. This is useful but not completely transparent for users. The cache and its updates are loaded as soon as the user runs the application, which could produce delays and annoying behavior. The API solves this problem by providing new methods to update the cache while the application is already running:

update()—This method initiates an update of the cache. It indicates to the browser to first download the manifest file and then continue with the rest of the files if a change in the manifest is detected (the files for the cache were modified).

swapCache()—This method switches to the most recent cache after an update. It doesn't run new scripts or replace resources but rather indicates to the browser that a new cache is available for future readings.

To update the cache, we call the `update()` method. The `updateready` and `noupdate` events are useful to know the result of the process. For the next example, we are going to use a new HTML document with two buttons to request the update and test the current Javascript code in the cache.

```
<!DOCTYPE html>
<html lang="en" manifest="mycache.appcache">
<head>
  <title>Offline API</title>
  <link rel="stylesheet" href="cache.css">
  <script src="cache.js"></script>
</head>
<body>
  <section id="databox">
    Offline Application
  </section>
  <input type="button" id="update" value="Update Cache">
  <input type="button" id="test" value="Test">
</body>
</html>
```

Listing 19-10: *HTML document to test the* `update()` *method*

The Javascript code implements techniques already studied; we just have to include two new functions for the buttons:

```
var cache, databox;
function initiate(){
  databox = document.getElementById('databox');

  var update = document.getElementById('update');
  update.addEventListener('click', updatecache);
  var test = document.getElementById('test');
  test.addEventListener('click', testcache);

  cache = applicationCache;
  cache.addEventListener('updateready', function(){ show(1); });
  cache.addEventListener('noupdate', function(){ show(2); });
}
function updatecache(){
  cache.update();
}
function testcache(){
  databox.innerHTML += '<br>change this message';
}
function show(value){
  switch(value){
    case 1:
      databox.innerHTML += '<br>Update Ready';
      break;
    case 2:
      databox.innerHTML += '<br>No Update Available';
      break;
  }
}
addEventListener('load', initiate);
```

Listing 19-11: *Updating the cache and checking the current version*

In the **initiate()** function, a listener for the **click** event is added to both buttons. Clicking the "Update Cache" button will call the **updatecache()** function and execute the **update()** method, and clicking the "Test" button will call the **testcache()** function and append a text to the **databox**. This is a text you can modify later to create a new version of the script and check whether or not it was updated.

> **Do It Yourself:** Create a new HTML document with the script of Listing 19-10. The manifest and the CSS files are the same as previous examples (unless you changed some file names, in which case you will have to update the file list in the manifest file). Copy the script of Listing 19-11 into a file called **cache.js**, and upload all these files to your server. Open the main document in your browser and test the application.

Once the HTML document has loaded, the window shows our typical **databox** and two buttons under it. As we explained before, the "Update Cache" button has the **click** event associated with the **updatecache()** function. If the button is clicked, the **update()** method is executed inside this function and the updating process starts. The browser downloads the manifest file and compares it with the same file already in the cache. If this file was modified, all the files listed inside are downloaded again. When the process is over, the **updateready** event is fired. This event calls the **show()** function with the value **1**, corresponding to the message "Update Ready". On the other hand, if the manifest file didn't change, no update is detected and the **noupdate** event is fired. This event calls the **show()** function with the value 2. In this case, the message "No Update Available" is shown in the **databox**.

You can test how the script works by modifying or adding comments in the manifest file. Every time you hit the button to update the cache after any modification, the message "Update Ready" will appear in the **databox**. You can also play with the text in the **testcache()** function to detect when an update is already running.

> **IMPORTANT:** This time there is no need to erase the cache from your browser to download a new version. The **update()** method forces the browser to download the manifest file and the rest of the files if an update is detected. However, the new cache is still not available until the user refreshes the page.

Chapter 20
Page Visibility API

20.1 The Visibility State

Web applications are getting more sophisticated and are demanding computer resources as never before. Web pages are no longer static documents; Javascript has turned them into full applications, capable of executing complex processes without interruption, and even without the user's intervention. But there are moments when these processes may be canceled or momentarily paused to effectively use resources and also to provide a better user experience. With the intention of producing conscious applications, HTML5 introduces the Page Visibility API. This API informs the application about the current visibility state of the document, reporting when the tab is hidden or the windows minimized, so it can decide what to do while nobody is watching.

Current State

Basically, the API provides a property to report the current state and an event to let the application know that something changed.

> **visibilityState**—This property returns the current visibility state of the document. The possible values are **hidden** or **visible** (some optional values such as **prerender** and **unloaded** may be also implemented by browsers).

> **visibilitychange**—This event is fired when the value of the **visibilityState** property changes.

```
<!DOCTYPE html>
<html lang="en">
<head>
  <title>Page Visibility API</title>
  <script>
    function initiate(){
      document.addEventListener('webkitvisibilitychange', showstate);
    }
    function showstate(){
      var element = document.getElementById('application');
      element.innerHTML += '<br>' + document.webkitVisibilityState;
    }
    addEventListener('load', initiate);
  </script>
</head>
```

```
<body>
  <section id="application">
    Move to another tab or minimize this window to change the visibility
state
  </section>
</body>
</html>
```

Listing 20-1: Informing the visibility state

In the script of Listing 20-1, the `showstate()` function is set to handle the `visibilitychange` event. When the event is fired, the function shows the value of the `visibilityState` property on the screen to inform the current state of the document. When the tab is replaced by another tab or the window is minimized, the value of the `visibilityState` property changes to `hidden`, and when the tab or the window is restored, the value is set back to `visible`.

> **IMPORTANT:** At the time of writing, the event and the property are prefixed by browsers. Google Chrome uses **webkitvisibilitychange** and **webkitVisibilityState**, and Mozilla Firefox uses **mozvisibilitychange** and **mozVisibilityState**. The examples of this chapter were prepared for Google Chrome.

A Better Experience

One of the reasons for the implementation of this API was the high consumption of resources by modern applications, but the API was also designed as a way to improve the user's experience. The next example shows you how to achieve the latter with just a few lines of code.

```
<!DOCTYPE html>
<html lang="en">
<head>
  <title>Page Visibility API</title>
  <script>
    var video;
    function initiate(){
      video = document.getElementById('media');
      document.addEventListener('webkitvisibilitychange', showstate);
      video.play();
    }
    function showstate(){
      var state = document.webkitVisibilityState;
      switch(state){
        case 'visible':
          video.play();
          break;
        case 'hidden':
          video.pause();
          break;
      }
    }
    addEventListener('load', initiate);
```

```
  </script>
</head>
<body>
  <video id="media" width="720" height="400">
    <source src="http://minkbooks.com/content/trailer.mp4">
    <source src="http://minkbooks.com/content/trailer.ogg">
  </video>
</body>
</html>
```

Listing 20-2: Responding to the visibility state

The script of Listing 20-2 plays a video while the document is visible and pauses it when it's not. We use the same functions from the previous example, except this time the value of the `visibilityState` property is checked by a `switch` statement and the `play()` or `pause()` methods are executed according to the case.

> **Do It Yourself:** Create an HTML file with the document of Listing 20-2. Open the file in your browser, and alternate between tabs to see the application in action. The video will pause when the document is not visible and resume when it is visible again.

Full Detector

For some reason, browsers do not change the value of the `visibilityState` property when the user opens a new browser window or program. The API is only capable of detecting the change in visibility when the tab is hidden by another tab or the window is minimized. To determine the visibility state in any circumstance, we can complement the API with the `blur` and `focus` events. These are traditional Javascript events fired when the window or any element in the document loses or gains focus, respectively. With the addition of a small function, we can combine all the tools available to build a better detector.

```
<!DOCTYPE html>
<html lang="en">
<head>
  <title>Page Visibility API</title>
  <script>
    var state;
    function initiate(){
      addEventListener('blur', function(){ changestate('hidden'); });
      addEventListener('focus', function(){ changestate('visible'); });
      document.addEventListener('webkitvisibilitychange', function(){
changestate(document.webkitVisibilityState); });
    }
    function changestate(newstate){
      if(state != newstate){
        state = newstate;
        showstate();
      }
    }
```

```
    function showstate(){
      var element = document.getElementById('application');
      element.innerHTML += '<br>' + state;
    }
    addEventListener('load', initiate);
  </script>
</head>
<body>
  <section id="application">
    Move to another window to change the visibility state
  </section>
</body>
</html>
```

Listing 20-3: *Combining the* blur, focus *and* visibilitychange *events*

In the **initiate()** function in Listing 20-3, listeners for the three events are added. The **changestate()** function is set to handle the event and process the value corresponding to the current state. This value is determined by each event. The **blur** event sends the value **hidden**; the **focus** event sends the value **visible**; and the **visibilitychange** event sends the current value of the **visibilityState** property. As a result, the **changestate()** function receives the right value, no matter how the document was hidden (by another tab, window or program). Using the **state** variable, the function compares the previous value with the new one, stores the new value in the variable and calls the **showstate()** function to show the state on the screen.

This process is a little more complicated than the previous one but considers every possible situation in which the document may be hidden and the state changed.

> **IMPORTANT:** It is not clear at the moment whether the API should operate like this or if the function performed by the **blur** and **focus** events will later be added to the specification. These events are not completely reliable, but the API seems to be focused only on tabs, ignoring windows. If the premises of HTML5 are followed, this situation should be corrected soon. For updates, please visit www.minkbooks.com/updates/.

Page Visibility API

Chapter 21
Ajax Level 2

21.1 XMLHttpRequest

The old Web paradigm demanded that websites and web applications access the server and provide all their information at once. If new information was required, the browser had to access the server and replace the old information with the new. This prompted the use of the word *Pages* for HTML documents. Documents replaced themselves like pages turned in a book.

This was the standard until someone found a better use for an old object, introduced first by Microsoft and later improved by Mozilla, called XMLHttpRequest. This object provides a way to access the server and retrieve information from Javascript without reloading the HTML document. In an article written in 2005, the name *Ajax* was coined for this procedure.

Because of its relevance in modern applications, HTML5 has introduced the new XMLHttpRequest Level 2 API to carry out Ajax. This new API incorporates features such as cross-origin communication and new events to control the evolution of the request. These improvements simplify scripts and provide new options, such as interacting with several servers from the same application or working with small pieces of data instead of entire files, to name a few. The most important element of this API is, of course, the XMLHttpRequest object. A constructor was specified to create this object:

> **XMLHttpRequest()**—This constructor returns an XMLHttpRequest object from which we can start a request and listen to the events to control the communication process.

The object created by the `XMLHttpRequest()` constructor has important methods to initiate and control the request:

> **open(method, url, async)**—This method configures a pending request. The `method` attribute specifies the HTTP method used to open the connection (`GET` or `POST`). The `url` attribute declares the location of the script that is going to process the request. And `async` is a Boolean value to make the communication synchronous (`false`) or asynchronous (`true`). The method can also include values for the user and a password when it is necessary.

> **send(data)**—This is the method that actually initiates the request. There are several versions of this method in an XMLHttpRequest object to process different kinds of data. The `data` attribute may be omitted, declared as an ArrayBuffer, a blob, a document, a string or a FormData object.

> **abort()**—This is a simple method to cancel the request.

Retrieving Data

Let's begin building an example to get information from a text file in the server using the GET method. We are going to need a new HTML document with a button to start the request:

```html
<!DOCTYPE html>
<html lang="en">
<head>
  <title>Ajax Level 2</title>
  <link rel="stylesheet" href="ajax.css">
  <script src="ajax.js"></script>
</head>
<body>
  <section id="formbox">
    <form name="form">
      <input type="button" id="button" value="Do It">
    </form>
  </section>
  <section id="databox"></section>
</body>
</html>
```

Listing 21-1: HTML document for Ajax requests

To make the codes as simple as possible, we keep our usual HTML structure and apply some essential styles for aesthetic purposes.

```css
#formbox{
  float: left;
  padding: 20px;
  border: 1px solid #999999;
}
#databox{
  float: left;
  width: 500px;
  margin-left: 20px;
  padding: 20px;
  border: 1px solid #999999;
}
```

Listing 21-2: Styles to shape boxes on the screen

Do It Yourself: Create an HTML file with the document of Listing 21-1 and a CSS file called **ajax.css** with the rules in Listing 21-2. To be able to test the following examples, you will have to upload all the files, including the Javascript file and the file to which the request is made, to your server. We are going to provide more instructions in each example.

The following script reads a file in the server and shows its content on the screen. No data are sent to the server; we just have to make a GET request and show the information retrieved.

```
var databox;
function initiate(){
  databox = document.getElementById('databox');

  var button = document.getElementById('button');
  button.addEventListener('click', read);
}
function read(){
  var url = "textfile.txt";
  var request = new XMLHttpRequest();
  request.addEventListener('load', show);
  request.open("GET", url, true);
  request.send(null);
}
function show(e){
  var data = e.target;
  if(data.status == 200){
    databox.innerHTML = data.responseText;
  }
}
addEventListener('load', initiate);
```

Listing 21-3: Reading a file

In this example, the `initiate()` function creates a reference to the `databox` and adds a listener to the button for the `click` event. When the "Do It" button is pressed, the `read()` function is executed. Here, we can see all the methods previously studied in action. First, the URL of the file to be read is declared. Because we haven't yet explained how to make cross-origin requests, this file has to be in the same domain (and in this example, also the same directory) as the Javascript code. In the next step, the object is created with the `XMLHttpRequest()` constructor and assigned to the `request` variable. This variable is used to add an event listener for the `load` event, and the `open()` and `send()` methods are used to configure and start the request. Since no data will be sent in this request, the `send()` method is empty (`null`), but the `open()` method needs its attributes to configure the request. Using this method, we declare the request as `GET`, the URL of the file to be read and the type of operation (`true` for asynchronous).

An asynchronous operation means that the browser will continue processing the code while the file is being read. The end of the operation will be informed through the `load` event. When the file has finally loaded, this event is fired and the `show()` function is called. This function checks the status of the operation through the value of the `status` property and then inserts the value of the `responseText` property into the `databox` to show the content of the file on the screen.

> **Do It Yourself:** To test this example, create a text file called `textfile.txt` and add some content to it. Upload this file and the rest of the files created with the codes of Listings 21-1, 21-2 and 21-3 to your server, and open the HTML document in your browser. After clicking the "Do It" button, the content of the text file is shown on the screen.

> **Review the Basics:** Servers return information to report the status of the request. This information is called HTTP status code and includes a number and a message describing the status. Javascript provides two properties to read this information: `status` and `statusText`. The `status` property returns the number of the status, and the

statusText property returns the message. The value **200**, used in the example of Listing 21-3, is one of several available. This value indicates that the request was successful. The message for this status is "OK". For a full list of HTTP status codes, visit our website and follow the links for this chapter.

Response Properties

There are three different types of properties we can use to get information returned by a request:

> **response**—This is a general purpose property. It returns the response of the request in the format specified by the value of the **responseType** property. This property may take five different values: **text, arraybuffer, blob, document** or **json**.
>
> **responseText**—This returns the response of the request as text.
>
> **responseXML**—This returns the response of the request as XML data.

The most useful of these properties for HTML5 applications is probably **response**. This property returns the data in the format declared previously by the **responseType** property. The **responseType** property is part of the XMLHttpRequest object and must be declared before the request is made. Here is a practical example:

```
var databox;
function initiate(){
  databox = document.getElementById('databox');

  var button = document.getElementById('button');
  button.addEventListener('click', read);
}
function read(){
  var url = "myimage.jpg";
  var request = new XMLHttpRequest();
  request.responseType = 'blob';
  request.addEventListener('load', show);
  request.open("GET", url, true);
  request.send(null);
}
function show(e){
  var data = e.target;
  if(data.status == 200){
    var image = URL.createObjectURL(data.response);
    databox.innerHTML = '<img src="' + image + '">';
  }
}
addEventListener('load', initiate);
```

Listing 21-4: *Reading an image from the server using the* blob responseType

In Listing 21-4, the **responseType** property for the request is set to **blob**. Now, the data received will be a blob that we can use to store in a file, to slice, to upload, etc. In this example we use it as the source for an **<img>** element and show the image downloaded on the screen. To turn the blob into an URL for the source of the image, we apply the `createObjectURL()` method introduced in Chapter 9.

Events

In addition to `load`, the specification includes specific events for the XMLHttpRequest object:

loadstart—This event is fired when the request starts.

progress—This event is fired periodically while sending or loading data.

abort—This event is fired when the request is aborted.

error—This event is fired when an error occurs during the request.

load—This event is fired when the request has been completed.

timeout—If a `timeout` value has been specified, this event will be fired when the request can't be completed in that specified period of time.

loadend—This event is fired when the request has been completed (either in success or failure).

The most attractive event of all may be **progress**. This event is fired approximately every 50 milliseconds to inform the user about the state of the request. By taking advantage of **progress**, we can notify the user about every step of the process and create professional communication applications.

```
var databox;
function initiate(){
  databox = document.getElementById('databox');

  var button = document.getElementById('button');
  button.addEventListener('click', read);
}
function read(){
  var url = "trailer.ogg";
  var request = new XMLHttpRequest();
  request.addEventListener('loadstart', start);
  request.addEventListener('progress', status);
  request.addEventListener('load', show);
  request.open("GET", url, true);
  request.send(null);
}
function start(){
  databox.innerHTML = '<progress value="0" max="100">0%</progress>';
}
function status(e){
  if(e.lengthComputable){
    var per = parseInt(e.loaded / e.total * 100);
    var progressbar = databox.querySelector("progress");
    progressbar.value = per;
    progressbar.innerHTML = per + '%';
  }
}
```

```
function show(e){
  var data = e.target;
  if(data.status == 200){
    databox.innerHTML = 'Done';
  }
}
addEventListener('load', initiate);
```

Listing 21-5: *Showing the progress of the request*

In Listing 21-5, the code uses three events, `loadstart`, `progress` and `load`, to control the request. The `loadstart` event calls the `start()` function to show the progress bar on the screen for the first time. While the file is being downloaded, the `progress` event executes the `status()` function several times. This function informs the user about the progress through the `<progress>` element and the value of the `progress` event's properties, studied in Chapter 16.

Finally, when the file has fully downloaded, the `load` event is fired and the `show()` function shows the string "Done" on the screen.

> **IMPORTANT:** We used `innerHTML` to add a new `<progress>` element to the document. While it's useful and convenient for our example, this is not a recommended practice. Usually elements are added to the DOM using the Javascript method `createElement()` along with `appendChild()`, as explained in Chapter 4.

> **Do It Yourself:** Depending on your Internet connection, to see the progress bar working, you might have to use large files. In the code in Listing 21-5, we declare the URL as the name of the video used in Chapter 6 to work with the `<video>` element. You can use your own or download the file at www.minkbooks.com/content/.

Sending Data

So far, we have been getting information from the server, but we haven't sent any data or used another HTTP method other than `GET`. In the following example, we are going to work with the `POST` method and a new object that allows us to send information using virtual form elements.

We haven't mentioned how to send data through a `GET` method because it's as simple as adding the values in the URL. You have to create a path for the `url` variable such as `textfile.txt?val1=1&val2=2`, and the values are sent along with the request. The `val1` and `val2` attributes of this example will be read as `GET` variables at the server. Of course, a text file can't process that information, so usually you will have a PHP file or any other server-side script to receive these values. However, for `POST` requests, it is not that simple.

A `POST` request includes all the information sent by a `GET` method but also a message body. The message body allows us to send any type of information of any length we need. An HTML form is normally the best way to provide this information, but for dynamic applications, this is probably not the best option or the most appropriate. To solve this issue, the API includes the FormData interface. This simple interface has a constructor and a method to get and work with FormData objects.

> **FormData(form)**—This constructor returns a FormData object used later by the `send()` method to send the information. The `form` attribute is optional. This attribute is a reference to an HTML form and provides an easy way to include an entire HTML form into the object.

append(name, value)—This method adds data to the FormData object. It takes a keyword/value pair as attributes. The **value** attribute can be either a string or a blob. The data returned represent a form field.

```
var databox;
function initiate(){
  databox = document.getElementById('databox');

  var button = document.getElementById('button');
  button.addEventListener('click', send);
}
function send(){
  var data = new FormData();
  data.append('name', 'John');
  data.append('lastname', 'Doe');

  var url = "process.php";
  var request = new XMLHttpRequest();
  request.addEventListener('load', show);
  request.open("POST", url, true);
  request.send(data);
}
function show(e){
  var data = e.target;
  if(data.status == 200){
    databox.innerHTML = data.responseText;
  }
}
addEventListener('load', initiate);
```

Listing 21-6: Sending a virtual form to the server

When information is sent to a server, it is with the purpose of processing it and producing a result. Usually, this result is saved in the server and some information is returned to provide feedback. In the example of Listing 21-6, we send data to the **process.php** file and show the information returned by that script on the screen.

To test this example, you can print the values received by **process.php** with a code like the following:

```
<?PHP
  print('Your name is: '.$_POST['name'].'<br>');
  print('Your last name is: '.$_POST['lastname']);
?>
```

Listing 21-7: Responding to a POST *request (*process.php*)*

Let's see first how the information is prepared for sending. In the **send()** function in Listing 21-6, the **FormData()** constructor is invoked, and the FormData object returned is stored in the **data** variable. Two keyword/value pairs are added to this object with the names **name** and **lastname** using the **append()** method. These values represent form input fields.

The initialization of the request is exactly the same as in previous scripts except this time the first attribute for the **open()** method is **POST** instead of **GET**, and the attribute of the **send()** method is the **data** object.

When the "Do It" button is clicked, the **send()** function is called and the form created in the FormData object is sent to the server. The **process.php** file receives this data (**name** and **lastname**) and returns a text to the browser with this information. The **show()** function is executed when the process is complete, and the information received is shown on the screen through the **responseText** property.

> **Do It Yourself:** This example requires several files to be uploaded to a server. We are going to use the same HTML document and CSS styles of Listings 21-1 and 21-2. The Javascript code in Listing 21-6 replaces the previous one. You also have to create a new file called **process.php** with the code in Listing 21-7 to respond to the request. Upload all these files to a server, and open the HTML document in your browser. By clicking the "Do It" button, you should be able to see the text returned by the **process.php** file on the screen.

Cross-Origin Requests

We have been working with scripts and data files in the same directory and the same domain, but the CORS technology studied in Chapter 10 also applies to XMLHttpRequest Level 2, allowing us to configure our server to accept cross-origin requests.

As we studied in Chapter 10, the access from one origin to another must be authorized at the server. The advantage with this API is that in cases where we are accessing server-side scripts, we can add the header to the script file instead of changing the server's configuration.

The solution for our previous example is as simple as adding the header **Access-Control-Allow-Origin** as the first line of the PHP script.

```php
<?PHP
  header('Access-Control-Allow-Origin: *');

  print('Your name is: '.$_POST['name'].'<br>');
  print('Your last name is: '.$_POST['lastname']);
?>
```

Listing 21-8: Allowing multiple origin requests

The value * for the **Access-Control-Allow-Origin** header represents multiple origins. The PHP code in Listing 21-8 may be accessed by any origin unless the value * is replaced by a specific origin.

> **IMPORTANT:** The PHP code in Listing 21-8 only adds the value at the header returned by the **process.php** file. To include this header in every file sent by the server, you have to modify the configuration files of your server. For more information, see Chapter 10.

Uploading Files

Uploading files to a server is one of the major concerns for web developers today. It's a feature required by almost every application online but has not been considered by browsers thus far. This API takes care of the situation by incorporating a new property to return an XMLHttpRequestUpload object not only to access all the methods, properties and events of XMLHttpRequest objects but also to control the upload processes.

> **upload**—This property returns an XMLHttpRequestUpload object. The property must be called from an existing XMLHttpRequest object.

To work with this, we are going to need a new HTML document with an `<input>` field to select the file to be uploaded:

```
<!DOCTYPE html>
<html lang="en">
<head>
  <title>Ajax Level 2</title>
  <link rel="stylesheet" href="ajax.css">
  <script src="ajax.js"></script>
</head>
<body>
  <section id="formbox">
    <form name="form">
      <label for="myfiles">File to Upload: </label><br>
      <input type="file" name="myfiles" id="myfiles">
    </form>
  </section>
  <section id="databox"></section>
</body>
</html>
```

Listing 21-9: HTML document to upload files

One way to upload a file is to use a file's reference and send it as a form field. The FormData object studied in a Listing 21-6 is capable of handling this type of data. The system automatically detects the type of information added to the FormData object and creates the proper headers for the request. The rest of the process is exactly the same as studied before in this chapter.

```
var databox;
function initiate(){
  databox = document.getElementById('databox');

  var myfiles = document.getElementById('myfiles');
  myfiles.addEventListener('change', upload);
}
function upload(e){
  var files = e.target.files;
  var myfile = files[0];
```

```
  var data = new FormData();
  data.append('file', myfile);

  var url = "process.php";
  var request = new XMLHttpRequest();
  request.addEventListener('loadstart', start);
  request.addEventListener('load', show);
  var xmlupload = request.upload;
  xmlupload.addEventListener('progress', status);
  request.open("POST", url, true);
  request.send(data);
}
function start(){
  databox.innerHTML = '<progress value="0" max-"100">0%</progress>';
}
function status(e){
  if(e.lengthComputable){
    var per = parseInt(e.loaded / e.total * 100);
    var progressbar = databox.querySelector("progress");
    progressbar.value = per;
    progressbar.innerHTML = per + '%';
  }
}
function show(e){
  var data = e.target;
  if(data.status == 200){
    databox.innerHTML = 'Done';
  }
}
addEventListener('load', initiate);
```

Listing 21-10: *Uploading a file with* `FormData()`

The main function in the script of Listing 21-10 is **upload()**. The function is called when the user selects a new file from the **<input>** element in the document (when the **change** event is fired). The file selected is received and stored in the **myfile** variable, exactly as in the File API in Chapter 16, and also in the Drag and Drop API in Chapter 13.

Once we have a reference to the file, the FormData object is created and the file is added to the object by the **append()** method. To send this form, we start a **POST** request and set all the event listeners for the request except for **progress**. The **progress** event checks the upload process, so we have to use the **upload** property first to get the necessary XMLHttpRequestUpload object. After this object is created, we are able to add the listener for the **progress** event and send the request.

The rest of the Javascript code carries out the same process as the example in Listing 21-5; in other words, a progress bar is shown on the screen when the process starts and then is updated according to the progress of this process.

Real-Life Application

Uploading one file at a time is probably not what most web developers have in mind nor is using the **<input>** element to select the files for uploading. Usually, every programmer wants their applications to be as intuitive as possible, and what better way to do this than combining techniques and methods they are already familiar with. By taking advantage of the Drag and

Drop API, we are going to create a real-life application to upload several files to the server at the same time just by dropping them into an area on the screen.

Let's create an HTML document with the drop box first:

```
<!DOCTYPE html>
<html lang="en">
<head>
  <title>Ajax Level 2</title>
  <link rel="stylesheet" href="ajax.css">
  <script src="ajax.js"></script>
</head>
<body>
  <section id="databox">
    <p>Drop Files Here</p>
  </section>
</body>
</html>
```

Listing 21-11: *Dropping area to upload files*

The Javascript code for this example combines two APIs and works constantly with anonymous functions to keep everything organized and within the same scope (inside the same function). We have to take the files dropped into the **databox** element and list them on the screen, prepare the form with the file to be sent, make an upload request for every file and update each progress bar while the files are being uploaded.

```
var databox;
function initiate(){
  databox = document.getElementById('databox');

  databox.addEventListener('dragenter', function(e){ e.preventDefault();
});
  databox.addEventListener('dragover', function(e){ e.preventDefault();
});
  databox.addEventListener('drop', dropped);
}
function dropped(e){
  e.preventDefault();
  var files = e.dataTransfer.files;
  if(files.length){
    var list = '';
    for(var f = 0; f < files.length; f++){
      var file = files[f];
      list += '<div>File: ' + file.name;
      list += '<br><span><progress value="0"
max="100">0%</progress></span>';
      list += '</div>';
    }
    databox.innerHTML = list;
```

```
    var count = 0;
    var upload = function(){
      var myfile = files[count];
      var data = new FormData();
      data.append('file', myfile);
      var url = "process.php";
      var request = new XMLHttpRequest();
      var xmlupload = request.upload;

      xmlupload.addEventListener('progress', function(e){
        if(e.lengthComputable){
          var child = count + 1;
          var per = parseInt(e.loaded / e.total * 100);
          var progressbar - databox.querySelector("div:nth-
child("+child+") > span > progress");
          progressbar.value = per;
          progressbar.innerHTML = per + '%';
        }
      });
      request.addEventListener('load', function(){
        var child = count + 1;
        var elem = databox.querySelector("div:nth-child(" + child + ") >
span");
        elem.innerHTML = 'Done!';

        count++;
        if(count < files.length){
          upload();
        }
      });
      request.open("POST", url, true);
      request.send(data);
    }
    upload();
  }
}
addEventListener('load', initiate);
```

Listing 21-12: Uploading files one by one

Okay, Listing 21-12 is not a nice script to follow, but it will be easier if we go step by step. As usual, everything starts from the **initiate()** function called as soon as the document has loaded. This function creates a reference to the **databox** that will be our drop box for this example and adds listeners for three events to control the drag and drop operation. To know more about the Drag and Drop API, see Chapter 13. Basically, the **dragenter** event is fired when the files that are being dragged enter the area of the drop box; the **dragover** event is fired periodically while the files are over the drop box; and the **drop** event is fired when the files are dropped into the drop box. We don't have to do anything for **dragenter** and **dragover** in this example, so these events are just canceled to prevent the browser's default behavior. The only event we respond to is **drop**. The **dropped()** function, set as the listener for this event, is executed every time something is dropped into the **databox**.

The first line in the **dropped()** function also uses the **preventDefault()** method to do what we want with the files dropped and not what the browser would do by default. Now that we have absolute control over the situation, it is time to process the files dropped. First, we get the files from the dataTransfer object. The value returned is an array of files that we store in the **files** variable. To ensure the files (and not another type of element) were dropped in our drop box, we check the value of the `length` property with the statement `if(files.length)`. If this value is different than 0 or `null`, it means that one or more files have been dropped, and we can proceed.

Now it's time to work with the files received. With a `for` loop, we navigate through the `files` array and create a list of `<div>` elements containing the file's name and a progress bar enclosed in `<span>` tags. Once the list is finished, the result is shown on the screen as the content of the `databox`.

It looks like the `dropped()` function does all the work, but inside this function, we create another one called `upload()` to handle the upload process for each file. So after showing the files on the screen, the next step is to create this function and call it for every file on the list.

The `upload()` function is created using an anonymous function. Inside this function, we first select a file from the array using the `count` variable as an index. This variable is initialized to 0, so the first time the `upload()` function is called, the first file of the list is selected and uploaded.

To upload every file, we use the same method as in previous examples. A reference to the file is stored in the `myfile` variable; a FormData object is created using the `FormData()` constructor; and the file is added to the object with the `append()` method.

This time, we only listen to two events to control the process: `progress` and `load`. Every time the `progress` event is fired, an anonymous function is called to update the status of the progress bar for the file that is being uploaded. To identify the `<progress>` element corresponding to that file, the `querySelector()` method with the `:nth-child()` pseudo-class is used. The index for the pseudo-class is calculated using the value of the `count` variable. This variable has the number of the index for the `files` array, but this index starts at 0, and the index used for the list of children accessed by `:nth-child()` starts at the value 1. To get the corresponding index value to find the right `<progress>` element, we add 1 to the value of `count`, store the result in the `child` variable and use this variable as the index.

Every time the previous process finishes, we have to inform the situation and move to the next file in the `files` array. For this purpose, in the anonymous function executed when the `load` event is fired, we increase the value of `count` by 1, replace the `<progress>` element by the string "Done!" and call the `upload()` function again in case there are more files to be processed.

If you follow the script line by line, you will see that the `upload()` function, after being declared, is called for the first time at the end of the `dropped()` function. Because the value of `count` was previously initialized to 0, the first file of the `files` array is processed first. Then, when the upload process for this file is complete, the `load` event is fired, and the anonymous function called to handle this event increases the value of `count` by 1 and executes the `upload()` function again to process the next file in the array. At the end, every file dropped in the drop box will have been uploaded to the server, one by one.

Ajax Level 2

Chapter 22

Web Messaging API

22.1 Cross-Document Messaging

The Web Messaging API allows applications from different origins to communicate with each other. This process is called Cross-Document Messaging. Applications running in different frames, tabs or windows can now communicate using this technology. The procedure is simple: we post a message from one document and process this message in the target document.

Posting a Message

To post messages, the API provides the `postMessage()` method:

> **postMessage(message, target)**—This method sends a message to another document. The `message` attribute is a string representing the message to be transmitted, and the `target` attribute is the domain of the target document (host name or a port, as we will see later). The target may be declared as a specific domain, as any document with the * symbol, or as the same as the origin using the / symbol. The method can also include an array of ports as a third attribute.

The communication method is asynchronous. To listen to the messages posted for a particular document, the API uses the `message` event, which includes a few properties to return the information:

> **data**—This property of the `message` event returns the content of the message.
>
> **origin**—This property of the `message` event returns the origin of the document that sent the message, usually the host name. This value can be used to send a message back.
>
> **source**—This property of the `message` event returns an object to identify the source of the message. This value can be used as a reference to the sender to answer the message, as we will see later.

Communicating with an iFrame

For an example of the API, we have to consider that the communication process occurs between different windows (windows, frames, tabs). Therefore, we must provide documents for each side. Our example includes an HTML document with an iframe and the proper Javascript codes for the main document and the document to be loaded inside the iframe. Let's start with the main HTML document:

```
<!DOCTYPE html>
<html lang="en">
<head>
  <title>Cross Document Messaging</title>
  <link rel="stylesheet" href="messaging.css">
  <script src="messaging.js"></script>
</head>
<body>
  <section id="formbox">
    <form name="form">
      <label for="name">Your name: </label>
      <input type="text" name="name" id="name" required>
      <input type="button" id="button" value="Send">
    </form>
  </section>
  <section id="databox">
    <iframe id="iframe" src="iframe.html" width="500"
height="350"></iframe>
  </section>
</body>
</html>
```

Listing 22-1: Main document with an iframe

As you can see, there are two **<section>** elements as in previous documents, but this time **databox** includes an **<iframe>** element that is loading the **iframe.html** file. We will get back to this later.

> **Review the Basics:** The **<iframe>** element replaces the deprecated set of **<frameset>** and **<frame>** tags. This element allows us to insert a document inside another document. The document for the **<iframe>** is declared in the **src** attribute. Anything inside an iframe responds as if it were located in the main window.

Let's add a few styles to the structure:

```
#formbox{
  float: left;
  padding: 20px;
  border: 1px solid #999999;
}
#databox{
  float: left;
  width: 500px;
  margin-left: 20px;
  padding: 20px;
  border: 1px solid #999999;
}
```

Listing 22-2: Styling the boxes (messaging.css)

The Javascript code for the main document has to take the value of the **name** input from the form and send it to the document inside the iframe using the **postMessage()** method:

```
function initiate(){
  var button = document.getElementById('button');
  button.addEventListener('click', send);
}
function send(){
  var name = document.getElementById('name').value;
  var iframe = document.getElementById('iframe');

  iframe.contentWindow.postMessage(name, '*');
}
addEventListener('load', initiate);
```

*Listing 22-3: Sending a message to the iframe (*messaging.js*)*

In the script in Listing 22-3, the message is composed with the value of the **name** input. The * symbol is used as a target to send this message to every document running inside the iframe (regardless of its origin).

> **Review the Basics:** The **postMessage()** method belongs to the Window object. To get the Window object of an iframe from the main document, we have to use the **contentWindow** property.

Once the "Send" button is clicked in the main document, the **send()** function is called, and the value of the input field is sent to the content of the iframe. Now it's time to take this message from the iframe and process it. We are going to create a small HTML document for the iframe to show this information on the screen.

```
<!DOCTYPE html>
<html lang="en">
<head>
  <title>iframe Window</title>
  <script src="iframe.js"></script>
</head>
<body>
  <section>
    <div><b>Message from main window:</b></div>
    <div id="databox"></div>
  </section>
</body>
</html>
```

*Listing 22-4: HTML document for the iframe (*iframe.html*)*

This document has its own **databox** that we can use to show the message on the screen and its own Javascript code to process the message:

```
function initiate(){
  addEventListener('message', receiver);
}
function receiver(e){
  var databox = document.getElementById('databox');
  databox.innerHTML = 'message from: ' + e.origin + '<br>';
  databox.innerHTML += 'message: ' + e.data;
}
addEventListener('load', initiate);
```

Listing 22-5: *Processing messages in the target (*iframe.js*)*

As we explained before, to listen to messages the API provides the **message** event and some properties. In the script of Listing 22-5, the **receiver()** function is set as the function to be called when the event is fired. This function shows the content of the message using the **data** property and information about the document that sent the message using the value of **origin**.

Remember that this Javascript code belongs to the HTML document for the iframe, and not the main document of Listing 22-1. These are two different documents with their own environment, scope and scripts: one is in the main browser window, and the other is inside the iframe.

> **Do It Yourself:** There are a total of five files that have to be created and uploaded to a server in order to test the example above. First, create a new HTML file with the code in Listing 22-1 for the main document. This document requires the **messaging.css** file with the styles in Listing 22-2 and the **messaging.js** file with the Javascript code in Listing 22-3. The document of Listing 22-1 has an **<iframe>** element with the **iframe.html** file as its source. You will need to create this file with the HTML code of Listing 22-4 and the corresponding **iframe.js** file with the Javascript code of Listing 22-5. Upload all the files to your server, open the first HTML document in your browser, and send your name to the iframe using the form.

Filters and Cross-Origin

So far our coding method has not followed what is considered to be best practice, especially with regard to security issues. The Javascript code in the main document is sending a message to a specific iframe but is not controlling which document is allowed to read it. (Any document inside the iframe will be able to read the message.) Also, the code in the iframe is not controlling the origin and is processing every message received. Both parts of the communication process must be improved to prevent abuse.

In the next example, we are going to correct this situation and show you how to answer a message from the target using another property of the **message** event called **source**.

```
<!DOCTYPE html>
<html lang="en">
<head>
  <title>Cross Document Messaging</title>
  <link rel="stylesheet" href="messaging.css">
  <script src="messaging.js"></script>
</head>
```

```
<body>
  <section id="formbox">
    <form name="form">
      <label for="name">Your name: </label>
      <input type="text" name="name" id="name" required>
      <input type="button" id="button" value="Send">
    </form>
  </section>
  <section id="databox">
    <iframe id="iframe" src="http://www.domain2.com/iframe.html"
width="500" height="350"></iframe>
  </section>
</body>
</html>
```

Listing 22-6: Communicating with specific origins/targets

In the last document, we not only provide the HTML file for the source of the iframe as we did before, but also declare the entire path to a different location (www.domain2.com). The main document, for example, will be at www.domain1.com and the iframe's content will be at www.domain2.com. To prevent abuse, we will have to declare these locations and be specific about who is able to read a message and from where. The following Javascript codes consider this situation:

```
function initiate(){
  var button = document.getElementById('button');
  button.addEventListener('click', send);

  addEventListener('message', receiver);
}
function send(){
  var name = document.getElementById('name').value;
  var iframe = document.getElementById('iframe');
  iframe.contentWindow.postMessage(name, 'http://www.domain2.com');
}
function receiver(e){
  if(e.origin == 'http://www.domain2.com'){
    document.getElementById('name').value = e.data;
  }
}
addEventListener('load', initiate);
```

Listing 22-7: Communicating with specific origins (`messaging.js`)

Pay attention to the **send()** function in the script of Listing 22-7. The **postMessage()** method now declares the specific target for the message (www.domain2.com). Only documents inside the iframe and from that specific origin will be able to read this message.

In the **initiate()** function in the script of Listing 22-7, we also add a listener for the **message** event. The purpose of the listener function **receiver()** is to listen to the answer sent by the document in the iframe. This will make sense later.

So let's look at the Javascript code for the iframe to see how a message from a specific origin is processed and how we answer this message. (We are going to use exactly the same HTML document of Listing 22-4 for the iframe.)

```
function initiate(){
  addEventListener('message', receiver);
}
function receiver(e){
  var databox = document.getElementById('databox');
  if(e.origin == 'http://www.domain1.com'){
    databox.innerHTML = 'valid message: ' + e.data;
    e.source.postMessage('message received', e.origin);
  }else{
    databox.innerHTML = 'invalid origin';
  }
}
addEventListener('load', initiate);
```

Listing 22-8: *Responding to the main document (*iframe.js*)*

The filter for the origin is as simple as comparing the value of the **origin** property with the domain we want to read messages from. Once the origin proves to be valid, the message is shown on the screen, and then an answer is sent back using the value of the **source** property. The **origin** property is also used to declare this answer, which is only available for the window that has sent the message. Now, you can go back to Listing 22-7 and check how the **receiver()** function processes this answer.

> **Do It Yourself:** This example is a bit tricky. We are using two different origins, so you need two different domains (or subdomains) to test the codes. Replace the domains in the codes for yours, then upload the codes for the main document to one domain and the codes for the iframe to the other and you will be able to see how these two documents from different domains are able to communicate

Chapter 23
WebSocket API

23.1 WebSockets

The WebSocket API provides connection support for faster and more effective bi-directional communication between browsers and servers. The connection is made through a TCP socket without sending HTTP headers, thus reducing the size of data transmitted in every call. The connection is also persistent, allowing servers to keep clients updated without a previous request, which means we don't have to call the server for updates. Instead, the server itself automatically sends us information about the current condition.

WebSocket might be thought of as an improved version of Ajax, but it is a totally different alternative for communication that allows the construction of real-time applications in a scalable platform—for example, multiplayer video games, chat rooms, etc.

The Javascript API is simple; a few methods and events are included to open and close the connection and send and listen for messages. However, by default no server provides this service and the response has to be customized to our needs, so we have to install our own WS server (WebSocket server) to be able to establish communication between the browser and the server that allocates our application.

WebSocket Server

If you are a savvy programmer you can probably figure out how to build your own WS server script, but for those who want to spend their time on something else, there are several scripts available to configure a WS server and have it ready to process WS requests. Depending on your preferences, you can opt for scripts made in PHP, Java, Ruby and others. For a complete list, visit our website and follow the links for this chapter.

For the purpose of this book, we are going to show you how to install a PHP server. There are several versions programmed in this language, but we are going to use a simple one called **phpws**.

> **IMPORTANT:** At the time of writing, only Google Chrome has enabled the websocket connections by default. We recommend you test these examples on Google Chrome and also search the Web for other versions of WS servers available. The phpws server requires at least PHP version 5.3 to run correctly, and your hosting account has to include shell access to be able to communicate with your server and run the PHP script (you can ask your hosting provider to enable shell access if you don't have it by default).

Installing and Running a WS Server

The phpws script includes several files to create the classes and methods you need to run your WS server. The library is available at http://code.google.com/p/phpws/, but to test these examples, all you need to do is to download the package we prepare for this chapter at www.minkbooks.com/content/. Download the **ws.rar** file, decompress it, and upload the **ws** folder onto your server using any FTP program (e.g., FileZilla). Inside this folder, you will find the **server.php** file with a modification of the original file called **demo.php**. We just added a bit of code to this file to adapt the script to our examples. You can change this code later to suit your own needs. Here is our function to process the messages:

```php
public function onMessage(IWebSocketConnection $user, IWebSocketMessage
$msg){
  $msg = trim($msg->getData());
  switch($msg){
    case 'hello':
      $msgback = WebSocketMessage::create("hello human");
      $user->sendMessage($msgback);
      break;
    case 'name':
      $msgback = WebSocketMessage::create("I don't have a name");
      $user->sendMessage($msgback);
      break;
    case 'age':
      $msgback = WebSocketMessage::create("I'm old");
      $user->sendMessage($msgback);
      break;
    case 'date':
      $msgback = WebSocketMessage::create("today is ".date("F j, Y"));
      $user->sendMessage($msgback);
      break;
    case 'time':
      $msgback = WebSocketMessage::create("the time is ".date("H:iA"));
      $user->sendMessage($msgback);
      break;
    case 'thanks':
      $msgback = WebSocketMessage::create("you're welcome");
      $user->sendMessage($msgback);
      break;
    case 'bye':
      $msgback = WebSocketMessage::create("have a nice day");
      $user->sendMessage($msgback);
      break;
    default:
      $msgback = WebSocketMessage::create("I don't understand");
      $user->sendMessage($msgback);
      break;
  }
}
```

*Listing 23-1: PHP function adapted to our examples (*server.php*)*

Once you have all these files in your server, it is time to run the script. WebSocket uses a persistent connection, so the WS server has to be running all the time, capturing requests and sending updates to users. To run the PHP file, you can access your server using an SSH connection, find the **ws** folder and insert the command **php server.php**.

> **Review the Basics:** SSH is a network protocol (Secure Shell) that you can use to access your server and control it remotely. It allows you to work with folders and files in your server and run scripts. One of the popular free applications that provide a console for Shell access is called PuTTY (available from www.chiark.greenend.org.uk/~sgtatham /putty/). After running PuTTY and inserting the domain of your server, a text console will pop up and ask for your login and password. Once inside the server, you have to access the **ws** folder and run the script as explained before.

The WS server is running and ready. Now, it is time to connect with the server from our web page.

Constructor

Before programming our Javascript code to interact with the WS server, let's see what the API provides for this purpose. The specification declares only one interface with a few methods, properties and events, plus a constructor to set the connection:

> **WebSocket(url)**—This constructor starts a connection between the application and the WS server targeted by the **url** attribute. It returns a WebSocket object referencing this connection. A second attribute may be specified to provide an array with communication sub-protocols.

Methods

The connection is initiated by the constructor, so there are only two methods to work with it:

> **send(data)**—This is the method necessary to send a message to the WS server. The **data** attribute represents a string with the information to be transmitted.
>
> **close()**—This is the method to close the connection.

Properties

A few properties inform us about the connection's configuration and status:

> **url**—This property returns the URL to which the application is connected.
>
> **protocol**—This property returns the sub-protocol used, if any.
>
> **readyState**—This property returns a number representing the state of the connection: 0 meaning the connection has not yet been established, 1 meaning the connection is opened, 2 meaning the connection is being closed, and 3 meaning the connection was closed.

bufferedAmount—This is a very useful property that allows us to know the data requested but not yet sent to the server. The value returned helps us regulate the amount of data and frequency of the requests in order to not saturate the server.

Events

To know the status of the connection and listen to messages sent by the server, we have to use events. The API provides the following:

open—This event is fired when the connection is opened.

message—This event is fired when there is a message from the server available.

error—This event is fired when an error occurs.

close—This event is fired when the connection is closed.

HTML Document

The `server.php` file we prepared for these examples has a method called `onMessage()` that processes a small list of predefined commands and sends back the proper answer (see Listing 23-1). For testing purposes, we are going to use a form to insert and send these commands to the server:

```
<!DOCTYPE html>
<html lang="en">
<head>
  <title>WebSocket</title>
  <link rel="stylesheet" href="websocket.css">
  <script src="websocket.js"></script>
</head>
<body>
  <section id="formbox">
    <form name="form">
      <label for="command">Command: </label><br>
      <input type="text" name="command" id="command"><br>
      <input type="button" id="button" value="Send">
    </form>
  </section>
  <section id="databox"></section>
</body>
</html>
```

Listing 23-2: HTML document to insert commands

We will also need a CSS file with the following styles and the name `websocket.css`:

```
#formbox{
  float: left;
  padding: 20px;
  border: 1px solid #999999;
}
```

```
#databox{
  float: left;
  width: 500px;
  height: 350px;
  overflow: auto;
  margin-left: 20px;
  padding: 20px;
  border: 1px solid #999999;
}
```

Listing 23-3: Styles for the boxes

Initiating Communication

As always, the Javascript code is responsible for the entire process. Let's create our first communication application to check how the API works.

```
var databox, socket;
function initiate(){
  databox = document.getElementById('databox');
  var button = document.getElementById('button');
  button.addEventListener('click', send);

  socket = new WebSocket("ws://YOUR_IP_ADDRESS:12345/ws/server.php");
  socket.addEventListener('message', received);
}
function received(e){
  var list = databox.innerHTML;
  databox.innerHTML = 'Received: ' + e.data + '<br>' + list;
}
function send(){
  var command = document.getElementById('command').value;
  socket.send(command);
}
addEventListener('load', initiate);
```

Listing 23-4: Sending messages to the server

> **IMPORTANT:** Replace YOUR_IP_ADDRESS by the IP of your server. You can always use your domain instead, but using the IP has the purpose of avoiding DNS translation. (You should always use this technique to access your application to avoid the time spent by the network translating the domain into the corresponding IP address.)

In the **initiate()** function of Listing 23-4, the WebSocket object is constructed and stored in the **socket** variable. The **url** attribute points to the location of the **server.php** file in your server. Also, the port of connection is declared in this URL. Usually, the host is specified with the IP number of the server, and the value of the port is 8000 or 8080, but that depends on your needs, the configuration of your server, the ports available, the location of the file in your server, etc.

After we get the WebSocket object, a listener for the **message** event is added to this object. Every time the WS server sends a message to the browser, the **message** event is fired and the **received()** function is called to handle the event. As in previous APIs, this event includes the `data` property that holds the content of the message. In the `received()` function, we use that property to show the message on the screen.

To send messages to the server, we include the `send()` function. The value of the `<input>` element named `command` is taken by this function and sent to the WS server using the `send()` method.

> **IMPORTANT:** The function we prepared for these examples checks the message received and compares its value with a list of predefined commands. The commands available are `hello`, `name`, `age`, `date`, `time`, `thanks` and `bye`. For instance, if you insert the command `hello` in the form, the server will send back the message "hello human". You can change this function to satisfy your needs. Study the script in Listing 23-1 to understand how this function works.

Full Application

In the last example, you can easily see how the communication process works for this API. The connection is started by the `WebSocket()` constructor, the `send()` method sends every message we want to be processed by the server, and the `message` event informs the application of the arrival of new messages from the server. However, we didn't close the connection, check for errors or even detect when the connection was ready to work. Let's now see an example that utilizes all the events provided by this API to inform the user about the status of the connection at every step of the process.

```
var databox, socket;
function initiate(){
  databox = document.getElementById('databox');
  var button = document.getElementById('button');
  button.addEventListener('click', send);

  socket = new WebSocket("ws://YOUR_IP_ADDRESS:12345/ws/server.php");
  socket.addEventListener('open', opened);
  socket.addEventListener('message', received);
  socket.addEventListener('close', closed);
  socket.addEventListener('error', showerror);
}
function opened(){
  databox.innerHTML = 'CONNECTION OPENED<br>';
  databox.innerHTML += 'Status: ' + socket.readyState;
}
function received(e){
  var list = databox.innerHTML;
  databox.innerHTML = 'Received: ' + e.data + '<br>' + list;
}
function closed(){
  var list = databox.innerHTML;
  databox.innerHTML = 'CONNECTION CLOSED<br>' + list;

  var button = document.getElementById('button');
  button.disabled = true;
}
```

```
function showerror(){
  var list = databox.innerHTML;
  databox.innerHTML = 'ERROR<br>' + list;
}
function send(){
  var command = document.getElementById('command').value;
  if(command == 'close'){
    socket.close();
  }else{
    socket.send(command);
  }
}
addEventListener('load', initiate);
```

Listing 23-5: *Informing the user about the state of the connection*

There are a few improvements in the script of Listing 23-5 from the previous example. Listeners for all the events available in the WebSocket object are added, and the proper functions to handle the events are created. We also show the status when the connection is opened using the value of the `readyState` property, close the connection using the `close()` method when the "close" command is sent from the form and disable the "Send" button when the connection is closed (`button.disabled = true`).

> **Do It Yourself:** This last example requires the HTML document and CSS styles of Listings 23-2 and 23-3. Open the HTML file in your browser, insert a command in the form, and click the "Send" button. You should get answers from the server according to the command inserted (`hello`, `name`, `age`, `date`, `time`, `thanks` and `bye`). Send the command "close" to close the connection.

> **IMPORTANT:** Remember that your WS server has to be running all the time to process requests.

WebSocket API

Chapter 24
WebRTC API

24.1 Here Comes the Revolution

Every API introduced in HTML5 has its own characteristics. There is something unique in each one that may be described by an adjective alone. Some are the most beautiful, some the most complex, some the most interesting. But the WebRTC API presented in this chapter is the one that epitomizes the word *revolutionary* in the subtitle of this book. If we have to pick just one API to create *revolutionary applications*, WebRTC is it.

The Old Paradigm

WebRTC means Web Real-Time Communication. It is no longer just about communication but rather a whole new kind of communication for the Web. This API lets developers create applications that connect users to each other without intermediaries. Applications implementing WebRTC can stream video, audio and data directly from one user to another, creating an effective peer-to-peer connection. This is a big shift in paradigms. Thus far, users were able to share information on the Web through a server. Servers were like big repositories of content accessible by a domain or an IP address. Users had to connect to these servers, download or upload information, and wait for other users to do the same on the other side. If we wanted to share a picture with a friend, for example, we had to upload the picture to a server and wait for our friend to connect to the same server and download the picture to his computer. The process is illustrated in Figure 24-1:

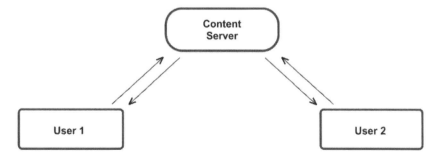

Figure 24-1: *Old paradigm*

There was no way for User 1 to send information to User 2 without using a server. Up to this point, every process required a server to store the information sent by one user and provide it (serve it) to another. Outside the Web, there were a lot of applications connecting users directly with each other, allowing them to send instant messages or make video calls, but the browser was incapable of doing this.

The New Paradigm

WebRTC brings a new paradigm to the Web. The API provides the technology to make peer-to-peer applications for the Web a reality. The process uses a signaling server to establish the connection, but the information is exchanged between users' browsers without further intervention, as shown in Figure 24-2:

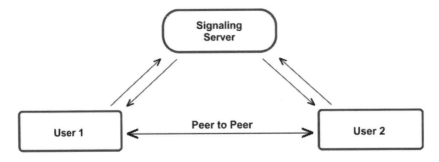

Figure 24-2: New paradigm

Servers are still necessary, but they are not the contents' providers anymore. The server now sends signals to start the connection, but the content is transmitted directly from one user's computer to another. Thanks to this technology, video and audio streaming, video calling, instant messaging and data sharing are features now available for applications running in the browser.

Requisites

There is one problem though. In the old paradigm, servers are publically accessible. They were assigned an IP address (or several) as identifiers, and also, domains that translate to those IPs make the access even easier. Servers are not only easy to find, but they are accessible all the time, from everywhere. If a server changes the IP, its domain is translated to the new IP almost instantly (it takes a few hours for the new information to propagate through the Net, but the change is instantaneous). User's computers, on the other hand, can't have a unique IP. They have private IPs that are later translated into public ones by a system called NAT (Network Address Translator). This system sets routes towards users' computers that are usually complex to follow and varies for each case. As if this weren't complicated enough, user's computers are also hidden behind firewalls, have different ports through which the data are transferred or even become inaccessible without a warning. Connecting one user to another requires information that browsers are incapable of providing. They need help.

Considering this situation, the WebRTC API was developed to work along with servers that check and return the information necessary for the application to access the user's computer. These servers work under a structure called ICE (Interactive Connectivity Establishment) to find the best way to connect one user to another. ICE is the name of a process that gets the information through different servers and systems. Figure 24-3 shows how the new structure is set.

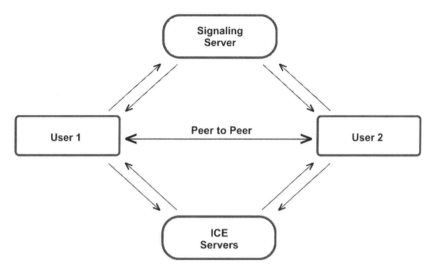

Figure 24-3: Including ICE Servers

ICE servers are usually STUN and TURN servers. A STUN server discovers and returns the public IP of the user's computer and also information about how the NAT for that computer was configured, while a TURN server provides a connection using an IP in the cloud when the other alternatives are not available. The systems at both ends of the communication process decide which connection is more efficient and proceed through that route.

The structure described in Figure 24-3 works as follows: the browsers of User 1 and 2 access the ICE servers to get the information that describes how each computer is seen on the Internet. Both applications access the signaling server and send their descriptions to each other. Once the information arrives and both sides agree on the route to follow, the peer-to-peer connection is established, and the users are connected without requiring intervention from servers anymore (unless they are disconnected and the connection has to be set again).

Peer Connection

The first step to create the peer connection is to provide the browser with the information about the connection, the data to be shared and the ICE servers to use. This is done by the properties, methods and events provided by the RTCPeerConnection object. The API provides the following constructor to get this object:

> **RTCPeerConnection(configuration)**—This constructor returns an RTCPeerConnection object. The object is used to provide the browser with the necessary information to establish a peer-to-peer connection. The **configuration** attribute is an object that specifies the information to find the ICE servers.

ICE Candidate

When the ICE process finds a way to communicate with a computer, the information retrieved is called an ICE Candidate. Candidates are set and added to the peer connection using the following:

RTCIceCandidate(candidateInitDict)—This constructor returns an RTCIceCandidate object. The `candidateInitDict` attribute provides the information to initialize the object (this is usually the information sent by the remote peer).

addIceCandidate(candidate)—This method adds a remote ICE Candidate to the peer connection. The `candidate` attribute is an object returned by the `RTCIceCandidate()` constructor.

iceState—This property returns the state of the ICE process for the current peer connection.

Offer and Answer

The communication between two peers is started by two processes called **offer** and **answer**. When an application wants to start a connection, it sends an offer to the application on the other side through the signaling server. If this offer is accepted, the second application sends back an answer. These are the methods provided by the API for this purpose:

createOffer(success, error)—This method is used to create an offer. It generates a blob containing the description of the local computer (called the SessionDescription). The description contains the media streams, codecs negotiated for the session, the ICE candidates and also a property describing its type (in this case `offer`). The SessionDescription obtained by this method is sent to the `success` function to be processed. This function is responsible for sending the offer to the remote peer.

createAnswer(success, error)—This method is used to create an answer. It generates a blob containing the description of the local computer (called the SessionDescription). The description contains the media streams, codecs negotiated for the session, the ICE candidates and also a property describing its type (in this case `answer`). The SessionDescription obtained by this method is sent to the `success` function to be processed. This function is responsible for sending the answer to the remote peer.

SessionDescription

As we just discussed, the description of each computer, including the media streams, codecs negotiated for the session and the ICE candidates, is called the SessionDescription. SessionDescriptions are sent from one user to another through the signaling server and then declared to the peer connection using the following methods:

setLocalDescription(description, success, error)—This method provides the SessionDescription of the local computer to the peer connection. The `description` attribute is the object returned by the `createOffer()` and `createAnswer()` methods. The `success` and `error` attributes are functions to be called in the case of success or failure.

setRemoteDescription(description)—This method provides the SessionDescription of the remote computer to the peer connection. The `description` attribute is an object returned by the `RTCSessionDescription()` constructor and the information received from the remote peer.

Media Streams

Basically, a peer-to-peer connection is made to share media streams and data. The process to transmit data involves the creation of data channels, as we will see later, but to add or remove media streams to a peer connection, we just have to apply the following methods:

addStream(stream)—This method adds a media stream to the peer connection. The `stream` attribute is a reference to the media stream (returned by methods such as `getUserMedia()`, for example).

removeStream(stream)—This method removes a media stream from the peer connection. The `stream` attribute is a reference to the media stream (returned by methods such as `getUserMedia()`, for example).

Events

The process of setting the peer-to-peer connection and getting information from one computer or another is asynchronous. Once the RTCPeerConnection object is created, we have to listen to events and wait for results. Here is a list of the events available:

negotiationneeded—This event is fired when a new session negotiation is necessary (e.g., a new offer has to be made).

icecandidate—This event is fired when a new ICE Candidate is available.

statechange—This event is fired when the state of the peer connection changes.

addstream—This event is fired when a media stream is added by the remote peer.

removestream—This event is fired when a media stream is removed by the remote peer.

gatheringchange—This event is fired when the state of the ICE process changes.

icechange—This event is fired when the state of the ICE changes (a new server was set, for example).

datachannel—This event is fired when a new data channel is added by the remote peer.

The End

Users have to have to ability to start and end a peer-to-peer connection. To terminate the connection, the API provides the following method:

close()—This method changes the state of the RTCPeerConnection object to `closed` and terminates any active streaming and ICE processing, closing the connection.

24.2 Implementing WebRTC

As we explained in the introduction to this chapter, the structure necessary to generate a peer-to-peer connection on the Web involves not only a Javascript application on each end but also servers to coordinate the connection. The API leaves how to configure the process, the technologies to use, and the type of servers and network in the hands of developers. So there is plenty to do besides program the application. Let's start with the signaling server.

> **IMPORTANT:** The examples for this chapter are based on a procedure we consider appropriate for the circumstance, but how the connection is performed, how the signaling is made and how the users are identified may change completely in different contexts. You have to decide whether or not implementing this procedure is right for your application.

Signaling Server

A signaling server is not the same as a content server. Signaling servers have to establish persistent connections to be able to inform the application when an offer or an answer is received. To illustrate, let's look at Figure 24-3 again. When User 1 wants to connect with User 2, the application on this computer has to send an offer to the signaling server requesting the connection, and the server has to be able to inform User 2 that a request was made. This process is only possible if a persistent connection was previously set by the server and both users. Therefore, a signaling server not only has the purpose of receiving and sending signals (offers and answers) but also has to establish a persistent connection before the configuration of the peer-to-peer connection to keep users informed (for example, a video call system wouldn't be possible if users weren't notified of an available incoming call).

The work of a signaling server doesn't stop there. It also has to control who is authorized to create a connection and who is able to connect with whom. WebRTC doesn't provide a standard method to do this; it is all in the hands of the developer. The good news is that there are several options available. We already studied how to create permanent connections with HTML5 in Chapter 23 using WebSockets. The WebSocket API is one alternative but not the only one. Google offers the Google Channel API, an API developed to create a persistent connection between applications and Google servers. And open-source servers that implement a technology called SIP (Session Initiation Protocol) are already available for free.

For our example, we decided to implement the same WebSocket server in PHP used in Chapter 23. The `onMessage()` function of the `server.php` file has to be modified to receive and send signals back to the right connection:

```php
public function onMessage(IWebSocketConnection $user, IWebSocketMessage $msg){
  $thisuser = $user->getId();
  $msg = trim($msg->getData());
  $msgback = WebSocketMessage::create($msg);
```

```
    foreach($this->server->getConnections() as $user){
      if($user->getId() != $thisuser){
        $user->sendMessage($msgback);
      }
    }
  }
}
```

Listing 24-1: New PHP function for the WebSocket server (`server.php`)

The server for our example is not controlling anything. It is doing the most basic step to help establish a peer-to-peer connection: it takes the message received from one user and sends it to the other. It is not useful for a real-life application, but it is enough to test our small application and understand how the process works.

> **Do It Yourself:** As in Chapter 23, we prepare a file with the WebSocket server ready to install and with the **server.php** file already adapted for the application. Go to www.minkbooks.com/content/, download the package **webrtc.rar**, and upload the **ws** folder inside this package to your server. You can to access your server through an SSH connection using a program like PuTTY (available from www.chiark.greenend.org.uk/~sgtatham/putty/), get into the **ws** folder, and type the command **php server.php** to run the WebSocket server. For more information, see Chapter 23.

ICE Servers

ICE servers are specified during the construction of the peer connection. The API provides a property to declare an array with the configuration of ICE servers for the **RTCPeerConnection()** constructor:

> **iceServers**—This property is used to specify the STUN and TURN servers available to be used by the ICE process.

The **iceServers** property's value is defined as an array of objects containing the following properties:

> **url**—This property declares the URL of the STUN or TURN server.
>
> **credential**—This property is used to define a credential for a TURN server.

The syntax to introduce this information is the following: **{"iceServers": [{"url": "stun: stun.mydomain.com:12345"}]}**, where **stun.mydomain.com** is the domain of a STUN server and **12345** is the port in which the server is available.

> **IMPORTANT:** We have to provide our own ICE servers to work with our application. The creation and configuration of STUN and TURN servers is beyond the scope of this book. In the examples in this chapter, we are going to work with a STUN server provided by Google for testing purposes. For more information on ICE servers, visit our website and follow the links for this chapter.

HTML Document

It is time to create our application. The most common use for a peer-to-peer connection is to generate a video call. We are going to create an HTML document with two **<video>** elements to show the video from the local camera in a small box on the left side of the screen and the video from the remote camera (the person we call) in a bigger box on the right. The document also includes the "Call" button to make the call and CSS styles to style the boxes.

```
<!DOCTYPE html>
<html>
<head>
  <title>WebRTC API</title>
  <style>
    #caller, #receiver{
      float: left;
      margin: 5px;
      padding: 5px;
      border: 1px solid #000000;
    }
  </style>
  <script src="webrtc.js"></script>
</head>
<body>
  <section id="caller">
    <video id="callermedia" width="150" height="150"></video>
    <br><input type="button" id="callbutton" value="Call">
  </section>
  <section id="receiver">
    <video id="receivermedia" width="500" height="500"></video>
  </section>
</body>
</html>
```

Listing 24-2: *HTML document to make video calls*

The script included in the **webrtc.js** file takes the video and audio streams from the local camera and microphone, assigns them to the **<video>** element with the **callermedia** id and sends the stream to the other user. When a media stream from the other end of the line arrives, the script assigns that stream to the second **<video>** element identified as **receivermedia**, and the communication is finally established.

Javascript Code

The Javascript code for this example has to set the peer connection, communicate with ICE servers, get the SessionDescription, send the offer and the answer, and add the local and remote media streams to the connection. But we are going to do this step by step. First, we need to create the persistent connection with the signaling server (in this case, a WebSocket server) and then capture the video stream from the local webcam and the audio stream from the local microphone.

```
var user, socket;
function initiate(){
  var callbutton = document.getElementById('callbutton');
  callbutton.addEventListener('click', makecall);

  socket = new WebSocket("ws://YOUR_IP_ADDRESS:12345/ws/server.php");
  socket.addEventListener('message', received);

  navigator.webkitGetUserMedia({video: true, audio: true}, setwebcam,
showerror);
}
```

Listing 24-3: Connecting with the WebSocket server and getting the media streams

In the initiate() function in Listing 24-3, we start by adding the makecall() function as the listener for the click event. Every time the "Call" button is clicked, this function is executed to send an offer and start the call.

Next, the application creates a persistent connection with the WebSocket server and adds a listener to the message event to listen to messages coming from the signaling server. This is useful for both sides of the line: the receiver will know when it is being called, and the caller will be able to listen to the answer.

Finally, the media streams from the local webcam and microphone are captured by the getUserMedia() method (see Chapter 9). In the case of success, we call the setwebcam() function, and in case an error occurs, the showerror() function is executed (the access to the webcam was denied, for example).

```
function setwebcam(stream){
  var video = document.getElementById("callermedia");
  video.setAttribute('src', URL.createObjectURL(stream));
  video.play();

  var servers = {"iceServers": [{"url": "stun: stun.l.google.com:
19302"}]};
  user = new webkitRTCPeerConnection(servers);
  user.addStream(stream);
  user.addEventListener('addstream', setremotestream);
  user.addEventListener('icecandidate', setice);
}
function showerror(){
  console.log('Error');
}
```

Listing 24-4: Starting the peer connection

The showerror() function is going to be called by several methods, so we just use it to show an error message in the console; but the setwebcam() function has more work to do. We have to set the peer connection and assign the media streams from the webcam and the microphone to the <video> element.

In the beginning of the setwebcam() function in Listing 24-4, the video and audio streams captured by the getUserMedia() method are assigned to the corresponding <video> element (the small video at the left of the screen) and then played by the play() method. The peer connection is initiated next by declaring the ICE servers available and creating the RTCPeerConnection object with this information. The STUN server provided by Google is set as our ICE server for this example. The RTCPeerConnection object provides the browser with the information necessary to establish the connection. Some of this information is immediately available, such as the local media stream, but the rest of the process is asynchronous, so we have to listen to events to capture that information when it becomes available. For this reason, after adding the local media stream to the object with the **addStream()** method, we add listeners to the **addstream** and **icecandidate** events. The **addstream** event will fire when a media stream is added by the remote peer, and the **icecandidate** event will fire when an ICE candidate is determined by the local peer.

For all this to happen, first the peer-to-peer connection has to be established. Here is the function we use to create the offer and initiate the call:

```
function makecall(){
  user.createOffer(setdescription, showerror);
}
```

Listing 24-5: Getting the SessionDescription

When the video and audio from the local webcam and microphone are already playing on the screen in both ends, we are ready to make a call. By clicking the "Call" button, we execute the **makecall()** function. This function generates the SessionDescription of the offer type and calls the **setdescription()** function with this information in the case of success. The **setdescription()** function receives the SessionDescription, sets that information as the local description and sends it to the remote peer to initiate the connection.

```
function setdescription(sessionDescription){
  user.setLocalDescription(sessionDescription);
  sendmsg(sessionDescription);
}
```

Listing 24-6: Sending an offer to a remote peer

The **setLocalDescription()** method is used in the function in Listing 24-6 to provide the browser with the information describing the local peer. This information is then sent by the **sendmsg()** function to the remote peer. This is the function in charge of sending messages to the WebSocket server to be able to establish the connection:

```
function sendmsg(message){
  var msg = JSON.stringify(message);
  socket.send(msg);
}
```

Listing 24-7: Sending signals to the remote peer

The **send()** method of the WebSocket API has its limitations. For this reason, before sending Javascript objects to the server, we have to convert them to JSON strings. In the function in Listing 24-7, we do this using the **JSON.stringify()** method.

Review the Basics: JSON (Javascript Object Notation) is a data format developed specifically for data sharing. A JSON value is text with a specific format that can be sent as a regular string but transformed into useful objects by almost any programming language. Javascript provides two methods to work with JSON: `JSON.stringify()` to convert Javascript objects to JSON strings and `JSON.parse()` to convert JSON strings to Javascript objects.

The `sendmsg()` function is in charge of the signaling process. Every time an offer is made, an answer is sent or ICE candidates are shared by peers, the information is transmitted to the WebSocket server through messages sent by this function. The format of these messages and how these signals are sent and processed depends on the developer. For our application, we decided to use the `type` property sent by SessionDescriptions to check the type of message received. Here is the function that receives and processes the signals:

```
function received(e){
  var msg = JSON.parse(e.data);
  switch(msg.type){
    case 'offer':
      user.setRemoteDescription(new RTCSessionDescription(msg));
      user.createAnswer(setdescription, showerror);
      break;
    case 'answer':
      user.setRemoteDescription(new RTCSessionDescription(msg));
      break;
    case 'candidate':
      var candidate = new RTCIceCandidate(msg.candidate);
      user.addIceCandidate(candidate);
  }
}
```

Listing 24-8: Processing the signals

The `received()` function in Listing 24-8 is called every time the `message` event of the WebSocket object is fired. This means that every time the WebSocket server sends a message to the application, this function is executed. Here we check for the value of the `type` property in every signal message and follow the procedure according to each case. If the value of the `type` property is `offer`, it means the application received an offer from a caller. In this case, we have to set the SessionDescription for the remote peer and send an answer with the `createAnswer()` method. But when the signal message is of the `answer` type, which means the call was accepted, we set the description of the remote peer and the connection is established. The last case of the `switch()` statement checks when a signal message is of the `candidate` type. In this case, the ICE candidate sent by the remote peer is added to the RTCPeerConnection object by the `addIceCandidate()` method.

IMPORTANT: The procedure we just described is the one we decided to use for this example. The WebRTC API doesn't define any standard procedure to process signal messages or even to send them (the use of the WebSocket server was our choice as well). You have to decide whether or not implementing this procedure is right for your application.

When the offer is accepted and the answer received, both computers share the media streams and information about the ICE servers to be used to establish the connection. This process fires the `addstream` and `icecandidate` events, executing the `setremotestream()` and the `setice()` functions at both ends:

```
function setremotestream(e){
  var video = document.getElementById("receivermedia");
  video.setAttribute('src', URL.createObjectURL(e.stream));
  video.play();
}
function setice(e){
  if (e.candidate) {
    var message = {
      type: 'candidate',
      candidate: e.candidate,
    };
    sendmsg(message);
  }
}
```

Listing 24-9: Responding to the addstream *and* icecandidate *events*

As soon as the RTCPeerConnection object is created, the browser starts negotiating with the ICE servers to get the information required to access the local computer. When this information is finally retrieved, the application is informed by the `icecandidate` event. In the `setice()` function in Listing 24-9, the information provided by the event is used to generate a signal message of the `candidate` type and send it to the remote peer. Notice that this time we had to explicitly declare the `type` property because the `candidate` object does not include it. This is a procedure we have to follow to be consistent with the rest of the signaling process we created before in the `received()` function.

After the peers agree on which route to follow for the connection, the streams are shared. The addition of a new media stream by one peer is informed to the other peer through the `addstream` event. When this event is fired, we simply assign the remote stream to a `<video>` element (the same way we did before for the local media stream from the webcam and the microphone). The `setremotestream()` function in Listing 24-9 creates the corresponding URL to point to the remote stream and assign it as the source of the `<video>` element identified as `receivermedia`. This is done at both ends of the connection, so every user has their own image on the left side of the screen and the image of the other person on the right.

The last thing we need to do for our application to be ready is to listen to the `load` event and execute the `initiate()` function as soon as the document has loaded:

```
addEventListener('load', initiate);
```

Listing 24-10: Listening to the load *event to start the application*

Do It Yourself: Copy the document of Listing 24-2 into an HTML file. Create a file called `webrtc.js`, and copy every Javascript code from Listing 24-3 to Listing 24-10 into this file. Upload both files to your server, run the WebSocket server as we explained before, and open the document in your browser. To connect with another person you will have

WebRTC API

to open the document on different computers, but to test the application you can just open it in different windows in the same computer.

IMPORTANT: Remember to replace the `YOUR_IP_ADDRESS` string by the IP of your server. For testing purposes it is also possible to use your domain, but in a professional application it is better to use the IP to avoid the time spent by the DNS translation process.

Real-Life Application

WebRTC is a very special API. It provides an extremely powerful feature that will change the Web as we know it, but it also leaves critical processes in the developer's hands. We have to control everything: whether the connection was already established or not, if the user is authorized to make the call, how the users are going to listen to possible calls, how they are going to be informed of these incoming calls, etc. The example we studied is as simple as it gets. We called the basic methods and created the simplest process necessary to establish a connection. Because of the nature of this API, how to translate it into a real-life application depends entirely on you— and how much time you have to spare.

24.3 Data Channels

The most revolutionary feature of the API is probably not the transmission of media streams but the transmission of data. This is done through data channels. These channels are created over an existing peer connection and allow users to share any kind of data, which we can turn into files or content at the other end.

Creating Data Channels

The API provides the following method to create data channels:

> **createDataChannel(label, configuration)**—This method returns a RTCDataChannel object to represent a data channel. The `label` and the `configuration` attributes identify the channel and an object to provide configuration parameters, respectively. The remote peer is informed of the creation of the channel by the `datachannel` event mentioned before.

The RTCDataChannel object includes the following properties, methods and events to configure and work with data channels:

> **label**—This property returns the label assigned to the channel when it was created.
>
> **reliable**—This property returns `true` if the channel was set as reliable when it was created, or `false` otherwise.
>
> **readyState**—This property returns the state of the channel.

bufferedAmount—This property allows us to know the data requested but not yet sent to the remote peer. The value returned may be used to regulate the amount of data and frequency of the requests in order not to saturate the connection.

binaryType—This property sets how the binary data is going to be shown to the script. It can take two values: `blob` or `arraybuffer`.

send(data)—This method sends the value of the `data` attribute to the remote peer. The data must be specified as a string, a blob or an ArrayBuffer.

close()—This method closes the data channel.

message—This event is fired when a new message is received through a data channel (new data was sent by the remote peer).

open—This event is fired when the channel is opened.

close—This event is fired when the channel is closed.

error—This event is fired when an error occurs.

Sending Data

To demonstrate how data channels work, we are going to add a chat room below the videos to let users send messages while they talk. The new HTML document will include two small boxes at the top for the videos, an input field and a button to write and send the messages, and a box below to show the conversation.

```
<!DOCTYPE html>
<html>
<head>
  <title>WebRTC API</title>
  <style>
    #caller, #receiver{
      float: left;
      margin: 5px;
      padding: 5px;
      border: 1px solid #000000;
    }
    #buttons{
      clear: both;
      width: 528px;
      text-align: center;
    }
    #databox{
      width: 526px;
      height: 300px;
      margin: 5px;
      padding: 5px;
      border: 1px solid #000000;
    }
  </style>
  <script src="webrtc.js"></script>
</head>
```

```
<body>
  <section id="caller">
    <video id="callermedia" width="250" height="200"></video>
  </section>
  <section id="receiver">
    <video id="receivermedia" width="250" height="200"></video>
  </section>
  <nav id="buttons">
    <input type="button" id="callbutton" value="Call">
    <input type="text" id="myinput" size="60" required>
    <input type="button" id="sendbutton" value="Send">
  </nav>
  <section id="databox"></section>
</body>
</html>
```

Listing 24-11: HTML document to test data channels

The Javascript code for the **webrtc.js** file is similar to the previous example but adds all the necessary functions to create the data channel and transfer messages from one peer to another.

```
var user, socket, channel, channelopen;
function initiate(){
  var callbutton = document.getElementById('callbutton');
  callbutton.addEventListener('click', makecall);
  var sendbutton = document.getElementById('sendbutton');
  sendbutton.addEventListener('click', sendmessage);

  socket = new WebSocket("ws://YOUR_IP_ADDRESS:12345/ws/server.php");
  socket.addEventListener('message', received);

  navigator.webkitGetUserMedia({video: true, audio: true}, setwebcam,
showerror);
}
function showerror(e){
  console.error(e);
}
function setwebcam(stream){
  var servers = {"iceServers": [{"url":
"stun:stun.l.google.com:19302"}]};
  user = new webkitRTCPeerConnection(servers);
  user.addEventListener('addstream', setremotestream);
  user.addEventListener('icecandidate', setice);
  user.ondatachannel = function(e){
    channel = e.channel;
    channel.onmessage = receivemessage;
    channelopen = true;
  };
  user.addStream(stream);

  var video = document.getElementById("callermedia");
  video.setAttribute('src', URL.createObjectURL(stream));
  video.play();
}
```

```
function received(e){
  var msg = JSON.parse(e.data);
  switch(msg.type){
    case 'offer':
      user.setRemoteDescription(new RTCSessionDescription(msg));
      user.createAnswer(setdescription, showerror);
      break;
    case 'answer':
      user.setRemoteDescription(new RTCSessionDescription(msg));
      channel = user.createDataChannel('data');
      channel.onopen = function(){ channelopen = true; };
      channel.onmessage = receivemessage;
      break;
    case 'candidate':
      var candidate = new RTCIceCandidate(msg.candidate);
      user.addIceCandidate(candidate);
  }
}
function sendmsg(message){
  var msg = JSON.stringify(message);
  socket.send(msg);
}
function makecall(){
  user.createOffer(setdescription, showerror);
}
function setdescription(sessionDescription){
  user.setLocalDescription(sessionDescription);
  sendmsg(sessionDescription);
}
function setremotestream(e){
  var video = document.getElementById("receivermedia");
  video.setAttribute('src', URL.createObjectURL(e.stream));
  video.play();
}
function setice(e){
  if (e.candidate){
    var message = {
      type: 'candidate',
      candidate: e.candidate,
    };
    sendmsg(message);
  }
}
function sendmessage(){
  var databox = document.getElementById('databox');
  if(!channelopen){
    databox.innerHTML = 'DataChannel is not ready, please try again';
  }else{
    var message = document.getElementById('myinput').value;
    var chatroom = databox.innerHTML;
    databox.innerHTML = 'Local Says: ' + message + '<br>';
    databox.innerHTML += chatroom;
    channel.send(message);
  }
}
```

```
function receivemessage(e){
  var databox = document.getElementById('databox');
  var chatroom = databox.innerHTML;
  databox.innerHTML = 'Remote Says: ' + e.data + '<br>';
  databox.innerHTML += chatroom;
}
addEventListener('load', initiate);
```

Listing 24-12: Creating the peer-to-peer connection with a data channel

The data channel has to be created by one of the peers using the `createDataChannel()` method. The procedure can only be done after the peer connection is ready. One way to detect this is to wait for an answer. When an answer is received, it means the connection was accepted and established. For this reason, we decided to create the data channel for this example in the `received()` function. When a message of the `answer` type is received from the signaling server, the data channel is created and assigned to the `channel` variable. This process is asynchronous: the channel is added to the peer connection and the browser informs to the application when the channel is ready through the `open` event. To inform to the rest of the application when the channel is ready to be used, we listen to this event and change the value of the `channelopen` variable to `true` when the event is fired. We also listen to the `message` event to check for messages coming from the other peer through this channel.

When a channel is created by one peer, the other peer detects this action by listening to the `datachannel` event. A handler for this event was registered in the `initiate()` function. The event returns an object with the `channel` property providing a reference to the new channel. This reference is stored in the `channel` variable and a handler for the `message` event is also registered on this side to check for messages coming through this channel.

Now, both peers have the data channel opened, a handler for the `message` event registered, and are ready to listen and send messages. Two functions were created for this purpose: `sendmessage()` and `receivemessage()`. These functions take the messages generated by the local and remote peers and insert them in the `databox` of each application. The `sendmessage()` function is executed every time the "Send" button is clicked. This function reads the `channelopen` variable to check whether or not the channel is already opened, and, if it is opened, takes the value of the input field `myinput`, shows it on the screen and sends it to the other peer with the `send()` method. When the message is received by the other peer, the `message` event is fired and the `receivemessage()` function is called. This function simply takes the value of the `data` property of the object returned by the event and shows it on the screen.

> **Do It Yourself:** Copy the document of Listing 24-11 into an HTML file and the script of Listing 24-12 in the `webrtc.js` file. Upload both files to your server, run the WebSocket server as we explained before, and open the HTML document in your browser. To connect with another person you will have to open the document on different computers, but to test the application you can just open it in different windows in the same computer. Insert a message in the input field and press the "Send" button. Remember to replace the `YOUR_IP_ADDRESS` string by the IP of your server.

> **IMPORTANT:** At the time of writing, the specification for data channels is under development, and this part of the API was not yet implemented in browsers. To test the last example, we used a polyfill developed by Jesús Leganés Combarro (pirannafs. blogspot.com) and available at https://github.com/piranna/DataChannel-polyfill. This script implements data channels using its own Websocket server. For this reason, the

script of Listing 24-12 might have to be modified to work with the official implementation. Please check our website for updates.

Chapter 25
Web Audio API

25.1 Audio Node Structure

Audio processing is not something we usually consider essential for the Web. Even with the possibility of creating rich graphic applications in 2D and 3D, the processing of audio may seem irrelevant. Wrong. No matter how versatile the `<video>` and `<audio>` elements are, only the ability of audio processing can turn them into professional tools. We may have a simple video to play, but with lack of equalization, it can look amateur. We may have a neat sound of a gun in our game, but only with variations in intensity are we able to make it sound like it was shot from the back of our 3D scene. We may have great engine sounds for the cars in our racing game, but the feeling that the car was passed may only be achieved by applying a Doppler effect.

HTML5 provides all the tools for developers to create full web applications. The ability to process sounds and any kind of audio sources is not only necessary but essential for this purpose. The Web Audio API is a full professional solution that introduces audio processing for the Web. It is a low-level API developed for audio engineers but is accessible to anyone. From now on, web developers have the tools to develop audio production applications and game audio engines so far reserved only for desktop computers and game consoles.

Audio Nodes

The Web Audio API uses a modular organization where everything is a node (officially called AudioNodes). Nodes represent every part of the audio system, from raw sound to the speakers. Nodes are connected to each other to form the final structure that will produce the sound.

Figure 25-1: *Basic node organization*

Figure 25-1 represents the most basic structure possible: a node containing the source of the audio and a node for the destination (speakers, headphones or whatever in the system is configured to make the actual sound). This is the most elementary structure, a node producing the sound and a node making the sound audible, but we may have more nodes with audio sources, filters, volume controls, delays, effects, etc. The structure may be as complex as our application requires.

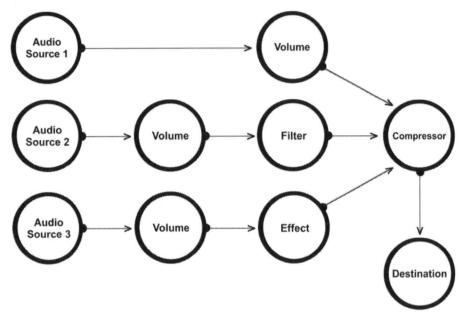

Figure 25-2: *A more elaborate audio system*

The first audio source node in Figure 25-2 is connected to the volume node (called GainNode), which in turn is connected to the compressor node (called DynamicsCompressorNode), which is finally connected to the destination node (speakers, headphones, etc). The volume of this audio source is going to be modified by the volume node, then compressed, automatically mixed with the rest of the sounds, and finally sent to the destination node and reproduced by the device's audio output (speakers, headphones, etc). The sources for audio 2 and 3 of this figure are going to follow a similar path, but they are going to pass through the filter node (called BiquadFilter) and the effect node (called ConvolverNode) before reaching the compressor node and destination.

Most nodes have an input and output connection to receive sound from a previous node, perform some kind of process and send the result to the next one. Our work is to create the nodes, provide the information each one requires to work properly and connect them.

Audio Context

This structure of nodes is set in an audio context. This is similar to the context created for the `<canvas>` element. The Audio API provides a constructor to get the AudioContext object:

> **AudioContext()**—This constructor returns an AudioContext object. The object provides methods to create every type of node available as well as some properties to configure the context and set the Destination node to access the device's audio output.

The following are the properties provided by the AudioContext object to configure the context and the audio system:

destination—This property returns an AudioDestinationNode that represents the destination node. This is the last node of an audio system, and its function is to provide access to the device's audio output.

currentTime—This property returns the time in seconds since the context was created.

activeSourceCount—This property returns the number of the AudioBufferSourceNode currently playing.

sampleRate—This property returns the rate (frames per second) at which the audio is being processed.

listener—This property returns an AudioListener object with properties and methods to calculate the position and orientation of the listener in a 3D scene.

Audio Sources

The most important nodes are probably the audio source nodes depicted as the starting point for every path in the previous figures. Without these initial sources of audio, we wouldn't have any sound to send to the speakers. These types of nodes may be created from different sources: audio buffers in memory, media streams or media elements. The API provides the following methods to get the objects to represent each source:

createBufferSource()—This method returns an AudioBufferSourceNode object. The object is created from an audio buffer in memory and provides its own properties and methods to play and configure the audio source.

createMediaStreamSource(stream)—This method returns a MediaStreamAudioSourceNode object. The object is created from a media stream. The `stream` attribute is a stream generated by methods like `getUserMedia()` (see Chapter 9).

createMediaElementSource(element)—This method returns a MediaElementAudioSourceNode object. The object is created from a media element. The `element` attribute is a reference to an `<audio>` or `<video>` element.

The `createMediaStreamSource()` and `createMediaElementSource()` methods work with streams and media elements that have their own controls to play, pause or stop the media, but the `createBufferSource()` method works with sounds in memory and needs its own properties and methods to play and configure the source:

start(time, offset, duration)—This method starts playing the sound assigned as the source of the node. The `time` attribute determines when the action will take place (in seconds). The `offset` and `duration` attributes are optional. They determine which part of the buffer must be played, starting from `offset` and as long as determined by `duration` (in seconds).

stop(time)—This method stops playing the sound assigned as the source of the node. The `time` attribute determines when the action will take place (in seconds).

loop—This property makes the sound assigned as the source of the node to play in a loop.

buffer—This property declares an audio buffer in memory as the source of the node.

The object returned by the `createBufferSource()` method doesn't work directly with audio files. The files have to be downloaded from the server, stored in memory as audio buffers and assigned to the audio source node by the `buffer` property. To turn the sounds from an audio file into a buffer in memory, the API provides the following methods:

createBuffer(arraybuffer, mixToMono)—This method creates an audio buffer from binary data. The `arraybuffer` attribute is the binary data from the audio file (ArrayBuffer type). The `mixToMono` attribute is a Boolean attribute that determines whether or not the audio channels will be mixed to mono (usually `false`).

decodeAudioData(arraybuffer, success, error)—This method creates an audio buffer from binary data asynchronously. The `arraybuffer` attribute is the binary data from the audio file (ArrayBuffer type). The `success` attribute is the function that will receive and process the buffer, and the `error` attribute is a function to process errors.

Information from audio buffers may be retrieved by the following properties:

duration—This property returns the duration of the buffer in seconds.

length—This property returns the length of the buffer in sample frames.

numberOfChannels—This property returns the number of channels available in the buffer.

sampleRate—This property returns the sample rate of the buffer in samples per second.

Connecting Nodes

There is one more thing we need to study before creating our first example: how to connect the nodes. AudioNodes have output and input connections that allow us to create a path for the sound to follow. The API provides two methods to organize this structure:

connect(node)—This method connects the output from one node to the input of another. The syntax is `output.connect(input)`, where `output` is a reference to the node that provides the output, and `input` is a reference to the node that receives the audio from that output.

disconnect()—This method disconnects the output of the node. The syntax is `output.disconnect()`, where `output` is a reference to the node to be disconnected.

25.2 Sounds for the Web

It is time to put all this theory into practice. Usually, sounds are part of complex Javascript codes, like those necessary to create a 3D video game or an audio production application, but for the following examples, we are going to use a modest HTML document to simplify the creation and implementation of AudioNodes.

```
<!DOCTYPE html>
<html lang="en">
<head>
  <title>Web Audio API</title>
  <script src="audio.js"></script>
</head>
<body>
  <section>
    <input type="button" id="button" value="Play" disabled="true">
  </section>
</body>
</html>
```

Listing 25-1: HTML document to play sounds

The HTML document includes the `audio.js` file with the Javascript code and a button to play the sounds. We are going to use this document for most of examples in this chapter.

Two Basic Nodes

As we explained before, a basic node structure requires a node for the source and another for the destination. The destination node is returned by the context's **destination** property, but the audio source requires some work. We have to download the audio file from the server, convert the content to audio buffer, use the buffer as the source for the node and finally connect both nodes to get the sound from the speakers.

For our example we are going to download a **WAV** file using Ajax and the XMLHttpRequest object.

```
var context;
function initiate(){
  var mybuffer;
  var button = document.getElementById('button');
  button.addEventListener('click', function(){ play(mybuffer); });

  context = new webkitAudioContext();

  var url = 'gunshot.wav';
  var request = new XMLHttpRequest();
  request.responseType = "arraybuffer";
  request.addEventListener('load', function(){
    if(request.status == 200){
      mybuffer = context.createBuffer(request.response, false);
      button.disabled = false;
    }
  });
  request.open("GET", url, true);
  request.send();
}
```

```
function play(mybuffer){
  var sourceNode = context.createBufferSource();
  sourceNode.buffer = mybuffer;
  sourceNode.connect(context.destination);
  sourceNode.start(0);
}
addEventListener("load", initiate);
```

Listing 25-2: *Playing an audio buffer*

As always, we have our **initiate()** function to run the application. The function starts by getting a reference to the HTML button and adding a listener to the **click** event to execute the **play()** function every time the button is clicked. Immediately after, the audio context is created by the **audioContext()** constructor and stored in the **context** variable. The **gunshot.wav** audio file is loaded next using Ajax.

The loading process for this file is the same we applied in the examples in Chapter 21, except this time the response type is set to **arraybuffer** because we need this type of data to create the buffer in memory. Once the file has completely downloaded and the **status** property of the request returns 200 (OK), the buffer is created from the value of the **response** property using the **createBuffer()** method. Now, the sound from the file is an audio buffer stored in the **mybuffer** variable and is ready to be provided as the source for an audio source node.

The whole audio system, including nodes and connections, has to be built every time we want to play a sound. So the **initiate()** function takes care of downloading the file and turning its content into an audio buffer in memory, but the rest is done by the **play()** function.

Every time the "Play" button is clicked, the audio system is created by the **play()** function. First, the audio source node is created by the **createBufferSource()** method, and then, the audio buffer is assigned as the value of the **buffer** property of this node. This process links the node to the audio buffer in memory. When this node is ready, it is connected to the destination node by the **connect()** method, and the sound represented by the node is finally played by the **start()** method.

Notice that the button is initially disabled, but it is enabled in the **initiate()** function after the data necessary to create the audio system is ready. This is just a process we decided to follow to simplify the example. Once enabled, every time the button is clicked, the audio system is created again and the sound from the **gunshot.wav** audio file is played. You can follow any procedure to download your files and inform the rest of the script when everything is ready. Usually, in professional applications, a loader script is responsible for downloading the files, setting the variables and informing the script about the progress. We will see some examples of this later.

> **Do It Yourself:** Copy the document of Listing 25-1 into an HTML file and the script of Listing 25-2 into a Javascript file called **audio.js**. You can download the **gunshot.wav** file from our website (www.minkbooks.com/content/) or use your own audio file. Upload all the files to your server, and open the document in your browser.

> **IMPORTANT:** At the time of writing, Google Chrome is the only browser that has an implementation available of this API. The browser uses the prefixed constructor **webkitAudioContext()** to generate the audio context. We will apply this constructor in the examples in this chapter, but you should check the state of the API to know when it becomes available in other browsers and whether or not the prefixed constructor is still necessary. For more information, visit our website and follow the links for this chapter.

Loops and Times

The **start()** method at the end of the **play()** function in the last example was called with the value **0**. When this value is set to **0** or is less than the value of the context's current time, the sound starts playing immediately. Once it is played, the **start()** method can't be called again to play the same audio source node, and we have to recreate the whole audio system to do this. This is the reason why we constructed the audio system in one function. Despite this restriction, there are different ways to play a sound several times without having to call the **play()** function over and over again. One alternative is to generate a loop for this audio source node setting the **loop** property to **true**:

```
function play(mybuffer){
  var sourceNode = context.createBufferSource();
  sourceNode.buffer = mybuffer;
  sourceNode.loop = true;
  sourceNode.connect(context.destination);
  sourceNode.start(0);
  sourceNode.stop(context.currentTime + 3);
}
addEventListener("load", initiate);
```

Listing 25-3: *Playing the audio source node in a loop*

The loop will run indefinitely until the **stop()** method is called. In the script of Listing 25-3, we use this method to stop the loop after 3 seconds. The time is set using the value returned by the **currentTime** property. By adding the value 3 to the current time, we order the browser to stop playing the sound 3 seconds from now.

> **Do It Yourself:** Replace the **play()** function in Listing 25-2 with the new function in Listing 25-3. Upload the **audio.js** file to your server, and open the document of Listing 25-1 in your browser.

Creating AudioNodes

Every node in the audio system is called AudioNode. The basic nodes we need to produce sound are the audio source node and the destination node created in previous examples, but these aren't the only nodes available. The API provides methods to build a variety of AudioNodes to process, analyze and even create sounds:

> **createAnalyser()**—This method creates an AnalyserNode. These types of nodes provide access to information from the audio source. The object returned includes several properties and methods for this purpose. It is often used to visualize the audio stream.

> **createGain()**—This method creates a GainNode. These types of nodes set the gain of the audio signal (the volume). The object returned provides the **gain** property to set the volume in values between **0.0** and **1.0**.

> **createDelay(maxDelayTime)**—This method creates a DelayNode. These types of nodes set a delay for the audio source, and. The optional attribute **maxDelayTime**

declares the maximum time for the delay in seconds. The object returned provides the `delayTime` property to set the delay in seconds.

createBiquadFilter()—This method creates a BiquadFilterNode. These types of nodes apply filters to the audio signal. The object returned provides properties, methods and also several constants to set the characteristics of the filter.

createWaveShaper()—This method creates a WaveShaperNode. These types of nodes apply a distortion effect based on a shaping curve. The object returned provides the `curve` property to declare the shaping curve (Float32Array type).

createPanner()—This method creates a PannerNode. These types of nodes are used to determine the position, orientation and speed of the sound in a three-dimensional space. The effect produced depends on the current values set for the listener. The object returned provides several methods and properties to configure the parameters of the node.

createConvolver()—This method creates a ConvolverNode. These types of nodes apply a convolution effect to the audio signal based on an impulse response. The object returned provides two properties: `buffer` and `normalize`. The `buffer` property is necessary to set the buffer to be used as the impulse response, and the `normalize` property receives a Boolean value to set whether or not the impulse response will be scaled.

createChannelSplitter(numberOfOutputs)—This method creates a ChannelSplitterNode. These types of nodes generate different outputs for each channel of the audio stream. The `numberOfOutputs` attribute declares the number of outputs to be generated.

createChannelMerger(numberOfInputs)—This method creates a ChannelMergerNode. These types of nodes combine channels from multiple audio streams into one. The `numberOfInputs` attribute declares the number of inputs to be merged.

createDynamicsCompressor()—This method creates a DynamicsCompressorNode. These types of nodes apply a compression effect to the audio signal. The object returned provides several properties to configure the effect.

createOscillator()—This method creates an OscillatorNode. These types of nodes generate waveforms for audio synthesis. The object returned provides several properties and methods to configure the waveform.

The applications of some of these methods require knowledge in audio engineering. The topic extends beyond the scope of this book, but we will show you how to implement the methods necessary for the construction of common audio applications and also 2D and 3D video games.

AudioParam

Besides the normal properties and methods every AudioNode object provides to configure the node, there is an interface defined by the API to set specific parameters. The AudioParam interface is like a control unit linked to the node ready to adjust its values at any time.

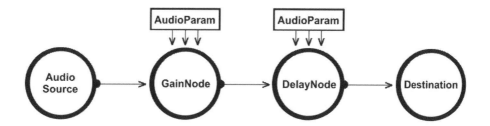

Figure 25-3: Nodes controlled by AudioParam properties and methods

The interface can set values immediately or be configured to do it later following a specific schedule. Listed below are the properties and methods provided for this purpose:

value—This property declares the value of the parameter as soon as it is defined.

setValueAtTime(value, startTime)—This method sets the value of the parameter at a given time. The `value` and `startTime` attributes declare the new value and the time in seconds, respectively.

linearRampToValueAtTime(value, endTime)—This method changes the value of the parameter gradually from the previous value to the one specified in the attributes. The `value` and `endTime` attributes declare the new value and the end time of the process in seconds, respectively.

exponentialRampToValueAtTime(value, endTime)—This method changes the current value of the parameter exponentially to the value specified in the attributes. The `value` and `endTime` attributes declare the new value and the end time of the process in seconds, respectively.

setTargetAtTime(target, startTime, timeConstant)—This method changes the value of the parameter exponentially to the value of the `target` attribute. The `startTime` attribute declares the start time of the process, and `timeConstant` sets the rate at which the previous value will approach the new one.

setValueCurveAtTime(values, startTime, duration)—This method changes the value of the parameter by arbitrary values selected from the array declared in the `values` attribute (Float32Array type). The `startTime` and `duration` attributes declare the start time of the process and the duration in seconds.

cancelScheduledValues(startTime)—This method cancels any previous scheduled change at the time specified by the `startTime` attribute.

GainNode

The first thing we generally want to do when playing a sound is turn the volume up or down. For this purpose, we are going to introduce a GainNode between the audio source node and the destination node created in previous examples.

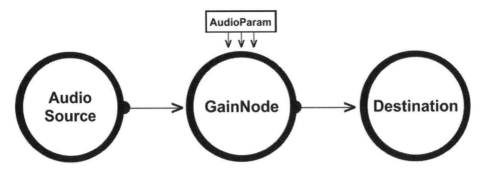

Figure 25-4: Adding a GainNode to control volume

When we add a new node to an audio system, the basic structure remains the same; we simply create the new node, provide the configuration values and connect it to the rest of the structure. In this case, the audio source node will be connected to the GainNode and the GainNode to the destination. Here is the script:

```
function play(mybuffer){
  var sourceNode = context.createBufferSource();
  sourceNode.buffer = mybuffer;

  var volumeNode = context.createGain();
  volumeNode.gain.value = 0.2;

  sourceNode.connect(volumeNode);
  volumeNode.connect(context.destination);
  sourceNode.start(0);
}
addEventListener("load", initiate);
```

Listing 25-4: Turning down the volume using a GainNode

The new **play()** function in Listing 25-4 includes a GainNode in our audio system. The node is created by the **createGain()** method and then, using the AudioParam's **value** property, a value of **0.2** is assigned to the node's **gain** property. The possible values for this property range from **0.0** to **1**. By default, the value of **gain** is 1, so the volume in this example is reduce to 20%.

The connections made at the end of the script include the new GainNode. First, the audio source node is connected to the GainNode (**sourceNode.connect(volumeNode)**), and then the GainNode is connected to the destination node (**volumeNode.connect (context.destination)**).

The value of the **gain** property for this example was set as a fixed value by the **value** property because the audio file contains only a short sound of a gunshot, but we could have used any of the AudioParam methods instead to increase or reduce the volume at different times (like at the end of a song, for example). Methods such as **exponentialRampToValueAtTime()** may be used in combination with the **duration** property of the buffers to mix songs, fading out one track and fading in the next.

> **Do It Yourself:** Replace the **play()** function in Listing 25-2 with the new function in Listing 25-4. Upload the **audio.js** file, the HTML document of Listing 25-1 and the audio file to your server, and open the document in your browser.

DelayNode

The purpose of a DelayNode is to delay the sound for the time specified by the `delayTime` property (and the AudioParam interface). In the following example, we are going to introduce this node to play the sound of the shotgun one second later.

```
function play(mybuffer){
  var sourceNode = context.createBufferSource();
  sourceNode.buffer = mybuffer;

  delayNode = context.createDelay();
  delayNode.delayTime.value = 1;

  sourceNode.connect(delayNode);
  delayNode.connect(context.destination);
  sourceNode.start(0);
}
addEventListener("load", initiate);
```

Listing 25-5: Introducing delay

The `play()` function in Listing 25-5 replaces the GainNode in the previous example with a DelayNode. The delay is declared as 1 second by the AudioParam's `value` property, and the connections are set following the same previous path: the audio source node is connected to the DelayNode, and this node is connected to the destination node.

This is not a great effect but is useful in some circumstances. A DelayNode produces better results when it is combined with other nodes, as in the following example:

```
function play(mybuffer){
  var sourceNode = context.createBufferSource();
  sourceNode.buffer = mybuffer;

  delayNode = context.createDelay();
  delayNode.delayTime.value = 0.3;

  volumeNode = context.createGain();
  volumeNode.gain.value = 0.2;

  sourceNode.connect(delayNode);
  delayNode.connect(volumeNode);
  volumeNode.connect(context.destination);
  sourceNode.connect(context.destination);
  sourceNode.start(0);
}
addEventListener("load", initiate);
```

Listing 25-6: Getting an echo effect with the DelayNode

In the `play()` function in Listing 25-6, a GainNode is added in the middle to reduce the volume of the delayed sound and generate an echo effect. Two paths are set for the audio source. In one path, the audio source node is connected to the DelayNode, the DelayNode to the

GainNode and the GainNode to the destination node. The sound on this path will have a low volume and will be played with a delay of 0.3 seconds. The second path for the source is a direct connection to the destination node. The sound on this path will play immediately at full volume.

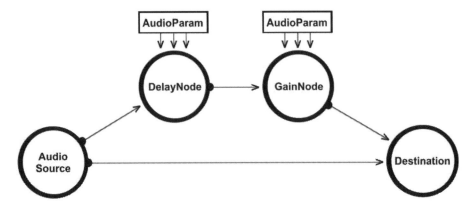

Figure 25-5: *Two paths for the same audio source*

Do It Yourself: Replace the `play()` function in Listing 25-2 with the new functions in Listings 25-5 and 25-6 to test each example. Upload the `audio.js` file, the HTML document of Listing 25-1 and the audio file to your server, and open the document in your browser.

BiquadFilterNode

The BiquadFilterNode lets us apply common filters to the audio signal. The node is created by the `createBiquadFilter()` method, and the type of filter is selected by the **type** property. The possible values for this property are **LOWPASS** (0), **HIGHPASS** (1), **BANDPASS** (2), **LOWSHELF** (3), **HIGHSHELF** (4), **PEAKING** (5), **NOTCH** (6) and **ALLPASS** (7). To configure the filter, the node also includes the **frequency**, **Q** and **gain** properties. The effect on the filter produced by the values of these properties depends on the filter's type.

```
function play(mybuffer){
  var sourceNode = context.createBufferSource();
  sourceNode.buffer = mybuffer;

  var filterNode = context.createBiquadFilter();
  filterNode.type = 1;
  filterNode.frequency.value = 1000;

  sourceNode.connect(filterNode);
  filterNode.connect(context.destination);
  sourceNode.start(0);
}
addEventListener("load", initiate);
```

Listing 25-7: *Adding a filter with the BiquadFilterNode*

In the example in Listing 25-7, we declare the type of the filter as LOWPASS (value 1) and set the cutoff frequency as 1000. This will cut off some frequencies of the spectrum making the gunshot sound like a toy gun.

The value of the frequency property is set by the AudioParam's **value** property. This may be replaced by any AudioParam's method to vary the frequency over time.

> **IMPORTANT:** The effect produced by the values of the **frequency**, **Q** and **gain** properties will depend on the filter selected. Some values won't produce any effect at all. For more information, read the API's specification. Links are available at www.minkbooks.com.

> **Do It Yourself:** Replace the **play()** function in Listing 25-2 with the new function in Listing 25-7. Upload the **audio.js** file, the HTML document of Listing 25-1 and the audio file to your server, and open the document in your browser.

DynamicsCompressorNode

Compressors smooth the audio, reducing the volume of loud sounds and raising the volume of quiet sounds. These types of nodes are usually connected at the end of the audio system with the purpose of coordinating the audio levels of the sources to make them sound unified. The Web Audio API includes the DynamicsCompressorNode to produce this effect on the audio signal. The node has several properties to limit and control the compression: **threshold** (decibels), **knee** (decibels), **ratio** (values from 1 to 20), **reduction** (decibels), **attack** (seconds) and **release** (seconds).

```
function play(mybuffer){
  var sourceNode = context.createBufferSource();
  sourceNode.buffer = mybuffer;

  var compressorNode = context.createDynamicsCompressor();
  compressorNode.threshold = -60;
  compressorNode.ratio = 10;

  sourceNode.connect(compressorNode);
  compressorNode.connect(context.destination);
  sourceNode.start(0);
}
addEventListener("load", initiate);
```

Listing 25-8: *Adding a dynamic compressor*

The script of Listing 25-8 shows how to create and configure the DynamicsCompressorNode, but it is not a common example of use. These types of nodes are usually implemented at the end of elaborate audio systems that include several audio sources.

> **Do It Yourself:** Replace the **play()** function in Listing 25-2 with the new function in Listing 25-8. Upload the **audio.js** file, the HTML document of Listing 25-1 and the audio file to your server, and open the document in your browser.

ConvolverNode

The ConvolverNode applies convolution effects to an audio signal. It is commonly used to simulate different acoustic spaces and achieve complex sound distortions, like a voice on a telephone, for example. The effect is achieved by calculating an impulse response using a second audio file. This audio file is usually a recording from the real acoustic space we are trying to simulate. Because of this requirement, to implement the effect, we have to download at least two audio files, one for the source and one for the impulse response. Let's see an example:

```
var context;
var mybuffers = [];
function initiate(){
  var button = document.getElementById('button');
  button.addEventListener('click', function(){ play(); });

  context = new webkitAudioContext();
  loadbuffers('gunshot.wav', 0);
  loadbuffers('garage.wav', 1);

  var control = function(){
    if(mybuffers.length >= 2){
      button.disabled = false;
    }else{
      setTimeout(control, 200);
    }
  }
  control();
}
function loadbuffers(url, id){
  var request = new XMLHttpRequest();
  request.responseType = "arraybuffer";
  request.addEventListener('load', function(){
    if(request.status == 200){
      mybuffers[id] = context.createBuffer(request.response, false);
    }
  });
  request.open("GET", url, true);
  request.send();
}
function play(){
  var sourceNode = context.createBufferSource();
  sourceNode.buffer = mybuffers[0];

  var convolverNode = context.createConvolver();
  convolverNode.buffer = mybuffers[1];

  sourceNode.connect(convolverNode);
  convolverNode.connect(context.destination);
  sourceNode.start(0);
}
addEventListener("load", initiate);
```

Listing 25-9: *Applying a convolution effect*

In the script of Listing 25-9, we recreate the entire Javascript code to include a small loader to be able to load the two audio files necessary for the effect (**gunshot.wav** and **garage.wav**). This time we have to move the Ajax code to a new function to download these files one by one and create the **control()** function to control the downloading process.

At the beginning of the **initiate()** function, the **loadbuffers()** function is called twice to download each file. A buffer is created from each file and stored in the **mybuffers** array. This process is checked by the **control()** function, and when the length of the array is equal or greater than **2**, the "Play" button is enabled.

The construction of the audio system in the **play()** function is similar to previous examples, except this time two nodes require audio buffers. Using the **buffer** property of each one we assign the corresponding item of the **mybuffers** array, and finally both nodes are connected.

> **Do It Yourself:** Copy the script of Listing 25-9 into the **audio.js** file, upload all the files to your server, and open the document of Listing 25-1 in your browser.

PannerNode and 3D Sound

Three-dimensional graphic libraries are incredible tools nowadays. The re-creation of real objects on a computer screen has reached a high level of perfection and realism. And as a result of WebGL, this amazing experience is now available on the Web. But graphics are not enough to re-create the real world. For this task, sounds also play a significant role. Sounds are not static in a 3D world; they change along with the changes in the position of the source, and they vary according to the speed of the source and its orientation. The PannerNode is a node design specifically to simulate the variations in sounds produced in a 3D scene.

The PannerNode is similar to other nodes, but the sounds must be configured considering the parameters of a 3D world. The object representing the node includes the following properties and methods for this purpose:

> **panningModel**—This property specifies the algorithm to use to position the audio in the 3D scene. The possible values are **EQUALPOWER**, **HRTF** and **SOUNDFIELD**.

> **distanceModel**—This property specifies the algorithm to use to reduce the volume of the sound according to the movement of the source. The possible values are **LINEAR_DISTANCE**, **INVERSE_DISTANCE** and **EXPONENTIAL_DISTANCE**.

> **refDistance**—This property specifies a reference value to calculate the distance between the source and the listener. It may be useful to adapt the node to the scale of our 3D scene. The default value is **1**.

> **maxDistance**—This property specifies the maximum distance between the source of the sound and the listener. After this limit, the sound will keep its current values.

> **rolloffFactor**—This property specifies the ratio in which the volume is reduced.

> **coneInnerAngle**—This property specifies the angle for directional audio sources. Inside this angle, the volume is not reduced.

> **coneOuterAngle**—This property specifies the angle for directional audio sources. Outside this angle, the volume is reduced to a value determined by the **coneOuterGain** property.

setPosition(x, y, z)—This method sets the position of the audio source relative to the listener. The **x**, **y** and **z** attributes declare the value for each coordinate.

setOrientation(x, y, z)—This method sets the direction for a directional audio source. The **x**, **y** and **z** attributes declare a direction vector.

setVelocity(x, y, z)—This method sets the speed and direction of the audio source. The **x**, **y** and **z** attributes declare a direction vector to represent the direction and also the speed of the source.

As you may have inferred by the descriptions of some of these properties and methods, most of the sounds in a 3D scene are relative to the listener. Because there is only one listener, its characteristics are defined by the audio context and not by a particular node. The object representing the listener is accessible through the `listener` property and provides the following properties and methods for configuration:

dopplerFactor—This property declares a value to configure the pitch shift for the Doppler effect.

speedOfSound—This property specifies the speed of the sound in meters per second. It is used to calculate the Doppler shift. The default value is `343.3`.

setPosition(x, y, z)—This method sets the position of the listener. The **x**, **y** and **z** attributes declare the value for each coordinate.

setOrientation(x, y, z, xUp, yUp, zUp)—This method sets the direction in which the listener is oriented. The **x**, **y** and **z** attributes declare a direction vector for the front of the listener, and the **xUp**, **yUp** and **zUp** attributes declare a direction vector for the top of the listener.

setVelocity(x, y, z)—This method sets the speed and direction of the listener. The **x**, **y** and **z** attributes declare a direction vector to represent the direction and also the speed of the listener.

Let's see how to apply all this in a 3D application using the Three.js library. The HTML document we have been using so far in this chapter has to be modified to include the `three.min.js` file and the `<canvas>` element.

```
<!DOCTYPE html>
<html lang="en">
<head>
  <title>Web Audio API</title>
  <script src="three.min.js"></script>
  <script src="audio.js"></script>
</head>
<body>
  <section>
    <canvas id="canvas" width="500" height="400"></canvas>
  </section>
</body>
</html>
```

Listing 25-10: *HTML document including the Three.js library*

The script for this example will draw a cube on the screen that we can move backwards and forwards using the mouse wheel. Here is the Javascript code for the `audio.js` file:

```javascript
var context, pannerNode, renderer, scene, camera, mesh;
function initiate(){
  var canvas = document.getElementById('canvas');
  var width = canvas.width;
  var height = canvas.height;

  renderer = new THREE.WebGLRenderer({canvas: canvas});
  scene = new THREE.Scene();
  camera = new THREE.PerspectiveCamera(45, width/height, 0.1, 10000);
  camera.position.set(0, 0, 150);

  var geometry = new THREE.CubeGeometry(50, 50, 50);
  var material = new THREE.MeshPhongMaterial({color: 0xCCCCFF});
  mesh = new THREE.Mesh(geometry, material);
  mesh.rotation.y = 0.5;
  mesh.rotation.x = 0.5;
  scene.add(mesh);

  var light = new THREE.SpotLight(0xFFFFFF, 1);
  light.position.set(0, 100, 250);
  scene.add(light);

  context = new webkitAudioContext();
  context.listener.setPosition(0, 0, 150);

  var url = 'engine.wav';
  var request = new XMLHttpRequest();
  request.responseType = "arraybuffer";
  request.addEventListener('load', function(){
    if(request.status == 200){
      var mybuffer = context.createBuffer(request.response, false);
      play(mybuffer);
      canvas.addEventListener('mousewheel', move, false);
      renderer.render(scene, camera);
    }
  });
  request.open("GET", url, true);
  request.send();
}
function play(mybuffer){
  var sourceNode = context.createBufferSource();
  sourceNode.buffer = mybuffer;
  sourceNode.loop = true;

  pannerNode = context.createPanner();
  pannerNode.refDistance = 100;

  sourceNode.connect(pannerNode);
  pannerNode.connect(context.destination);
  sourceNode.start(0);
}
```

```
function move(e){
  mesh.position.z += e.wheelDeltaY / 5;
  pannerNode.setPosition(mesh.position.x, mesh.position.y,
mesh.position.z);
  renderer.render(scene, camera);
}
addEventListener('load', initiate, false);
```

Listing 25-11: Calculating the position of the sound in a 3D scene

The `initiate()` function in Listing 25-11 initializes all the elements of the 3D scene and downloads the **engine.wav** file with the sound for our cube. Notice that after creating the audio context with the **audioContext()** constructor, the position for the listener is set with the **setPosition()** method. This is done in the initialization process because in this example the listener keeps the same position the whole time, but this will probably change in other applications.

After the file is downloaded and the audio buffer is created, a listener for the **mousewheel** event is added to execute the **move()** function every time the wheel of the mouse is rotated. This function updates the position of the cube on the **z** axis according to the direction in which the wheel was moved, and then it sets the new coordinates for the audio source. The effect will make the cube look like the real source of the sound.

In the **play()** function, the PannerNode is created and included in the audio system. We use the **refDistance** property to set the values for the node relative to the scale of our 3D scene.

> **Do It Yourself:** Create a new HTML file with the document of Listing 25-10, copy the script of Listing 25-11 into the **audio.js** file, upload all the files to your server, and open the document in your browser. The links to download the **engine.wav** file are available at www.minkbooks.com/content/.

AnalyserNode

It would be extremely difficult to implement all the tools provided by the Web Audio API in a professional environment if we weren't able to visualize the results on the screen. To do this, the API includes the AnalyserNode. This node implements an algorithm called FFT (fast Fourier transform) to turn the waveform of the audio signal into an array of values representing magnitude versus frequency in a specific period of time. The values returned may be used to analyze the signal or create charts to show its values on the screen. The AnalyserNode provides properties and methods to retrieve and process the information:

fftSize—This property specifies the size of the FFT (the size of the block of data to be analyzed). The value must be a power of 2 (e.g., 128, 256, 512, 1024, etc.).

frequencyBinCount—This property returns the number of frequency values provided by the FFT.

minDecibels—This property specifies the minimum power value for the FFT.

maxDecibels—This property specifies the maximum power value for the FFT.

smoothingTimeConstant—This property declares a period of time in which the analyser will get an average value of the frequencies. It takes a value from 0 to 1.

getFloatFrequencyData(array)—This method retrieves the current frequency data from the audio signal and stores it in the **array** attribute as floating-point values. The **array** attribute is a reference to a floating-point array already created.

getByteFrequencyData(array)— This method retrieves the current frequency data from the audio signal and stores it in the **array** attribute as unsigned byte values. The **array** attribute is a reference to an unsigned byte array already created.

getByteTimeDomainData(array)— This method retrieves the current waveform data from the audio signal and stores it in the **array** attribute as floating-point values. The **array** attribute is a reference to a floating-point array already created.

The data produced by these properties and methods may be used to update a chart on the screen and show the evolution of the audio signal. To see how to implement an AnalyserNode, we are going to use a **<canvas>** element to visualize the sound taken from a **<video>** element. Here is the HTML document for this example:

```
<!DOCTYPE html>
<html lang="en">
<head>
  <title>Web Audio API</title>
  <style>
    section{
      float: left;
    }
  </style>
  <script src="audio.js"></script>
</head>
<body>
  <section>
    <video id="media" width="483" height="272" controls>
      <source src="http://www.minkbooks.com/content/trailer2.mp4">
      <source src="http://www.minkbooks.com/content/trailer2.ogg">
    </video>
  </section>
  <section>
    <canvas id="canvas" width="500" height="272"></canvas>
  </section>
</body>
</html>
```

Listing 25-12: HTML document to test AnalyserNode

As we explained before, when the source is a media element, the audio source node has to be created with the **createMediaElementSource()** method. In the following Javascript code, we will apply this and the **createAnalyser()** methods to get the nodes we need for our audio system:

```
var canvas, context, analyserNode;
function initiate(){
  var video = document.getElementById('media');
  var elem = document.getElementById('canvas');
```

```
canvas = elem.getContext('2d');
context = new webkitAudioContext();

var sourceNode = context.createMediaElementSource(video);
analyserNode = context.createAnalyser();
analyserNode.fftSize = 512;
analyserNode.smoothingTimeConstant = 0.9;

sourceNode.connect(analyserNode);
analyserNode.connect(context.destination);

showgraphic();
}
function showgraphic(){
  var data = new Uint8Array(analyserNode.frequencyBinCount);
  analyserNode.getByteFrequencyData(data);

  canvas.clearRect(0, 0, 500, 400);
  canvas.beginPath();
  for(var f = 0; f < analyserNode.frequencyBinCount; f++){
    canvas.fillRect(f * 5, 272 - data[f], 3, data[f]);
  }
  canvas.stroke();

  webkitRequestAnimationFrame(showgraphic);
}
addEventListener('load', initiate, false);
```

Listing 25-13: *Drawing the chart on a* <canvas> *element*

To limit the size of the data retrieved and smooth the chart on the screen, in the script of Listing 25-13 the size for the FFT is set as **512**, and a period of time of **0.9** is established by the **smoothingTimeConstant** property. After the nodes are created, configured and connected, the audio system is ready to provide information from the audio signal. The **showchart()** function is created to process this data. This function creates an empty array of the type Uint8Array and the size determined by the **frequencyBinCount** property, and then it calls the **getByteFrequencyData()** method to populate the array with values from the audio signal. Because of the type of array, the values stored will be integers from **0** to **256** (8-bit integers). In the **for** loop, next, we use these values to calculate the size of the bars that represent the corresponding frequencies and draw them on the canvas.

Figure 25-6: *Audio chart for the video created from an AnalyserNode*
© Copyright 2008, Blender Foundation / www.bigbuckbunny.org

Review the Basics: Javascript variables are usually defined without taking into consideration the type of data they are going to work with, but some new methods take only values provided in a specific type. The `Uint8Array()` constructor, implemented in the example of Listing 25-13, is just one of the constructors introduced by the language to provide new array types to satisfy the requirements of the HTML5 APIs. For more information on the subject, visit our website and follow the links for this chapter.

Do It Yourself: Create a new HTML file with the document of Listing 25-12, copy the script of Listing 25-13 into the `audio.js` file, and open the document in your browser.

Web Audio API

Chapter 26
Web Workers API

26.1 Doing the Hard Work

Javascript has become the primary tool for building successful applications on the Web. As we explained in Chapter 4, it is no longer just an alternative for the creation of nice (or sometimes annoying) tricks for web pages. The language is already an essential part of the Web and a technology everybody has to understand and implement.

Javascript has already reached the status of a general-purpose language and, as a result, has been forced to provide elemental features that by nature it doesn't have. Since its creation, the language was intended to be processed one code at a time. The absence of multithreading (processing multiple codes simultaneously) reduces efficiency and limits the scope of the technology, turning the emulation of desktop applications on the Web into an impossible task.

Web Workers is an API designed for the specific purpose of turning Javascript into a multithreading language and solving this problem. Now, with HTML5, we are able to execute time-consuming operations in the background while the main script runs uninterrupted on the web page, always able to process the user's input and keep the document responsive.

Creating a Worker

The way Web Workers works is simple: the worker is built in a separate Javascript file, and the codes communicate with each other through messages. But before communicating with the worker, we have to get an object pointing to the file in which the code for the worker is located.

> **Worker(scriptURL)**—This constructor returns a Worker object. The `scriptURL` attribute is the URL of the file with the code (worker) that will be processed in the background.

Usually, the message sent to the worker from the main code is the information we want to be processed, and the messages sent back by the worker represents the result of this processing. To send and receive these messages, the API takes advantage of techniques implemented in the Web Messaging API. Events and methods that you already know are used to send and receive messages from one code to another:

> **postMessage(message)**—This method is the same studied in Chapter 22 for the Web Messaging API, but it is now implemented for the Worker object. It sends a message to or from the worker code. The `message` attribute is any Javascript value, such a string or a number, and also binary data, such a File object or an ArrayBuffer, representing the message to be transmitted.

message—This event listens for messages sent to the code. As with the `postMessage()` method, it can be applied to the worker or to the main code. It returns an object with the **data** property to retrieve the content of the message.

Sending and Receiving Messages

To learn how workers and the main Javascript code communicate with each other, we are going to use a simple HTML document to send our name as a message to the worker and print the answer. Even a basic example of Web Workers like this one requires at least three files: the main document, the main code and the Javascript file with the code for the worker.

```
<!DOCTYPE html>
<html lang="en">
<head>
  <title>Web Workers</title>
  <link rel="stylesheet" href="webworkers.css">
  <script src="webworkers.js"></script>
</head>
<body>
  <section id="formbox">
    <form name="form">
      <label for="name">Name: </label><br>
      <input type="text" name="name" id="name"><br>
      <input type="button" id="button" value="Send">
    </form>
  </section>
  <section id="databox"></section>
</body>
</html>
```

Listing 26-1: HTML document to test Web Workers

In the main document of Listing 26-1, we include a CSS file called **webworkers.css** with the following rules:

```
#formbox{
  float: left;
  padding: 20px;
  border: 1px solid #999999;
}
#databox{
  float: left;
  width: 500px;
  margin-left: 20px;
  padding: 20px;
  border: 1px solid #999999;
}
```

Listing 26-2: Styling the boxes (webworkers.css)

Web Workers API

The Javascript for the main document has to be able to send the information we want to be processed by the worker. This code also has to be able to listen for the answer.

```
var worker, databox;
function initiate(){
   databox = document.getElementById('databox');
   var button = document.getElementById('button');
   button.addEventListener('click', send);

   worker = new Worker('worker.js');
   worker.addEventListener('message', received);
}
function send(){
   var name = document.getElementById('name').value;
   worker.postMessage(name);
}
function received(e){
   databox.innerHTML = e.data;
}
addEventListener('load', initiate);
```

Listing 26-3: *Loading the worker (*webworkers.js*)*

Listing 26-3 presents the code for our document (the one that goes inside the **webworkers.js** file). After the creation of the necessary references for the **databox** and the button in the **initiate()** function, the Worker object is constructed. The **Worker()** constructor takes the **worker.js** file as the file with the code for the worker and returns a Worker object with this reference. Every interaction with the object will, actually, be an interaction with the code in this particular file.

Once we get the proper object, a listener for the **message** event is added to listen for messages coming from the worker. When a message is received, the **received()** function is called, and the value of the **data** property (the message) is shown on the screen.

The other part of the communication is conducted by the **send()** function. When the user clicks the "Send" button, the value of the **name** input is taken and sent as a message for the worker using the **postMessage()** method.

With the **received()** and **send()** functions in charge of communications, we are ready to send messages to the worker and process its answers. Now it's time to prepare the worker:

```
addEventListener('message', received);

function received(e){
   var answer = 'Your name is '+e.data;
   postMessage(answer);
}
```

Listing 26-4: *Creating the worker (*worker.js*)*

As well in the script of Listing 26-3, the code for the worker has to listen constantly for messages coming from the main code using the **message** event. The first line in Listing 26-4 adds a listener for this event to the worker. Every time the event is fired (a message is received), the `received()` function is executed. In this function, the value of the **data** property is added to a predefined string and sent back to the main code using again the **postMessage()** method.

> **Do It Yourself:** Compare the scripts of Listings 26-3 and 26-4 (the main code and the worker). Check how the communication process works and how the same method and event are applied for this purpose in both codes. Create the files using Listings 26-1, 26-2, 26-3 and 26-4, upload them to your server, and open the HTML document in your browser.

This worker is, of course, elementary. Nothing is really processed; the only processing performed is the construction of a string from the message received that is immediately sent back as the answer. However, this example is useful for understanding how the codes communicate with each other and how to take advantage of this API.

Despite their simplicity, there are a few important things to consider before creating your own workers. Messages are the only possible way to communicate directly with workers. Also, workers can't access the document or manipulate any HTML element, and Javascript functions and variables from the main code are not accessible to workers. Workers are like canned codes, only allowed to process information received through messages and send the result back using the same mechanism.

Detecting Errors

Despite all the limitations mentioned, workers are still flexible and powerful. We can use functions, native methods and entire APIs from inside a worker. Considering how complex a worker may become, the Web Workers API incorporates a specific event to check for errors and return as much information as possible about the situation.

> **error**—This event is fired by the Worker object in the main code every time an error occurs in the worker. It uses three properties to provide information: **message**, **filename** and **lineno**. The **message** property represents the error message. It's a string that tells us what went wrong. The **filename** property shows the name of the file with the code that caused the error. This is useful when external files are loaded by the worker, as we will see later. And the **lineno** property returns the line number in which the error occurred.

Let's create a script to show errors returned by a worker:

```
var worker, databox;
function initiate(){
  databox = document.getElementById('databox');
  var button = document.getElementById('button');
  button.addEventListener('click', send);

  worker = new Worker('worker.js');
  worker.addEventListener('error', error);
}
```

```
function send(){
  var name = document.getElementById('name').value;
  worker.postMessage(name);
}
function error(e){
  databox.innerHTML = 'ERROR: ' + e.message + '<br>';
  databox.innerHTML += 'Filename: ' + e.filename + '<br>';
  databox.innerHTML += 'Line Number: ' + e.lineno;
}
addEventListener('load', initiate);
```

Listing 26-5: *Listening to the* `error` *event (*`webworkers.js`*)*

The Javascript code in Listing 26-5 is similar to the main code of Listing 26-3. It constructs a worker, but it only uses the **error** event because we don't want to listen for answers from the worker this time but rather check for errors. It's useless, of course, but it will show you how the errors are returned and what kind of information is provided in these situations.

To deliberately generate an error, we will call a non-existent function within the worker:

```
addEventListener('message', received);

function received(e){
  test();
}
```

Listing 26-6: *Producing an error (*`worker.js`*)*

In the worker, we have to use the **message** event to listen for messages coming from the main code because it begins the process. When a message is received the **received()** function is executed, and the non-existent **test()** function is called, generating an error.

As soon as the error occurs, the **error** event is fired in the main code, and the **error()** function is called, showing the values on the screen of the three properties provided by the event. Check the code in Listing 26-5 to see how the function takes and processes this information.

> **Do It Yourself:** For this example, we are using the HTML document and CSS rules of Listings 26-1 and 26-2. Copy the script of Listing 26-5 in the **webworkers.js** file and the script of Listing 26-6 in the **worker.js** file. Open the document of Listing 26-1 in your browser, and send any random string to the worker using the form to activate the process. The error returned by the worker will be shown on the screen.

Terminating Workers

Workers are special units of code that always run in the background, waiting for information to be processed. Most of the time, workers will be required in specific circumstances and for limited periods of time. Usually, their services won't be necessary or required all the time, and it is good practice to stop or terminate their processing if we no longer need them. The API provides two different methods for this purpose:

terminate()—This method terminates the worker from the main code.

close()—This method terminates the worker from inside the worker.

When a worker is terminated, any process running at that moment is aborted, and any task in the event loop is discarded. To test both methods, we are going to create a small application that works exactly as our first example, but it also responds to two specific commands: "close1" and "close2". If the strings "close1" or "close2" are sent from the form, the worker will be terminated by the main code or the code of the worker using `terminate()` or `close()`, respectively.

```
var worker, databox;
function initiate(){
  databox = document.getElementById('databox');
  var button = document.getElementById('button');
  button.addEventListener('click', send);

  worker = new Worker('worker.js');
  worker.addEventListener('message', received);
}
function send(){
  var name = document.getElementById('name').value;
  if(name == 'close1'){
    worker.terminate();
    databox.innerHTML = 'Worker Terminated';
  }else{
    worker.postMessage(name);
  }
}
function received(e){
  databox.innerHTML = e.data;
}
addEventListener('load', initiate);
```

Listing 26-7: Terminating the worker from the main code (`webworkers.js`)

The only difference between the script of Listing 26-7 and the one in Listing 26-3 is the addition of the `if` statement to check for the insertion of the "close1" command. If this command is inserted in the form, the `terminate()` method is executed, and a message is shown on the screen indicating the termination of the worker. On the other hand, if the string is different from the command expected, it is sent as a message to the worker.

The code for the worker will perform a similar task. If the message received contains the string "close2", the worker will terminate itself using the `close()` method or send a message back otherwise.

```
addEventListener('message', received);

function received(e){
  if(e.data == 'close2'){
    postMessage('Worker Terminated');
    close();
  }else{
```

```
    var answer = 'Your name is ' + e.data;
    postMessage(answer);
  }
}
```

Listing 26-8: Terminating the worker from the worker script

> **Do It Yourself:** Use the same HTML document and CSS rules of Listings 26-1 and 26-2. Copy the script of Listing 26-7 into the **webworkers.js** file and the script of Listing 26-8 into the **worker.js** file. Open the document in your browser, and using the form, send the commands "close1" or "close2". After this, the worker will no longer respond.

Synchronous APIs

Workers may have limitations in working with the main document and accessing its elements, but when it comes to processing and functionality, as we mentioned before, they are ready for the task. For instance, we can use regular methods such as **setTimeout()** or **setInterval()**, load additional information from servers using **XMLHttpRequest** and also access other APIs to create powerful codes. The last possibility is the most promising of all, but it has a catch: we will have to learn a different implementation of the APIs available for workers.

When we studied some APIs in earlier chapters, the implementation presented was the one called asynchronous. Most APIs have asynchronous and synchronous versions available. These different versions of the same API perform the same tasks but use specific methods according to the way they are processed. Asynchronous APIs are useful when the operations performed are time consuming and require resources the main document can't provide at that moment. The asynchronous operations are performed in the background while the main code continues processing without interruption. Because workers are new threads running at the same time as the main code, they are already asynchronous, and these types of operations are no longer necessary.

> **IMPORTANT:** Several APIs have synchronous versions, such as File API and IndexedDB API, but currently most of them are under development or are unstable. Visit the links on our website for more information on this subject.

Importing Scripts

Something worth mentioning is the possibility of loading external Javascript files from a worker. A worker can hold all the code necessary to perform any task we need, but because several workers may be created for a single document, there is a chance that some parts of this code will become redundant. We can select these parts, put them into a single file and load that file from every worker with the new **importScripts()** method:

> **importScripts(file)**—This method loads an external Javascript file to incorporate new code into a worker. The **file** attribute indicates the path of the file to be included.

The way the **importScripts()** method works is similar to older methods from other languages, such as **include()** from PHP, for example. The code in the file is incorporated into the worker as if it were part of the original worker's file.

To use the new `importScripts()` method, you have to declare it at the beginning of the worker. The code for the worker won't be ready until these files have completely loaded.

```
importScripts('morecodes.js');

addEventListener('message', received);

function received(e){
  test();
}
```

Listing 26-9: Loading external Javascript codes for the worker

The script of Listing 26-9 is non-functional but is an example of how to use the `importScripts()` method. In this hypothetical situation, the file `morecodes.js` containing the function `test()` is loaded as soon as the worker's file has loaded. After this process, the `test()` function (and any other function inside the `morecodes.js` file) becomes available for the rest of the worker's code.

Shared Worker

The worker we have seen so far is called a Dedicated Worker. This type of worker only responds to the main code from which it was created. There is another type of worker called a Shared Worker, which responds to multiple documents from the same origin. Working with multiple connections means that we can share the same worker from different windows, tabs or frames, and keep everything updated and synchronized. The API provides a second constructor to get the SharedWorker object:

> **SharedWorker(scriptURL)**—This constructor replaces the previous `Worker()` constructor used for Dedicated Workers. As usual, the `scriptURL` attribute declares the path of the Javascript file with the code for the worker. An optional second attribute could be added to specify a `name` for the worker.

The connections are made through ports, and these ports can be saved inside the worker for future reference. To work with Shared Workers and ports, this part of the API incorporates new properties, events and methods:

> **port**—When the SharedWorker object is constructed, a new port is created for this document and assigned to the `port` property. This property will be used later to reference the port and communicate with the worker.

> **connect**—This is a specific event to check for new connections from inside the worker. The event will be fired every time a document starts a connection with the worker. It is useful to keep track of all the connections available for the worker (to reference all the documents that are using this worker).

> **start()**—This method is available for MessagePort objects (one of the objects returned in the construction of a shared worker), and its function is to begin dispatching messages received through a port. After the construction of the SharedWorker object, this method must be called to start the connection.

Web Workers API

The `SharedWorker()` constructor returns a SharedWorker object and a MessagePort object with the value of the port through which the connection to the worker will be made. The communication with the shared worker must be done through the port referenced by the value of the `port` property.

To test Shared Workers, we will have to use at least two different documents from the same origin, two Javascript codes for each document and one file for the worker.

The HTML document for our example includes an iframe to load a second document in the same window. Both the main document and the document within the iframe will share the same worker.

```
<!DOCTYPE html>
<html lang="en">
<head>
  <title>Web Workers</title>
  <link rel="stylesheet" href="webworkers.css">
  <script src="webworkers.js"></script>
</head>
<body>
  <section id="formbox">
    <form name="form">
      <label for="name">Name: </label>
      <input type="text" name="name" id="name">
      <input type="button" id="button" value="Send">
    </form>
  </section>
  <section id="databox">
    <iframe id="iframe" src="iframe.html" width="500"
height="350"></iframe>
  </section>
</body>
</html>
```

Listing 26-10: HTML document to test shared workers

The document we have to create for the iframe must be a simple HTML document with a `<section>` element to recreate our familiar `databox` and a `<script>` tag to include the `iframe.js` file containing the script to connect with the worker.

```
<!DOCTYPE html>
<html lang="en">
<head>
  <title>iframe Window</title>
  <script src="iframe.js"></script>
</head>
<body>
  <section id="databox"></section>
</body>
</html>
```

Listing 26-11: HTML document for the iframe (`iframe.html`)

Each HTML document has its own Javascript code to start the connection with the worker and process its answers. These codes have to construct the SharedWorker object and use the port referenced by the value of the **port** property to send and receive messages. First, let's see the script corresponding to the main document:

```
var worker;
function initiate(){
   var button = document.getElementById('button');
   button.addEventListener('click', send);
   worker = new SharedWorker('worker.js');
   worker.port.addEventListener('message', received);
   worker.port.start();
}
function received(e){
   alert(e.data);
}
function send(){
   var name = document.getElementById('name').value;
   worker.port.postMessage(name);
}
addEventListener('load', initiate);
```

Listing 26-12: *Connecting to the worker from the main document (*webworkers.js*)*

Every document that wants to work with a shared worker has to create the SharedWorker object and set a connection with the worker. In the script of Listing 26-12, the object is constructed using the **worker.js** file, and then the communication is established through the corresponding port using the **port** property.

After a listener for the **message** event is added to listen for answers from the worker, the **start()** method is called to begin dispatching messages. The connection to a shared worker is not really established until this method is executed.

Notice that the **send()** function is similar to previous examples, except this time the communication is made through the value of the **port** property.

For the iframe, the code doesn't change too much:

```
function initiate(){
   var worker = new SharedWorker('worker.js');
   worker.port.addEventListener('message', received);
   worker.port.start();
}
function received(e){
   var databox = document.getElementById('databox');
   databox.innerHTML = e.data;
}
addEventListener('load', initiate);
```

Listing 26-13: *Connecting to the worker from the iframe (*iframe.js*)*

In both scripts, the SharedWorker object is constructed referencing the same file (**worker.js**), and the connection has to be established using the **port** property (albeit through different ports). The only noticeable difference between the code for the main document and the code for the iframe is how the response from the worker is processed. In the main document, the **received()** function pops up an alert message (see Listing 26-12), while within the iframe, the answer is printed as a simple text inside the **databox** (see Listing 26-13).

Now it is time to see how the shared worker handles every connection and sends messages back to the proper document. Remember that there is only one worker for both documents (hence shared worker). Every request for a connection to the worker has to be differentiated and saved for future reference. We are going to store the references to the ports for each document in an array called **myports**.

```
var myports = new Array();
addEventListener('connect', connect);

function connect(e){
  myports.push(e.ports[0]);
  e.ports[0].onmessage = send;
}
function send(e){
  for(var f = 0; f < myports.length; f++){
    myports[f].postMessage('Your Name is ' + e.data);
  }
}
```

Listing 26-14: The Javascript code for the shared worker (`worker.js`*)*

This procedure is similar to the one for Dedicated Workers. This time we have to consider which document we are going to answer, because several may be connected to the worker at the same time. To do this, the **connect** event provides the **ports** array with the value of the newly created port (the array only contains this value located at index 0).

Every time a code requests a connection to the worker, the **connect** event is fired. In the script of Listing 26-14, this event calls the **connect()** function. In this function, we perform two operations: First, the value of the port is taken from the **ports** property (index 0) and stored in the **myports** array (initialized at the beginning of the worker). Second, the **onmessage** event property is registered for this particular port, and the **send()** function is set to be called when a message is received.

As a result, every time a message is sent to the worker from the main code, regardless of from which document, the **send()** function in the worker is executed. In this function, we use a **for** loop to retrieve, from the **myports** array, all the ports opened for this worker and send a message to each document connected. The process is the same as for Dedicated Workers, but this time several documents are answered instead of just one.

> **Do It Yourself:** To test this example, you have to create several files and upload them to your server. Create an HTML file with the document of Listing 26-10. This document will load the same **webworkers.css** file used throughout this chapter, the **webworkers.js** file with the script of Listing 26-12 and the **iframe.html** file as the source of the iframe with the script of Listing 26-11. You also have to create a file called **worker.js** for the worker with the code of Listing 26-14. Once all these files are saved and uploaded to the server, open the first file in your browser. Use the form to send a message to the worker, and see how both documents (the main document and the document in the iframe) process the answer.

Web Workers API

Conclusion

Working for the World

This book is about HTML5. It is a guide for developers, designers and programmers who want to build revolutionary websites and applications. It is for the genius everyone has inside. For Masterminds. But we are in a transition; a moment in time in which old technologies are merging with new ones, and markets are falling behind. While millions and millions of copies of new browsers are downloaded from the Web, millions and millions of people are unaware of their existence. The market is full of old computers running Windows 98 and Internet Explorer 6, or worse.

Creating for the Web has always been a challenge, and it's not getting any easier. Despite the long, hard efforts to build and implement standards for the Web, even new browsers do not consistently support them. And old browsers with no standards at all are still there, running all around the world, making our lives difficult.

So it's time to discuss what we can do to bring HTML5 to the public, to innovate and create, to be Masterminds in a world that seems indifferent. It's time to see how we can work with new technologies and make them available to everyone.

The Alternatives

When it comes to alternatives, we have to decide which position to take. We can be rude, polite, smart or hard workers. A rude developer would say, "Hey, this was programmed to work in new browsers. New browsers are free, don't be lazy; download a copy." The polite developer would say, "This was developed taking advantage of new technologies; if you want to enjoy my work to its full potential, upgrade your browser. In the meantime, here is an old version you can use." The smart developer would say, "We make cutting-edge technology available for everyone. You don't need to do anything; we did it for you." And finally, a dedicated developer would say, "This is a version of our website adapted to your browser; here is another version with more features special for new browsers; and here is the experimental version of our super-evolved application only available for the beta version of this specific browser."

For the most useful and practical approach, there are options available when the user's browser is not ready for HTML5:

> **Inform**—Ask the user to upgrade the browser if some of the features your application needs are not available.
>
> **Adapt**—Select different styles and scripts for the document according to the features available in the user's browser.
>
> **Redirect**—Redirect users to an entirely new document designed especially for older browsers.
>
> **Emulate**—Use libraries to make HTML5 features available in old browsers.

Modernizr

Regardless of what option you choose, the first step is to detect whether or not the HTML5 features your application needs are available in the user's browser. The features are independent and easy to identify, but the techniques required to detect them are as diverse as the features themselves. Developers must consider different browsers and versions and depend on codes that are often unreliable.

A small library called Modernizr was developed to solve this problem. This library creates an object called Modernizr that offers properties for every HTML5 feature. These properties return a Boolean value that will be **true** or **false** depending on whether or not the features are available.

The library is open-source, made in Javascript and available for free from www.modernizr.com. You just download the Javascript file and include it in the head of your document, as in the following example:

```
<!DOCTYPE html>
<html lang="en">
<head>
  <title>Modernizr</title>
  <script src="modernizr.min.js"></script>
  <script src="ourscript.js"></script>
</head>
<body>
  <section id="databox">
    content
  </section>
</body>
</html>
```

Listing C-1: Including Modernizr in our documents

The file called **modernizr.min.js** is a copy of the file for the Modernizr library downloaded from the Modernizr website (www.modernizr.com). The second file included in the HTML document in Listing C-1 is our own Javascript code to check the values of the properties provided by the library.

```
function initiate(){
  var databox = document.getElementById('databox');
  if(Modernizr.boxshadow){
    databox.innerHTML = 'Box Shadow is available';
  }else{
    databox.innerHTML = 'Box Shadow is NOT available';
  }
}
addEventListener('load', initiate);
```

Listing C-2: Detecting the availability of CSS styles for box shadows

As you can see in the script of Listing C-2, we can detect any HTML5 feature using an `if` statement and the corresponding property of the Modernizr object. Every feature has its own property available.

> **IMPORTANT:** This is a short introduction to this useful library. By using Modernizr, for example, you can also select a set of CSS styles from CSS files without using Javascript. Modernizr provides special classes to implement in our style sheets to select the proper CSS properties according to the features available. To learn more, visit www.modernizr.com.

Libraries

Once the features available are detected, you have the option of only using what has been detected to work in the user's browser or recommending the user upgrade his or her software. However, imagine you are a stubborn developer or a mad programmer who (along with your users and clients) doesn't care about the browser vendors, browser version, beta versions, unimplemented features or anything else—you just want to run the latest technology available, no matter what!

Well, this is where independent libraries can help. Dozens of programmers around the world are probably more stubborn than you and your clients, and they are developing and improving libraries to emulate HTML5 features in old browsers, especially Javascript APIs. Thanks to their efforts, we already have new HTML elements, CSS3 selectors and styles and even complex APIs such as Canvas or Web Storage available in every browser in the market.

These libraries are usually called polyfills, and there is an up-to-date list available at www.github.com/Modernizr/Modernizr/wiki/HTML5-Cross-browser-Polyfills.

Google Chrome Frame

Google Chrome Frame is probably a last resort. It was a good idea initially, but now, it is better to recommend users upgrade their browsers rather than making them download a plug-in like Google Chrome Frame.

Google Chrome Frame was specifically developed for older versions of Internet Explorer. It was designed to bring all the power and possibility of Google Chrome into browsers that are not prepared for these technologies but are still running on users' computers. By inserting a simple HTML tag in your documents, a message is shown to your users to recommend they install the Google Chrome Frame before running your website or application. After this simple step, all the features supported by Google Chrome are automatically available. However, since users had to download software from the Web anyways, why not download a new browser version? Especially now that Internet Explorer has its own HTML5 compatible version available for free. Now, with so many browsers HTML5 ready, it is better to guide users to this new software than to send them to obscure and confusing plug-ins.

This alternative shouldn't be your first, but it can still be useful in some circumstances. To know more about Google Chrome Frame and learn how to use it, visit http://code.google.com/chrome/chromeframe/.

Working for the Cloud

In this new world of mobile devices and cloud computing, no matter how current the browser, we will always have something new to worry about. The iPhone was likely the innovation that started it all. Since its launch, several things have changed for the Web, and all kinds of devices, like the iPad and others, have emerged to expand this new market. Thanks to this radical change in the electronic world, mobile Internet access has become commonplace. These new devices are now an important focus for websites and web applications, and the diversity of platforms, screens and interfaces has forced developers to adapt their products to every specific case.

These days, independent of what kind of technology we use, our websites and applications must still be adapted to every possible platform to preserve consistency and make our work available to everyone. Fortunately, HTML always considered this situation and provided the `media` attribute in the `<link>` element to select external resources according to predetermined parameters:

```
<!DOCTYPE html>
<html lang="en">
<head>
  <title>Main Document</title>
  <link rel="stylesheet" href="webstyles.css" media="all and (min-width:
769px)">
  <link rel="stylesheet" href="tablet.css" media="all and (min-width:
321px) and (max-width: 768px)">
  <link rel="stylesheet" href="phone.css" media="all and (min-width: 0px)
and (max-width: 320px)">
</head>
<body>
  ...
</body>
</html>
```

Listing C-3: *Including different CSS files for different devices*

Selecting CSS styles is an easy way to get our job done. According to the device or the size of the screen, the CSS files are loaded and the proper styles applied. HTML elements can be resized and entire documents adapted and rendered into a specific space and circumstances.

In Listing C-3, three different CSS files are incorporated for three different situations. The situations are detected by the values of the attribute `media` in every `<link>` tag. By using the properties `min-width` and `max-width,` we are able to determine the CSS file that will be applied to this document according to the resolution of the screen on which the document is being displayed. In this example, three devices are considered: a small smartphone, a tablet PC, and a full-scale computer. The values used are usually found in these devices. If the horizontal size of the screen is between 0 and 320 pixels, the `phone.css` file is loaded; for a resolution between 321 and 768 pixels, the `tablet.css` file is loaded; and finally, for a resolution larger than 768 pixels, the `webstyles.css` file is used to render the document.

Of course, the adaptation process does not involve only CSS styles. The interfaces provided by these devices are slightly different from a desktop computer because physical parts, such as the keyword and mouse, are eliminated. Regular events such as `click` or `mouseover` have been modified or in some cases replaced by touch events. And there is another important feature usually present in mobile devices that allows the user to change the orientation of the screen and therefore the space available for the document. All these changes from the old computer interface make it almost impossible to get a good adaptation of the design and operability just by adding or modifying some CSS rules. Javascript has to be used to adapt codes or even detect the situation and redirect users to a version of the website specific for the device that is accessing the application.

> **IMPORTANT:** This topic is beyond the scope of this book. For more information, please visit our website and follow the links for this chapter.

APIs Not Included

For different reasons, we were not able to include all the APIs provided by HTML5 in this book. But a few of them are important enough to at least let you know are available:

> **Clipboard API**—This API provides access to the system clipboard. It provides events to control each possible action (copy, cut and paste) and also access to an interface used in the Drag and Drop API to set and retrieve the data involved in the process.

> **Device Orientation API**—This API provides access to the information offered by the device regarding orientation and movement.

> **Quota Management API**—As we mentioned in Chapter 16, the Quota Management API lets applications request storage space or check the space available.

> **SVG API**—This API, Scalable Vector Graphics, brings the possibility to generate vector graphics to the Web. Due to the success of Flash (a vector graphic plug-in), this API was viewed as a good choice at the beginning, but there is a downside. Contrary to the rest of the specifications, this one is based on XML rather than Javascript. While everybody was trying to simplify markup, this API introduced more complexity, following a totally different path. For this reason, it wasn't included, but you should evaluate it yourself.

HTML5 is called a living standard. The specifications are constantly changing and expanding. In the link section of the MinkBooks website, you will find links to every specification page. Visit these pages often to check for the current state of each one and to expand your knowledge of these technologies.

What You Should Know

The technologies explained in this book, especially the Javascript language, are extremely flexible and can be implemented in so many ways that it is impossible to show you every option available. Although, here are a few things you should know:

- The way we organize our Javascript code and how we implement the tools provided by the language is usually called **pattern**. In this book, we implemented a simple pattern, but there are innumerable alternatives available, and even entire books focus on this subject. You should learn more about patterns to decide what is better for your projects.

- The `prototype` property, provided by Javascript to modify prototypes in a prototype chain, is extensively used in examples on the Web. The programming pattern applied in our examples avoids the use of this property, but you should learn more about it.
- In this book we just scratched the surface of some complex APIs. For some of them, an entire book would be required to describe all their features. As you implement them, we recommend you expand your knowledge by reviewing their official specifications (visit the links section of www.minkbooks.com).

Final Words from the Author

There will be always developers who will say, "If you use technologies that are not available for 5% of the browsers on the market, you are going to lose 5% of customers." My answer is, "If you have clients to satisfy, then adapt, redirect or emulate; but if you work for yourself, inform."

You always have to find a way to succeed. If you work for others, in order to succeed you have to provide a full working solution, a product that the clients of your client are able to access, no matter what computers, browsers or systems they have. But if you work for yourself, you have to create the best; you have to innovate and be ahead of everyone, independent of what the 5% of the users have installed on their computers. You have to work for the 20% that have already downloaded the latest version of Mozilla Firefox, the 15% that already have Google Chrome running on their PCs, the 10% that have Safari on their mobile devices. You have millions of users ready to become your customers. While the developer asked you why you would lose the 5% of the market, I ask you why you would lose the chance to succeed.

You will never capture 100% of the market, and that is a fact. You are not developing your websites in Chinese or Portuguese. You are not working for 100% of the market; you are already working for a small part of it. Why continue limiting yourself? Develop for the market that allows you to succeed. Develop for that portion of the market that is continuously growing and will let you free your genius inside. In the same way that you don't worry about markets that speak other languages, don't worry about the part of the market that is still using old technologies. Inform them. Let them know what they are missing. Take advantage of the latest technologies available, and be a Mastermind. Develop for the future, and you will succeed.

INDEX

3053305R00270

Made in the USA
San Bernardino, CA
30 June 2013